بسم الله الرحمن الرحيم

Shaykhu'l-Islām
Aḥmad ibn 'Abdu'l-Ḥalīm ibn Taymiyyah

The Decisive Criterion Between

The FRIENDS of ALLĀH and the FRIENDS of SHAYṬĀN

being a translation of his
'al-Furqān bayna Awliyā' ar-Raḥmān wa awliyā' ash-Shayṭān'

دار السنة

"Unquestionably, for the Awliyā' of Allāh there will be no fear concerning them, nor will they grieve - those who believed and were fearing Allāh. For them are good tidings in the worldly life and in the Hereafter."

[YŪNUS (10): 62-63]

THE DECISIVE CRITERION BETWEEN THE

Friends Of Allāh & The Friends Of Shayṭān

by

SHAYKHUL-ISLĀM

IBN TAYMIYYAH

Translated from the original Arabic by Abū Rumaysah

دار السنة

Dār as-Sunnah Publishers

BIRMINGHAM

Third Edition Published in Great Britain, December 2010 / Muharram 1432H
by Dār as-Sunnah Publishers

DĀR AS-SUNNAH PUBLISHERS
P.O. Box 9818, Birmingham, B11 4WA, United Kingdom
W: www.darassunnah.com.
E: info@darussunnah.com
E: daar-us-sunnah@mail.com

British Library Cataloguing in publication Data.
A catalogue record for this book is available from the British Library.

Title: The Decisive Criterion Between the Friends of Allāh
and the Friends of Shayṭān
by Shaykhu'l-Islām Aḥmad ibn 'Abdu'l-Ḥalīm ibn Taymiyyah
Translated from the original Arabic by Abū Rumaysah

ISBN 1-904336-16-7
Paper-back

Typeset by: Dār as-Sunnah Publishers
Printed in Turkey

First Edition, 1421 AH/2000 CE
Second Edition, 1426 AH/2005 CE
Third Edition, 1431 AH/2010 CE

CONTENTS

CHAPTER ELEVEN

The Prophets are Superior to the *Awliyā* who are not Prophets 185

CHAPTER TWELVE

The Confusion Between the Universal Reality and the Religious Reality 238

Transliteration Table

Consonants. Arabic

initial: unexpressed medial and final:

ء ʾ	د d	ض ḍ	ك k
ب b	ذ dh	ط ṭ	ل l
ت t	ر r	ظ ẓ	م m
ث th	ز z	ع ʿ	ن n
ج j	س s	غ gh	هـ h
ح ḥ	ش sh	ف f	و w
خ kh	ص ṣ	ق q	ي y

Vowels, diphthongs, etc.

Short:	ـَ a	ـِ i	ـُ u
long:	ـَا ā	ـُو ū	ـِي ī
diphthongs:		ـَوْ aw	
		ـَيْ ay	

TRANSLATOR'S FOREWORD

ALL PRAISE AND THANKS ARE DUE TO ALLĀH, the Most Beneficent, the Most Merciful and Master of the Day of Judgement. I bear witness that there is none worthy of worship save Allāh Alone Who has no partner, the Lord of the universe and the Originator of the heavens and the earth. I bear witness that Muḥammad (ﷺ) is His servant and Messenger, who was sent as a mercy for mankind and a proof for those traversing the path to Allāh.

'Indeed the enmity between man and *Shayṭān* is old, commencing from the time that Ādam (*'alayhi as-salām*) was created - from the time that he was ordered to prostrate to him. *Shayṭān* refused, became arrogant and hence disobeyed his Lord. His arrogance and pride led him to commit a whole host of sins, it made him expend every effort in misleading the children of Adam and made him beautify and embellish sins such that they accepted them and eagerly committed them. Due to this, Allāh, the Exalted, revealed the Books, sent the Messengers and enjoined His servants to various injunctions and admonitions in order to secure them from the evil of *Shayṭān*. In the light of His advice, profound injunctions and severe warnings, mankind became separated into two groups: a group who were guided and a group who deserved to be misguided. The group who were guided are the inhabitants of Paradise and the group who were misguided are the denizens of the Fire. The inhabitants of Paradise are the *Awliyā'* of the Most Merciful and the denizens of the Fire are the *awliyā'* of *Shayṭān*.

وَمَن يَتَّخِذِ ٱلشَّيْطَٰنَ وَلِيًّا
مِّن دُونِ ٱللَّهِ فَقَدْ خَسِرَ خُسْرَانًا مُّبِينًا ﴿١١٩﴾

Whoever takes Shayṭān as an ally instead of Allāh has certainly sustained a clear loss.

[*An-Nisā'* (4): 119]

Presented to the reader is the book *'al-Furqān bayna Awliyā' ar-Raḥmān wa awliyā' ash-Shayṭān'* [1] at a time in which *Shayṭān* has overcome the majority of mankind and knowledge of the differences between the *Awliyā'* of the Most Merciful and the *awliyā'* of *Shayṭān* is seldom found.' [2] In it, the author explained, in detail, the most important differences between the two categories of *awliyā'*, tackling the subject from various different angles and thoroughly refuting those who have gone astray in this matter. He discussed the issue of miracles and furnished the principles he laid out with examples of miracles performed by both groups of the *awliyā'*. Furthermore, he clarified some of the most important aspects of the Muslim belief, in all of this depending entirely upon the Book, *Sunnah* and understanding of the *Salaf*. May Allāh have mercy upon him and reward him well.

Methodology Employed in the Translation:

1. The main edition used for the translation was that published with the notes, *ḥadīth* documentation and analysis of Fawāz

[1] The Definitive Criterion Between the *Awliyā'* of the Most Merciful and the *awliyā'* of *Shayṭān*.

[2] Adapted from 'Abdul-Qādir al-Arna'uṭ's introduction to his notes upon 'al-furqān' [*Maktaba Dār al-Bayān*, 1405/1985].

Aḥmad Zumarlī [*Dār Kutūb al-ʿArabī*, 1st edition, 1415/1995].

2. The *ḥadīth* documentation and analysis of this edition was extremely detailed and was summarised by the translator as follows:
    a. Only two or three of the most famous reference books for the *ḥadīth* being documented were mentioned.

    b. If the *ḥadīth* was to be found in a collection that has been translated into English, reference was made to the translation and to every occurrence of the h̲adeeth in that translation. Hence, for example, if a *ḥadīth* occurs in six different places in *Ṣaḥīḥ* Bukhārī, then all six places were mentioned.

    c. Only the conclusion of the analysis of the *ḥadīth* was mentioned - was it *ṣaḥīḥ*, *ḥasan* or *ḍaʿīf*.

    d. After this, the names of all the Companions who narrated the *ḥadīth*, or a similar *ḥadīth*, were mentioned along with just one reference book in which they were contained.

    e. Any additional points of benefit were also mentioned, sometimes translated verbatim and sometimes summarised depending upon their length or value.

3. Two other editions were also employed for both the translation and notes. These were:

    a. The edition published with the notes of Muṣṭapha bin al-ʿAdawī, [*Maktabah al-Īmān*]

    b. The edition published with the notes of ʿAbdur-Raḥmān

bin 'Abdul-Karīm al-Yaḥyā [*Dār al-Faḍīlah*, 1st edition, 1420/1999]

4. These secondary editions were used to add additional notes of benefit not found in the main edition discussed above. Therefore any footnotes preceded by:

    a. {F} Refer to the edition of Zumarlī
    b. {M} Refer to the edition of al-'Adawī
    c. {Y} Refer to the edition of al-Yaḥyā
    d. {T} Refer to additional notes added by the translator.

5. If no clear verdict on a *ḥadīth* was given, the works of Muḥammad Nāṣir ad-Dīn al-Albānī were resorted to.

6. Major differences in the texts between the various editions of the book were also pointed out in footnotes.

7. Chapter headings and sub-headings were added to the book based upon those found in the two secondary editions of the book. They are not from the work of the author, may Allāh have mercy upon him. The purpose of these headings was to facilitate the reading of the book and to allow the reader to follow the logical development of an argument that the author was pursuing. To this purpose, the translator felt it necessary to add one or two additional sub-headings.

8. A brief summary of each chapter was included at its end, this summary was adapted from the edition of al-Yaḥyā.

9. Indexes of Qur'ānic verses cited, *aḥādīth*, brief biographies of all personages mentioned in the text and descriptions of place names were also appended to the book.

IBN TAYMIYYAH

May Allāh have mercy upon him

HE is Aḥmad ibn ʻAbdu'l-Ḥalīm ibn ʻAbdu'l-Salām ibn ʻAbdullāh ibn Abū Qāsim ibn Taymiyyah al-Ḥarrānī Taqī al-Dīn Abū al-ʻAbbās ibn Shihāb al-Dīn. He was born in Ḥarrān, an old city within the Arabian Peninsula between Syria[1] and Iraq, on the tenth or the twelfth of the month *Rabīʻu'l-Awwal* in the year 661H. He and his family were later forced to flee to Damascus due to the occupation by the Tartars.

He came from a family of scholars, his father and grandfather were both scholars as were three of his brothers: ʻAbdu'l-Raḥmān, ʻAbdullāh and his half-brother, Muḥammad.

During his early studies of Islām, he never ceased to amaze his teachers at the strength of his memory, keen intelligence and depth of understanding. It is said that he was first allowed to give legal verdicts at the age of nineteen and he began teaching at *Dār al-Ḥadīth al-Sukriyyah* at the age of twenty-two.

[1] Ar. *Shām*, in those days represented the areas of Syria, Jordan and Palestine.

He became famous for his knowledge of ḥadīth, indeed he was a *Ḥāfiẓ* (Ḥadīth Master), and for his knowledge of the Qur'ān and its related sciences, he impressed all with his circles on *tafsīr.* He also attained expertise in *Usūl al-Fiqh* and *Fiqh*, knowledge of the differences of opinions present amongst the scholars, writing, mathematics, history, astronomy and medicine. Many of the scholars of his time testified that he had attained the rank of *Mujtahid.*

He always showed a great concern for the affairs and welfare of the Muslims and this manifested itself greatly in his efforts during the *Jihād* against the Tartars, Christians and *Rawāfiḍah* wherein his displays of bravery, courage and inspiring talks were one of the most important factors in the Muslims victory against their enemies. These efforts won the praise and admiration of many scholars and indeed the ensuing generations of Muslims to this very day.

Aside from the physical *Jihād*, ibn Taymiyyah launched an intellectual struggle against the various deviant sects and heretical ideas of his day. He refuted the *Shī'a*, the People of Theological Rhetoric (*Ahl al-Kalām*) - such as the *Jahmiyyah*, *Mu'tazilah* and many of *Ashā'irah*, the philosophers who promoted the school of the early Greeks (*falāsifa*), the majority of *Ṣūfi* sects and paths and the adherents of other religions. His criticisms were not based on a lack of understanding, rather he first gained an in-depth knowledge of each of these schools and as such his critique of them was systematic, acute and valid. For example it is said that his refutation of Greek philosophy was one of the most devastating attacks ever leveled against them. His refutation of Christianity was outstanding and his rebuttal of the *Shī'a* completely demolished their beliefs and innovations from root to branch.[2]

---

[2] When this is understood, the critique levelled against him by some that 'his learning exceeded his intellect' can safely be relegated to the trash bin.

Needless to say, these refutations, and his very direct methods of refuting, made him many enemies and as a result his life was full of trials and persecutions. His enemies were careful to look for anything by which they could attack him and they eventually found what they were looking for in his works of belief entitled *'Aqīdah al-Wāsiṭiyyah** and *'Aqīdah al-Ḥamawiyyah.* Due to their total misunderstanding of what he wrote, they accused him of anthropomorphism and had him imprisoned on more than one occasion. Ibn Kathīr mentions that some scholars sat with ibn Taymiyyah to debate with him concerning his *'Aqīdah al-Wāsiṭiyyah* and the debate ending with their agreeing with him in what he had written.[3] Similarly ibn Kathīr mentions that some scholars debated with him concerning *'Aqīdah al-Ḥamawiyyah* and his replies to their accusations could not be rebutted.[4] Ibn Taymiyyah was again imprisoned because of a legal ruling he gave concerning divorce, and yet again he was later imprisoned for a legal verdict he issued prohibiting making journeys for the purpose of visiting graves. It was during this imprisonment that he passed away.

With regards his personality and worship, he exerted a huge and lasting influence on all who met him and he was known for his worship and glorification of the Islāmic laws, both inwardly and outwardly. His complete reliance upon Allāh can be best summed up in what his student, ibn al-Qayyim, relates from him when he was told that his enemies had plotted to kill him or imprison him,

> If they kill me it will be martyrdom for me. If they expel

---

* See: *'A Textbook on Orthodox Sunni Creed, the Creed of al-Wāsitiyyah - being a translation of al-'Aqīdah al-Wāsitiyyah'* [trans. Abu Rumaysah, Dār as-Sunnah, 1430/2009].

[3] Ibn Kathīr, *Bidāyah wa an-Nihāyah* [Vol. 14, under the heading *'Aqd Majālis al-Thalātha*].

[4] Ibn Kathīr [14/5].

> me, it will be migration for me; if they expel me to Cyprus, I will call its people to Allāh so that they answer me. If they imprison me, it will be a place of worship for me.[5]

Ibn al-Qayyim himself said,

> Allāh knows, I have never seen anyone who had a better life than his. Despite the difficulties and all that expunges comfort and luxury, nay, things completely opposite to them; despite imprisonment, intimidation and oppression, ibn Taymiyyah had a purer life than anyone could. He was the most generous, the strongest of heart and the most joyful of souls, with the radiance of bliss in his face. When we were seized with fear and our thoughts turned negative, and the earth grew narrow for us, we would go to him. No sooner did we look at him and hear his words, all these feelings would leave us to be replaced by relief, strength, certainty and tranquillity.[6]

Al-Bazzār said,

> I was of those who knew well his habits, he would not talk to anyone unnecessarily after the prayer of Fajr and would remain performing the *dhikr* of Allāh in a low voice which perhaps could just be heard by one sitting next to him; and frequently would he direct his gaze to the sky. This he would do until the Sun had risen high and the time in which it is prohibited to pray was over.[7]

He also said,

---

[5] *Nāhiyah min Ḥayāh Shaykh al-Islām* [p. 30].

[6] Ibn al-Qayyim, *Al-Wābil al-Ṣayyib* [p. 69].

[7] Bazzār, *al-A'lām al-'Aliyyah* [p. 40]

> I have not seen him mention any of the pleasures and attractions of this world, he did not delve into worldly conversations and he never asked for any of its livelihood. Instead he directed his attentions and conversations to seeking the Hereafter and what could get him closer to Allāh.[8]

Once, the ruler Muḥammad ibn Qalāwūn accused him of wanting to wrench kingship from him due to his large following to which he replied,

> I would do that! By Allāh, your kingship and the kingship of Moghul is not even worth two meagre coins in my eyes![9]

His Teachers[10]

He studied under a great number of scholars and he himself mentioned a number of them as related by Dhahabī directly from him.[11] This particular chronicle of teachers includes forty-one male scholars and four female scholars. The total number of scholars whom he took knowledge from exceeds two hundred.[12]

---

[8] Bazzār [p.52].

[9] Bazzār [p. 74].

[10] Refer to: *Majmū' Fatāwā Shaykh al-Islām* [18/76-121]; *Dhayl ibn Rajab* [2/387]; Ibn Kathīr [14/136-137]; Dhahabī, *Tadhkirah al-Ḥuffādh* [3/1496]; Ibn Ḥajr al-'Asqalānī, *al-Durar al-Kāminah fi A'yān al-Mi'ah al-Thāminah* [1/154].

[11] *Majmū' al-Fatāwā* [18/76-121].

[12] *Al-'Uqūd al-Durriyyah* [p. 3]; *al-Kawākib al-Durriyyah* [p. 52].

The following is a selection of some of his teachers:

- Abū al-'Abbās Aḥmad ibn 'Abdu'l-Dā'im al-Maqdasī
- Abū Naṣr 'Abdu'l-'Azīz ibn 'Abdu'l-Mun'im
- Abū Muḥammad Ismā'īl ibn Ibrāhīm at-Tanūkhī
- Al-Manjā ibn 'Uthmān al-Tanūkhī al-Dimashqī
- Abu al-'Abbās al-Mu'ammil ibn Muḥammad al-Bālisī
- Abū 'Abdullāh Muḥammad ibn Abū Bakr ibn Sulaymān al-Āmirī
- Abū al-Faraj 'Abdu'l-Raḥmān ibn Sulaymān al-Baghdādī
- Sharaf ad-Dīn al-Maqdasī, Aḥmad ibn Aḥmad al-Shāfi'ī
- Muḥammad ibn 'Abdu-l-Qawī al-Maqdasī
- Taqī ad-Dīn al-Wāsiṭī, Ibrāhīm ibn 'Alī as-Ṣāliḥī al-Ḥanbalī
- His paternal aunt, Sitt ad-Dār bint 'Abdu'l-Salām ibn Taymiyyah

His Students

He had many students and those who were affected by him are many, some of his students were:

- Ibn al-Qayyim al-Jawziyyah, Muḥammad ibn Abū Bakr.
- Al-Dhahabī, Muḥammad ibn Aḥmad.
- Al-Mizzī, Yūsuf ibn 'Abdu'l-Raḥmān.
- Ibn Kathīr, Ismā'īl ibn 'Umar.
- Ibn 'Abdu'l-Hādī, Muḥammad ibn Aḥmad.
- Al-Bazzār, 'Umar ibn 'Alī.
- Ibn Qāḍī al-Jabal, Aḥmad ibn Ḥusain.
- Ibn Faḍlillāh al-Amrī, Aḥmad ibn Yaḥyā.
- Muḥammad ibn al-Manj, ibn 'Uthmān al-Tanūkhī.
- Yūsuf ibn 'Abdu'l-Maḥmūd ibn 'Abdu'l-Salām al-Battī.

- Ibn al-Wardī, Zayn al-Dīn 'Umar.
- 'Umar al-Ḥarrānī, Zayn al-Dīn Abū Ḥafs.
- Ibn Mufliḥ, Shams al-Dīn Abū 'Abdullāh.

The Praise of the Scholars for him

Many scholars praised ibn Taymiyyah, not only for his scholarly achievements but also for his active participation in *Jihād* and the affairs relating to public welfare, his abundant concern for others and his worship. Below is a selection of some of these statements:

1. Dhahabī said,

> It was amazing when he mentioned an issue over which there was a difference of opinion and when he gave evidence and decided the strongest opinion - he could perform *ijtihād* due to his fulfilling its conditions. I have not seen one who was quicker than he at recalling a verse which pertained to the issue that he derived from it, nor a man who was stronger in recalling texts and referring them to their sources. The *Sunnah* was in front of his eyes and upon the tip of his tongue with eloquent phrases and an open eye.
>
> He was a sign from the signs of Allāh in *tafsīr* and expounding upon it. With regards to the foundation of the religion and knowledge of the differing opinions [on an issue], he was unequalled - this alongside his generosity, courage and lack of attention to the joys of the soul.
>
> Quite possibly his legal rulings in the various sciences reached three hundred volumes, indeed more and he was always saying the truth for the sake of Allāh, not caring for the blame that came to him.

Whosoever associates with him and knows him well accuses me of falling short with regards to him. Whosoever opposes him and differs with him accuses me of exaggeration, and I have been wronged by both parties - his companions and his opponents.

He was white skinned with black hair and a black beard with a few grey hairs. His hair reached his earlobes and his eyes were eloquent tongues. He had broad shoulders and a loud, clear voice with a fast recitation. He was quick to anger but overcame it with patience and forbearance.

I have not seen his like for supplications [to Allāh], his seeking succour with Him and his abundant concern for others. However I do not believe him to be infallible, rather I differ with him on both fundamental and subsidiary matters, for he - despite his vast learning, extreme courage, fluid mind and regard for the sanctity of the religion - was a man from amongst men. He could be overcome with sharpness and anger in discussion, and attack his opponents [verbally] hence planting enmity in their souls towards him.

If only he were gentle to his opponents then there would have been a word of agreement over him - for indeed their great scholars bowed to his learning, acknowledged his ability, lack of mistakes and conceded that he was an ocean having no limits and a treasure having no equivalent...

He used to preserve the prayers and fasts, glorifying the laws outwardly and inwardly. He did not give legal rulings out of poor understanding for he was extremely intelligent, nor out of lack of knowledge for he was an overflowing ocean. Neither did he play with the religion but derived evidence from the Qur'ān, *Sunnah* and *Qiyās* (analogy), he proved [his stances] and argued following the footsteps of the *Imāms* who preceded him, so he has a reward if he erred and two rewards if he was correct.

He fell ill in the castle [wherein he was imprisoned] with a serious disease until he died on the night of Monday 20th *Dhū-l-Qaʿdah*, and they prayed over him in the *Masjid* of Damascus. Afterwards many talked about the number that attended his funeral prayer, and the least number given was fifty thousand.[13]

2. Ibn Ḥajr al-ʿAsqalānī said,

> The *Shaykh* of our *Shaykhs*, *al-Ḥāfiẓ* Abū al-Yuʿmarī [ibn Sayyid al-Nās] said in his biography of ibn Taymiyyah, 'al-Mizzī encouraged me to express my opinion on *Shaykh al-Islām* Taqī ad-Dīn. I found him to be from those who had acquired a fortune of knowledge in the sciences that he had. He used to completely memorise and implement the *Sunan* and *Āthār* (narrations). Should he speak about *tafsīr*, he would carry its flag, and should he pass a legal ruling in *fiqh*, he knew its limits. Should he speak about a ḥadīth, he was the seat of its knowledge and fully cognisant of its narrations. Should he give a lecture on religions and sects, none was seen who was more comprehensive or meticulous than he. He surpassed his contemporaries in every science, you would not see one like him and his own eye did not see one like himself...' [14]

3. Ibn Ḥajr also said,

> The acclaim of Taqī al-Dīn is more renown then that of

[13] Ibn Ḥajr, [under the biography of ibn Taymiyyah].

[14] Ibid.

the Sun and titling him *Shaykh al-Islām* of his era remains until our time upon the virtuous tongues. It will continue tomorrow just as it was yesterday. No one refutes this but a person who is ignorant of his prestige or one who turns away from justice...

...those of his stances that were rejected from him were not said by him due to mere whims and desires and neither did he obstinately and deliberately persist in them after the evidence was established against him. Here are his works overflowing with refutations of those who held to *tajsīm* (anthropomorphism), yet despite this he is a man who makes mistakes and is also correct. So that which he is correct in - and that is the majority - is to benefited from and Allāh's Mercy should be sought for him due to it, and that which he is incorrect in should not be blindly followed. Indeed he is excused for his mistakes because he is one of the *Imāms* of his time and it has been testified that he fulfilled the conditions of *ijtihād*...

From the astonishing qualities of this man was that he was the severest of people against the People of Innovation, the *Rawāfiḍah*, the *Ḥulūliyyah* and the *Ittiḥādiyyah*. His works on this are many and famous and his *fatāwā* on them cannot be counted, so how the eyes of these innovators must have found joy when they heard those who declared him to be a *kāfir*! And how delighted they must have been when they saw those who did not declare him to be a *kāfir* in turn being labeled *kāfir*! It is obligatory upon the one who has donned the robe of knowledge and possesses intelligence that he consider the words of a man based upon his well-known books or from the tongues of those who are trusted to accurately convey his words. Then he should isolate from all of this what is rejected and warn against it with the intention of giving sincere advice and to praise him for his excellent qualities and for what he was correct in, as is the way of the scholars.

> If there were no virtues of *Shaykh* Taqī al-Dīn except for his famous student *Shaykh* Shams al-Dīn ibn al-Qayyim al-Jawziyyah, writer of many works, from which both his opponents and supporters benefited, then this would be a sufficient indication of his [ibn Taymiyyah's] great position. And how could it be otherwise when the Shāfiʿī *Imāms* and others, not to speak of the Ḥanbalīs, of his time testified to his prominence in the [Islāmic] sciences...[15]

4. Ibn Kathīr said,

> The least he would do when he heard something was to memorise it and then busy himself with learning it. He was intelligent and had much committed to memory, he became an *Imām* in *tafsīr* and everything linked to it and knowledgeable in *fiqh*. Indeed it was said that he was more knowledgeable of the *fiqh* of the *madhhabs* than the followers of those very same *madhhabs* in his time and other than his time. He was a scholar in *Uṣūl* and the branches of the religion, in grammar, the language and other textual and intellectual sciences.... no scholar of a science would speak to him except that he thought that that science was the specialty of ibn Taymiyyah. As for ḥadīth then he was the carrier of its flag, a *Ḥāfiẓ*, able to distinguish the weak from the strong, fully acquainted with the narrators....[16]

He also said,

> He was, may Allāh have mercy upon him, from the great-

[15] From Ibn Ḥajr's endorsement of *Radd al-Wāfir* contained at the end of the book.

[16] Ibn Kathīr, [14/118-119].

est of scholars but also from those who err and are correct. However his errors with respect to his correct rulings were like a drop in a huge ocean and they are forgiven him as is authentically reported by Bukhārī,

> "When a ruler makes a ruling, and he is correct then he has two rewards, and if he has erred then he has one reward."

5. Al-Mizzī said,

> I have not seen the likes of him and his own eye had not seen the likes of himself. I have not seen one who was more knowledgeable than he of the Book and the Sunnah of His Messenger, nor one who followed them more closely.[17]

6. Ibn Rajab al-Ḥanbalī said,

> He is the *Imām*, the legal Jurist, the *Mujtahid*, the Scholar of Ḥadīth, the *Ḥāfiẓ*, the Explainer of the Qur'ān, the Ascetic, Taqī al-Dīn Abū al-'Abbās *Shaykh al-Islām*, the most knowledgeable of the knowledgeable. It is not possible to exaggerate his renown when he is mentioned and his fame does not require us to write a lengthy tract on him. He, may Allāh have mercy upon him, was unique in his time with respect to understanding the Qur'ān and knowledge of the realities of faith....[18]

[17] Bahjatul Baiṭār, *Ḥayāt Shaykh al-Islām ibn Taymiyyah* [p. 21].

[18] ibn Rajab, [2/387-392].

His Sayings

Shaykh al-Islām was famous for stating profound statements, below is a selection of some of them;

- Every punishment from Him is pure justice and every blessing from Him is pure grace.[19]
- Whoever desires everlasting bliss, let him adhere firmly to the threshold of servitude[20]
- The Lord loves to be loved.[21]
- Guidance is not attained except with knowledge and correct direction is not attained except with patience.[22]
- In this world there is a paradise, whoever does not enter it will not enter the Paradise of the Hereafter.[23]
- The one who is [truly] imprisoned is the one whose heart is imprisoned from Allāh and the captivated one is the one whose desires have enslaved him.[24]

---

[19] *Majmū' Fatāwā* [10/85]

[20] ibn al-Qayyim, *Madārij* [1/531]

[21] *Majmū' Fatāwā* [1/54]

[22] *Majmū' Fatāwā* [10/40]

[23] ibn al-Qayyim, *al-Wābil* [p. 69]

[24] Ibn al-Qayyim, *al-Wābil* [p. 69].

- This whole religion revolves around knowing the truth and acting by it, and action must be accompanied by patience.[25]

- Worship is founded upon the Legal Law and following it, not upon ones base desires and innovation.[26]

- If you do not taste the sweetness of an action in your heart, suspect it, for the Lord, Exalted is He, is the Appreciative.[27]

- The more the servant loves his Master, the less will he love other objects and they will decrease in number. The less the servant loves his Master, the more will he love other objects and they will increase in number.[28]

- Perpetually is the servant either the recipient of a blessing from Allāh, in which case he is need of gratitude; or he is the perpetrator of a sin, in which case he is in need of repentance; he is always moving from one blessing to another and is always in need of repentance.[29]

- Sins cause harm and repentance removes the cause.[30]

- Bearing witness to *tawḥīd* opens the door of good and repent-

[25] *Majmūʿ Fatāwā* [10/38]

[26] *Majmūʿ Fatāwā* [1/80]

[27] ibn al-Qayyim, *al-Madārij* [2/68]

[28] *Majmūʿ Fatāwā* [1/94]

[29] *Majmūʿ Fatāwā* [10/88]

[30] *Majmūʿ Fatāwā* [10/255]

ance from sins closes the door of evil.[31]

- The *Jihād* against the soul is the foundation for the *Jihād* against the disbelievers and hypocrites.[32]

- A man will never fear something besides Allāh unless it be due to a disease in his heart.[33]

- Trials and tribulation are like feeling the heat and cold, when one knows that they cannot be avoided, he will not feel anger at their onset, nor will he be distressed or disheartened.[34]

- The perfection of *tawḥīd* is found when there remains nothing in the heart except Allāh, the servant is left loving those He loves and what He loves, hating those He hates and what He hates, showing allegiance to those He has allegiance to, showing enmity to those He shows enmity towards, ordering what He orders and prohibiting what He prohibits.[35]

- In this world, man finds in the remembrance of Allāh, praising Him and worshipping Him, a delight that is incomparable to anything else.[36]

---

[31] *Majmūʿ Fatāwā* [10/256]

[32] ibn al-Qayyim, *ar-Rawḍah* [p. 478]

[33] Bazzār [p. 74]

[34] ibn al-Qayyim, *al-Madārij* [3/289]

[35] ibn al-Qayyim, *al-Madārij* [3/485]

[36] *Minhāj as-Sunnah* [5/389]

- The objective of asceticism is to leave all that harms the servants Hereafter and the objective of worship is to do all that will benefit his Hereafter.[37]

- Sins are like chains and locks preventing their perpetrator from roaming the vast garden of *tawḥīd* and reaping the fruits of righteous actions.[38]

- What can my enemies do to me? I have in my breast both my heaven and my garden. If I travel they are with me, never leaving me. Imprisonment for me is a chance to be alone with my Lord. To be killed is martyrdom and to be exiled from my land is a spiritual journey.[39]

His Death

Ibn Taymiyyah died while imprisoned on the twentieth of *Dhū-l-Qaʿdah* of the year 728H, after ultimately being banned from reading or writing. He fell sick for the few days preceding his death.

His funeral was attended by a huge congregation despite the many lies and slanders being spread about him by certain innovators of his time. Al-Bazzār says,

> Once the people had heard of his death, not a single person in Damascus who was able to attend the prayer and wanted to remained except that he appeared and was

[37] *Majmūʿ Fatāwā* [14/458]

[38] *Majmūʿ Fatāwā* [14/49]

[39] ibn al-Qayyim, *Wābil* [p. 69]

> present for it. As a result, the markets in Damascus were closed and all transactions of livelihood were stopped...Governors, heads, scholars, jurists all came out. They say that none of the majority of the people failed to turn up - according to my knowledge - except three individuals; they were well known for their enmity for ibn Taymiyyah and thus, hid away from the people out of fear for their lives.[40]

Ibn Kathīr said,

> There were so many people in front of his funeral, behind it, to its right and to its left. None but Allāh could enumerate them, and then someone shouted, 'this is how the funerals of the *Imāms* of the *Sunnah* are to be!' At that the people started to cry... when the call to prayer for *Ẓuhr* was proclaimed they prayed after it straight away against the usual norm. Once they finished prayer, the deputy *khaṭīb* came out - as the main *khaṭīb* was absent and in Egypt - and he led the prayer over ibn Taymiyyah... then the people poured out from everywhere and all the doors of the *Masjid*... and they assembled at *al-Khayl* market. [41]

His Works

Ibn Taymiyyah was a prolific writer and authored many works spanning a broad range of topics. The sum of his writings were thought to consist of hundreds of volumes and even though a large number of them have been lost, many are still available and in print. A number

[40] Bazzār [pp. 82-83].

[41] Ibn Kathīr [14/138].

of his works have also been translated and below is a list of these works followed by some of his works in Arabic. [42]

The books of, or about, ibn Taymiyyah available in the English language:

1. *Ibn Taymiyyah on Public and Private Law in Islam or Public Policy in Islamic Jurisprudence* [tr. Omar A. Farrukh, Khayats, 1966]
2. *A Seventh Century Sunni Creed: The Aqida al-Wastiya of ibn Taymiya* [tr. Merlin Swartz, the Hague: Mouton, 1973]
3. *Public Duties in Islam* [tr. Muhtar Holland, The Islamic Foundation, 1402/1982]
4. *Ibn Taymiyyah's Essay on the Jinn* [tr. Abu Ameenah Bilal Philips, 1409/1989]
5. *The Concise Legacy* [tr. Farhat Abbaas, Jam'iyyah Ihyaa Minhaaj as-Sunnah, 1415/1994]
6. *Introduction to the Principles of Tafseer* [tr. Muhammad Abdul Haqq Ansari, al-Hidaayah, 1414/1993]
7. *The Friends of Allāh and the Friends of Shayṭān* [trans. Abu Rumaysah, Daar as-Sunnah, 1421/2000].
8. *Ibn Taymiyyah Against the Greek Logicians* [tr. Wal B. Hallaq, Oxford University Press, 1993]
9. *A Textbook on Orthodox Sunni Creed, the Creed of al-Wāsitiyyah - being a translation of al-'Aqīdah al-Wāsitiyyah* [trans. Abu Rumaysah, Dār as-Sunnah, 1430/2009]..
10. *Fundamentals of Enjoining Good & Forbidding Evil* [tr. Abu Khalil & Muhammad al-Jibali, al-Qur'an & Sunnah Society of North America, 1997]
11. *Mukhatasar Iqtidaa as-Siraat al-Mustaqeem* [Dar-us-Salam Publications, 1416/1996]
12. *The Book of Eemaan* [compiled from the works of ibn Taymiyyah by Dr. Muhammad Nasim Yasim, al-Firdous Ltd.,

[42] None of the lists detailed below are meant to be exhaustive.

1997]

13. *Diseases of the Hearts and their Cures* [tr. Abu Rumaysah, Daar us-Sunnah, 1418/1998]
14. *Ibn Taymiyyah's Letters from Prison* [tr. Abu Ammar, Message of Islam, 1419/1998]
15. *The Waasitah Between Allaah & The Creation* [tr. Abu Iyaad Amjad Rafiq, Invitation to Islaam, 1998]
16. *Al-Ubudiyyah* [tr. Nasir ud-Deen Khattaab,]; also translated as *Ibn Taymiyyah's Essay on Servitude* [tr. Abu Safwan Fareed ibn Haibatan, al-Hidaayah, 1420/1999]
17. *Kitab al-Iman: Book of Faith* [tr. Salman Hasan al-Ani, Iman Publishing House, 1999]
18. *Ibn Taimiya's Struggle Against Popular Religion: with an annotated translation of his Kitab Iqtida as-Sirat al-Mustaqim Mukhalafat Ashab al-Jahim* [Muhammad Umar Memon, the Hague: Mouton, 1976]
19. *Ibn Taymiyyah and his Projects of Reform* [Serajul Haque, Islamic Foundation of Bangladesh, 1982]
20. *Ibn Taymiyyah's Ethics* [Victor E. Makari, Scholars Press, 1983]
21. *A Muslim Theologian's Response to Christianity: Ibn Taymiyyah's al-Jawab as-Sahih* [ed. Thomas F. Michel, Caravan Books, 1985]
22. *Economic Concepts of Ibn Taymiyyah* [Abdul Azim Islahi, The Islamic Foundation, 1408/1988]
23. *The Political Thought of ibn Taymiyyah* [prof. Qamaruddin Khan, Adam Publishers & Distributers, 1992]
24. *Ibn Taymiyyah & The Islamization of Knowledge* [Taha Jabir al-Alwani, IIIT, 1994]
25. *The Relief from Distress* - An explanation to the *duʿā* of Yūnus[trans. Abu Rumaysah, Daar us-Sunnah, 1425/2005].

The available Arabic works of ibn Taymiyyah are many, from amongst them:

1. *Majmū' Fatāwā ibn Taymiyyah* [compiled by 'Abdur-Raḥmān ibn Qāsim and his son, Muḥammad in thirty-seven volumes] containing many monographs and treatise that he wrote.
2. *Fatāwā al-Kubrā*, in five volumes
3. *Fatāwā al-Miṣriyyah*
4. *Al-Jawāb as-Ṣaḥīḥ li man Baddala Dīn al-Masīḥ*, in six volumes
5. *Minhāj as-Sunnah an-Nabawiyyah*, in six volumes
6. *Darr Ta'āruḍ al-'Aql wa-n-Naql*, in twelve volumes
7. *As-Ṣārim al-Maslūl 'alā Shātim ar-Rasūl*, in three volumes
8. *Naqd at-Ta'sīs*
9. *Iqtiḍā as-Ṣirāṭ al-Mustaqīm li Mukhālafah Aṣḥāb al-Jaḥīm*, in two volumes
10. *Al-Istiqāmah*
11. *Naqd Marātib al-Ijmā'*
12. *ar-Radd 'alā al-Manṭiqiyyīn*
13. *ar-Radd 'alā al-Akhnā'ī*
14. *ar-Radd 'alā al-Bakrī*
15. *an-Nubuwwāt*
16. *Qā'idah 'Adhīmah fi-l-Farq bayn 'Ibādah Ahl al-Islām wa-l-Īmān wa 'Ibādah Ahl ash-Shirk wa-n-Nifāq*
17. *Al-Qawā'id an-Nūrāniyyah al-Fiqhiyyah*
18. *Tafsīr ibn Taymiyyah*, compiled by 'Abdu-r-Raḥmān 'Umayrī, in seven volumes.

INTRODUCTION

ALL PRAISE AND THANKS ARE DUE TO ALLĀH, we seek His Help and we seek His Forgiveness.[1] We take refuge with Him from the evil of our souls and the evil of our actions. Whosoever Allāh guides, there is none who can misguide him, and whosoever Allāh leaves astray, there is none who can guide him. We bear witness that there is no deity worthy of worship except for Allāh Alone Who has no partner, and we bear witness that Muḥammad (ﷺ) is His servant and messenger. He sent him with true guidance and the religion of Truth such that it may become manifest and supreme over all other religions and sufficient is Allāh as a Witness.

He sent him just preceding the Last Hour as a giver of glad tidings and a warner, a caller to Allāh with His Permission and an illuminating torch [of light]. Through him He replaced misguidance with guidance, blindness with sight and aimless wandering with clear direction. Through him unseeing eyes were opened, deaf ears were released and sealed hearts were unlocked. Through him He distinguished Truth from falsehood, guidance from misguidance, clear

[1] {F} In some printed editions of *'al-Furqān'* the additional words 'and we seek His guidance' are found. However our Shaykh [al-Albānī] pointed out in his *'aṣ-Ṣaḥīḥah'* [1/5] that this wording finds no basis in any of the various routes by which this *khuṭbah* has been reported.

direction from aimless wandering, the believers from the disbelievers, the blissful People of Paradise from the wretched denizens of the Fire and the friends of Allāh from the enemies of Allāh.

Therefore whosoever Muḥammad (ﷺ) testified to be amongst the *Awliyā'* [2] of Allāh is indeed from the *Awliyā'* of the Most Merciful and whosoever he testified to be amongst the enemies of Allāh is indeed from the *awliyā'* of *Shayṭān.*

[The *Awliyā'* of the Most Merciful and the *Awliyā'* of *Shayṭān*]

Allāh, the Glorious and Exalted, has clearly explained in His Book and in the *Sunnah* of His Messenger (ﷺ) that He has *Awliyā'* from amongst mankind just as *Shayṭān* has his *awliyā'* and He distinguished and differentiated between the *Awliyā'* of the Most Merciful and the *awliyā'* of *Shayṭān*. Allāh, the Exalted says,

أَلَآ إِنَّ أَوْلِيَآءَ ٱللَّهِ لَا خَوْفٌ عَلَيْهِمْ وَلَا هُمْ يَحْزَنُونَ
﴿٦٢﴾ ٱلَّذِينَ ءَامَنُوا۟ وَكَانُوا۟ يَتَّقُونَ ﴿٦٣﴾ لَهُمُ ٱلْبُشْرَىٰ
فِى ٱلْحَيَوٰةِ ٱلدُّنْيَا وَفِى ٱلْءَاخِرَةِ ۚ لَا تَبْدِيلَ لِكَلِمَٰتِ ٱللَّهِ ۚ
ذَٰلِكَ هُوَ ٱلْفَوْزُ ٱلْعَظِيمُ ﴿٦٤﴾

> Unquestionably, for the *Awliyā'* of Allāh there will be no fear concerning them, nor will they grieve - those who believed and were fearing Allāh. For them are good tidings in the worldly life and in the Hereafter. No change is there in the words [i.e. decrees] of Allāh, that is the great

[2] {T} The word *Awliyā'* [أولياء](sing: *Waliy*) can be loosely translated as friends or allies. It will be explained more fully later, but throughout this work the word will be left untranslated.

achievement.

[*Yūnus* (10): 62-64]

ٱللَّهُ وَلِيُّ ٱلَّذِينَ ءَامَنُوا۟ يُخْرِجُهُم مِّنَ ٱلظُّلُمَٰتِ إِلَى ٱلنُّورِ ۖ
وَٱلَّذِينَ كَفَرُوٓا۟ أَوْلِيَآؤُهُمُ ٱلطَّٰغُوتُ يُخْرِجُونَهُم مِّنَ
ٱلنُّورِ إِلَى ٱلظُّلُمَٰتِ ۗ أُو۟لَٰٓئِكَ أَصْحَٰبُ ٱلنَّارِ ۖ هُمْ فِيهَا
خَٰلِدُونَ ﴿٢٥٧﴾

Allāh is the Ally (*Waliy*) of those who believe. He brings them out from the darknesses into the light. As for those who disbelieve - their *awliyā'* are all the false deities (*ṭāghut*), they take them out of the light and into the darknesses. Those are the companions of the Fire; they will abide eternally therein.

[*Al-Baqarah* (2): 257]

۞ يَٰٓأَيُّهَا ٱلَّذِينَ ءَامَنُوا۟ لَا تَتَّخِذُوا۟ ٱلْيَهُودَ وَٱلنَّصَٰرَىٰٓ أَوْلِيَآءَ ۘ بَعْضُهُمْ
أَوْلِيَآءُ بَعْضٍ ۚ وَمَن يَتَوَلَّهُم مِّنكُمْ فَإِنَّهُۥ مِنْهُمْ ۗ إِنَّ ٱللَّهَ لَا يَهْدِى ٱلْقَوْمَ
ٱلظَّٰلِمِينَ ﴿٥١﴾ فَتَرَى ٱلَّذِينَ فِى قُلُوبِهِم مَّرَضٌ يُسَٰرِعُونَ فِيهِمْ
يَقُولُونَ نَخْشَىٰٓ أَن تُصِيبَنَا دَآئِرَةٌ ۚ فَعَسَى ٱللَّهُ أَن يَأْتِىَ بِٱلْفَتْحِ أَوْ أَمْرٍ
مِّنْ عِندِهِۦ فَيُصْبِحُوا۟ عَلَىٰ مَآ أَسَرُّوا۟ فِىٓ أَنفُسِهِمْ نَٰدِمِينَ ﴿٥٢﴾
وَيَقُولُ ٱلَّذِينَ ءَامَنُوٓا۟ أَهَٰٓؤُلَآءِ ٱلَّذِينَ أَقْسَمُوا۟ بِٱللَّهِ جَهْدَ أَيْمَٰنِهِمْ ۙ
إِنَّهُمْ لَمَعَكُمْ ۚ حَبِطَتْ أَعْمَٰلُهُمْ فَأَصْبَحُوا۟ خَٰسِرِينَ ﴿٥٣﴾ يَٰٓأَيُّهَا
ٱلَّذِينَ ءَامَنُوا۟ مَن يَرْتَدَّ مِنكُمْ عَن دِينِهِۦ فَسَوْفَ يَأْتِى ٱللَّهُ بِقَوْمٍ يُحِبُّهُمْ
سَبِيلِ ٱللَّهِ وَلَا يَخَافُونَ لَوْمَةَ لَآئِمٍ ۚ ذَٰلِكَ فَضْلُ ٱللَّهِ يُؤْتِيهِ مَن يَشَآءُ ۚ
وَٱللَّهُ وَٰسِعٌ عَلِيمٌ ﴿٥٤﴾ إِنَّمَا وَلِيُّكُمُ ٱللَّهُ وَرَسُولُهُۥ وَٱلَّذِينَ ءَامَنُوا۟ ٱلَّذِينَ
يُقِيمُونَ ٱلصَّلَوٰةَ وَيُؤْتُونَ ٱلزَّكَوٰةَ وَهُمْ رَٰكِعُونَ ﴿٥٥﴾ وَمَن يَتَوَلَّ ٱللَّهَ
وَرَسُولَهُۥ وَٱلَّذِينَ ءَامَنُوا۟ فَإِنَّ حِزْبَ ٱللَّهِ هُمُ ٱلْغَٰلِبُونَ ﴿٥٦﴾

O you who have believed! Do not take the Jews and Christians as *awliyā'*, they are in fact *awliyā'* only of one another. And whoever is an ally to them among you - then indeed he is [one] of them. Indeed Allāh guides not the wrongdoing people. So you see those in whose hearts is a disease hastening [to join with] them saying, 'we are afraid a misfortune may strike us.' But perhaps Allāh will bring conquest or a decision from Him and they will become regretful over what they have been concealing within themselves. And those who believe will say, 'are these the ones who swore by Allāh their strongest oaths that indeed they were with you?' Their deeds have become worthless and they have become losers. O you who have believed! Whoever of you should revert from his religion - Allāh will bring forth [in place of them] a people He will Love and who will love Him, [who are] humble towards the believers and powerful against the disbelievers; they strive in the cause of Allāh and do not fear the blame of the critic. That is the favour of Allāh; He bestows it upon whom He Wills. Allāh is All-Encompassing and Knowing. Your *Waliy* is none but Allāh and His Messenger and those who have believed - those who establish the prayer, give the *zakāh* and bow down [in worship]. And whosoever is as *waliy* of Allāh and His Messenger and those who have believed, then indeed it is the party of Allāh who will be victorious.

[*Al-Mā'idah* (5): 51-56]

هُنَالِكَ ٱلْوَلَٰيَةُ لِلَّهِ ٱلْحَقِّ

There the authority [*wilāya*] is completely for Allāh, the Truth.

[*Al-Kahf* (18): 44]

And He, the Exalted, mentioned the *awliyā'* of Shayṭān with His words,

فَإِذَا قَرَأْتَ الْقُرْآنَ
فَاسْتَعِذْ بِاللَّهِ مِنَ الشَّيْطَانِ الرَّجِيمِ ﴿٩٨﴾ إِنَّهُ لَيْسَ لَهُ سُلْطَانٌ
عَلَى الَّذِينَ آمَنُوا وَعَلَىٰ رَبِّهِمْ يَتَوَكَّلُونَ ﴿٩٩﴾ إِنَّمَا
سُلْطَانُهُ عَلَى الَّذِينَ يَتَوَلَّوْنَهُ وَالَّذِينَ هُم بِهِ مُشْرِكُونَ

So when you recite the Qur'ān, [first] seek refuge with Allāh from Shayṭān, the Accursed. Indeed he has no authority over those who have believed and rely upon their Lord. His authority is only over those who take him as an ally and those who associate partners with Allāh through him.

[*An-Naḥl* (16): 98-100]

الَّذِينَ آمَنُوا يُقَاتِلُونَ فِي سَبِيلِ اللَّهِ ۖ وَالَّذِينَ كَفَرُوا
يُقَاتِلُونَ فِي سَبِيلِ الطَّاغُوتِ فَقَاتِلُوا أَوْلِيَاءَ الشَّيْطَانِ ۖ إِنَّ كَيْدَ
الشَّيْطَانِ كَانَ ضَعِيفًا ﴿٧٦﴾

Those who believe fight in the way of Allāh, and those who disbelieve fight in the cause of *ṭāghūt. So* fight against the *awliyā'* of Shayṭān, indeed the plot of Shayṭān has ever been weak.

[*An-Nisā'* (4): 76]

وَإِذْ قُلْنَا لِلْمَلَائِكَةِ اسْجُدُوا
لِآدَمَ فَسَجَدُوا إِلَّا إِبْلِيسَ كَانَ مِنَ الْجِنِّ فَفَسَقَ عَنْ أَمْرِ رَبِّهِ ۗ
أَفَتَتَّخِذُونَهُ وَذُرِّيَّتَهُ أَوْلِيَاءَ مِن دُونِي وَهُمْ لَكُمْ عَدُوٌّ ۚ
بِئْسَ لِلظَّالِمِينَ بَدَلًا ﴿٥٠﴾

And [mention] when we said to the Angels, 'Prostrate to Ādam,' and they prostrated, except for Iblīs, he was of the Jinn and departed from the command of his Lord.

Then will you take him and his descendants as *awliyā'* other than Me while they are your enemies? Wretched it is for the wrongdoers as an exchange.

[*Al-Kahf* (18): 50]

وَمَن يَتَّخِذِ ٱلشَّيْطَٰنَ وَلِيًّا
مِّن دُونِ ٱللَّهِ فَقَدْ خَسِرَ خُسْرَانًا مُّبِينًا ﴿١١٩﴾

And whoever takes *Shayṭān* as a *waliy* instead of Allāh has certainly sustained a clear loss.

[*An-Nisā'* (4): 119]

ٱلَّذِينَ قَالَ لَهُمُ ٱلنَّاسُ إِنَّ ٱلنَّاسَ قَدْ جَمَعُوا۟ لَكُمْ فَٱخْشَوْهُمْ
فَزَادَهُمْ إِيمَٰنًا وَقَالُوا۟ حَسْبُنَا ٱللَّهُ وَنِعْمَ ٱلْوَكِيلُ ﴿١٧٣﴾
فَٱنقَلَبُوا۟ بِنِعْمَةٍ مِّنَ ٱللَّهِ وَفَضْلٍ لَّمْ يَمْسَسْهُمْ سُوٓءٌ وَٱتَّبَعُوا۟
رِضْوَٰنَ ٱللَّهِ ۗ وَٱللَّهُ ذُو فَضْلٍ عَظِيمٍ ﴿١٧٤﴾ إِنَّمَا ذَٰلِكُمُ ٱلشَّيْطَٰنُ
يُخَوِّفُ أَوْلِيَآءَهُۥ فَلَا تَخَافُوهُمْ وَخَافُونِ إِن كُنتُم مُّؤْمِنِينَ ﴿١٧٥﴾

Those to whom [some] people said, 'Indeed the people have gathered against you, so fear them.' But it [only] increased them in faith and they said, 'Sufficient for us is Allāh and [He is] the best Disposer of affairs.' So they returned with favour and bounty from Allāh, no harm having touched them, and they pursued the good Pleasure of Allāh, and Allāh is the possessor of great bounty. It is only Shayṭān who inculcates fear [in you] of his *awliyā'*. So fear them not, but fear Me, if you are [indeed] believers.

[*Āli 'Imrān* (3): 173-175]

إِنَّا جَعَلْنَا ٱلشَّيَٰطِينَ أَوْلِيَآءَ لِلَّذِينَ لَا يُؤْمِنُونَ ﴿٢٧﴾ وَإِذَا فَعَلُوا۟
فَٰحِشَةً قَالُوا۟ وَجَدْنَا عَلَيْهَآ ءَابَآءَنَا وَٱللَّهُ أَمَرَنَا بِهَا ۗ قُلْ إِنَّ ٱللَّهَ
لَا يَأْمُرُ بِٱلْفَحْشَآءِ ۖ أَتَقُولُونَ عَلَى ٱللَّهِ مَا لَا تَعْلَمُونَ ﴿٢٨﴾ قُلْ
أَمَرَ رَبِّى بِٱلْقِسْطِ ۖ وَأَقِيمُوا۟ وُجُوهَكُمْ عِندَ كُلِّ مَسْجِدٍ
وَٱدْعُوهُ مُخْلِصِينَ لَهُ ٱلدِّينَ ۚ كَمَا بَدَأَكُمْ تَعُودُونَ ﴿٢٩﴾ فَرِيقًا
هَدَىٰ وَفَرِيقًا حَقَّ عَلَيْهِمُ ٱلضَّلَٰلَةُ ۗ إِنَّهُمُ ٱتَّخَذُوا۟ ٱلشَّيَٰطِينَ
أَوْلِيَآءَ مِن دُونِ ٱللَّهِ وَيَحْسَبُونَ أَنَّهُم مُّهْتَدُونَ ﴿٣٠﴾

We have made the devils *awliyā'* to those who do not believe. And when they commit an immorality, they say, 'We found our fathers doing it and Allāh has ordered us do it.' Say, 'Indeed Allāh does not order immorality. Do you say about Allāh that which you do not know?' Say, 'My Lord has ordered justice and that you maintain yourselves [in worship of Him] at every place [or time] of prostration, and invoke Him making your religion sincere to Him.' Just as He originated you, so will you return [to life] - A group [of you] He guided and a group deserved [to be in] error. Indeed they [the latter group] had taken the devils as *awliyā'* instead of Allāh while thinking they were guided.

[*Al-A'rāf* (7): 27-30]

وَإِنَّ ٱلشَّيَٰطِينَ لَيُوحُونَ إِلَىٰٓ
أَوْلِيَآئِهِمْ لِيُجَٰدِلُوكُمْ ۖ وَإِنْ أَطَعْتُمُوهُمْ إِنَّكُمْ لَمُشْرِكُونَ ﴿١٢١﴾

And indeed do the devils inspire their *awliyā'* [among men] to dispute with you. And if you were to obey them, indeed you would be associators [of others with Him].

[*Al-An'ām* (6): 121]

Al-Khalīl [Abraham] (*ʿalayhi as-salām*) said,

يَٰٓأَبَتِ إِنِّيٓ أَخَافُ أَن يَمَسَّكَ عَذَابٞ مِّنَ ٱلرَّحۡمَٰنِ
فَتَكُونَ لِلشَّيۡطَٰنِ وَلِيّٗا ﴿٤٥﴾

O my father, indeed I fear that there will touch you a punishment from the Most Merciful so you would be to Shayṭān a companion (*waliy*) [in Hellfire].

[*Maryam* (19): 45]

Allāh, the Exalted said,

يَٰٓأَيُّهَا ٱلَّذِينَ ءَامَنُواْ لَا تَتَّخِذُواْ عَدُوِّي وَعَدُوَّكُمۡ أَوۡلِيَآءَ تُلۡقُونَ
إِلَيۡهِم بِٱلۡمَوَدَّةِ وَقَدۡ كَفَرُواْ بِمَا جَآءَكُم مِّنَ ٱلۡحَقِّ يُخۡرِجُونَ ٱلرَّسُولَ
وَإِيَّاكُمۡ أَن تُؤۡمِنُواْ بِٱللَّهِ رَبِّكُمۡ إِن كُنتُمۡ خَرَجۡتُمۡ جِهَٰدٗا فِي سَبِيلِي
وَٱبۡتِغَآءَ مَرۡضَاتِيۚ تُسِرُّونَ إِلَيۡهِم بِٱلۡمَوَدَّةِ وَأَنَا۠ أَعۡلَمُ بِمَآ أَخۡفَيۡتُمۡ
وَمَآ أَعۡلَنتُمۡۚ وَمَن يَفۡعَلۡهُ مِنكُمۡ فَقَدۡ ضَلَّ سَوَآءَ ٱلسَّبِيلِ ﴿١﴾ إِن
يَثۡقَفُوكُمۡ يَكُونُواْ لَكُمۡ أَعۡدَآءٗ وَيَبۡسُطُوٓاْ إِلَيۡكُمۡ أَيۡدِيَهُمۡ وَأَلۡسِنَتَهُم
بِٱلسُّوٓءِ وَوَدُّواْ لَوۡ تَكۡفُرُونَ ﴿٢﴾ لَن تَنفَعَكُمۡ أَرۡحَامُكُمۡ وَلَآ أَوۡلَٰدُكُمۡۚ
يَوۡمَ ٱلۡقِيَٰمَةِ يَفۡصِلُ بَيۡنَكُمۡۚ وَٱللَّهُ بِمَا تَعۡمَلُونَ بَصِيرٞ ﴿٣﴾ قَدۡ
كَانَتۡ لَكُمۡ أُسۡوَةٌ حَسَنَةٞ فِيٓ إِبۡرَٰهِيمَ وَٱلَّذِينَ مَعَهُۥٓ إِذۡ قَالُواْ لِقَوۡمِهِمۡ
إِنَّا بُرَءَٰٓؤُاْ مِنكُمۡ وَمِمَّا تَعۡبُدُونَ مِن دُونِ ٱللَّهِ كَفَرۡنَا بِكُمۡ وَبَدَا بَيۡنَنَا
وَبَيۡنَكُمُ ٱلۡعَدَٰوَةُ وَٱلۡبَغۡضَآءُ أَبَدًا حَتَّىٰ تُؤۡمِنُواْ بِٱللَّهِ وَحۡدَهُۥٓ إِلَّا
قَوۡلَ إِبۡرَٰهِيمَ لِأَبِيهِ لَأَسۡتَغۡفِرَنَّ لَكَ وَمَآ أَمۡلِكُ لَكَ مِنَ ٱللَّهِ مِن شَيۡءٖۖ
رَّبَّنَا عَلَيۡكَ تَوَكَّلۡنَا وَإِلَيۡكَ أَنَبۡنَا وَإِلَيۡكَ ٱلۡمَصِيرُ ﴿٤﴾ رَبَّنَا لَا تَجۡعَلۡنَا
فِتۡنَةٗ لِّلَّذِينَ كَفَرُواْ وَٱغۡفِرۡ لَنَا رَبَّنَآۖ إِنَّكَ أَنتَ ٱلۡعَزِيزُ ٱلۡحَكِيمُ ﴿٥﴾

O you who have believed! Do not take my enemies and your enemies as *awliyāʾ*, extending to them affection while they have disbelieved in what came to you of the Truth, having driven out the Prophet and yourselves [only] because you believe in Allāh, your Lord. If you have come out for *Jihād* in My cause and to seek means to My good Pleasure, [take them not as friends]. You confide to them affection, but I am most knowing of what you have confided and what you have declared. And whoever does this amongst you has certainly strayed from the soundness of the way. If they gain dominance over you, they would be to you as enemies and extend against you their hands and their tongues with evil and they wish you would disbelieve. Never will your relatives or your children benefit you [and on] the Day of Resurrection He will judge between you, Allāh is Seeing of all that you do. There has already been an excellent pattern in Abraham and those with him when they said to their people, 'Indeed, we are free from you and whatever you worship besides Allāh. We have rejected you and there has appeared between us and you animosity and hatred forever until you believe in Allāh Alone,' except for the saying Abraham to his father, 'I will ask forgiveness for you, but I have no [power to do] anything against Allāh for you. Our Lord! Upon You we have relied and to You have we turned in repentance and to You is the destination. Our Lord! Make us not a trial for the disbelievers and forgive us, our Lord. Indeed, it is You Who is Exalted in Might, the Wise.

[*Al-Mumtaḥinah* (60): 1-5]

CHAPTER ONE

[The Obligation to Differentiate the *Awliyā'* of Allāh from the *awliyā'* of *Shayṭān*]

WHEN IT IS UNDERSTOOD that there are amongst mankind those who are the *Awliyā'* of the Most Merciful and those who are the *awliyā'* of Shayṭān, it becomes necessary to distinguish between the two, in the same way that Allāh and His Messenger (ﷺ) distinguished between the two.

[1.1 The Description of the *Awliyā'* of the Most Merciful]

Therefore the *Awliyā'* of Allāh are the pious, God-fearing believers. Allāh, the Exalted says,

أَلَآ إِنَّ أَوۡلِيَآءَ ٱللَّهِ لَا خَوۡفٌ عَلَيۡهِمۡ وَلَا هُمۡ يَحۡزَنُونَ
﴿٦٢﴾ ٱلَّذِينَ ءَامَنُواْ وَكَانُواْ يَتَّقُونَ ﴿٦٣﴾

> Unquestionably, for the *Awliyā'* of Allāh there will be no fear concerning them, nor will they grieve - those who believed and were fearing Allāh.
>
> [*Yūnus* (10): 62-63]

In the *ṣaḥīḥ* ḥadīth, reported by Bukhārī and others, from Abū Hurayrah (*raḍiyAllāhu 'anhu*) that the Prophet (ﷺ) said,

«يقول الله : من عادى لي ولياً فقد بارزني بالمحاربة - أو فقد آذنته بالحرب - وما تقرّب إليّ عبدي بمثل أداءِ ما افترضتُ عليه، ولا يزال عبدي يتقرب إليّ بالنوافل حتى أُحبَّهُ. فإذا أحببته، كنتُ سَمْعَهُ الذي يسمع به، وبصره الذي يبصر به، ويده التي يبطش بها، ورجله التي يمشي بها»

"Allāh says, 'Whosoever has mutual animosity with a friend (Waliy) of Mine, then he has declared war on Me - or I declare war on him. My servant does not draw close to Me with anything as he does by carrying out what I have made obligatory upon him. My servant continues to draw near to Me by performing optional deeds such that I love him. And when I love him, I am his hearing by which he hears, his sight by which he sees, his hand with which he strikes and his leg with which he walks. Were he to ask of Me, I would surely give him and were he to ask Me for refuge, I would surely grant it to him. I am never so hesitant to do something as I am to take the soul of my believing servant, he dislikes death and I Dislike to harm him but he must die.'" [1]

---

[1] {F} Reported by al-Bukhārī [Eng. Trans. 8/336 no. 509] and ibn Ḥibbān [no. 347]. The wording of Bukhārī is, "Allāh says, '*Whosoever has mutual animosity with a friend (Waliy) of Mine, then I declare war on him. My servant does not draw close to Me with anything more beloved to Me than what I have made obligatory upon him. My servant continues to draw near to Me by performing optional deeds such that I love him. And when I love him I am his hearing by which he hears, his sight by which he sees, his hand with which he strikes, and his leg with which he walks. Were he to ask of Me, I would surely give him; and were he to ask Me for refuge, I would surely grant it to him. I am never so hesitant to do something as I am to take the soul of my believing servant, he dislikes death and I Dislike to harm him.*' "

Similar *aḥādīth* have also been reported from 'Ā'ishah by Aḥmad [6/256]; Abū Umāmah by at-Ṭabarānī; 'Alī by al-Ismā'īlī, *'Musnad 'Alī'*; Ibn 'Abbās by at-Ṭabarānī; Anas by at-Ṭabarānī; and Maymūnah by Abū Ya'lā.

{Y} The wording, *'then he has declared war on Me,'* has not been reported by al-Bukhārī, rather it is reported by at-Ṭabarānī from Abū Umāmah and al-Bayhaqī =

In another report the wording is,

«فبي يسمع وبي يبصر، وبي يبطش، وبي يمشي»

"So it is for My sake that he hears, it is for My sake that he sees, it is for My sake that he strikes and it is for My sake that he walks."[2]

This is the most authentic *ḥadīth* that has been reported concerning the *Awliyā'* and in it the Prophet (ﷺ) explained that whosoever displays enmity to a *Waliy* of Allāh has declared war against Allāh.

In another *ḥadīth* it is mentioned,

«وإني لاثار لاوليائي كما يثار الليث الحرب»

"Indeed I will fight for My Awliyā' like the fighting of a ferocious, angry lion." [3]

Meaning that I will fight against those who display enmity [to My *Awliyā'*] on their behalf in the same way that the ferocious, angry lion fights. This is because the *Awliyā'* of Allāh are those who have believed in Him and befriended Him. They love what He Loves, hate what He Hates, are pleased with what Pleases Him and are angered by what Angers Him. They command what He commands, they prohibit what He prohibits, they give to those whom He Loves to be given and they withhold from those who He Loves to be withheld from. It is reported in at-Tirmidhī and others that the Prophet (ﷺ) said,

=

from Abū Hurayrah.

The wording, *'but he must die,'* is also not reported by Bukhārī but by at-Ṭabarānī from Anas.

[2] {Y} Reported by al-Hakīm at-Tirmidhī, *'Khatm al-Awliyā'*.

[3] {Y} Reported by al-Baghawī, *'Sharh as-Sunnah'* [no. 1249] and *al-Ḥāfiẓ* ibn Ḥajr, *'Fatḥ'* [11/293] indicated that it is *ḍa'īf* .

«أوثق عـرى الايمـان: الحب في الله والبغض فـي الله»

"The firmest bond of Faith is to love for the sake of Allāh and to hate for the sake of Allāh." [4]

In another *ḥadīth* reported by Abū Dāwūd, the Prophet (ﷺ) said,

«مـن أحـب لله،
وأبـغض لله، وأعطى لله، ومنع لله، فقد استكمل الإيمان»

"Whosoever loves for Allāh, hates for Allāh, gives for Allāh and withholds for Allāh has perfected faith." [5]

---

[4] {F} At-Tirmidhī [no. 2521], Aḥmad [3/438-440], Abū Ya'lā [no. 1485, 1500] and al-Ḥākim [2/164].

The wording of at-Tirmidhī is, '*Whosoever gives for Allāh, withholds for Allāh, loves for Allāh, hates for Allāh, and marries for Allāh has perfected his faith.*'

Then he ruled the ḥadīth to be *ḥasan*. I say: the *isnād* is *ḥasan inshaAllāh*. The ḥadīth has witnesses that further strengthen it such as the following ḥadīth.

Important note: you, O noble reader, will have noticed that the wording that *Shaykh al-Islām* attributed to at-Tirmidhī is different from the one found there, and maybe the reason for this was that he was quoting from memory, may Allāh have mercy upon him. The wording that *Shaykh al-Islām* quoted is found in the ḥadīth narrated by Barā'a bin 'Āzib from the Prophet (ﷺ) recorded by ibn Abī Shaybah, '*al-Īmān*' [no. 110], Aḥmad [4/286] and others.

Similar *aḥādīth* have been reported from ibn Mas'ūd by at-Ṭabarānī [no. 10531] with the wording of Barā'a; 'Amr bin al-Jamū' by Aḥmad [3/430]; and Abū Dharr by Aḥmad [5/146]. All of the above *isnāds* are problematic.

{T} Shaykh al-Albānī says about the ḥadīth of ibn Mas'ūd, "However at-Ṭabarānī, '*al-Kabīr*' reports it from ibn Mas'ūd from the Prophet (ﷺ) via another *isnād* and it is *ḥasan*, especially since a witness for it has preceded in the ḥadīth of Barā'a bin 'Āzib.' - ibn Abī Shaybah, '*Kitāb al-Īmān*' [no. 134], *taḥqīq* al-Albānī

[5] {F} Abū Dāwūd [Eng. Trans. 3/1312 no. 4664] and al-Baghawī, '*Sharḥ as-Sunnah*' [no. 3469] who has the additional words, '*Indeed the most noble of you are the ones who have the best manners and indeed good manners are part of faith.*'

I say: its *isnād* is *ḥasan*.

[1.2 The Basic Meaning of *Wilāyah*]

Al-Wilāyah (الولاية), or loyalty, is the opposite of *al-'Adāwah* (العداوة), or enmity. The essential meaning of *al-Wilāyah* is love and closeness whereas the essential meaning *al-'Adāwā* is hatred and distance. It is also postulated that the *Waliy* is called so because of his *muwālah*, or persistence and regularity in performing actions of obedience, meaning by this his following up [good actions] with more [good actions]. The first analysis is more correct.[6]

The *Waliy* , therefore, is one who is close. It is said, 'This is *yalī* to that,' meaning close to. Also in this respect is his (ﷺ) saying,

«ألحقوا
الفرائض بأهلها فما أبقت الفرائض فلأولى رجل ذكر»

"Give the assigned portions [of the inheritance] to their rightful owners, then that which remains should be given to the nearest (awlā) male man." [7]

Meaning the closest male relation to the deceased. He stressed

---

[6] {F} I say: the *waw*, *lām, yā* making up the word *Waliya* means to be close. Derived from this is the word *walyu*, which means closeness. It is said, 'He became distant after being close (*walyu*).' It is also said, 'He sat close to me (*yalīni*).' Therefore everyone who is next to you or close to you is a *waliy*.

In *'as-Ṣiḥāḥ'* it is mentioned that the *waliy* is the opposite of the *'aduww*, or enemy.

Ar-Rāghib said, '*al-Walā* and *at-Tawālī* means that two or more things occur such that anything that is not in them does not come between them.'

The word can be applied to closeness from the perspective of place, origin, religion and from the perspective of friendship, aid and belief.

Refer to: *'Mu'jam Maqāyīs al-Lughah'* [6/141]; ar-Rāghib, *'al-Mufradāt'* [pp. 533-534]; *'Al-Kulliyyāt'* [5/4]; *'Lisān al-'Arab'* [15/406-407]; *'Nuzhatul A'yun an-Nawāẓir'* [pp. 613-614].

[7] {F} Reported by al-Bukhārī [Eng. Trans. 8/477 no. 724, 8/479 no. 727, 8/481 no. 729, 8/487 no. 738] and Muslim [Eng. Trans. 3/852 no.'s 3929-3931].

this by mentioning the word male [alongside the word man] in order to clarify that the above ruling is specific to men only and that women are not included. In a similar vein, he (ﷺ) said with regards to the *zakāh*,

«فابن لبون ذكر»

"[...Then give] a male son of a milk-giving camel that is in its third year." [8]

Since the *Waliy* of Allāh is the one who conforms to and follows Allāh in all that He Loves and is Pleased with, Hates and is Displeased with, orders and prohibits, [it is not then surprising that] the enemy of the *Waliy* becomes His enemy. Allāh, the Exalted says,

يَٰٓأَيُّهَا ٱلَّذِينَ ءَامَنُوا۟ لَا تَتَّخِذُوا۟ عَدُوِّى وَعَدُوَّكُمْ أَوْلِيَآءَ تُلْقُونَ

O you who have believed! Do not take my enemies and your enemies as *Awliyā'*...

[*Al-Mumtaḥinah* (60): 1]

Therefore the one who shows enmity to the *Awliyā'* of Allāh has shown enmity to Him, and the one who has shown enmity to Him has declared war on Him. This is why he said,

«ومن عادى لي ولياً فقد بارزني بالمحاربة»

"Whosoever has mutual animosity with a friend (Waliy) of Mine, then he has declared war on Me."

[1.3 The Best and Most Noble of the *Awliyā'*]

The best and most noble of the *Awliyā'* of Allāh are His Prophets.

[8] {Y} Reported by Abū Dāwūd [Eng. Trans. 2/410 no. 1567], an-Nasā'ī [5/18] and ibn Mājah [no. 1800]

{T} and the ḥadīth is to be found in al-Albānī, *'Ṣaḥīḥ Abū Dāwūd'* [no.1385].

The best and most noble of the Prophets are the Messengers amongst them and the best of the Messengers are those of firm determination (*Ūlul 'Azm*), these being Noah, Abraham, Moses, Jesus and Muḥammad (ﷺ). Allāh, the Exalted says,

۞ شَرَعَ لَكُم مِّنَ الدِّينِ مَا وَصَّىٰ بِهِۦ نُوحًا وَالَّذِىٓ أَوْحَيْنَآ
إِلَيْكَ وَمَا وَصَّيْنَا بِهِۦٓ إِبْرَٰهِيمَ وَمُوسَىٰ وَعِيسَىٰٓ أَنْ أَقِيمُوا الدِّينَ
وَلَا تَتَفَرَّقُوا فِيهِ

> He has ordained for you the same religion that He enjoined upon Noah and that which We revealed to you, and what We enjoined upon Abraham, Moses and Jesus - to establish the religion and not be divided therein.
>
> [*Ash-Shūrā* (42): 13]

وَإِذْ أَخَذْنَا مِنَ النَّبِيِّـۧنَ مِيثَٰقَهُمْ وَمِنكَ وَمِن نُّوحٍ وَإِبْرَٰهِيمَ
وَمُوسَىٰ وَعِيسَى ابْنِ مَرْيَمَ وَأَخَذْنَا مِنْهُم مِّيثَٰقًا غَلِيظًا ﴿٧﴾
لِّيَسْـَٔلَ الصَّٰدِقِينَ عَن صِدْقِهِمْ وَأَعَدَّ لِلْكَٰفِرِينَ عَذَابًا أَلِيمًا

> And [mention] when We took from the Prophets their covenant and from you and from Noah, Abraham, Moses and Jesus, the son of Mary; and We took from them a solemn covenant. That He may question the truthful about their truth. And He has prepared for the disbelievers a painful punishment.
>
> [*Al-Aḥzāb* (33): 7-8]

The best and most noble of the Messengers of firm determination is Muḥammad (ﷺ), the seal of the Prophets, the Imām of the pious and God-fearing, Master of the children of Ādam, the Imām of the Prophets when they gathered and their spokesman when they came in delegations. He is the owner of the Praiseworthy Station - (*Maqām al-Maḥmūd*) for which he will be shown [permissible] envy [9] by the first and succeeding peoples, carrier of the banner of praise, possessor of the Fount - (*ḥawḍ*) at which the believers will gather and drink from [on the Last Day], the intercessor for the creation on the Day of Judgement and the owner of the rank of intercession - (*wasīlah*) and noble standing - (*faḍīlah*). He is the one who Allāh sent with the best of His Books, legislated for him the best laws of His religion and made his nation the best of nations brought forth for mankind. He gathered together all the noble and virtuous qualities for him and his nation that were only to be found scattered amongst the nations before him. They were the last of the nations to have been created yet the first of the nations to be resurrected as was mentioned by him (ﷺ),

> "*We are the last ones, the first ones on the Day of Resurrection even though they were given the Book before us and we were given it after them. This is their day over which they have differed* - meaning Friday - *which Allāh has guided us to. The people then follow after us; tomorrow for the Jews, and the day after tomorrow for the Christians.*" [10]

He (ﷺ) said,

«أنا أوّل من تنشقّ عنه الأرض»

[9] {T} Ar. *Ghubṭa*, referring to the permissible form of envy where the envier wishes to have the same blessings as the envied but without desiring to see them removed from the envied. This is opposed to *ḥasad*, the blameworthy form of envy where the envier wishes to see the blessings removed from the envied.

[10] {F} Reported by al-Bukhārī [Eng. Trans. 1/150 no. 239, 2/1 no. 1, 2/9 no. 21, 4/128 no. 204, 4/457 no. 693, 8/406 no. 621, 9/18 no. 26, 9/131 no. 160, 9/435 no. 587] and Muslim [Eng. Trans. 2/405 no.'s 1858-1861].

"I am the first one who the earth will give up." [11]

He (ﷺ) also said,

«آتي بـاب الجنـة
فأستفتح، فيقول الخازن: من أنت؟ فـأقول: أنـا محمد.
فيقـول: بك أُمـرت أن لا أفتح لأحد قبلك»

" I will come to the door of Paradise and attempt to open it. The guard will ask, 'Who are you?' I will reply, 'I am Muḥammad.' Thereupon he will say, 'You are the one for whom I was ordered to open and to no one else before you.'"[12]

[1.4 *Wilāyah* is Conditional Upon Following the Prophet (ﷺ) Inwardly and Outwardly]

The noble qualities of the Prophet (ﷺ) and his nation are many and from the point that Allāh commissioned him [as a Prophet], He appointed him as the determining factor between His *Awliyā'* and His enemies. Therefore no one can be a *Waliy* of Allāh until he believes in him, all that he came with and follows him both inwardly and outwardly. Whosoever claims to have love for Allāh, closeness and loyalty to Him, yet does not follow the Prophet (ﷺ) is in reality not from the *Awliyā'* of Allāh. Indeed whosoever opposes him (ﷺ) is from the enemies of Allāh and the *awliyā'* of Shayṭān. Allāh, the Exalted says,

قُلْ إِن كُنتُمْ تُحِبُّونَ ٱللَّهَ فَٱتَّبِعُونِى يُحْبِبْكُمُ ٱللَّهُ

Say: If you truly love Allāh then follow me, Allāh will

---

[11] {F} Reported by al-Bukhārī [Eng. Trans. 3/351 no. 595, 4/400 no. 610, 6/128 no. 162, 9/38 no. 52, 9/385 no. 524] and Muslim [Eng. Trans. 4/1230 no. 5655 - {T} although the relevant section of the ḥadīth has not been translated].

[12] {F} Reported by Muslim [Eng. Trans. 1/134 no. 284] and Aḥmad [3/136].

Love you...

[*Āli 'Imrān* (3): 31]

Al-Ḥasan al-Baṣrī (*raḍiyAllāhu 'anhu*) said,

> 'A people claimed that they loved Allāh, so Allāh revealed this verse in order to test them.'[13]

In this verse Allāh has made clear that whosoever follows the Messenger, then Allāh will Love him but whosoever claims to love Allāh, yet does not follow the Messenger (ﷺ), is not from the *Awliyā'* of Allāh. This is despite that fact that many people deceive themselves into thinking, about themselves or others, that they are the *Awliyā'* of Allāh, even though they are not in reality. For example the Jews and the Christians, they claim that they are the *Awliyā'* of Allāh and that none shall enter Paradise except those who are with them, indeed they even go as far as claiming to be the children of Allāh and His beloved! Allāh says,

وَقَالَتِ ٱلْيَهُودُ وَٱلنَّصَٰرَىٰ نَحْنُ أَبْنَٰٓؤُا۟ ٱللَّهِ وَأَحِبَّٰٓؤُهُۥ ۚ قُلْ
فَلِمَ يُعَذِّبُكُم بِذُنُوبِكُم ۖ بَلْ أَنتُم بَشَرٌ مِّمَّنْ خَلَقَ ۚ

[13] {F} Reported by ibn Jarīr, *'Tafsīr'* [3/231] with the words, 'A group of people during the time of the Prophet (ﷺ) said, 'O Muḥammad! Truly we love our Lord.' Thereupon Allāh revealed the verse,

قُلْ إِن كُنتُمْ تُحِبُّونَ ٱللَّهَ فَٱتَّبِعُونِى يُحْبِبْكُمُ ٱللَّهُ

> Say: If you truly love Allāh then follow me, Allāh will Love you...,

hence making the following of His Prophet, Muḥammad, a sign of those who love Him and [appointing] punishment for those who oppose him.' It is *mursal*.

It is also reported by ibn Jarīr [3/231] and ibn al-Mundhir via the route of Abū 'Ubayd an-Nājī - who is very weak (*wāhin*) - from Ḥasan.

Refer to: *'Ad-Durr al-Manthūr'* [2/17]; *'Tafsīr al-Baghawī'* [1/233]; ibn Kathīr [1/358].

> But the Jews and Christians say, 'We are the children of Allāh and His beloved.' Say, 'Then why does he punish you for your sins?' Rather you are human beings from those He has created.
>
> [*Al-Mā'idah* (5): 18]

وَقَالُوا لَن يَدْخُلَ الْجَنَّةَ إِلَّا مَن كَانَ هُودًا أَوْ نَصَارَىٰ ۗ
تِلْكَ أَمَانِيُّهُمْ ۗ قُلْ هَاتُوا بُرْهَانَكُمْ إِن كُنتُمْ
صَادِقِينَ ﴿١١١﴾ بَلَىٰ مَنْ أَسْلَمَ وَجْهَهُ لِلَّهِ وَهُوَ مُحْسِنٌ
فَلَهُ أَجْرُهُ عِندَ رَبِّهِ وَلَا خَوْفٌ عَلَيْهِمْ وَلَا هُمْ يَحْزَنُونَ ﴿١١٢﴾

> They say, 'None will enter Paradise except one who is a Jew or a Christian.' This is merely their wishful thinking. Say, 'Produce your proof if you should be truthful.' Yes, [on the contrary], whoever submits his face to Allāh while being a doer of good will have his reward with his Lord and no fear will there be concerning them, neither will they grieve.
>
> [*Al-Baqarah* (2): 111-112]

The polytheist Arabs used to claim that they were the 'People of Allāh' because they lived in Mecca, neighbouring the House, and they used to exult in this and pride themselves over all others. Allāh, the Exalted says,

قَدْ كَانَتْ آيَاتِي
تُتْلَىٰ عَلَيْكُمْ فَكُنتُمْ عَلَىٰ أَعْقَابِكُمْ تَنكِصُونَ ﴿٦٦﴾ مُسْتَكْبِرِينَ
بِهِ سَامِرًا تَهْجُرُونَ ﴿٦٧﴾

> My verses had already been recited to you, but you used to turn back on your heels in arrogance regarding it [the revelation], conversing by night and speaking evil.
>
> [*Al-Mu'minūn* (23): 66-67]

وَإِذْ يَمْكُرُ بِكَ ٱلَّذِينَ
كَفَرُوا۟ لِيُثْبِتُوكَ أَوْ يَقْتُلُوكَ أَوْ يُخْرِجُوكَ ۚ وَيَمْكُرُونَ وَيَمْكُرُ
ٱللَّهُ ۖ وَٱللَّهُ خَيْرُ ٱلْمَـٰكِرِينَ ﴿٣٠﴾ وَإِذَا تُتْلَىٰ عَلَيْهِمْ ءَايَـٰتُنَا
قَالُوا۟ قَدْ سَمِعْنَا لَوْ نَشَآءُ لَقُلْنَا مِثْلَ هَـٰذَآ ۙ إِنْ هَـٰذَآ إِلَّآ
أَسَـٰطِيرُ ٱلْأَوَّلِينَ ﴿٣١﴾ وَإِذْ قَالُوا۟ ٱللَّهُمَّ إِن كَانَ هَـٰذَا
هُوَ ٱلْحَقَّ مِنْ عِندِكَ فَأَمْطِرْ عَلَيْنَا حِجَارَةً مِّنَ ٱلسَّمَآءِ
أَوِ ٱئْتِنَا بِعَذَابٍ أَلِيمٍ ﴿٣٢﴾ وَمَا كَانَ ٱللَّهُ لِيُعَذِّبَهُمْ
وَأَنتَ فِيهِمْ ۚ وَمَا كَانَ ٱللَّهُ مُعَذِّبَهُمْ وَهُمْ يَسْتَغْفِرُونَ ﴿٣٣﴾
وَمَا لَهُمْ أَلَّا يُعَذِّبَهُمُ ٱللَّهُ وَهُمْ يَصُدُّونَ عَنِ ٱلْمَسْجِدِ
ٱلْحَرَامِ وَمَا كَانُوٓا۟ أَوْلِيَآءَهُۥٓ ۚ إِنْ أَوْلِيَآؤُهُۥٓ إِلَّا ٱلْمُتَّقُونَ
وَلَـٰكِنَّ أَكْثَرَهُمْ لَا يَعْلَمُونَ ﴿٣٤﴾

> And [remember] when those who disbelieved plotted against you to restrain you or kill you or evict you [from Mecca]. But they plan, and Allāh plans and Allāh is the best of planners.... But why should Allāh not punish them while they obstruct [people] from the Holy Mosque and they were not [fit to be] its guardians? Its [true] guardians are not but the righteous, but most of them do not know.
> [*Al-Anfāl* (8): 30-34]

So He, Glorious is He, explained that the polytheists are not His *Awliyā'* and neither are they the *Awliyā'* of His House, rather His *Awliyā'* are only the pious and God-fearing.

It is established in the Two Ṣaḥīḥs from 'Amr bin al-'Ās (*raḍiyAllāhu 'anhu*) who said, I heard the Messenger of Allāh (ﷺ) saying loudly and not in secret,

«إن آل فلان ليسوا لي بأولياء - يعني طائفة من
أقاربه - إنما وليي الله وصالح المؤمنين»

"*Indeed the family of so-and-so are not my Awliyā* - referring to a group of his close relations - *indeed my Waliy is only Allāh and the righteous believers.*" [14]

This is in complete conformity to the saying of Allāh, the Exalted,

فَإِنَّ ٱللَّهَ هُوَ مَوْلَىٰهُ وَجِبْرِيلُ وَصَٰلِحُ ٱلْمُؤْمِنِينَ

Then indeed Allāh is his Protector (*Mawlā*), and Gabriel and the righteous of the believers.

[*At-Taḥrīm* (66): 4]

The righteous of the believers are the pious, God-fearing believers - the *Awliyā'* of Allāh. Included amongst these are Abū Bakr, 'Umar, 'Uthmān, 'Alī and all of those who gave the Pledge of Allegiance with which Allāh was well pleased - *bay'atul riḍwān* - those who gave the pledge under the tree.[15] These people numbered four-

---

[14] {F} Reported by al-Bukhārī [Eng. Trans. 8/14 no. 19] and Muslim [Eng. Trans. 1/140 no. 417]

[15] {T} Allāh says,

۞ لَّقَدْ رَضِيَ ٱللَّهُ عَنِ
ٱلْمُؤْمِنِينَ إِذْ يُبَايِعُونَكَ تَحْتَ ٱلشَّجَرَةِ فَعَلِمَ مَا فِى قُلُوبِهِمْ
فَأَنزَلَ ٱلسَّكِينَةَ عَلَيْهِمْ وَأَثَٰبَهُمْ فَتْحًا قَرِيبًا ﴿١٨﴾

Indeed Allāh was well pleased with the believers when they pledged allegiance to you under the tree, and He knew what was in their hearts, so He sent down tranquility upon them and rewarded them with an imminent conquest.

[*Al-Fatḥ* (48): 18]

teen hundred[16] and all of them are in Paradise as is established in the *Ṣaḥīḥ* from the Prophet (ﷺ) that he said,

«لا يدخل النارَ أحدٌ ممن بايعَ تحت الشجرة»

"No one who gave the pledge of allegiance under the tree shall enter the Fire." [17]

This fact is also mentioned in another *ḥadīth*,

«إن أوليائي المتقون أيّاً كانوا وحيث كانوا»

"My Awliyā' are the pious and God-fearing, whosoever they may be and wheresoever they may be." [18]

In a similar vein [to the Jews, Christians and polytheists] are those from amongst the disbelievers who also claim to be *Awliyā'* of Allāh, although in reality they are not but instead are enemies of Allāh.

Similarly there are from the hypocrites [those who would claim to be a *Waliy* of Allāh]. Such people who openly display Islām, those

---

[16] {F} The narrations differ as to the exact number who gave the pledge of allegiance under the tree and it is reported that they were fourteen hundred or fifteen hundred. *Al-Ḥāfiẓ* [ibn Ḥajr] said in *'al-Fatḥ'* [7/440], 'The numbers are reconciled by understanding that they were more than fourteen hundred in number and this reconciliation is strengthened by a third report from Barā'a bin Āzib who said, 'They were fourteen hundred or more.' It was this reconciliation that an-Nawawī depended upon.'

[17] {F} Reported by Abū Dāwūd [Eng. Trans. 3/1305 no. 4636] and at-Tirmidhī [no. 3860]. I say: its *isnād* is *ṣaḥīḥ*.

A similar ḥadīth has also been reported from Umm Mubashshir in Ṣaḥīḥ Muslim [Eng. Trans. 4/1332 no. 6090].

[18] {F} Reported by Aḥmad [5/235] and at-Tabarānī, *'al-Kabīr'* [no. 241]. I say: its *isnād* is *ḥasan*.

Al-Haythamī, *'Majma' az-Zawā'id'* [10/232] said, 'Its *isnād* is good'.

who outwardly acknowledge the testimony that none has the right to be worshipped save Allāh, that Muḥammad is the Messenger of Allāh and that he has been sent to the whole of mankind - indeed both the races of mankind and Jinn. However, inwardly they conceal that which nullifies this such as their not really acknowledging that he is the Messenger of Allāh and that instead he is a king who enjoins a great following, who is governing the people by way of his intellect and views and is no different to other kings. Or they believe that he is the Messenger of Allāh but he has only been sent to the illiterate people [the Arabs] and not to the People of the Book as stated by many Jews and Christians. Or they believe that he has been sent to the generality of the creation but Allāh has a special elite, His *Awliyā'*, to whom he was not sent and they are in no need of him, rather such people have a route to Allāh that does not go via him (ﷺ) as was the case of Moses and Khiḍr.[19] Or they believe that they can take from Allāh all that they require, and benefit from what they have acquired such that they are in no need of intermediaries [with respect to conveying the revelation]. Or they believe that he has truly been sent, but he has been sent with mere outward, superficial laws and they agree to conform to these. However, as for the inner realities then he was not sent with these, or he not know them, or they have more knowledge of them than him, or they know them as he knows them but they have acquired this knowledge in a way that was not his way.

---

[19] {Y} He is the companion of Moses, it is said that he was a Prophet or a righteous servant - however the majority are of the opinion that he was a Prophet. This is because the realities behind his actions can only be known through revelation and because a person does not learn or follow except one who is above him and it is not possible that a non-prophet be above a Prophet. His name and life are greatly differed over and this difference is detailed by ibn Kathīr. Refer to: *'Tafsīr al-Qurṭubī'* [11/16] and *'al-Bidāyah wan Nihāyah'* [1/355].

[1.5 The People of *Ṣuffah*]

Some of these may even say, 'The *Ahlus Ṣuffah* were in no need of him and he was not sent to them.' Others from amongst these say, 'Allāh revealed to the *Ahlus Ṣuffah* inwardly all that He revealed to him on the night of the *Mi'rāj*, and hence they achieved the same status as him.' These people, by saying this, betray the profound depths of their ignorance for they do not know that the Night's Journey occurred [while he (ﷺ)] was in Mecca, as Allāh, the Exalted says,

سُبْحَٰنَ ٱلَّذِىٓ أَسْرَىٰ بِعَبْدِهِۦ لَيْلًا مِّنَ ٱلْمَسْجِدِ ٱلْحَرَامِ
إِلَى ٱلْمَسْجِدِ ٱلْأَقْصَا ٱلَّذِى بَٰرَكْنَا حَوْلَهُۥ لِنُرِيَهُۥ مِنْ ءَايَٰتِنَآ

> Exalted is He who took His servant by night from the *Masjid al--Ḥarām* to the *Masjid al-Aqṣā* whose surroundings We have blessed...
>
> [*Al-Isrā'* (17): 1]

However the [*Ahlus*] *Ṣuffah* did not exist until [after the Prophet (ﷺ) migrated to] Madīnah. The *Ahlus Ṣuffah* were a people who resided in the northern part of his (ﷺ) *Masjid* , they were strangers [to Madīnah] who had no family or friends with whom they could live. This is because the believers used to migrate to the Prophet (ﷺ) to Madīnah, so whosoever was able to find a place of residence set up his abode there, but the one who was unable to, stayed in the *Masjid* until it became easy for him to move to another place.

Because of this the *Ahlus Ṣuffah* were never a specific group of people who permanently resided in *as-Ṣuffah*, [rather their numbers varied] such that sometimes they were small in number and other times many in number. A man would stay there for some time and then move on to another place. Those who resided there were just like the remainder of the people, they had no specific quality that would make them stand out with regards their knowledge or religion. Indeed from them were those who apostated and were killed by the Prophet (ﷺ), an example of this lies with the people who came from ʿUraynah and found it difficult to acclimatise to Madīnah and as a result fell ill. The Prophet (ﷺ) ordered them to go to those camels whose udders were heavy with milk and to drink their milk and urine. After they had recovered, they murdered the shepherd who was tending to the camels and drove them away. The Prophet (ﷺ) dispatched a delegation to pursue them and they brought them to him [after having captured them]. He ordered that their hands and feet be amputated and that their eyes be cauterised, then he left them in *al-Ḥurrah* [20] [desperately] asking for water but finding none who would give them drink [until they died].

The ḥadīth about them is to be found in the Two Ṣaḥīḥs being reported from Anas,[21] and it is mentioned therein that they were residing in *as-Ṣuffah*. Therefore, the likes of these people would reside there just as the best of the Muslims would also reside there, such as Saʿd bin Abī Waqqāṣ (*raḍiyAllāhu ʿanhu*) who was the best of those who lived there after which he moved on. Abū Hurayrah (*raḍiyAllāhu ʿanhu*) also lived there. Abū ʿAbdur-Raḥmān as-Sulamī collected the history of all those who lived in *as-Ṣuffah*.

As for the *Anṣār* [22] then they never constituted part of the *Ahlus*

---

[20] {T} A well-known rocky place in Madīnah. They were left there because this place was close to where they had committed the crime. Refer to *'al-Fatḥ'* [1/449].

[21] {F} Reported by al-Bukhārī [Eng. Trans. 1/148 no. 234, 5/354 no. 505, 6/106 no. 134, 8/519 no. 794-796, 9/25 no. 37] and Muslim [Eng. Trans. 3/893 no.'s 4130-4137].

[22] {T} The *Anṣār* is a term referring to a group of the Muslims already residing the Madīnah, who aided those who migrated there.

Ṣuffah and likewise the seniors of the *Muhājirūn*[23] such as Abū Bakr, 'Umar, 'Uthmān, 'Alī, Ṭalḥah, az-Zubair, 'Abdur-Raḥmān bin Auf, Abū 'Ubaidah bin al-Jarrāḥ and others.[24]

[1.5.1 Some Fabricated *Aḥādīth* Concerning the *Awliyā'*]

It is reported that a servant of al-Mughīrah bin Shu'bah used to reside therein and that the Prophet (ﷺ) said about him,

«هذا واحد من السبعة»

"This is one of the seven."[25]

This ḥadīth is a lie by agreement of the People of Knowledge even though Abu Nu'aym has reported it in his *'al-Ḥilyah.'* The same applies to every ḥadīth reported from the Prophet (ﷺ) concerning the number of the *Awliyā', al-Abdāl* (الأبدال)the Substitutes,[26] *an-*

---

[23] {T} The *Muhājirūn* is a term referring to those Muslims who migrated to Madīnah.

[24] {T} Meaning, therefore, that in the eyes of these people the elite of the people were not to be found amongst the elite of the Companions!

[25] {M} Reported by Abū Nu'aym, *'al-Ḥilyah'* [2/24] under the biography of Hilāl, the servant of al-Mughīrah. His biography can also be found in *'al-Iṣābah'* [3/575-576].

{T} The seven refers to the number of the *Abdāl* as per al-Jarjānī, *'at- Ta'rīfāt'* [p. 93].

[26] {Y} *Al-Abdāl* is derived from *at-tabdīl,* to change or alter. According to the *Ṣufis* the *Abdāl* are seven people. When one of them travels to a place he leaves behind him a body which carries his form so that nobody knows that he has left. They are upon the heart of Abraham (*'alayhi as-salām*).

Refer to: *'Tahdhīb al-Lughah'* [14/132]; as-Samarqandī, *'Istilāḥāt as-Ṣūfiyyah'*[p. 8].

{T} In *'al-Qāmūs al-Muḥīt'*[p. 1247] it is mentioned that, 'The *Abdāl* are a people =

Nuqabā' (النقباء) the Leaders,[27] *an-Nujabā'* (النجباء) the Nobles,[28] *al-Awtād* (الاوتاد) the Poles[29] and *al-Aqṭāb* (الاقطاب) The Axis.[30] Exam-

=

through whom Allāh, the Mighty and Magnificent, will establish the earth. They are seventy in number, forty in Syria and thirty elsewhere. Not one of them dies except that another takes his place.' In *'an-Nihāyah fī Gharīb al-Ḥadīth'* [1/107] it is mentioned that the *Abdāl* are called so because each time one of them dies, he is substituted by another.

[27] {Y} *An-Naqīb* in the language means the one entrusted or the one responsible for looking after something. In the terminology of the *Ṣūfīs* it refers to those who have realised the inner or secret Name [of Allāh] and hence gaze into the depths of man and come to know their innersmost secrets and thoughts due to the veils being lifted for them. They are three hundred in number.

Refer to: *'Tahdhīb al-Lughah'* [9/197]; al-Jarjānī, *'at-Ta'rīfāt'* [p. 266].

[28] {Y} *An-Najīb* in the language refers to a person who is kind and generous, of noble lineage who carries on the noble ways of his ancestors. In the terminology of the *Ṣūfīs* it refers to those who have undertaken the responsibilty of carrying and resolving the burdens of man that normal human capabilities do not allow to be resolved. This is because of them being singled out due to their compassion and mercy and hence they only act for the sake of others.

Refer to: *'Tahdhīb al-Lughah'* [11/125]; *'at-Ta'rīfāt'* [p. 259].

[29] {Y} *Al-Watad* refers to the peg that is driven into the earth to support a tent, its plural is *awtād*. In the terminology of the *Ṣufīs* its refers to four individuals who are located at the four extremes of the earth - the north, south, east and west - and it is through them that Allāh preserves those regions of the earth due to their being the place to which Allāh, the Exalted, looks.

Refer to: *'Lisān al-Arab'* [3/444]; *'Istilāḥāt as-Ṣūfiyyah'* [p. 7].

[30] {Y} *Al-Quṭb* in the language refers to the center around which the spokes of the wheel revolve. The *Quṭb* of a people refers to their master. In the terminology of the *Ṣūfīs* it refers to the individual who is the place to which Allāh Looks in the world in every time and he is upon the heart of Isrāfīl.

Refer to: *'Tahdhīb al-Lughah'* [9/4]; *'at-Ta'rīfāt'* [p. 185].

{T} As-Ṣana'anī, after quoting the definitions of these terms as given by Jarjānī, states,

=

ples of this would be [the *aḥādīth* mentioning that they are] four, seven, twelve, forty, seventy, three hundred, or three hundred and thirteen in number, or that the *Quṭb* (القطب) Axis is one - nothing of this is authentic from the Prophet (ﷺ) [31] and such names were not mentioned by the *Salaf* with the exception of the term *al-Abdāl*.[32]

A ḥadīth concerning them, stating that they are forty in number and that they are from Syria, has been reported in the *Musnad* [of Aḥmad] from 'Alī, may Allāh ennoble his face.[33] This ḥadīth is

=

> We have only quoted these definitions so that the one who comes across them, and still possesses some knowledge of his religion and faith in Allāh, His Messengers and what His Messengers came with, will know that all of them are divorced from that which the Messengers came with and was revealed in the Books of Allāh, the Exalted. He will know that these are stances from amongst the stances held by those who deny Allāh and His Messengers just as he will know that they are the words of the worshippers of servants and that they revolve around the same principles adhered to by those who believe in the divinity of stars. - As-Ṣana'ānī, *'Al-Inṣāf fī Ḥaqīqah al-Awliyā'* [p. 15]

[31] {F} Refer to: *'al-Manār al-Munīf'* [p. 136]; *'al-Maqāṣid al-Ḥasanah'* [pp. 8-10]; *'Al-Lā'ī al-Maṣnū 'ah'* [2/330-332].

[32] {F} Such as the saying of ash-Shāfi'ī concerning some people, 'We used to count him amongst the *Abdāl*' and the saying of al-Bukhārī and others, 'They were in no doubt that he was from the *Abdāl*.' Refer to *'al-Maqāṣid al-Ḥasanah'* [p. 9].

[33] {F} Reported by Aḥmad [2/171] and its *isnād* is *ḍa'īf* due to its being *munqaṭi'*. Shuraiḥ bin 'Ubaid al-Ḥamsī did not meet 'Alī, he only met some of the *Ṣaḥābah* who were the last to pass away. Refer to *'at-Tahdhīb'* [4/328-329]; and Aḥmad Shākir, *'Sharḥ al-Musnad'* [2/171].

The text of the narration reads, 'The people of Syria were mentioned in the presence of 'Alī while he was in Iraq.' They said, 'Curse them O Leader of the

=

munqaṭi' and is not established [authentic]. It is known that 'Alī and those of the Companions who were with him were better and more noble than Mu'āwiyah and those who were with him in Syria. Therefore the best and most noble of mankind would not be found in the army of Mu'āwiyah (*raḍiyAllāhu 'anhu*) to the exception of the army of 'Alī (*raḍiyAllāhu 'anhu*).

Bukhārī and Muslim report from Abū Sa'īd (*raḍiyAllāhu 'anhu*) from the Prophet (ﷺ) that he said,

«تمرق مارقة من الدين على حين فُرقة من
المسلمين يقتلهم أولى الطائفتين بالحق»

> *"A group will desert the religion at a time when a split occurs between the Muslims. They will be killed by the closer of the two parties to the truth."* [34]

This group refers to the *Khawārij*, the *Ḥururiyyah*,[35] who deserted

=

Believers!' He said, "no, for I heard the Messenger of Allāh (ﷺ) saying,

> *'The Abdāl will be in Syria, they are forty in number and each time one of them dies, Allāh replaces him with another. By means of them Allāh brings down the rain, gives [the Muslims] victory over their enemies, and averts punishment from the people of Syria.'"*

[34] {Y} Reported by Bukhārī [Eng. Trans. 4/519 no. 808] and Muslim [Eng. Trans. 2/513 no.'s 2325-2327].

The words, *'They will be killed by the closer of the two parties to the truth'* are not found in Bukhārī, just in Muslim.

[35] {Y} They are the one who fought against 'Alī at Ṣiffīn. They were called *Ḥururiyyah* because they withdrew to Ḥururā after returning from Ṣiffīn. At that time they numbered twelve thousand. 'Alī (*raḍiyAllāhu 'anhu*) argued with them and some of them returned [to *Ahlus Sunnah*] and he fought the remainder, utterly defeating them. Refer to: *'al-Farq bayna al-Firaq'* [pp. 75-81] and *'al-Fatāwā'* [3/279].

when the split occurred between the Muslims during the *Khilāfah* (Caliphate) of 'Alī. They were fought by 'Alī bin Abī Ṭālib (*raḍiyAllāhu 'anhu*) and those with him, hence this authentic ḥadīth clearly proves that 'Alī and those with him were closer to the truth than Mu'āwiyah (*raḍiyAllāhu 'anhu*) and those with him. So how is it that the *Abdāl* be found in the lesser of the two parties and not in the better?

[Another inauthentic ḥadīth] is that which is reported from the Prophet (ﷺ) that when he heard a poet recite,

The serpent of base desires has bitten my liver
There is no doctor for it, nor one who could perform *ruqyā*
Except for the Beloved whose love has encompassed
all my heart[36]
For with Him lies my ruqyā and purification.

He (ﷺ) was overtaken with spiritual ecstasy (*wajd*) such that his cloak fell off his shoulders. This narration is a lie by agreement of the Scholars of Ḥadīth.[37] An even greater lie is what some of them

[36] {T} Ar: *Shaghfah.* Ibn al-Qayyim has described the various levels of love with his words, 'the starting point of love (*maḥabbah*) is the heart being devoted and dependant upon that which it beholds. This then intensifies to become fervent longing (*sabābah*) whereby the heart becomes totally dependant and devoted to the [object of its desire]. Then this further intensifies and becomes infatuation (*gharāmah*) which clings to the heart like the one seeking repayment of a debt clings firmly to the one who has to pay the debt. Then this intensifies and becomes passionate love (*'ishk*) and this is a love that transgresses all bounds. Then this further intensifies and becomes crazed passion (*shaghafa*) and this a love that encompasses every tiny part of the heart. Then this intensifies and becomes worshipful love (*tatayyuma*). *Tatayyum* means worship and it is said: *tayyama Allāh* i.e. he worshipped Allāh.' - *'al-Muntaqā min Ighāthatul Lahfān fī Maṣāyid ash-Shayṭān'* [p. 103] of ibn al-Qayyim, summarised by 'Alī Ḥasan.

[37] {F} This fabricated narration occurs in as-Sahrawardī, *''Awārif al-Ma'arif'* [p. 121].

report [in another version of this *ḥadīth*] that he ripped apart his cloak [in ecstasy] and that Jibrīl took a piece of this cloak and hung it on the Throne. This narration, along with those like it, are known by the People of Knowledge and cognisance of the Messenger (ﷺ) to be the most obvious of lies against him.

The same applies to what they report from ʿUmar (*raḍiyAllāhu ʿanhu*) that he said, 'the Prophet (ﷺ) and Abū Bakr used to talk to each other and I would be amongst them like one who had no comprehension of what they said.'[38] Again this narration is a lie and fabricated by agreement of the Scholars of Ḥadīth.

The point of this discussion is to show that there are amongst the people those who accept his message, generally and outwardly but inwardly believe that which nullifies their [outward show of belief], and hence become hypocrites. Such a person goes on to claim about himself and those like him that they are the *Awliyā'* of Allāh despite their inner disbelief in what the Messenger of Allāh (ﷺ) came with - either through rejection or ignorance.

This is similar to the belief of many Jews and Christians that they are the *Awliyā'* of Allāh, that Muḥammad is truly the Messenger of Allāh, but he was only sent to those other than the People of the Book and as such they are not obligated to follow him, reasoning that Allāh had already sent Messengers to them before him.

All of these people are disbelievers, even though they believe that their particular party are the *Awliyā'* of Allāh, for the true *Awliyā'* of

---

Refer to: *'al-Maqāṣid al-Ḥasanah'* [p. 333]; *'at-Tamyīz'* [p. 129]; *'al-Asrār al-Marfūʿah'* [pp. 272-275]; as-Suyuṭī, *'al-Ḥāwī'* [1/566]; *'ad-Durar al-Muntathirah'* [p. 282]; *'Tanzīh ash-Sharīʿah'* [2/233].

[38] {F} Refer to: *'Aḥādīth al-Quṣṣāṣ'* [pp. 77-78]; *'Tanzīh ash-Sharīʿah'* [1/407]; *'al-Fawā'id al-Majmūʿah'* [p. 335]; *'al-Manār al-Munīf'* [p. 115].

Allāh are those He has described as deserving His Love and closeness,

أَلَآ إِنَّ أَوْلِيَآءَ ٱللَّهِ لَا خَوْفٌ عَلَيْهِمْ وَلَا هُمْ يَحْزَنُونَ
﴿٦٢﴾ ٱلَّذِينَ ءَامَنُوا۟ وَكَانُوا۟ يَتَّقُونَ ﴿٦٣﴾

Unquestionably, for the *Awliyā'* of Allāh there will be no fear concerning them, nor will they grieve - those who believed and were fearing Allāh.

[*Yūnus* (10): 62-63]

[1.6 True Faith]

[True] Faith must include belief in Allāh, His Angels, His Books, His Messengers and the Last Day. It must also include belief in every Messenger that Allāh sent and every Book that Allāh revealed, as He, the Exalted says,

قُولُوٓا۟ ءَامَنَّا بِٱللَّهِ وَمَآ
أُنزِلَ إِلَيْنَا وَمَآ أُنزِلَ إِلَىٰٓ إِبْرَٰهِـۧمَ وَإِسْمَـٰعِيلَ وَإِسْحَـٰقَ وَيَعْقُوبَ
وَٱلْأَسْبَاطِ وَمَآ أُوتِىَ مُوسَىٰ وَعِيسَىٰ وَمَآ أُوتِىَ ٱلنَّبِيُّونَ
مِن رَّبِّهِمْ لَا نُفَرِّقُ بَيْنَ أَحَدٍ مِّنْهُمْ وَنَحْنُ لَهُۥ مُسْلِمُونَ ﴿١٣٦﴾
فَإِنْ ءَامَنُوا۟ بِمِثْلِ مَآ ءَامَنتُم بِهِۦ فَقَدِ ٱهْتَدَوا۟ ۖ وَّإِن تَوَلَّوْا۟ فَإِنَّمَا
هُمْ فِى شِقَاقٍ ۖ فَسَيَكْفِيكَهُمُ ٱللَّهُ ۚ وَهُوَ ٱلسَّمِيعُ ٱلْعَلِيمُ

Say, 'We have believed in Allāh and what has been revealed to us and what has been revealed to Abraham and Ishmael and Isaac and Jacob and the Descendants and what was given to Moses and Jesus and what was given to the prophets from their Lord. We make no distinction between any of them, and we are Muslims [having submitted] to Him.' So if they believe in the same way as you believe, then they have been rightly guided; but if they turn away, they are only in dissension and Allāh will be sufficient for you against them. He is the Hearing, the Knowing.

[*Al-Baqarah* (2): 136-137]

ءَامَنَ ٱلرَّسُولُ بِمَآ أُنزِلَ
إِلَيۡهِ مِن رَّبِّهِۦ وَٱلۡمُؤۡمِنُونَۚ كُلٌّ ءَامَنَ بِٱللَّهِ وَمَلَٰٓئِكَتِهِۦ وَكُتُبِهِۦ
وَرُسُلِهِۦ لَا نُفَرِّقُ بَيۡنَ أَحَدٖ مِّن رُّسُلِهِۦۚ وَقَالُواْ سَمِعۡنَا
وَأَطَعۡنَاۖ غُفۡرَانَكَ رَبَّنَا وَإِلَيۡكَ ٱلۡمَصِيرُ ﴿٢٨٥﴾ لَا يُكَلِّفُ
ٱللَّهُ نَفۡسًا إِلَّا وُسۡعَهَاۚ لَهَا مَا كَسَبَتۡ وَعَلَيۡهَا مَا ٱكۡتَسَبَتۡۗ
رَبَّنَا لَا تُؤَاخِذۡنَآ إِن نَّسِينَآ أَوۡ أَخۡطَأۡنَاۚ رَبَّنَا وَلَا تَحۡمِلۡ
عَلَيۡنَآ إِصۡرٗا كَمَا حَمَلۡتَهُۥ عَلَى ٱلَّذِينَ مِن قَبۡلِنَاۚ رَبَّنَا وَلَا
تُحَمِّلۡنَا مَا لَا طَاقَةَ لَنَا بِهِۦۖ وَٱعۡفُ عَنَّا وَٱغۡفِرۡ لَنَا وَٱرۡحَمۡنَآۚ
أَنتَ مَوۡلَىٰنَا فَٱنصُرۡنَا عَلَى ٱلۡقَوۡمِ ٱلۡكَٰفِرِينَ ﴿٢٨٦﴾

The Messenger has believed in what was revealed to him from his Lord, and [so have] the believers. All of them have believed in Allāh and His Angels and His Books and His Messengers, [saying], 'We make no distinction between any of His Messengers.' And they say, 'We hear and we obey. [We seek] Your forgiveness, our Lord, and to You is the [final] destination.' Allāh does not charge a soul except [with that within] its capacity. It will have [the consequence of] what [good] it has gained, and it will bear [the consequence of] what [evil] it has earned. 'Our Lord, do not impose blame upon us if we have forgotten or erred. Our Lord, and lay not upon us a burden like that which You laid upon those before us. Our Lord, and burden us not with that which we have no ability to bear.

Pardon us; forgive us; and have mercy upon us. You are our Protector, so give us victory over the disbelieving people.'

[*Al-Baqarah* (2): 285-286]

الٓمٓ ﴿١﴾ ذَٰلِكَ ٱلْكِتَٰبُ لَا رَيْبَ فِيهِ هُدًى
لِّلْمُتَّقِينَ ﴿٢﴾ ٱلَّذِينَ يُؤْمِنُونَ بِٱلْغَيْبِ وَيُقِيمُونَ ٱلصَّلَوٰةَ
وَمِمَّا رَزَقْنَٰهُمْ يُنفِقُونَ ﴿٣﴾ وَٱلَّذِينَ يُؤْمِنُونَ بِمَآ أُنزِلَ
إِلَيْكَ وَمَآ أُنزِلَ مِن قَبْلِكَ وَبِٱلْءَاخِرَةِ هُمْ يُوقِنُونَ ﴿٤﴾
أُوْلَٰٓئِكَ عَلَىٰ هُدًى مِّن رَّبِّهِمْ وَأُوْلَٰٓئِكَ
هُمُ ٱلْمُفْلِحُونَ ﴿٥﴾

Alif, Lām, Mīm. This is the Book about which there is no doubt, a guidance for those who fear Allāh - who believe in the unseen, establish the prayer and spend out of what We have provided for them. Who believe in what has been revealed to you and what was revealed before you, and of the Hereafter they are certain [in faith]. Those are upon [right] guidance from their Lord, and it is those who are successful.

[*Al-Baqarah* (2): 1-5]

Therefore true Faith must include the belief that Muḥammad (ﷺ) is the Seal of the Prophets, that there is no Prophet after him, and that he was sent to the entirety of the two races - the Jinn and mankind. So anyone who does not believe in what he came with is not a believer, let alone being one of the pious, God-fearing *Awliyā'* of Allāh! Furthermore, whosoever believes in a part of what he came with and disbelieves in the remainder is also a disbeliever and in no way a believer. Allāh, the Exalted says,

إِنَّ ٱلَّذِينَ يَكۡفُرُونَ
بِٱللَّهِ وَرُسُلِهِۦ وَيُرِيدُونَ أَن يُفَرِّقُواْ بَيۡنَ ٱللَّهِ وَرُسُلِهِۦ
وَيَقُولُونَ نُؤۡمِنُ بِبَعۡضٖ وَنَكۡفُرُ بِبَعۡضٖ وَيُرِيدُونَ
أَن يَتَّخِذُواْ بَيۡنَ ذَٰلِكَ سَبِيلًا ﴿١٥٠﴾ أُوْلَٰٓئِكَ هُمُ ٱلۡكَٰفِرُونَ
حَقّٗاۚ وَأَعۡتَدۡنَا لِلۡكَٰفِرِينَ عَذَابٗا مُّهِينٗا ﴿١٥١﴾ وَٱلَّذِينَ ءَامَنُواْ
بِٱللَّهِ وَرُسُلِهِۦ وَلَمۡ يُفَرِّقُواْ بَيۡنَ أَحَدٖ مِّنۡهُمۡ أُوْلَٰٓئِكَ سَوۡفَ
يُؤۡتِيهِمۡ أُجُورَهُمۡۚ وَكَانَ ٱللَّهُ غَفُورٗا رَّحِيمٗا ﴿١٥٢﴾

> Indeed, those who disbelieve in Allāh and His Messengers and wish to discriminate between Allāh and His Messengers and say, 'We believe in some and disbelieve in others,' and wish to adopt a way between - those are the disbelievers, truly. And We have prepared for the disbelievers a humiliating punishment. But those who believe in Allāh and His Messengers and do not discriminate between any of them - to those He is going to give their rewards. And ever is Allāh Forgiving and Merciful.
> [*An-Nisā'* (4): 150-152]

Part of believing in him (ﷺ) is to believe that he is the intermediary between Allāh and His creation with regards to conveying His command and prohibition, promise and threat and what He declared to be lawful and prohibited. Hence the lawful is what Allāh and His Messenger declared to be lawful, the prohibited is what Allāh and His Messenger declared to be prohibited, and the religion comprises only that which Allāh and His Messenger (ﷺ) legislated. Therefore whosoever believes that there is a person from amongst the *Awliyā'* who has a route to Allāh, other than through following Muḥammad (ﷺ), is a disbeliever and from the *awliyā'* of Shayṭān.

As for Allāh creating the creation, His providing for them, His answering their supplications, His guiding their hearts, His helping them against their enemies, and other such things that promote benefit and repress harm - then this is for Allāh Alone. He does this through setting up whatsoever causes (*asbāb*) He Wills [that would lead to acquisition of these benefits] and the mediation of the Messengers has no role to play in this whatsoever.

[1.7 The Obligation to Believe Everything the Messenger Came With]

Furthermore, if a person were to reach the heights of asceticism (*zuhd*), worship (*'ibādah*) and knowledge (*'ilm*), yet not believe in everything that Muḥammad (ﷺ) came with then neither can he be a believer, nor a *Waliy* of Allāh, the Exalted. An example of this lies with the Rabbis and Monks from amongst the scholars and worshippers of the Jews and Christians. The same applies to those who are attributed to knowledge and worship amongst the polytheists - the polytheists of the Arabs, Turks, Indians and others such as those [thought to be] the wise men of India and Turkey. Such a person may possess knowledge, asceticism or worship in his religion but is not a believer in everything that Muḥammad (ﷺ) came with, as such he is in reality a disbeliever and an enemy of Allāh, even if a group of people believe him to be a *Waliy* of Allāh. The same also applies to the wise men of Persia found amongst the Magians - they too are disbelievers as are the wise-men of Greece such as Aristotle (*Aristu*) and those like him, all of these people are polytheists who used to worship idols and the stars. Aristotle lived three hundred years before the Messiah (*'alayhi as-salām*) and was a minister for Alexander, son of Philip the Macedonian, about whom the Roman, Greek, Jewish and Christian historians wrote.

This Alexander is not *Dhūl Qarnain* who Allāh mentioned in His

Book, as surmised by some people, which in turn led them to believe that Aristotle was a minister of *Dhūl Qarnain.* They fell into this error because they saw that his name was Alexander just as *Dhūl Qarnain* [39] was possibly also called Alexander - this was the presumption of ibn Sīnā and those with him. The matter is not like this - this polytheist Alexander, whose minister was Aristotle, lived after the other, this Alexander was not the one who built the barrier and nor did he travel to the lands of *Ya'jūj* and *Ma'jūj* (the Gog and

---

[39] {F} They have differed about *Dhūl Qarnain* from a number of perspectives.

1. The reason for his being called *Dhūl Qarnain.*

It is said, 'Because he had in his head the likeness of two horns.'

Wahb bin Munabbih said, 'He used to have two horns of iron on his head' but this is *ḍa'īf.*

Some of the People of the Book said, 'Because he was the king of the Romans and the Persians.'

It is also said, 'Because he reached the rising and setting places of the sun (i.e. the whole earth) and reigned over all that lay between them.' This seems to be most likely and it is the opinion of az-Zuhrī. Other opinions have also been mentioned.

2. They differed as to whether he was a Prophet or not.

Some of the *Salaf* said, 'He was a righteous servant' and 'Alī said, 'He was not a Prophet, a Messenger or an Angel, rather he was a righteous servant.' It is also postulated that he was a Prophet or an Angel but these are strange positions.

3. They differed over his name.

It is reported from ibn 'Abbās that his name was 'Abdullāh bin ad-Ḍaḥḥāk bin Sa'd. It is also said that his name was Mus'ab bin 'Abdullāh.

In a ḥadīth it is mentioned that he was from Ḥumayr, that his mother was Roman and that he used to be called, 'The son of philosophy' because of his keen intellect.

As-Suhaylī said, 'His name was Marzubān bin Marzubah as stated by ibn Hishām.' Other opinions have also been mentioned.

Qataadah said: *Dhūl Qarnain* is Alexander, his father was the first of the Chosroes and was a child of Sām bin Nuh (*'alayhi as-salām*).

As for the second *Dhūl Qarnain* then he is Alexander son of Philip, the Macedonian who lived a long time after the first.

Refer to: *'al-Bidāyah wan Nihāyah'* [2/103-106]; *'Tafsīr al-Baghawī'* [3/178]; *'Tafsīr ibn Kathīr'* [3/100]; *'Zād al-Masīr'* [5/183-185]; *'al-Baḥr al-Muḥīṭ'* [6/157-159]; *'al-Kāmil fī at-Tārīkh'* [1/161].

Magog). It is this [polytheist] Alexander who finds mention in the well-known annals of Rome.

[1.8 The Influence of the Devils Over Their *Awliyā'*]

Amongst all the categories of polytheists - the polytheists of Arabia, India, Turkey, Greece and others, there are found those who exert themselves in acquiring knowledge, asceticism, and worship, but these people do not follow the Messengers and neither do they believe in what they came with. They do not consider to be true what they inform and nor do they obey them in that which they command, hence these people are neither believers and nor are they the *Awliyā'* of Allāh. The devils descend upon and accompany these people and through them they are able to unveil certain [unseen] realities to the people and perform some miraculous feats[40] of the type performed by magicians. Hence these people are nothing more than types of fortune-tellers and magicians upon whom the devils descend, Allāh, the Exalted says,

---

[40] {Y} *Khāriqul Ādah*, or miraculous feats, when performed by Prophets are technically termed *mu'jizāt* [sing. *mu'jizah*] and no one else is capable of performing a similar feat, they are of a number of different types and the author has mentioned some of the *mu'jizāt* of the Messenger (ﷺ) at the end of the book. When they are performed by the *Awliyā'* they are called *karāmāt* [sing. *karāmah*] and the author has mentioned a number of the *karāmāt* performed by the *Ṣaḥābah* and *Tābi'īn* at the end of the book. When they are performed by a *waliy* of Shayṭān then they fall under some type of deception, illusion or action performed by the devils, the author has mentioned examples of these at the end of the book.

Other terms are *mukhāṭabah* which refers to the servant hearing that which no one else can hear; *mushāhada* which is his seeing that which no one else can see; and *mukāshafah* which is his knowing what no one else knows.

This is in accordance to the terminology of the later scholars, as for the earlier scholars such as *Imām* Aḥmad then they used to call any miraculous feat, *mu'jizah* and refer to it as an *āyah* (sign).

Refer to: Al-Jarjānī, *'at-Ta'rīfāt'* [p. 184] and ibn Taymiyyah, *'Majmū' Fatāwā'* [11/311].

هَلْ أُنَبِّئُكُمْ عَلَىٰ مَن تَنَزَّلُ ٱلشَّيَٰطِينُ ﴿٢٢١﴾ تَنَزَّلُ عَلَىٰ
كُلِّ أَفَّاكٍ أَثِيمٍ ﴿٢٢٢﴾ يُلْقُونَ ٱلسَّمْعَ وَأَكْثَرُهُمْ كَٰذِبُونَ ﴿٢٢٣﴾

Shall I inform you upon whom the devils descend? They descend upon every sinful liar. They pass on what is heard and most of them are liars.

[*Ash-Shu'arā'* (26): 221-223]

All of the above mentioned types of people are to be imputed with unveilings and miraculous occurrences because they are not followers of the Messengers, as such they must lie and deceive in what they do just as their devils lie to them. There must be in their actions that which is sin and transgression such as various types of *shirk*, oppression, indecent acts, extremism or innovations in worship.

It is for this reason that the devils descend upon them and accompany them and hence they become the *awliyā'* of Shayṭān and not the *Awliyā'* of the Most Merciful. Allāh, the Exalted says,

وَمَن يَعْشُ عَن ذِكْرِ ٱلرَّحْمَٰنِ نُقَيِّضْ لَهُۥ شَيْطَٰنًا
فَهُوَ لَهُۥ قَرِينٌ ﴿٣٦﴾

And whoever is blinded from remembrance of the Most Merciful - We appoint for him a devil, and he is to him a companion.

[*Az-Zukhruf* (43): 36]

The remembrance (*dhikr*) of the Most Merciful is the remembrance He sent the Messenger (ﷺ) with, such as the Qur'ān. Therefore whosoever does not believe in the Qur'ān, accept its narratives to be true and believe in the obligation of its commands has turned away from it and as a result is assigned a devil who accompanies him.

Allāh, the Exalted says,

وَهَٰذَا ذِكْرٌ مُّبَارَكٌ أَنزَلْنَٰهُ ۚ أَفَأَنتُمْ لَهُۥ
مُنكِرُونَ ﴿٥٠﴾

And this [Qur'ān] is a blessed message which We have sent down. Then are you with it unacquainted?
[*Al-Anbiyā'* (21): 50]

وَمَنْ أَعْرَضَ عَن
ذِكْرِى فَإِنَّ لَهُۥ مَعِيشَةً ضَنكًا وَنَحْشُرُهُۥ يَوْمَ ٱلْقِيَٰمَةِ
أَعْمَىٰ ﴿١٢٤﴾ قَالَ رَبِّ لِمَ حَشَرْتَنِىٓ أَعْمَىٰ وَقَدْ كُنتُ بَصِيرًا ﴿١٢٥﴾
قَالَ كَذَٰلِكَ أَتَتْكَ ءَايَٰتُنَا فَنَسِيتَهَا ۖ وَكَذَٰلِكَ ٱلْيَوْمَ تُنسَىٰ ﴿١٢٦﴾

And whoever turns away from My remembrance - indeed, he will have a depressed life, and We will gather him on the Day of Resurrection blind. He will say, 'My Lord, why have You raised me blind while I was [once] seeing?' [Allāh] will say, 'Thus did Our signs come to you, and you forgot them; thus will you this Day be forgotten.'
[*Ṭā Hā* (20): 124-126]

This proves that His remembrance is His verses that He revealed. This is why if a person were to remember Allāh continuously, day and night, along with fulfilling the pinnacle of asceticism, worship of Him and exert himself for this purpose, yet does not follow His remembrance that He revealed - which is the Qur'ān - such a person is from the *awliyā'* of Shayṭān, even if he were to fly through the air and walk on water for indeed, it is the Shayṭān who carries him through the air. This is explained further in another place.

In Summary

- The description of the *Awliyā'* as doing all that Allāh Loves and is Pleased with.
- An explanation of the words *Wilāyah* and *'Adāwah*.
- It is obligatory to differentiate the *Awliyā'* of Allāh from the *awliyā'* of Shayṭān.
- The best of the *Awliyā'* are the Messengers and Prophets and the best of them is Muḥammad (ﷺ).
- Discussion of his (ﷺ) noble qualities and that all good qualities were combined in him.
- His nation is the best of nations and his *Sharī'ah* is the best of laws.
- *Wilāyah* is conditional upon following the Prophet (ﷺ) both inwardly and outwardly.
- Discussion of the false claimants to *Wilāyah* and that they are false because they contradict fundamental principles of Islām.
- Clarification of false beliefs concerning the *Awliyā'*.
- False beliefs concerning the *Ahlus Ṣuffah* and clarification that there was nothing special about them with regards their religion.
- Discussion of fabricated *aḥādīth* concerning the *Awliyā'*.
- Essential aspects of the Muslim faith and that true faith must include belief in Allāh, His Angels, His Books, His Messengers and the Last Day.

CHAPTER TWO

[People can Possess Faith and a Characteristic of Hypocrisy]

AMONGST THE PEOPLE ARE THOSE WHO have faith but also possess a characteristic of hypocrisy as is reported in the Two Ṣaḥīḥs from ʿAbdullāh bin ʿAmr (*raḍiyAllāhu ʿanhu*) that the Prophet (ﷺ) said,

«اربعٌ من كنَّ فيه ومن كانت فيه خَصْلَةٌ منهنّ، كانت
فيه خصلةٌ من النفاق حتى يَدَعها: إذا حدَّث كذب،
وإذا وعد أخلف، وإذا اؤتمن خان، وإذا عاهد غدر»

> *"There are four [qualities], whosoever has them is a hypocrite and whosoever has a characteristic of these four possesses a characteristic of hypocrisy until he leaves it: when he speaks he lies, when he promises he breaks it, when he makes a covenant he proves treacherous, and when he argues he behaves in an imprudent and uncouth manner."* [1]

Also in the Two Ṣaḥīḥs it is reported from Abū Hurayrah

[1] {F} Reported by Bukhārī [Eng. Trans. 1/31 no. 33, 3/382 no. 639, 4/269 no. 403] and Muslim [Eng. Trans. 1/40 no. 111].

(*raḍiyAllāhu ʿanhu*) that the Prophet (ﷺ) said,

«الإيمان بضع وستون -
أو بِضع وسبعون شعبة - أعلاها قول: لا إله إلا الله، وأدناها
إماطةُ الأذى عن الطريق، والحياءُ شعبة من الإيمان»

> *"Faith has sixty or seventy and odd branches. The most lofty of them is the saying, 'none has the right to be worshipped save Allāh,' and the least of them is to remove something harmful from the road and modesty is a branch of faith."* [2]

Hence the Prophet (ﷺ) explained that whosoever has a characteristic of these qualities [mentioned in the first ḥadīth] then he has a characteristic of hypocrisy until he leaves it.

It is also established in the Two Ṣaḥīḥs that he (ﷺ) said to Abū Dharr (*raḍiyAllāhu ʿanhu*),

«إنك امرؤٌ فيك جاهلية». فقال:
يا رسول الله! أعلى كِبَر سني؟ قال: «نعم»

> *"Indeed you still contain [some qualities] of the Pre-Islāmic ignorance.'* [3] He asked, 'despite my old age?' He replied, *'yes.'"* [4]

It is established from him (ﷺ) in the Ṣaḥīḥ that he said,

---

[2] {F} Reported by Bukhārī [Eng. Trans. 1/18 no. 8] and Muslim [Eng. Trans. 1/27 no. 56].

[3] {T} Ar. *Jāhiliyyah*. Technically this refers to the condition of a people before the guidance of Allāh reaches them, or the state of a people that prevents them from accepting the guidance of Allāh.

[4] {F} Reported by Bukhārī [Eng. Trans. 1/29 no. 29, 3/434 no. 721, 8/46 no. 76] and Muslim [Eng. Trans. 3/884 no.'s 4092-4094].

«أربع في أمتي من أمر الجاهلية: الفخرُ في الأحساب، والطعنُ في الأنساب، والنياحة على الميت، والإستسقاءُ بالنجوم»

"There are four things [found] in my nation that are from the affairs of jāhiliyyah: boasting about social status, abusing genealogies, wailing over the dead and seeking rain through the stars." [5]

It is reported in the Two Ṣaḥīḥs from Abū Hurayrah (*raḍiyAllāhu ʿanhu*) that the Prophet (ﷺ) said,

«آية المنافق ثلاث: إذا حدث كذب، وإذا وعد أخلف، وإذا اؤتمن خان»

"The signs of the hypocrite are three: when he speaks he lies, when he promises he breaks it and when he is entrusted with something he proves treacherous." [6]

In Ṣaḥīḥ Muslim [there occurs the additional wording],

«وإن صام وصلى وزعم أنه مسلم»

"Even if he fasts, prays and thinks that he is a Muslim." [7]

Al-Bukhārī mentions from ibn Abī Mulaykah that he said,

أدركت ثلاثين من أصحاب محمد - ﷺ - كلهم يخاف النفاق على نفسه

[5] {F} Reported by Muslim [Eng. Trans. 2/444 no. 2033] and Aḥmad [5/342-344].

[6] {F} Reported by Bukhārī [Eng. Trans. 1/31 no. 32, 3/524 no. 847, 4/8 no. 12, 8/76 no. 117] and Muslim [Eng. Trans. 1/40 no.'s 112-115].

[7] {F} Reported by Muslim [Eng. Trans. 1/41 no. 115].

> "I have met thirty of the Companions of Muḥammad (ﷺ) all of them fearing hypocrisy for themselves." [8]

Allāh, the Exalted says,

وَمَآ أَصَٰبَكُمْ يَوْمَ ٱلْتَقَى ٱلْجَمْعَانِ فَبِإِذْنِ ٱللَّهِ وَلِيَعْلَمَ ٱلْمُؤْمِنِينَ
﴿١٦٦﴾ وَلِيَعْلَمَ ٱلَّذِينَ نَافَقُوا۟ ۚ وَقِيلَ لَهُمْ تَعَالَوْا۟ قَٰتِلُوا۟ فِى سَبِيلِ ٱللَّهِ
أَوِ ٱدْفَعُوا۟ ۖ قَالُوا۟ لَوْ نَعْلَمُ قِتَالًا لَّٱتَّبَعْنَٰكُمْ ۗ هُمْ لِلْكُفْرِ
يَوْمَئِذٍ أَقْرَبُ مِنْهُمْ لِلْإِيمَٰنِ ۚ

> And what struck you on the day the two armies met [at Uhud] was by the permission of Allāh so that He might make evident the [true] believers and that He might make evident those who are the hypocrites. For it was said to them, 'Come, fight in the Way of Allāh or [at least] defend.' They said, 'If we had known [there would be] fighting we would have followed you.' They were nearer to disbelief that day than to faith.
>
> [*Āli 'Imrān* (3): 166-167]

So He declared these people to be closer to disbelief than belief [on that day], thus it becomes known that they had mixed faith with disbelief, and that their disbelief was the stronger of the two. [Likewise] others who have mixed faith with disbelief could find that their faith is the stronger of the two.

[2.1 The Increase and Decrease of Faith]

Now, when it is known that the *Awliyā'* of Allāh are the pious, God-fearing believers, then [know that] the servants love of and

---

[8] {F} Reported by Bukhārī [Eng. Trans. 1/40 chpt. 37] as a *mu'allaq* narration, designating it with certainty and quoted its complete *isnād* in *'Tārīkh al-Kabīr'* [3/1/137]

closeness to Allāh (*wilāyah*) will be determined by the amount of faith and *taqwā* he has. Therefore the one who is more complete with regards his faith and *taqwā* is closer to and has greater love of Allāh, the Exalted. Hence the people are of varying degrees in their closeness to, and love of Allāh, the Mighty and Magnificent, varying in accordance to their degrees of completion in faith and *taqwā*. Similarly people are of varying degrees with regards their enmity to Allāh, which is determined in accordance to their level of disbelief and hypocrisy. Allāh, the Exalted says,

وَإِذَا مَآ أُنزِلَتْ سُورَةٌ فَمِنْهُم مَّن يَقُولُ أَيُّكُمْ زَادَتْهُ هَٰذِهِۦٓ
إِيمَٰنًا ۚ فَأَمَّا ٱلَّذِينَ ءَامَنُوا۟ فَزَادَتْهُمْ إِيمَٰنًا وَهُمْ يَسْتَبْشِرُونَ
﴿١٢٤﴾ وَأَمَّا ٱلَّذِينَ فِى قُلُوبِهِم مَّرَضٌ فَزَادَتْهُمْ رِجْسًا
إِلَىٰ رِجْسِهِمْ وَمَاتُوا۟ وَهُمْ كَٰفِرُونَ ﴿١٢٥﴾

> And whenever a *Sūrah* is revealed, there are among them [the hypocrites] those who say, 'Which of you has this increased in faith?' As for those who have believed, it has increased them in faith and they rejoice. But as for those in whose hearts is a disease, it has [only] increased them in evil [in addition] to their evil and they will have died while they are disbelievers.
>
> [*At-Tawbah* (9): 124-125]

إِنَّمَا ٱلنَّسِىٓءُ زِيَادَةٌ فِى ٱلْكُفْرِ ۖ

> Indeed, the postponing [of restriction within the sacred months] is an increase in disbelief.
>
> [*At-Tawbah* (9): 37]

وَٱلَّذِينَ ٱهْتَدَوْا۟ زَادَهُمْ هُدًى وَءَاتَىٰهُمْ تَقْوَىٰهُمْ ﴿١٧﴾

> And those who are guided - He increases them in guidance and grants them their righteousness.
>
> [*Muhammad* (47): 17]

He, the Exalted, says with regards the hypocrites,

فِي قُلُوبِهِم مَّرَضٌ فَزَادَهُمُ ٱللَّهُ مَرَضًا

> In their hearts is a disease, so Allāh has increased their disease.
>
> [*Al-Baqarah* (2): 10]

In conclusion, Allāh, the Glorious and Exalted, has explained that a single person could have some measure of closeness and allegiance to Allāh in accordance to his level of faith and also have some measure of enmity to Allāh in accordance to his level of disbelief and hypocrisy. Allāh, the Exalted says,

وَيَزْدَادَ ٱلَّذِينَ ءَامَنُوٓا۟ إِيمَٰنًا

> And those who have believed will increase in faith.
>
> [*Al-Muddaththir* (74): 31]

لِيَزْدَادُوٓا۟ إِيمَٰنًا مَّعَ إِيمَٰنِهِمْ

> ...so that they would increase in faith along with their [present] faith.
>
> [*Al-Fatḥ* (48): 4]

In Summary

- A single person can contain both faith and hypocrisy.
- Therefore the *Awliyā'* are of differing levels.
- And the enemies of Allāh are also of differing levels.

CHAPTER THREE

[The *Awliyā'* of Allāh are of Two Categories]

[3.1 The Levels of *Wilāyah*]

THE *AWLIYĀ'* OF ALLĀH ARE OF TWO categories: the Forerunners, who have been brought close to Allāh[1] and the Companions of the Right, who take a medium course [such that they do what Allāh commands and leave what He prohibits].[2] Allāh has mentioned them in a number of places in His Noble Book - in the beginning of *Sūrah al-Wāq'iah* and at its end, in *Sūrah al-Insān*, *Muṭaffifīn* and in *Sūrah Fāṭir*. In *Sūrah al-Wāq'iah*, Allāh, the Glorious and Exalted, has mentioned the Greater Judgement Day in the beginning of the chapter and the Lesser Judgement Day at its end. He said at the beginning of this *Sūrah*,

---

[1] Ar: *sābiqūn muqarrabūn* [سابقون، مقرّبون]

[2] Ar: *aṣhābul yamīn muqtasidūn* [اصحاب يمين مقتصدون]

إِذَا وَقَعَتِ ٱلْوَاقِعَةُ ﴿١﴾ لَيْسَ لِوَقْعَتِهَا كَاذِبَةٌ ﴿٢﴾ خَافِضَةٌ رَّافِعَةٌ
﴿٣﴾ إِذَا رُجَّتِ ٱلْأَرْضُ رَجًّا ﴿٤﴾ وَبُسَّتِ ٱلْجِبَالُ بَسًّا ﴿٥﴾
فَكَانَتْ هَبَآءً مُّنۢبَثًّا ﴿٦﴾ وَكُنتُمْ أَزْوَٰجًا ثَلَٰثَةً ﴿٧﴾ فَأَصْحَٰبُ
ٱلْمَيْمَنَةِ مَآ أَصْحَٰبُ ٱلْمَيْمَنَةِ ﴿٨﴾ وَأَصْحَٰبُ ٱلْمَشْـَٔمَةِ مَآ أَصْحَٰبُ
ٱلْمَشْـَٔمَةِ ﴿٩﴾ وَٱلسَّٰبِقُونَ ٱلسَّٰبِقُونَ ﴿١٠﴾ أُوْلَٰٓئِكَ ٱلْمُقَرَّبُونَ ﴿١١﴾
فِى جَنَّٰتِ ٱلنَّعِيمِ ﴿١٢﴾ ثُلَّةٌ مِّنَ ٱلْأَوَّلِينَ ﴿١٣﴾ وَقَلِيلٌ مِّنَ ٱلْآخِرِينَ

> When the Occurrence occurs - there is, at its occurrence, no denial. It will bring down [some] and raise up [others]. When the earth is shaken with convulsion, and the mountains are crumbled, breaking down and become dust dispersing, you will become [of] three kinds: The Companions of the Right - what of the Companions of the Right? And the Companions of the Left - what of the Companions of the Left? And the Forerunners, the Forerunners - they are the ones brought near [to Allāh]. In Gardens of Pleasure, a large company of the former people but a few of the later people.
>
> [*Al-Wāqʿiah* (56): 1-14]

This is how mankind will be divided when the Greater Judgement Day is established, in which Allāh will gather together the first and the last [of mankind]. This event has been described by Allāh, the Glorious, in more than one place in His Book. Then Allāh, the Exalted says at the end of this *Sūrah*,

فَلَوْلَآ
إِذَا بَلَغَتِ ٱلْحُلْقُومَ ﴿٨٣﴾ وَأَنتُمْ حِينَئِذٍ تَنظُرُونَ ﴿٨٤﴾ وَنَحْنُ أَقْرَبُ
إِلَيْهِ مِنكُمْ وَلَٰكِن لَّا تُبْصِرُونَ ﴿٨٥﴾ فَلَوْلَآ إِن كُنتُمْ غَيْرَ مَدِينِينَ
﴿٨٦﴾ تَرْجِعُونَهَآ إِن كُنتُمْ صَٰدِقِينَ ﴿٨٧﴾ فَأَمَّآ إِن كَانَ مِنَ ٱلْمُقَرَّبِينَ
﴿٨٨﴾ فَرَوْحٌ وَرَيْحَانٌ وَجَنَّتُ نَعِيمٍ ﴿٨٩﴾ وَأَمَّآ إِن كَانَ مِنْ أَصْحَٰبِ
ٱلْيَمِينِ ﴿٩٠﴾ فَسَلَٰمٌ لَّكَ مِنْ أَصْحَٰبِ ٱلْيَمِينِ ﴿٩١﴾ وَأَمَّآ إِن كَانَ مِنَ
ٱلْمُكَذِّبِينَ ٱلضَّآلِّينَ ﴿٩٢﴾ فَنُزُلٌ مِّنْ حَمِيمٍ ﴿٩٣﴾ وَتَصْلِيَةُ جَحِيمٍ
﴿٩٤﴾ إِنَّ هَٰذَا لَهُوَ حَقُّ ٱلْيَقِينِ ﴿٩٥﴾ فَسَبِّحْ بِٱسْمِ رَبِّكَ ٱلْعَظِيمِ ﴿٩٦﴾

Then why, when it [the soul at death] reaches the throat, and you are at that moment looking on - and We are nearer to him that you but you do not see - then why do you not, if you are not to be recompensed, bring it back if indeed you are truthful? And if he [the deceased] was of those brought near to Allāh, then [for him is] rest and bounty and a Garden of Pleasure. And if he was of the Companions of the Right, then [the Angels will say], 'Peace for you; [you are] from the Companions of the Right.' But if he was of the deniers [who were] astray, then [for him is] hospitality of scalding water and burning in Hellfire. Indeed, this is the true certainty, so glorify the Name of your Lord, the Most Great.

[*Al-Wāqiʿah* (56): 83-96]

Allāh, the Exalted says in *Sūrah al-Insān*,

إِنَّا هَدَيْنَٰهُ ٱلسَّبِيلَ إِمَّا شَاكِرًا وَإِمَّا كَفُورًا ﴿٣﴾
إِنَّآ أَعْتَدْنَا لِلْكَٰفِرِينَ سَلَٰسِلَا۟ وَأَغْلَٰلًا وَسَعِيرًا ﴿٤﴾ إِنَّ
ٱلْأَبْرَارَ يَشْرَبُونَ مِن كَأْسٍ كَانَ مِزَاجُهَا كَافُورًا ﴿٥﴾
عَيْنًا يَشْرَبُ بِهَا عِبَادُ ٱللَّهِ يُفَجِّرُونَهَا تَفْجِيرًا ﴿٦﴾ يُوفُونَ بِٱلنَّذْرِ وَيَخَافُونَ
يَوْمًا كَانَ شَرُّهُۥ مُسْتَطِيرًا ﴿٧﴾ وَيُطْعِمُونَ ٱلطَّعَامَ عَلَىٰ حُبِّهِۦ مِسْكِينًا
وَيَتِيمًا وَأَسِيرًا ﴿٨﴾ إِنَّمَا نُطْعِمُكُمْ لِوَجْهِ ٱللَّهِ لَا نُرِيدُ مِنكُمْ جَزَآءً وَلَا شُكُورًا
﴿٩﴾ إِنَّا نَخَافُ مِن رَّبِّنَا يَوْمًا عَبُوسًا قَمْطَرِيرًا ﴿١٠﴾ فَوَقَىٰهُمُ ٱللَّهُ شَرَّ ذَٰلِكَ
ٱلْيَوْمِ وَلَقَّىٰهُمْ نَضْرَةً وَسُرُورًا ﴿١١﴾ وَجَزَىٰهُم بِمَا صَبَرُوا۟ جَنَّةً وَحَرِيرًا
﴿١٢﴾ مُّتَّكِـِٔينَ فِيهَا عَلَى ٱلْأَرَآئِكِ ۖ لَا يَرَوْنَ فِيهَا شَمْسًا وَلَا زَمْهَرِيرًا ﴿١٣﴾

Indeed We have guided him to the way, be he grateful or be he ungrateful. Indeed We have prepared for the disbelievers chains and shackles and a blaze. Indeed the righteous will drink from a cup [of wine] whose mixture is of *Kāfūr*. A spring of which the [righteous] servants of Allāh will drink; they will make it gush forth in force [and abundance]. They [are those who] fulfil [their] vows and fear a Day whose evil will be widespread. They give food, in spite of love for it, to the needy, the orphan and the captive. [Saying in their hearts], 'We feed you only for the Face of Allāh. We wish not from you reward or gratitude. Indeed We fear from our Lord a Day austere and distressful.' So Allāh will protect them from the evil of that Day, grant them radiance and happiness and will reward them for what they patiently endured [with] a garden [in Paradise] and silk [garments]...

[*Al-Insān* (76): 3-12]

Similarly He says in *Sūrah Al-Muṭaffifīn*,

كَلَّآ إِنَّ كِتَٰبَ ٱلْفُجَّارِ لَفِى سِجِّينٍ ﴿٧﴾ وَمَآ أَدْرَىٰكَ مَا سِجِّينٌ ﴿٨﴾ كِتَٰبٌ
مَّرْقُومٌ ﴿٩﴾ وَيْلٌ يَوْمَئِذٍ لِّلْمُكَذِّبِينَ ﴿١٠﴾ ٱلَّذِينَ يُكَذِّبُونَ بِيَوْمِ ٱلدِّينِ ﴿١١﴾
وَمَا يُكَذِّبُ بِهِۦٓ إِلَّا كُلُّ مُعْتَدٍ أَثِيمٍ ﴿١٢﴾ إِذَا تُتْلَىٰ عَلَيْهِ ءَايَٰتُنَا قَالَ أَسَٰطِيرُ
ٱلْأَوَّلِينَ ﴿١٣﴾ كَلَّا ۖ بَلْ ۜ رَانَ عَلَىٰ قُلُوبِهِم مَّا كَانُوا۟ يَكْسِبُونَ ﴿١٤﴾ كَلَّآ إِنَّهُمْ
عَن رَّبِّهِمْ يَوْمَئِذٍ لَّمَحْجُوبُونَ ﴿١٥﴾ ثُمَّ إِنَّهُمْ لَصَالُوا۟ ٱلْجَحِيمِ ﴿١٦﴾ ثُمَّ يُقَالُ
هَٰذَا ٱلَّذِى كُنتُم بِهِۦ تُكَذِّبُونَ ﴿١٧﴾ كَلَّآ إِنَّ كِتَٰبَ ٱلْأَبْرَارِ لَفِى عِلِّيِّينَ
﴿١٨﴾ وَمَآ أَدْرَىٰكَ مَا عِلِّيُّونَ ﴿١٩﴾ كِتَٰبٌ مَّرْقُومٌ ﴿٢٠﴾ يَشْهَدُهُ ٱلْمُقَرَّبُونَ
﴿٢١﴾ إِنَّ ٱلْأَبْرَارَ لَفِى نَعِيمٍ ﴿٢٢﴾ عَلَى ٱلْأَرَآئِكِ يَنظُرُونَ ﴿٢٣﴾ تَعْرِفُ فِى
وُجُوهِهِمْ نَضْرَةَ ٱلنَّعِيمِ ﴿٢٤﴾ يُسْقَوْنَ مِن رَّحِيقٍ مَّخْتُومٍ ﴿٢٥﴾
خِتَٰمُهُۥ مِسْكٌ ۚ وَفِى ذَٰلِكَ فَلْيَتَنَافَسِ ٱلْمُتَنَٰفِسُونَ ﴿٢٦﴾ وَمِزَاجُهُۥ
مِن تَسْنِيمٍ ﴿٢٧﴾ عَيْنًا يَشْرَبُ بِهَا ٱلْمُقَرَّبُونَ ﴿٢٨﴾

No! Indeed the record of the wicked is in *Sijjīn*. And what can make you know what is *Sijjīn*? It is [their destination recorded in a] register inscribed. Woe that Day to the deniers, those who deny the Recompense, and none denies it except every sinful transgressor. When Our verses are recited to him he says, 'Tales of the ancient!' No! Rather, the stain of that which they were earning has covered their hearts. No! Indeed, from their Lord that Day they will be partitioned. Then indeed they will [enter and] burn in Hellfire. Then it will be said to them, 'This is what you used to deny.'

No! Indeed, the record of the righteous is in *Illiyyūn*. And what can make you know what is *Illiyyūn*? It is [their destination recorded in a] register inscribed. Which is witnessed by those brought near [to Allāh]. Indeed, the righteous will be in pleasure, on adorned couches, observing.

> You will recognise in their faces the radiance of pleasure. They will be given to drink [pure] wine [which was] sealed. The last of it is musk. So for this let those who would compete, compete! And its mixture is of *Tasnīm*, a spring from which those near [to Allāh] will drink.
>
> [*Al-Muṭaffifīn*(83): 7-28]

It is reported from ibn 'Abbās (*raḍiyAllāhu 'anhumā*) and others of the *Salaf* that they said,

يُمــزج
لأصحاب اليمين مزجاً، ويشرب بها المقرّبون صرفاً

> "A mixture is prepared for the Companions of the Right [containing *tasnīm*, which they proceed to drink] whereas those brought close drink the pure [drink of *tasnīm*] directly."[3]

What they said is correct for Allāh, the Exalted says,

يَشْرَبُ بِهَا

> They will drink with it (*bihā*)
>
> [*Al-Muṭaffifīn* (83): 7-26]

and He does not say, 'they will drink from it - *minhā* [يشربـون منها].' This is because the verse includes the meaning of drinking as well as quenching ones thirst. It is possible that the one drinking could drink and yet not have his thirst quenched. When one says, 'They drink from it,' this statement does not carry the meaning of satiating the thirst, however when one says, 'They drink with it'- [يشربـون بها], then the meaning is that their thirst has been satiated. Therefore those brought close have their thirst quenched by this drink by virtue of

[3] {M} This is also reported from ibn Mas'ud and Hudhayfah as recorded in *'ad-Durr al-Manthūr'* [6/328].

their drinking it in its state of purity such that they do not require anything else besides it, but this is not the case for the Companions of the Right for whom a mixture [containing *tasnīm*] is prepared. Allāh, the Exalted says in *Sūrah al-Insān*,

كَانَ مِزَاجُهَا كَافُورًا ﴿٥﴾
عَيْنًا يَشْرَبُ بِهَا عِبَادُ ٱللَّهِ يُفَجِّرُونَهَا تَفْجِيرًا ﴿٦﴾

> ...a cup [of wine] whose mixture is of *Kāfūr*. A spring of which the [righteous] servants of Allāh will drink; they will make it gush forth in force [and abundance].
> [*Al-Insān* (76): 5-6]

The servants of Allāh mentioned here are those brought near as mentioned in the previously mentioned *Sūrah*. [Their special reward] is because the recompense is of the same type as the action - be it good or bad. The Prophet (ﷺ) said,

«من نَفَّس عن مؤمن كربة من كرب الدنيا، نفّس الله عنه كربة من كرب يوم القيامة، ومن يسّر على معسر يسّر الله عليه في الدنيا والآخرة، ومن ستر مسلماً في عون أخيه، ومن سلك طريقاً يلتمس فيه علماً سهّل الله له ستره الله في الدنيا والآخرة، والله في عون العبد ما كان العبد به طريقاً إلى الجنة، وما اجتمع قومٌ في بيت من بيوت الله، يتلون كتابَ الله ويتدارسونه بينهم، إلا نزلت عليهم السكينة، وغشيتهم الرحمة، وحفّتهم الملائكة، وذكرهم اللّهُ فيمن عنده، ومن بطّأ به عملُهُ لم يُسرع به نسبه».

"Whoever relieves a believers of a distress from the distressful aspects of this world, Allāh will rescue him from a difficulty of the difficulties of the Hereafter. Whoever alleviates [the situation of]

one in dire straits who cannot repay his debt, Allāh will alleviate his lot both in this world and the Hereafter. Whoever conceals [the faults of] a Muslim, Allāh will conceal [his faults] in this life and the Hereafter. Allāh is Helping the servant as long as the servant is helping his brother. Whoever follows a path in order to seek knowledge, Allāh will make easy for him, due to this, a path to Paradise. No people gather together in a house amongst the houses of Allāh, reciting the Book of Allāh and studying it amongst themselves, except that tranquillity descends upon them, mercy covers them, the Angels surround them and Allāh makes mention of them to those in His presence. Whoever is slowed by his deeds will not be hastened forward by his lineage." [4]

And he (ﷺ) said,

«الراحمون يرحمهم
الرحمن، ارحموا مَنْ في الأرضِ يرحمكم مَنْ في السماءِ»

"The Most Merciful bestows Mercy upon the merciful [of his servants]. Show mercy to those who are on the earth, and the One Who is Above the heaven will bestow Mercy upon you." [5]

At-Tirmidhī ruled the ḥadīth to be *ṣaḥīḥ*.

In another authentic ḥadīth reported in the *Sunan*, Allāh, the Exalted says,

«أنا الرحمٰن، خلقت الرحمة، وشققتُ
لها اسماً من اسمي، فمن وصلها وصلته، ومن قطعها بتته»

"I am the Most Merciful (ar-Raḥmān), I created the womb (ar-

---

[4] {F} Reported by Muslim [Eng. Trans. 4/1417 no. 6518] and Abū Dāwūd [Eng. Trans. 3/1376 no. 4928].

[5] {F} Reported by Abū Dāwūd [Eng. Trans. 1/1375 no. 4923] and at-Tirmidhī [no. 1924].

I say: the ḥadīth is *ṣaḥīḥ* due to witnesses.

raḥm) and derived its name from My Name. So whosoever joins its ties, I will join him and whosoever breaks its ties, I will cut him off."[6]

And he (ﷺ) said,

«ومن وصل صفّاً وصله الله، ومن قطع صفّاً قطعه الله»

"Whosoever joins a row [in prayer] Allāh will join him and whosoever breaks a row in prayer, Allāh will cut him off."[7]

The *aḥādīth* carrying this meaning are many.

[3.2 The Actions of Those Brought Close and the People of the Right]

So the *Awliyā'* of Allāh, the Exalted are of two categories: those brought close and the Companions of the Right. The Prophet (ﷺ) mentioned the actions of both these categories in the ḥadīth concerning the *Awliyā'*,

«يقول الله: من عادى لي ولياً فقد بارزني بالمحاربة ولا يـزال عبدي يتقـرب إليّ بالنوافل حتى أُحبَّهُ. فإذا أحببته، آذنته بالحرب ـ وما تقرّب إليّ عبدي بمثل أداءِ ما افترضتُ عليه، كنتُ سَمْعَهُ الذي يسمع به، وبصره الذي يبصر به، ويده التي يبطش بها، ورجله التي يمشي بها»

---

[6] {F} Reported by Abū Dāwūd [Eng. Trans. 2/445 no. 1690, 1691] and at-Tirmidhī [no. 1907].

I say: the ḥadīth is *ṣaḥīḥ*.

[7] {F} Reported by Abū Dāwūd [Eng. Trans. 1/173 no. 666] and an-Nasā'ī [*Kitāb al-Imāmah*, chpt. 31].

I say: the ḥadīth is *ṣaḥīḥ*.

> "Allāh, the Exalted says, '*Whosoever has mutual animosity with a friend (Waliy) of Mine, then he has declared war on Me. My servant does not draw close to Me with anything as he does by carrying out what I have made obligatory upon him. My servant continues to draw near to Me be performing optional deeds such that I love him. And when I love him, I am his hearing by which he hears, his sight by which he sees, his hand with which he strikes, and his leg with which he walks.*'"

So the righteous (*abrār*) refers to the Companions of the Right, those who seek to draw close to Allāh by performing the obligations. They do what Allāh has ordered and leave what He has prohibited. They do not exert themselves by performing the recommended actions of worship and neither do they refrain from unnecessary permissible actions.

As for the Forerunners who are brought close then they seek to draw closer to Allāh by performing optional actions of worship after having performed the obligations. They perform the obligations and the recommendations, they leave the unlawful and the disliked. These people, since they seek to draw close to Him by doing all that is within their capability, become beloved to the Lord who Loves them with complete Love, as Allāh, the Exalted says [in this ḥadīth],

ولا يزال عبدي يتقرب إليّ بالنوافل حتى أُحبَّهُ. فإذا أُحببته،

"My servant continues to draw near to Me be performing optional deeds such that I love him."

Meaning unrestricted and unqualified love. In a similar way, Allāh, the Exalted says,

اهْدِنَا
الصِّرَاطَ الْمُسْتَقِيمَ ﴿٦﴾ صِرَاطَ الَّذِينَ أَنْعَمْتَ
عَلَيْهِمْ غَيْرِ الْمَغْضُوبِ عَلَيْهِمْ
وَلَا الضَّالِّينَ ﴿٧﴾

> Guide us to the Straight Path. The Path of those whom You have favoured. Not the path of those who have earned [Your] Anger and neither of those who have gone astray.
>
> [*Al-Fātiḥah* (1): 6-7]

Meaning: Favoured them with an unrestricted, unqualified and complete favour, a favour such as mentioned in His, the Exalted's saying,

وَمَن يُطِعِ اللَّهَ وَالرَّسُولَ فَأُولَٰئِكَ مَعَ الَّذِينَ أَنْعَمَ اللَّهُ عَلَيْهِم
مِّنَ النَّبِيِّينَ وَالصِّدِّيقِينَ وَالشُّهَدَاءِ وَالصَّالِحِينَ ۚ وَحَسُنَ
أُولَٰئِكَ رَفِيقًا ﴿٦٩﴾

> And whoever obeys Allāh and the Messenger - those will be with the ones upon whom Allāh has bestowed favour; of the Prophets, the steadfast affirmers of the truth, the martyrs and the righteous. And truly excellent are those as companions.
>
> [*An-Nisā'* (4): 69]

With regards to these people who have been brought close, the permissible actions become actions of obedience by which they further seek to draw closer to Allāh, Mighty and Magnificent. Hence every single one of their actions is for Allāh, therefore [as a fitting reward] they will drink [from *tasnīm*] directly because they acted only for His sake. As for those who take a medium course then some of their actions are performed purely for their own sakes and they are neither punished nor rewarded for these actions. Therefore they do not drink the pure [*tasnīm*], rather a mixture is prepared for them containing the drink of those brought near, and the extent of this mixture is determined by the extent they mixed the deeds performed for themselves and deeds performed for Allāh in this life.

[3.3 The Servant-Messenger and the Prophet-King]

In the same respect as this division is the division of the Prophets into Servant-Messengers and Prophet-Kings. Allāh, the Glorious, gave Muḥammad (ﷺ) the choice of being a servant of Allāh and a Messenger or being a Prophet and king and he chose to be a Servant-Messenger. Examples of Prophet-Kings lie with David, Solomon and their likes (*'alayhim aṣ-ṣalāh was salām*). Allāh, the Exalted says concerning the story of Solomon,

قَالَ رَبِّ ٱغْفِرْ
لِي وَهَبْ لِي مُلْكًا لَّا يَنۢبَغِي لِأَحَدٍ مِّنۢ بَعْدِيٓ ۖ إِنَّكَ أَنتَ ٱلْوَهَّابُ ﴿٣٥﴾
فَسَخَّرْنَا لَهُ ٱلرِّيحَ تَجْرِي بِأَمْرِهِۦ رُخَآءً حَيْثُ أَصَابَ ﴿٣٦﴾ وَٱلشَّيَٰطِينَ
كُلَّ بَنَّآءٍ وَغَوَّاصٍ ﴿٣٧﴾ وَءَاخَرِينَ مُقَرَّنِينَ فِي ٱلْأَصْفَادِ ﴿٣٨﴾ هَٰذَا
عَطَآؤُنَا فَٱمْنُنْ أَوْ أَمْسِكْ بِغَيْرِ حِسَابٍ ﴿٣٩﴾

> He said, 'My Lord, forgive me and grant me a kingdom such as will not belong to anyone after me. Indeed, You are the Bestower.' So We subjected to him the wind blowing gently by his command wherever he directed. And [also] the devils [of jinn] - every builder and diver and others bound together in shackles. [We said], 'This is Our gift, so grant or withhold without account.'
>
> [*Ṣād* (38): 35-39]

Meaning, 'Give what you wish and withhold what you wish, either way you will not be judged for this.' Therefore the Prophet-King does what Allāh made obligatory upon him, leaves what Allāh made unlawful for him and is free to act as he wills and desires with regards to the worldly authority and wealth granted him without incurring any sin.

As for the Servant-Messenger then he does not give to anyone except by order of his Lord, he does not give to whosoever he wishes and neither does he withhold from whosoever he wishes. Rather he gives to those whom His Lord ordered him to give and grants positions of authority to those whom his Lord ordered him to grant. As such all of his actions constitute worship of Allāh, the Exalted. It is reported in Ṣaḥīḥ al-Bukhārī from Abū Hurayrah (*raḍiyAllāhu ʿanhu*) that the Prophet (ﷺ) said,

> *"I, by Allāh, do not give to anyone nor withhold from anyone, I am only a distributor and place [the distribution] where I am ordered."*[8]

This is why Allāh has jointly mentioned the property that is legislated to collect [9] with Him and His Messenger,

قُلِ ٱلْأَنفَالُ لِلَّهِ وَٱلرَّسُولِ

> Say, 'The [decision concerning] bounties of war is for Allāh and the Messenger.'
>
> [*Al-Anfāl* (8): 1]

---

[8] {F} Reported by Bukhārī [Eng. Trans. 4/223 no. 346] and Aḥmad [2/482].

[9] {Y} This property is of three types:

1. That which the Muslims obtained from the polytheists while they were at war with them. Allāh has called this *anfāl* or *ghanāʾim*.
2. That which the Muslims obtained via land tax or *jizya*. Technically this is called *faiʾ*.
3. That which is obtained from the Muslims by way of *zakāh* etc. This is technically called *ṣadaqah*.

> مَّآ أَفَآءَ ٱللَّهُ عَلَىٰ رَسُولِهِۦ مِنْ أَهْلِ ٱلْقُرَىٰ فَلِلَّهِ وَلِلرَّسُولِ
>
> And what Allāh restored [of property] to His Messenger from the people of the towns - it is for Allāh and for the Messenger.
>
> [*Al-Ḥashr* (59): 7]

> ۞ وَٱعْلَمُوٓاْ أَنَّمَا غَنِمْتُم مِّن شَىْءٍ فَأَنَّ لِلَّهِ خُمُسَهُۥ وَلِلرَّسُولِ
>
> And know that anything you obtain of war booty - then indeed for Allāh is one fifth and for the Messenger.
>
> [*Al-Anfāl* (8): 41]

It is for this reason that the most obviously correct opinion of the scholars is that such property should be distributed in the way loved by Allāh and His Messenger as dictated by the *ijtihād* of the Muslim leader. This is the chosen opinion of Mālik and others from the *Salaf* and has also been mentioned in one report from Aḥmad. It is also said concerning this property that it should be distributed amongst the five categories as is the opinion of ash-Shāfiʿī and Aḥmad in the well-known opinion of his.[10] It is also said that it should be distributed amongst three categories as is mentioned by Abū Ḥanīfah, may Allāh have mercy upon him.[11]

The purpose of this discussion is to show that the Servant-Messenger is better than the Prophet-King, just as Abraham, Moses, Jesus and Muḥammad *(ʿalayhim aṣ-ṣalāh was salām)* are better than Joseph, David, and Solomon *(ʿalayhim aṣ-ṣalāh was salām)*. In the same way the Forerunners, those brought close are better than the righteous, the Companions of the Right.

---

[10] {T} Meaning Allāh and His Messenger (ﷺ), the close relatives of the Messenger (ﷺ) who are *Banū Hāshim* and *Banū Muṭṭalib*, the orphans, the needy and the wayfarers as per *al-Anfāl* (8): 41

[11] {T} Meaning the orphans, the needy and the wayfarer.

Therefore, whosoever fulfils what Allāh has obligated upon him and does whatsoever permissible actions he wishes to do, then he is from the Companions of the Right. But whosoever does only that which Allāh Loves and is Pleased with and intends that the permissible actions aid him in performing that which Allāh has ordered him with, then he is from the Forerunners.

In Summary

- The division of the *Awliyā'* into Forerunners and those who take a middle way.
- The Forerunners perform the optional actions of worship and do everything for the sake of Allāh. Those who take a middle way perform only the obligations and do other things for their own sakes.
- The reward befits the action and hence the reward of the Forerunners is that they drink directly from the well of *tasnīm* in Paradise.
- The Prophets are similarly divided into the Servant-Messenger and Prophet-King and their actions are also similarly distinguished.
- The Servant-Messenger is better than the Prophet-King and the Forerunners are better than those who take a medium way.

CHAPTER FOUR

[*Tafsīr to Sūrah Fāṭir*]

ALLĀH, THE EXALTED HAS MENTIONED his *Awliyā'*, both those who take a medium path and the Forerunners, in *Sūrah Fāṭir*,

ثُمَّ أَوْرَثْنَا الْكِتَٰبَ
الَّذِينَ اصْطَفَيْنَا مِنْ عِبَادِنَا فَمِنْهُمْ ظَالِمٌ لِّنَفْسِهِۦ وَمِنْهُم
مُّقْتَصِدٌ وَمِنْهُمْ سَابِقٌۢ بِالْخَيْرَٰتِ بِإِذْنِ اللَّهِ ذَٰلِكَ هُوَ
الْفَضْلُ الْكَبِيرُ ﴿٣٢﴾ جَنَّٰتُ عَدْنٍ يَدْخُلُونَهَا يُحَلَّوْنَ
فِيهَا مِنْ أَسَاوِرَ مِن ذَهَبٍ وَلُؤْلُؤًا وَلِبَاسُهُمْ فِيهَا حَرِيرٌ ﴿٣٣﴾
وَقَالُوا الْحَمْدُ لِلَّهِ الَّذِىٓ أَذْهَبَ عَنَّا الْحَزَنَ إِنَّ رَبَّنَا لَغَفُورٌ
شَكُورٌ ﴿٣٤﴾ الَّذِىٓ أَحَلَّنَا دَارَ الْمُقَامَةِ مِن فَضْلِهِۦ لَا يَمَسُّنَا
فِيهَا نَصَبٌ وَلَا يَمَسُّنَا فِيهَا لُغُوبٌ ﴿٣٥﴾

Then We caused to inherit the Book those We have chosen of Our servants; and among them is he who wrongs himself, and among them is he who takes a medium course, and among them is he who is foremost in good deeds by permission of Allāh. That [inheritance] is the great bounty. [For them are] gardens of perpetual resi-

> dence which they will enter. They will be adorned therein with bracelets of gold and pearls, and their garments therein will be silk. And they will say, 'Praise and thanks be to Allāh, who has removed from us [all] sorrow. Indeed our Lord is Forgiving and Appreciative - He Who has settled us in the abode of eternity out of His bounty. There touches us not in it any fatigue, and there touches us not in it weariness [of mind].'
>
> [*Fāṭir* (35): 32-35]

These three categories mentioned in this verse are only to be found in the nation of Muḥammad (ﷺ) specifically as Allāh, the Exalted said,

ثُمَّ أَوْرَثْنَا ٱلْكِتَٰبَ
ٱلَّذِينَ ٱصْطَفَيْنَا مِنْ عِبَادِنَا ۖ فَمِنْهُمْ ظَالِمٌ لِّنَفْسِهِۦ وَمِنْهُم
مُّقْتَصِدٌ وَمِنْهُمْ سَابِقٌۢ بِٱلْخَيْرَٰتِ بِإِذْنِ ٱللَّهِ ۚ ذَٰلِكَ هُوَ
ٱلْفَضْلُ ٱلْكَبِيرُ ﴿٣٢﴾

> Then We caused to inherit the Book those We have chosen of Our servants; and among them is he who wrongs himself, and among them is he who takes a medium course, and among them is he who is foremost in good deeds by permission of Allāh. That [inheritance] is the great bounty.
>
> [*Fāṭir* (35): 32]

It is the nation of Muḥammad (ﷺ) who inherited the Book after the previous nations. This [inheritance] is not merely specific to those who have memorised the Qur'ān, rather all those who have believed in the Qur'ān are included and they have been divided into three categories: he who wrongs himself; he who takes a medium course; and he who is foremost. As for the previously quoted verses from *Sūrah al-Wāqi'ah*, *al-Muṭaffifīn* and *al-Infiṭār* then these include all of the previous nations - both the disbelievers and believers.

So this is the division of the nation of Muḥammad (ﷺ):

1. He who wrongs himself: meaning those who commit sins and persist in them.

2. He who takes a medium course: meaning those who perform the obligations and avoid the unlawful.

3. He who is foremost in doing good deeds: meaning those who perform the obligations and supererogatory actions.

Whosoever repents from his sins, regardless of which sin it may be, in a correct manner then this does not eject him from being included amongst those who take a medium course or even those who are the Forerunners. Allāh, the Exalted says,

﴿ وَسَارِعُوٓا۟ إِلَىٰ مَغْفِرَةٍ مِّن رَّبِّكُمْ وَجَنَّةٍ عَرْضُهَا
ٱلسَّمَـٰوَٰتُ وَٱلْأَرْضُ أُعِدَّتْ لِلْمُتَّقِينَ ﴿١٣٣﴾ ٱلَّذِينَ يُنفِقُونَ
فِى ٱلسَّرَّآءِ وَٱلضَّرَّآءِ وَٱلْكَـٰظِمِينَ ٱلْغَيْظَ وَٱلْعَافِينَ
عَنِ ٱلنَّاسِ ۗ وَٱللَّهُ يُحِبُّ ٱلْمُحْسِنِينَ ﴿١٣٤﴾ وَٱلَّذِينَ إِذَا
فَعَلُوا۟ فَـٰحِشَةً أَوْ ظَلَمُوٓا۟ أَنفُسَهُمْ ذَكَرُوا۟ ٱللَّهَ فَٱسْتَغْفَرُوا۟
لِذُنُوبِهِمْ وَمَن يَغْفِرُ ٱلذُّنُوبَ إِلَّا ٱللَّهُ وَلَمْ يُصِرُّوا۟ عَلَىٰ
مَا فَعَلُوا۟ وَهُمْ يَعْلَمُونَ ﴿١٣٥﴾ أُو۟لَـٰٓئِكَ جَزَآؤُهُم مَّغْفِرَةٌ
مِّن رَّبِّهِمْ وَجَنَّـٰتٌ تَجْرِى مِن تَحْتِهَا ٱلْأَنْهَـٰرُ خَـٰلِدِينَ
فِيهَا ۚ وَنِعْمَ أَجْرُ ٱلْعَـٰمِلِينَ ﴿١٣٦﴾

And hasten to forgiveness from your Lord and a Garden

> as wide as the heavens and the earth, prepared for the righteous. Those who spend [in the cause of Allāh] during ease and hardship, who restrain anger and pardon the people - and Allāh Loves those who do good. And those who, if they commit an immoral deed or wrong themselves, remember Allāh and seek forgiveness for their sins - and who is there who can forgive sins except Allāh? - those [who] do not persist in what they have done while they know. Those - their reward is forgiveness from their Lord and gardens beneath which rivers flow wherein they will abide forever. Excellent indeed is the reward of the [righteous] workers.
>
> [*Āli 'Imrān* (3): 133-136]

The verse [previously quoted],

جَنَّٰتُ عَدْنٍ يَدْخُلُونَهَا

> [For them are] gardens of perpetual residence which they will enter.
>
> [*Fāṭir* (35): 33]

is one of the verses that *Ahlus-Sunnah* use to prove that no one from amongst the adherents of *Tawḥīd* will remain in Hellfire forever.

[4.1 The People of Major Sins Entering and Leaving the Fire]

As for many of those who have committed major sins entering the Fire, then this is something that has been reported via multiple routes from the Prophet (ﷺ). In the same way their eventually coming out of the Fire has also been reported via multiple routes. The same applies to the intercession (*shafā'a*) of our Prophet, Muḥammad (ﷺ), for those who have committed major sins, the taking out from the Fire those who our Prophet (ﷺ) interceded for, and the intercession of other than him.

Therefore those who state that the people who have committed major sins will remain in the Fire forever, and incorrectly interpret the verse to refer only to those who are the Forerunners, postulating that those who take a medium course or wrong themselves will not enter Paradise as has been stated by some of the *Muʿtazilah*, taking an opposing path to the *Murjiʿah* who are not certain that any of those who commit major sins shall enter the Fire, thinking that it is possible that all of them can enter Paradise without first being punished - then both of these stances contradict the *mutawātir Sunnah* of the Prophet (ﷺ) and the consensus of the *Salaf* of this nation and their *Imāms*.

The saying of Allāh, the Exalted, in two verses of His Book proves the invalidity of the opinion of both these groups. Allāh, the Exalted says,

إِنَّ ٱللَّهَ لَا يَغْفِرُ أَن يُشْرَكَ بِهِۦ وَيَغْفِرُ مَا دُونَ
ذَٰلِكَ لِمَن يَشَآءُ

> Indeed Allāh does not forgive committing *shirk* with Him, but He forgives what is less than that for whomsoever He Wills.
>
> [*An-Nisāʾ* (4): 48, 116]

Allāh informs us that He will not forgive *shirk* but that He will forgive what is less than it for whomsoever He Wills. It is not possible that this verse refers to the penitent as stated by some of the *Muʿtazilah* because it is known that Allāh will forgive *shirk* and what is less than it for the one who repents from it - as such this case is not dependant upon the Will of Allāh.[1] This is why when Allāh, the

[1] {T} Hence this verse refers to those who have died without repenting for their =

Exalted, mentions forgiveness for the penitent, He says,

﴿ قُلْ يَٰعِبَادِيَ ٱلَّذِينَ أَسْرَفُوا۟ عَلَىٰٓ أَنفُسِهِمْ لَا تَقْنَطُوا۟ مِن رَّحْمَةِ ٱللَّهِ ۚ إِنَّ ٱللَّهَ يَغْفِرُ ٱلذُّنُوبَ جَمِيعًا ۚ إِنَّهُۥ هُوَ ٱلْغَفُورُ ٱلرَّحِيمُ

> Say, 'O My servants who have transgressed against themselves, do not despair of the mercy of Allāh, indeed Allāh forgives all sins. Indeed, it is He who is the Forgiving, the Merciful.'
>
> [*Az-Zumar* (39): 53]

Here, Allāh generalised the forgiveness and left it unrestricted for indeed, Allāh forgives any sin of His servant that he repents from. Hence whosoever repents from *shirk*, Allāh will forgive him; whosoever repents from having committed a major sin, Allāh will forgive him; indeed any sin that the servant repents from, Allāh will forgive him.

So in this verse concerning repentance,[2] Allāh generalised and left it unrestricted whereas in the previous verse Allāh specified and made it dependant. He specified *shirk* saying that He would not forgive it and made everything other than it dependant upon His Will.

From amongst [the types of] *shirk* is to deny the Creator, this goes to prove the invalidity of those who have certainty that every sinner will be forgiven assuming that He used the word *shirk* to alert one of that which is greater than it such as the denial of the Creator. [This

=
sins, therefore those amongst these who have committed *shirk* shall not be forgiven but as for other than these, it is up to Allāh, if He Wills He will forgive them and if He Wills He will punish them. As for those who repented in this life for their sins, including *shirk*, then Allāh will forgive them.

[2] {T} Ar. *Āyah at-Tawbah*, which is the title given this verse.

also proves the invalidity of those who say] that it is possible that He not punish any sin, for if this were the case then He would not have mentioned that He forgives some [sins] and not others. If every person who wronged himself was automatically forgiven, without the need of repentance or righteous deeds that would serve as expiation for the sin, then He would not have made this dependant upon His Will.

In conclusion the saying of Allāh, the Exalted,

وَيَغْفِرُ مَا دُونَ ذَٰلِكَ لِمَن يَشَآءُ

> ...but He forgives what is less than that for whomsoever He Wills.
>
> [*An-Nisā'* (4): 48, 116]

proves that He forgives some and not others thereby proving the futility of those who negate His Forgiveness in totality or affirm it for all.

In Summary

- Explanation of the different categories of people found amongst this nation.
- Who are the Fore-runners?
- Who are those who take a medium way?
- Who are those who oppress themselves?
- Clarification that these three categories are specific to the nation of Muḥammad (ﷺ) and refutation of the *Murji'ah* and the *Mu'tazilah* with regards this last category.

- *Ahlus Sunnah* hold that Allāh forgives those who sincerely ask His forgiveness. Those who die without asking for forgiveness for their sins are under the Will of Allāh, if He wishes He will forgive them and if He wishes He will punish them. In this latter case, He will not forgive *shirk*.

CHAPTER FIVE

[The Differing Levels of *Wilāyah* is Based Upon the Differing Levels of Faith and *Taqwā*]

SINCE THE *AWLIYĀ'* OF ALLĀH, THE MIGHTY and Magnificent, are the pious, God-fearing believers and the people are of varying degrees with respect to their faith and piety then it follows that they are also of varying levels with respect to their love of, and closeness to Allāh in accordance to their level of faith and piety. In the same way when these people used to be of varying degrees with respect to disbelief and hypocrisy, they used to be of varying levels with respect to their enmity of Allāh in accordance to their level of disbelief and hypocrisy.

The foundation of faith and piety lies in having faith in the Messengers and this in turn can be succinctly summarised to having faith in the Seal of the Prophets, Muḥammad (ﷺ), for having faith in him necessarily includes believing in all the Books and Messengers of Allāh.

[5.1 The Pre-Requisite of Deserving Punishment]

The foundation of disbelief and hypocrisy lies in disbelieving in the Messengers and what they came with and it is this disbelief whose adherent deserves punishment in the Hereafter. Allāh, the Exalted has informed us in His Book that He does not punish anyone except after the conveyance of the Message. Allāh, the Exalted says,

وَمَا كُنَّا مُعَذِّبِينَ حَتَّىٰ نَبْعَثَ رَسُولًا ﴿١٥﴾

And never would We punish until We sent a Messenger.
[*Al-Isrā'* (17): 15]

﴿ إِنَّا أَوْحَيْنَا إِلَيْكَ كَمَا أَوْحَيْنَا إِلَىٰ نُوحٍ وَالنَّبِيِّينَ مِن بَعْدِهِ ۚ
وَأَوْحَيْنَا إِلَىٰ إِبْرَاهِيمَ وَإِسْمَاعِيلَ وَإِسْحَاقَ وَيَعْقُوبَ
وَالْأَسْبَاطِ وَعِيسَىٰ وَأَيُّوبَ وَيُونُسَ وَهَارُونَ وَسُلَيْمَانَ ۚ
وَآتَيْنَا دَاوُودَ زَبُورًا ﴿١٦٣﴾ وَرُسُلًا قَدْ قَصَصْنَاهُمْ عَلَيْكَ
مِن قَبْلُ وَرُسُلًا لَّمْ نَقْصُصْهُمْ عَلَيْكَ ۚ وَكَلَّمَ اللَّهُ مُوسَىٰ
تَكْلِيمًا ﴿١٦٤﴾ رُّسُلًا مُّبَشِّرِينَ وَمُنذِرِينَ لِئَلَّا يَكُونَ
لِلنَّاسِ عَلَى اللَّهِ حُجَّةٌ بَعْدَ الرُّسُلِ ۚ وَكَانَ اللَّهُ عَزِيزًا حَكِيمًا

Indeed, We have revealed to you [O Muḥammad (ﷺ)] as we revealed to Noah and the Prophets after him. And We revealed to Abraham, Ishmael, Isaac, Jacob, the Descendants, Jesus, Job, Jonah, Aaron, and Solomon; and to David We gave the book [of Psalms]. [We sent] Messengers about whom We have related [their stories] to you before and the Messengers about whom We have not related to you. And Allāh spoke to Moses with directly. [We sent] Messengers as bringers of good tidings and warners so that mankind will have no argument against Allāh after the Messengers. And ever is Allāh Exalted in Might and

Wise.

[*An-Nisā'* (4): 163-165]

Allāh says concerning the denizens of the Fire,

تكاد تميز
من الغيظ كلما ألقي فيها فوج سألهم خزنتها ألم يأتكم نذير ﴿٨﴾
قالوا بلى قد جاءنا نذير فكذبنا وقلنا ما نزل الله من شيء إن أنتم
إلا في ضلال كبير ﴿٩﴾

...Every time a company is thrown into it, its keepers ask them, 'Did there not come to you a warner?' They will say, 'Yes, a warner had come to us, but we denied and said, 'Allāh has not sent down anything. You are not but in great error.'

[*Al-Mulk* (67): 8-9]

Therefore He informed us that each time a company is thrown into the Fire they admit that a warner had come to them but they disbelieved in him. This goes to prove that only those who denied the warner will be thrown into the Fire. Allāh says, during the course of His discussion with Iblīs,

لأملأن جهنم منك وممن تبعك
منهم أجمعين ﴿٨٥﴾

I will surely fill Hell with you and those of them who follow you altogether.

[*Ṣād* (38): 85]

Therefore He informed us that He would fill Hell with Iblīs and those who followed him. This goes to show that if they will fill it then those other than them will not enter it and hence it becomes known that none shall enter Hell except the followers of Shayṭān:

This proves that those who have not committed a sin shall not enter it, for those who do not follow Shayṭān do not commit sins.

In conclusion the above discussion proves that none shall enter Hell except for those against whom the evidence has been established by way of the Messengers.

In Summary

- Explanation of the foundation of faith and that this can be succinctly summarised to believing in Muḥammad (ﷺ).
- The foundation of disbelief lies in disbelieving in the Messenger (ﷺ).
- The people who deserve the punishment of Allāh are those who have the evidence established against them.

CHAPTER SIX

[The Differing Levels of *Wilāyah*]

[6.1 Faith can be General or Specific]

FROM AMONGST THE PEOPLE ARE THOSE who believe in the Messengers in a general sense. As for the specific sense, with all of its details, then it is possible that much of what the Messengers came with has reached [those who possess this specific faith] whereas some of it has not. These people believe in what has reached them from the Messengers and they have no knowledge of that which has not reached them, but were it to have reached them they would have believed in it - in such cases they suffice in having a generic faith. If such a person were to act in accordance to what he knows that Allāh has ordered him with, conjoined with his faith and *taqwā* then he is also one of the *Awliyā'* of Allāh, the Exalted. His degree of love and closeness to Allāh is determined in accordance to his faith and *taqwā.* As for that portion of knowledge for which the proof has not been established against him then Allāh, the Exalted, does not require of him more than he can bear such as would necessitate his knowing it and having detailed faith in it. He will not punish him for leaving this portion but he has lost out on completing his love and closeness to Allāh in proportion to the portion he has missed.

[6.2 The Differing Levels of the People of Paradise]

So whosoever knows what the Messenger came with, and believes in him in the specific, detailed sense and acts in accordance to what he knows, such a person is more complete with respect to his faith, love and closeness to Allāh than the one who does not know this with all of its details and hence does not act by it. Both these categories of people are the *Awliyā'* of Allāh, the Exalted, but Paradise has varying levels, varying greatly with respect to their superiority,[1] and the pious, God-fearing *Awliyā'* of Allāh will reside in these levels as per their degree of faith and *taqwā*. Allāh, the Blessed and Exalted says,

مَّن كَانَ يُرِيدُ ٱلْعَاجِلَةَ عَجَّلْنَا لَهُۥ فِيهَا مَا نَشَآءُ لِمَن نُّرِيدُ ثُمَّ
جَعَلْنَا لَهُۥ جَهَنَّمَ يَصْلَىٰهَا مَذْمُومًا مَّدْحُورًا ﴿١٨﴾ وَمَنْ أَرَادَ
ٱلْـَٔاخِرَةَ وَسَعَىٰ لَهَا سَعْيَهَا وَهُوَ مُؤْمِنٌ فَأُو۟لَـٰٓئِكَ كَانَ
سَعْيُهُم مَّشْكُورًا ﴿١٩﴾ كُلًّا نُّمِدُّ هَـٰٓؤُلَآءِ وَهَـٰٓؤُلَآءِ مِنْ عَطَآءِ
رَبِّكَ ۚ وَمَا كَانَ عَطَآءُ رَبِّكَ مَحْظُورًا ﴿٢٠﴾ ٱنظُرْ كَيْفَ فَضَّلْنَا
بَعْضَهُمْ عَلَىٰ بَعْضٍ ۚ وَلَلْـَٔاخِرَةُ أَكْبَرُ دَرَجَـٰتٍ وَأَكْبَرُ تَفْضِيلًا

> Whoever should desire the immediate [worldly gratification] - We readily grant from it what We will to whom We intend. Then We have made Hell for him which he will [enter to] burn therein, censured and banished. But whosoever desires the Hereafter and strives for it while being a believer - it is those whose effort is ever appreciated [by

---

[1] {M} Bukhārī [Eng. Trans. 4/39 no. 48] reports from Abū Hurayrah (*raḍiyAllāhu 'anhu*) that the Messenger of Allāh (ﷺ) said,

> *"...indeed Paradise has one hundred levels which Allāh has reserved for those who fight in His Way, the distance between each level is like the distance between the heavens and the earth."*

> Allāh]. To each [category] - to these and to those - We extend from the gift of your Lord and never has the gift of your Lord been restricted. Look how We have favoured [in provision] some of you over others but the Hereafter is greater in degrees [of difference] and greater in distinction.
>
> [*Al-Isrā'* (17): 18-21]

Hence Allāh, the Glorious and Exalted, explains that He extends his gifts to those who desire the world and to those who desire the Hereafter and that his giving has never been held back, not from the righteous or the sinful. Then He, the Exalted says,

انظُرْ كَيْفَ فَضَّلْنَا
بَعْضَهُمْ عَلَىٰ بَعْضٍ وَلَلْآخِرَةُ أَكْبَرُ دَرَجَٰتٍ وَأَكْبَرُ تَفْضِيلًا

> Look how We have favoured [in provision] some of you over others but the Hereafter is greater in degrees [of difference] and greater in distinction.
>
> [*Al-Isrā'* (17): 21]

So Allāh, the Glorious, explains that the inhabitants of the Hereafter will be of greater degrees in difference than the people were in the worldly life and that these degrees are more marked in their distinction. Allāh has explained the differing degrees of His Prophets (*'alayhim as-salām*), and in the same way, all of His servants are of varying degrees. Allāh, the Exalted says,

۞ تِلْكَ ٱلرُّسُلُ فَضَّلْنَا بَعْضَهُمْ عَلَىٰ بَعْضٍ مِّنْهُم مَّن كَلَّمَ ٱللَّهُ
وَرَفَعَ بَعْضَهُمْ دَرَجَٰتٍ وَءَاتَيْنَا عِيسَى ٱبْنَ مَرْيَمَ ٱلْبَيِّنَٰتِ
وَأَيَّدْنَٰهُ بِرُوحِ ٱلْقُدُسِ وَلَوْ شَآءَ ٱللَّهُ مَا ٱقْتَتَلَ ٱلَّذِينَ
مِنۢ بَعْدِهِم مِّنۢ بَعْدِ مَا جَآءَتْهُمُ ٱلْبَيِّنَٰتُ وَلَٰكِنِ ٱخْتَلَفُوا۟
فَمِنْهُم مَّنْ ءَامَنَ وَمِنْهُم مَّن كَفَرَ وَلَوْ شَآءَ ٱللَّهُ مَا ٱقْتَتَلُوا۟
وَلَٰكِنَّ ٱللَّهَ يَفْعَلُ مَا يُرِيدُ ﴿٢٥٣﴾

Those Messengers - some of them We caused to exceed others. Among them were those to whom Allāh spoke, and some of them He raised in degree. And We gave Jesus, the son of Mary, clear proofs and We supported him with the Pure Spirit...

[*Al-Baqarah* (2): 253]

وَلَقَدْ فَضَّلْنَا بَعْضَ ٱلنَّبِيِّـۧنَ عَلَىٰ بَعْضٍ
وَءَاتَيْنَا دَاوُۥدَ زَبُورًا ﴿٥٥﴾

And We have made some of the Prophets exceed others and to David We gave the book.

[*Al-Isrā'* (17): 55]

In Ṣaḥīḥ Muslim from Abū Hurayrah (*raḍiyAllāhu 'anhu*) that the Prophet (ﷺ) said,

«المؤمن القويّ خيرٌ وأحب إلى الله من المؤمن الضعيف،
وفي كل خير، احرص على ما ينفعك، واستعن بالله، ولا
تعجز، وإن أصابك شيءٌ، فلا تقل: لو أني فعلت لكان
كذا وكذا؛ ولكن قل: قدّر الله وما شاء فعل،

"The strong believer is more beloved to Allāh than the weak and in

both there is good. Be desirous and seek after that which would benefit you and ask the help of Allāh and do not despair. If you are afflicted with something then do not say, 'If only I had done [this] then such and such would have happened,' rather say, 'Allāh decreed and did what He Willed.' Indeed, 'If only' opens the actions of Shayṭān." [2]

In the Two Ṣaḥīḥs from Abū Hurayrah (*raḍiyAllāhu 'anhu*) and 'Amr bin al-'Ās (*raḍiyAllāhu 'anhu*) that the Prophet (ﷺ) said,

«إذا اجتهد الحاكم فأصاب فله أجران، وإن أخطأ فله أجر»

"When the ruler strives to pass a verdict and is correct then he has two rewards, and if he strives to pass a verdict and is incorrect then he has one reward." [3]

Allāh, the Exalted says,

لَا يَسْتَوِى مِنكُم مَّنْ أَنفَقَ مِن قَبْلِ ٱلْفَتْحِ وَقَٰتَلَ

Not equal among you are those who spent before the conquest [of Mecca] and fought [and those who did so after it].

[*Al-Ḥadīd* (57): 10]

---

[2] {F} Ṣaḥīḥ Muslim [Eng. Trans. 4/1401 no. 6441] and Ibn Mājah [no.'s 79, 4168].

[3] {F} The ḥadīth of Abu Hurayrah has been reported by Bukhārī [Eng. Trans. 9/330 no. 450] and Muslim [Eng. Trans. 3/930 no. 4262]

{T} but the reference to the ḥadīth of Abu Hurayrah has been left untranslated in the English translation of Bukhārī.

{F} The ḥadīth of 'Amr bin al-'Ās has been reported by Bukhārī [Eng. Trans. 9/330 no. 450] and Muslim [Eng. Trans. 3/930 no. 4261].

لَا يَسْتَوِي الْقَاعِدُونَ مِنَ الْمُؤْمِنِينَ غَيْرُ أُولِي الضَّرَرِ وَالْمُجَاهِدُونَ
فِي سَبِيلِ اللَّهِ بِأَمْوَالِهِمْ وَأَنْفُسِهِمْ ۚ فَضَّلَ اللَّهُ الْمُجَاهِدِينَ بِأَمْوَالِهِمْ
وَأَنْفُسِهِمْ عَلَى الْقَاعِدِينَ دَرَجَةً ۚ وَكُلًّا وَعَدَ اللَّهُ الْحُسْنَىٰ ۚ وَفَضَّلَ اللَّهُ
الْمُجَاهِدِينَ عَلَى الْقَاعِدِينَ أَجْرًا عَظِيمًا ﴿٩٥﴾ دَرَجَاتٍ مِنْهُ وَمَغْفِرَةً
وَرَحْمَةً ۚ وَكَانَ اللَّهُ غَفُورًا رَحِيمًا ﴿٩٦﴾

Not equal are those believers remaining [at home] - other than the disabled - and the *Mujāhidīn* [who strive and fight] in the cause of Allāh with their wealth and their lives. Allāh has preferred the *Mujāhidīn* [who strive] with their wealth and lives over those who remain [behind] by degrees. And to all Allāh has promised the best [reward]. But Allāh has preferred the *Mujāhidīn* over those who remain [behind] with a great reward - degrees [of high position] from Him and forgiveness and mercy. And Allāh is ever Forgiving and Merciful.

[*An-Nisā'* (4): 95-96]

۞ أَجَعَلْتُمْ سِقَايَةَ
الْحَاجِّ وَعِمَارَةَ الْمَسْجِدِ الْحَرَامِ كَمَنْ آمَنَ بِاللَّهِ وَالْيَوْمِ الْآخِرِ
وَجَاهَدَ فِي سَبِيلِ اللَّهِ ۚ لَا يَسْتَوُونَ عِنْدَ اللَّهِ ۗ وَاللَّهُ لَا يَهْدِي الْقَوْمَ
الظَّالِمِينَ ﴿١٩﴾ الَّذِينَ آمَنُوا وَهَاجَرُوا وَجَاهَدُوا فِي سَبِيلِ اللَّهِ
بِأَمْوَالِهِمْ وَأَنْفُسِهِمْ أَعْظَمُ دَرَجَةً عِنْدَ اللَّهِ ۚ وَأُولَٰئِكَ هُمُ الْفَائِزُونَ ﴿٢٠﴾

Have you made the providing of water for the pilgrim and the maintenance of the *Masjid al-Ḥarām* equal to [the deeds of] one who believes in Allāh and the Last Day and strives in the cause of Allāh? They are not equal in the sight of Allāh and Allāh does not guide the wrongdoing people. The ones who have believed, emigrated and striven in the cause of Allāh with their wealth and their lives are greater in rank in the sight of Allāh and it is those who are the attainers [of success].

[*At-Tawbah* (9): 19-20]

أَمَّنْ هُوَ قَٰنِتٌ ءَانَآءَ ٱلَّيْلِ سَاجِدًا وَقَآئِمًا يَحْذَرُ
ٱلْءَاخِرَةَ وَيَرْجُوا۟ رَحْمَةَ رَبِّهِۦ ۗ قُلْ هَلْ يَسْتَوِى ٱلَّذِينَ يَعْلَمُونَ وَٱلَّذِينَ
لَا يَعْلَمُونَ ۗ إِنَّمَا يَتَذَكَّرُ أُو۟لُوا۟ ٱلْأَلْبَٰبِ ﴿٩﴾

Is one who is devoutly obedient during periods of the night, prostrating and standing [in prayer], fearing the Hereafter and hoping for the mercy of his Lord, [like one who does not]? Say, 'are those who know equal to those who do not know?' It is only the people of understanding who will take heed.

[*Az-Zumar* (39): 9]

يَرْفَعِ ٱللَّهُ ٱلَّذِينَ ءَامَنُوا۟
مِنكُمْ وَٱلَّذِينَ أُوتُوا۟ ٱلْعِلْمَ دَرَجَٰتٍ ۚ وَٱللَّهُ بِمَا تَعْمَلُونَ خَبِيرٌ ﴿١١﴾

Allāh will raise those who have believed among you and those who were given knowledge by degrees...

[*Al-Mujādilah* (58): 11]

In Summary

- Faith can be general or detailed.
- Detailed faith is to have knowledge of what the Messenger (ﷺ) came with and to act upon it.
- The more detailed a faith that a person possesses the greater his *wilāyah* to Allāh.
- Paradise has varying levels and the *Awliyā'* will reside in them as per their degree of *wilāyah*.
- The Prophets are also of varying degrees.

CHAPTER SEVEN

[*Taqwā* is a Pre-Requisite for *Wilāyah*]

IT IS NOW KNOWN THAT THE SERVANT can never be a *Waliy* of Allāh unless he be a pious, God-fearing believer due to the saying of the Exalted,

أَلَآ إِنَّ أَوْلِيَآءَ ٱللَّهِ لَا خَوْفٌ عَلَيْهِمْ وَلَا هُمْ يَحْزَنُونَ ﴿٦٢﴾ ٱلَّذِينَ ءَامَنُوا۟ وَكَانُوا۟ يَتَّقُونَ ﴿٦٣﴾

> Unquestionably, for the *Awliyā'* of Allāh there will be no fear concerning them, nor will they grieve - those who believed and were fearing Allāh.
>
> [*Yūnus* (10): 62-63]

And in the famous ḥadīth of Ṣaḥīḥ Bukhārī, whose mention has preceded, Allāh, the Blessed and Exalted says in it,

ولا يـزال عبدي يتقـرب إليّ بالنوافل حتى أحبّه.

> *"My servant continues to draw near to Me by performing optional deeds such that I love him."*

It is also known that the servant can never be a pious, God-fearing believer unless he seeks to draw close to Allāh by performing the obligatory duties and hence becomes one of the righteous, the People of the Right. Then after this the servant continues to draw closer to Allāh by performing the optional deeds until he becomes one of the Forerunners, those who have been brought close.

[7.1 Can Children or the Insane be *Awliyā*?]

It is further known that none of the disbelievers or hypocrites can ever be a *Waliy* of Allāh and in the same way those whose faith and worship is not valid, even if one were to assume about them that they carry no sin such as the children of the disbelievers and those to whom the Call has not been conveyed.[1] This holds true even

[1] {F} *Al-Ḥāfiẓ* ibn Qayyim al-Jawziyyah said in *'Ṭarīq al-Hijratayn'* [pp. 633-634] while explaining the differing levels of the morally responsible people (*mukallafīn*) in the Hereafter,

"The Fourtheenth Level: a people who have no actions of obedience or disobedience and neither do they have faith or disbelief. These people are of different types, from them are those to whom the Call has not reached in any form or fashion, from them are the insane who cannot comprehend anything nor differentiate between good and evil, from them are the deaf who cannot hear at all, and from them are the children of the polytheists who died before they reached the age of discernment.

The nation has differed greatly over this level of people and the greatest divergence is to be found concerning the issue of the children of the polytheists. As for the children of the Muslims then Imām Aḥmad said, 'There is no difference concerning them,' meaning that they are in Paradise.

Ibn 'Abdul Barr reported from a group of scholars that they refrained giving a verdict [concerning the children of the Muslims] and said that all children were subject to the Will of Allāh. He went on to say,

> And this is the opinion of a large group of the Legal Jurists and Scholars of Ḥadīth, from amongst them: Ḥammād bin Zayd; Ḥammād bin Salamah; ibn al-Mubārak; and Isḥāq bin Rāhawayah. They said, 'This is in accordance to what Mālik recorded in his Muwaṭṭa in the chapters concerning *Qadr* and the *aḥādīth* he included therein and like the view of the majority of his Companions.'

=

though it can be said about these types of people that they will not be punished until a Messenger is sent to them - they cannot be from the *Awliyā'* of Allāh unless they are one of the pious, God-fearing believers. Therefore whosoever does not seek to draw close to Allāh by performing good deeds and leaving evil deeds cannot be one of the *Awliyā'* of Allāh. The same holds true for the insane and children for the Prophet (ﷺ) said,

«يرفع القلم عن ثلاثة: عن المجنون حتى يفيق،
وعن الصبي حتى يحتلم، وعن النائم حتى يستيقظ»

"The Pen has been lifted from three: the insane until he regains his sanity; the child until he reaches puberty; and from the one who is asleep until he awakens."

This ḥadīth has been reported by the authors of the *Sunans* from

---

=

There is nothing directly reported from Mālik concerning this but many of his later followers were of the opinion that the children of the Muslims are in Paradise and the children of the polytheists are subject to the Will of Allāh. As for the children of the polytheists then there are eight different opinions voiced...."

Then he, may Allāh have mercy upon him, went on to discuss each opinion along with the evidences presented by their proponents, and here is a list of these eight opinions:

1. Refraining from giving a verdict on them.
2. That they are in the Fire.
3. That they are in Paradise.
4. That they are in a station between the two stations of Paradise and Hell.
5. That they are subject to the Will of Allāh.
6. That they are the servants of the inhabitants of Paradise and their properties.
7. Their ruling is the same as the ruling of their fathers in the wordly life and the Hereafter.
8. They will be tried on the Day of Judgement and a Messenger will be sent then and to all those to whom the Call did not reach. So if they obey him they will enter Paradise and if they disobey him they will enter the Fire. Therefore, based upon this, some of them will be in Paradise and others in the Fire.

'Ā'ishah and 'Alī (*raḍiyAllāhu 'anhumā*) [2] and the People of Knowledge have unanimously accepted it. However, the child who is able to discern right from wrong will have his worship accepted and be rewarded for it in the eyes of the majority of the scholars.

As for the one who is insane, from whom the pen has been lifted, then nothing of his worship is accepted by agreement of the scholars.[3] Therefore his faith, disbelief, prayer or other acts of worship are not accepted. Indeed, in the eyes of the generality of intelligent people, such a person is not capable of undertaking the affairs of this world such as trade and manufacturing. He is not fit to be a cloth seller, a perfumer, a blacksmith or a carpenter. His contracts are invalid by agreement of the scholars just as are his transactions of buying and selling, his marriage, divorce, confession, testimony or any other of his statements. Instead all of his words are to be regarded as useless and idle speech that have no significance or bearing on *Sharī'ah* rulings, reward or punishment. This is not the case

---

[2] {F} The ḥadīth of 'Alī has been reported by Abū Dāwūd [Eng. Trans. 3/1226 no. 4385], an-Nasā'ī, *'al-Kubrā'* [7343-7344], and Aḥmad [1/154-157]. Bukhārī [Eng. Trans. 7/146 chpt. 11, 8/527 chpt. 8] also reports it as a saying of 'Alī.

The ḥadīth of 'Ā'ishah has been reported by Abū Dāwūd [Eng. Trans. 3/1226 no. 4384], an-Nasā'ī [6/156], ibn Mājah [no. 2041] and Aḥmad [6/100, 101, 144].

Similar *aḥādīth* have been reported from Abū Qatādah by al-Ḥākim [4/389]; Abū Hurayrah by al-Bazzār [no. 1540]; Thawbān and Shaddād bin Aws by aṭ-Ṭabarānī, *'Musnad ash-Shāmiyyīn'* [no. 386]; and Anas by Abu ash-Shaykh, *'Ṭabaqāt al-Muḥaddithīn'* [no. 1000].

The ḥadīth is *ṣaḥīḥ* when taking into consideration all of its routes and witnesses.

[3] {F} *Al-Ḥāfiẓ*, *'al-Fatḥ'* [12/121-122] said, "The legal Jurists have taken to the implications of these *aḥādīth* except that ibn Hibbān mentioned that the meaning of lifting the pens is that the evil they commit is not written but the good is. Our *shaykh* said in *'Sharḥ at-Tirmidhī,'* "This is clear in the case of the child but not applicable to the insane and one who is sleeping because they are included amongst those whose worship cannot be accepted due to the absence of their awareness.""

with a child who can discern right from wrong for in certain circumstances and on certain occasions that are proven by [legal] texts and consensus his words are given consideration, there also exist other circumstances which have been differed over [as to whether or not his words are acceptable].

When it is known that the faith, *taqwā* and drawing close to Allāh by performing the obligatory and optional actions of one who is insane are not valid, and it is known that he cannot be a *Waliy* of Allāh, then it is not permissible to believe that such a person is a *Waliy* of Allāh. This is more so the case when the only proof that one has for believing him to be a *waliy* is his unveiling [certain hidden realities] concerning a particular individual or his doing something such as pointing towards someone who subsequently dies or faints. The reason for this is that it is known that the disbelievers and hypocrites from amongst the polytheists and the People of the Book can also perform satanic feats and unveil certain [hidden] realities. Such feats can be found amongst the soothsayers, magicians and worshippers of the polytheists and the People of the Book. Therefore it is not permissible for anyone to merely depend on the likes of these feats alone to prove that a particular individual is a *Waliy* of Allāh, even if he knows of nothing from this person that would nullify his being a *waliy*. Now if this is the case with regards to one who has done nothing that would nullify his being a *waliy*, then what of one from whom it is known that he has nullified the possibility of being a *Waliy* of Allāh such as one about whom it is known that he does not believe in the obligation of following the Prophet (ﷺ) both inwardly and outwardly, and instead believes that he should follow the outward aspects of the *Sharī'ah* and not the inner reality, or he believes that the *Awliyā'* of Allāh have a route to Allāh that is different to the route of the Prophets (*'alayhim aṣ-ṣalāh was salām*), or he says that the Prophets restricted and made narrow the path [to Allāh], or that they are role-models for the general masses but not the elite, or other such things that are stated by some of those who claim *wilāyah*. Such people contain a level of disbelief that nullifies faith not to mention nullifying the possibility of being a *Waliy* of Allāh, the Mighty and Magnificent! Hence whosoever uses their miraculous feats to prove [these beliefs] then such a person is more misguided than the Jews and the Christians.

The same is true of one who is insane, for the very fact of his being insane nullifies the validity of his faith and worship which are the pre-requisites of being a *Waliy* of Allāh. As for the one who becomes insane sometimes and sane at other times, then if he is a believer in Allāh and His Messenger at the time of his sanity, performing the obligations and avoiding the prohibited - his periods of insanity do not prevent Allāh rewarding him for his faith and *taqwā* that he had while being sane, and his degree of love and closeness to Allāh will be in accordance to that. In a similar way, the one who becomes insane after having faith and *taqwā* will be rewarded by Allāh for it and it will not be rendered null and void by this insanity that he has been afflicted with due to no sin that he has committed, and the Pen is lifted from him in the state of his insanity.

Based upon what has preceded, the one who outwardly shows that he is a *waliy*, yet does not perform the obligations and avoid the prohibited, indeed he does that which nullifies his claim, then it is not possible for anyone to say that he is a *Waliy* of Allāh. Such a claimant, if he is not insane but rather disorientated without any trace of insanity, or he loses his intellect through insanity sometimes and is sane at other times, and he does not perform the obligations [while being sane] and instead believes that it is not obligatory upon him to follow the Messenger (ﷺ) then he is a disbeliever.

If the claimant is indeed insane, inwardly and outwardly, then the Pen has been lifted from him and though he is not liable to the punishment that is meted out to the disbelievers, he is also not deserving of the miracles (*karāmah*) that Allāh, the Mighty and Magnificent, grants the People of Faith and *Taqwā*. In both cases it is not permissible for anyone to believe that such a claimant is truly a *Waliy* of Allāh. However if he does have a period of sanity and he is a pious, God-fearing believer during that period then his degree of love and closeness to Allāh will be determined in accordance to this. If, during the period of his sanity, he contains some degree of disbelief and hypocrisy, or he is a disbeliever or a hypocrite and then becomes insane, he will be punished for this and his insanity does not render null and void his previous disbelief or hypocrisy.

In Summary

- Faith and *taqwā* are pre-requisites for *wilāyah*.
- The disbeliever or hypocrite can never be a *Waliy*.
- The one whose worship is not valid can never be a *Waliy*.
- The rules and regulations dealing with the insane in this regard.

CHAPTER EIGHT

[The *Awliyā'* of Allāh Have no Distinguishing Features With Regards the Outward, Permissible Aspects]

THERE IS NOTHING ABOUT THE *Awliyā'* that would outwardly distinguish them from the rest of mankind with respect to the permissible issues. Therefore, with regards to the permissible aspects of clothing, they do not wear anything specific and neither are they known for having a shaved head or shortened hair, or braiding their hair - if this is permissible. The case is as [the proverb] reads,

How many truthful believers are there in course garments,
yet how many heretics[1] are there

---

[1] {Y} The word *Zindīq*, or heretic, is famously understood to refer to those who do not follow a religious law and believe that time is eternal. In the eyes of the Mālikī, Shāfi'ī and Ḥanbalī Legal Jurists it refers to those who openly show Islām yet conceal disbelief, at the time of the Prophet (ﷺ) such people were called Hypocrites, but later in the technical terminology of the *Sharī'ah* they were called heretics. In the eyes of the Ḥanafī Legal Jurists it refers to one who does not adhere to a religion.

Refer to *'al-Qāmūs al-Fiqhī'* [pg. 160].

[resplendent] in finery.

Instead they are to be found amongst every category of the nation of Muḥammad (ﷺ) provided that they are not from the People of Innovation and [Persistent] Sin. They are found amongst the people of the Qur'ān, the People of Knowledge, the People of *Jihād* and the Sword, the traders, manufacturers and farmers. Allāh, the Exalted, mentions the categories of the nation of Muḥammad (ﷺ) with His words,

﴿إِنَّ رَبَّكَ يَعْلَمُ أَنَّكَ تَقُومُ أَدْنَىٰ مِن ثُلُثَيِ الَّيْلِ وَنِصْفَهُۥ وَثُلُثَهُۥ وَطَآئِفَةٌ
مِّنَ الَّذِينَ مَعَكَ وَاللَّهُ يُقَدِّرُ الَّيْلَ وَالنَّهَارَ عَلِمَ أَن لَّن تُحْصُوهُ فَتَابَ
عَلَيْكُمْ فَاقْرَءُوا مَا تَيَسَّرَ مِنَ الْقُرْءَانِ عَلِمَ أَن سَيَكُونُ مِنكُم مَّرْضَىٰ
وَءَاخَرُونَ يَضْرِبُونَ فِي الْأَرْضِ يَبْتَغُونَ مِن فَضْلِ اللَّهِ وَءَاخَرُونَ
يُقَٰتِلُونَ فِي سَبِيلِ اللَّهِ فَاقْرَءُوا مَا تَيَسَّرَ مِنْهُ وَأَقِيمُوا الصَّلَوٰةَ وَءَاتُوا
الزَّكَوٰةَ وَأَقْرِضُوا اللَّهَ قَرْضًا حَسَنًا وَمَا تُقَدِّمُوا لِأَنفُسِكُم مِّنْ خَيْرٍ تَجِدُوهُ
عِندَ اللَّهِ هُوَ خَيْرًا وَأَعْظَمَ أَجْرًا وَاسْتَغْفِرُوا اللَّهَ إِنَّ اللَّهَ غَفُورٌ رَّحِيمٌ ﴿٢٠﴾

Indeed, your Lord knows that you stand [in prayer] almost two thirds of the night, or half of it, or a third of it, and [so do] a group of those with you. And Allāh determines [the extent of] the night and day. He has known that you [Muslims] will not be able to [continuously perform] it and has turned to you in forgiveness, so recite what is easy [for you] of the Qur'ān. He has known that there will be among you those who are ill and others travelling throughout the land seeking [something] of the bounty of Allāh and others fighting for the cause of Allāh. So recite what is easy from it...

[*Al-Muzzammil* (73): 20]

[8.1 The Terms *Ṣūfi* and *Fuqarā'*]

The *Salaf* used to call the people possessing religion and knowledge, *Qurrā'* (القرّاء) - reciters' and this term included the scholars and ascetics, then after this the names *as-Ṣūfiyyah* (الصوفية) and *Fuqarā'* (الفقراء) were invented. The term *as-Ṣūfiyyah* refers to an ascription to garments of wool - *Ṣūf* (صوف) according to the most correct opinion.[2]

It is also postulated that the ascription is to the finest and purest - *ṣafwah* (صفوة) of Legal Jurists[3]; or to Ṣafwa bin Murr bin Add bin Ṭābikha, a tribe of the Arabs who were known to be ascetics; or to the People of *Suffah* (الصفّة); or to purity -*ṣafā'* (الصفاء); or to the choicest of the people - *ṣafwah* (الصفوة); or the first row - *ṣaff* (الصف) before Allāh, the Exalted. All of these opinions are weak for if it was as they thought then the term would be *Ṣuffiy* (صُفّي), or *Ṣafā'ī* (صَفَائي), or *Ṣafwī* (صَفْوي), or *Ṣaffī* (صَفّي) and not *Ṣūfī* (صوفي).

The term *Fuqarā'* (الفقراء) came to be applied to those who were traversing the Path [to Allāh] and it is a newly invented terminology. The people have debated as to which of the two terms is better - the term *Ṣūfī* (صوفي) or the term *al-Faqīr* (الفقير).[4]

They have also debated concerning the rich man who expresses gratitude to Allāh and the poor man who is patient as to which of the two is better. This is an issue which has been debated of old

---

[2] {M} A comprehensive discussion concerning the derivation of the word *Taṣawwuf* can be be found in Abu Nu'aym, *'al-Ḥilya'* [1/17].

[3] {T} This is the wording in some texts of *'al-Furqān'*, in other texts the wording is 'the purest of the pure' or 'the hair at the bottom of the nape' (*ṣafwa al-qafā*).

[4] {T} *al-Faqīr*, or impoverished and poor, is the singular to *al-Fuqarā'*. One of its verbal nouns is *al-faqr*, or poverty.

between al-Junaid and Abū al-'Abbās bin 'Aṭā' and two opinions have been reported from Aḥmad concerning it. The correct opinion in all of this lies with what Allāh, the Blessed and Exalted says,

يَٰٓأَيُّهَا ٱلنَّاسُ إِنَّا خَلَقْنَٰكُم مِّن ذَكَرٍ وَأُنثَىٰ وَجَعَلْنَٰكُمْ شُعُوبًا وَقَبَآئِلَ لِتَعَارَفُوٓاْ إِنَّ أَكْرَمَكُمْ عِندَ ٱللَّهِ أَتْقَىٰكُمْ إِنَّ ٱللَّهَ عَلِيمٌ خَبِيرٌ ﴿١٣﴾

> O mankind, indeed We have created you male and female and made you peoples and tribes that you may know one another. Indeed the most noble of you in the Sight of Allāh is the most righteous and God-fearing of you...
>
> [*Al-Ḥujurāt* (49): 13]

It is reported in the Ṣaḥīḥ from Abū Hurayrah that,

عن النبي ﷺ، أنه سُئِل: أي الناس أفضل؟ قال: «أتقاهم»، قيل له: ليس عن هذا نسألك، فقال: «يوسف نبي الله، ابن يعقوب نبي الله، ابن إسحاق نبي الله، ابن إبراهيم خليل الله». فقيل له: ليس عن هذا نسألك. فقال: «عن معادن العرب تسألوني؟ الناس معادن كمعادن الذهب والفضة، خيارهم في الجاهلية خيارهم في الإسلام، إذا فقهوا»

> The Prophet (ﷺ) was asked, 'Who amongst the people is the best?' He replied, '*The most pious and God-fearing of them.*' It was said to him, 'We were not asking you about this.' He said, '*Joseph, the Prophet of Allāh, the son of Jacob, the Prophet of Allāh, the son of Isḥāq, the Prophet of Allāh, the son of Abraham, the Beloved of Allāh.*' It was said to him, 'We were not asking you about this.' He asked, '*Then is it about the classes of the Arabs that you are asking me? People are like*

minerals, similar to gold and silver - the best of them in Jāhilyyah are the best of them in Islām provided they have understanding [of Islām].'" [5]

Therefore the Book and *Sunnah* prove that the most noble people in the Sight of Allāh are the most pious and God-fearing.

It is reported in the *Sunan* from the Prophet (ﷺ) that he said,

«لا فضل لعربي على عجمي، ولا لعجمي على عربي، ولا لأسود على أبيض، ولا لأبيض على أسود إلا بالتقوى، كلكم لآدم وآدم من تراب»

"There is no superiority of an Arab over a non-Arab, nor a non-Arab over an Arab, nor the Black over the White, nor the White over the Black except through taqwā. All of you are from Ādam and Ādam was created from earth." [6]

It is also reported from him (ﷺ) that he said,

«إن الله تعالى أذهب عنكم عُبِّيَّة الجاهلية، وفخرها بالآباء، الناس رجلان: مؤمن تقي، وفاجر شقي»

"Indeed Allāh, the Exalted has removed from you the arrogance and pride of Jāhiliyyah and its boasting about lineage. The people are of two types: a pious, God-fearing believer, or a miserable sinner." [7]

---

[5] {F} Reported by Bukhārī [Eng. Trans. 4/366 no. 572, 4/388 no. 593, 4/390 no. 597, 4/460 no. 696] and Muslim [Eng. Trans. 4/1267 no. 5862].

[6] {F} This ḥadīth is not to be found in any of the *Sunan*, rather it is found in Aḥmad [5/411] with a *ṣaḥīḥ isnād*.

[7] {F} Reported by Abū Dāwūd [Eng. Trans. 3/1418 no. 5097], at-Tirmidhī [no. 3955-2956] and Aḥmad [2/361-524].
I say: its *isnād* is *ḥasan inshaAllāh*.

So whosoever, from any of the categories [of the nation of Muḥammad (ﷺ)] is the more pious and God-fearing then he is more noble in the Sight of Allāh and in the case that they have the same amount of *taqwā* then they are of the same ranking.

In the *Sharīʿah*, the word *al-Faqr* means one of two things, *al-Faqr* (the poverty) of wealth or *al-Faqr* (the need) that the creation has of the Creator. Allāh, the Exalted says,

﴿ إِنَّمَا ٱلصَّدَقَٰتُ لِلْفُقَرَآءِ وَٱلْمَسَٰكِينِ

Charity is only for the *fuqarā'* [the poor who do not beg].
[*At-Tawbah* (9): 60]

﴿ يَٰٓأَيُّهَا ٱلنَّاسُ أَنتُمُ ٱلْفُقَرَآءُ إِلَى ٱللَّهِ

O mankind! It is you who are *fuqarā'* [standing in need] of Allāh.
[*Fāṭir* (35): 15]

[8.1.1 The *Fuqarā'* who have been Praised]

Allāh, the Exalted, has commended two groups of the *Fuqarā'* in his Book, those who [deserve to be given] charity and those who [deserve to be given] from the war booty. Allāh says with regards the first group,

﴿ لِلْفُقَرَآءِ ٱلَّذِينَ أُحْصِرُوا۟ فِى سَبِيلِ ٱللَّهِ
لَا يَسْتَطِيعُونَ ضَرْبًا فِى ٱلْأَرْضِ يَحْسَبُهُمُ
ٱلْجَاهِلُ أَغْنِيَآءَ مِنَ ٱلتَّعَفُّفِ تَعْرِفُهُم بِسِيمَٰهُمْ
لَا يَسْـَٔلُونَ ٱلنَّاسَ إِلْحَافًا ۗ وَمَا تُنفِقُوا۟ مِنْ خَيْرٍ
فَإِنَّ ٱللَّهَ بِهِۦ عَلِيمٌ ﴿٢٧٣﴾

> [Charity is] for the *Fuqarā* [the poor], who are restricted [from travel] in the Way of Allāh and cannot move about in the land [for trade or work]. The one who does not know them thinks that they are rich because of their modesty. You will know them by their mark - they do not beg of people at all...
>
> [*Al-Baqarah* (2): 273]

And He says with regards the second group, which is the more noble of the two,

لِلْفُقَرَآءِ ٱلْمُهَٰجِرِينَ ٱلَّذِينَ أُخْرِجُوا۟ مِن دِيَٰرِهِمْ وَأَمْوَٰلِهِمْ يَبْتَغُونَ فَضْلًا مِّنَ ٱللَّهِ وَرِضْوَٰنًا وَيَنصُرُونَ ٱللَّهَ وَرَسُولَهُۥٓ ۚ أُو۟لَٰٓئِكَ هُمُ ٱلصَّٰدِقُونَ ﴿٨﴾

> [And there is also a share in this booty] for the poor emigrants who were expelled from their homes and their property, seeking the Bounty of Allāh and His Pleasure, helping Allāh and His Messenger. Such indeed are the truthful.
>
> [*Al-Ḥashr* (59): 8]

This is the description of the *Muhājirūn*, those who migrated from evil deeds and fought the enemies of Allāh both inwardly and outwardly. This is as the Prophet (ﷺ) said,

«المؤمن من أمنه الناسُ على دمائهم وأموالهم، والمسلم من سلِم المسلمون من لسانه ويده، والمهاجر من هجر ما نهى اللّٰه عنه، والمجاهد من جاهد نفسه في ذات الله»

> *"The believer is one to whom the people would entrust their blood and properties. The Muslim is one from whose tongue and hand the rest of the Muslims are secure. The Muhājir is one who migrates from that which Allāh forbade. The Mujāhid is the one who strives*

against his self for the sake of Allāh." [8]

[8.2 We Have Returned From the Lesser *Jihād* to the Greatest *Jihād*]

As for the hadīth that some of them narrate that the Prophet (ﷺ) said concerning the military expedition of Tabuk,

«رجعنا من الجهاد الأصغر إلى الجهاد الأكبر»

"We have returned from the Lesser Jihād to the Greatest Jihād." [9]

---

[8] {F} Reported by Aḥmad [6/21-22] from Fādālah bin 'Ubaid that the Prophet (ﷺ) said,

> *"Should I not inform you about the believer? He is the one to whom the people would entrust their blood and properties. The Muslim is one from whose tongue and hand the rest of the Muslims are secure. The Mujāhid is the one who exertes himself in the obedience of Allāh. The Muhājir is one who migrates from errors and sins."*

It is also reported by an-Nasā'ī, *'Sunan al-Kubrā'* as mentioned in *'at-Tuḥfah'* [8/262]; ibn Mājah [no. 3934] mentioning only the believer and the *Muhājir*; al-Bazzār [no. 1143] in its entirety; and ibn Ḥibbān [no. 25] in its entirety.

The *isnād* is *ṣaḥīḥ*. Similar *aḥādīth* have been reported by ibn 'Amr, Jābir, Mu'ādh al-Juhanī, Anas, Abū Hurayrah, and 'Amr bin 'Absa.

{Y} In one text of *'al-Furqān'* the wording of the ḥadīth reads, *'The Mujāhid is the one who exertes himself in the obedience of Allāh,'* therefore having the same wording as Aḥmad.

[9] {F} *Al-Ḥāfiẓ* ibn Ḥajr, *'Tasdīd al-Qūs'* said, 'It is widely quoted, but it is from the words of Ibrāhīm bin Abī Ablā [as mentioned] in *'al-Kunā'* of an-Nasā'ī.'

The ḥadīth has been mentioned in *'al-Iḥyā'* and al-'Irāqī attributed it to al-Bayhaqī from the ḥadīth of Jābir, then he said, 'This *isnād* contains weakness.' The [full wording] has been reported by al-Khaṭīb, *'at-Tārīkh'* from Jābir who said, 'The Prophet (ﷺ) returned from one of their military expeditions and said, *'you have returned in the best of ways, you have returned from the Lesser Jihād to the Greatest Jihād.'* They asked, 'What is the Greatest *Jihād*?' He replied, *'The servant striving against his*

=

Then this has no basis and it has not been reported by anyone who has knowledge of the sayings and actions of the Prophet (ﷺ). Undertaking *Jihād* against the disbelievers is from the greatest of actions, indeed it is the best action that a person could opt to perform. Allāh, the Exalted says,

لَّا يَسْتَوِي الْقَاعِدُونَ مِنَ الْمُؤْمِنِينَ غَيْرُ أُولِي الضَّرَرِ وَالْمُجَاهِدُونَ
فِي سَبِيلِ اللَّهِ بِأَمْوَالِهِمْ وَأَنفُسِهِمْ ۚ فَضَّلَ اللَّهُ الْمُجَاهِدِينَ بِأَمْوَالِهِمْ
وَأَنفُسِهِمْ عَلَى الْقَاعِدِينَ دَرَجَةً ۚ وَكُلًّا وَعَدَ اللَّهُ الْحُسْنَىٰ ۚ وَفَضَّلَ اللَّهُ
الْمُجَاهِدِينَ عَلَى الْقَاعِدِينَ أَجْرًا عَظِيمًا ﴿٩٥﴾ دَرَجَاتٍ مِّنْهُ وَمَغْفِرَةً
وَرَحْمَةً ۚ وَكَانَ اللَّهُ غَفُورًا رَّحِيمًا ﴿٩٦﴾

> Not equal are those believers remaining [at home] - other than the disabled - and the *Mujāhidīn* [who strive and fight] in the cause of Allāh with their wealth and their lives. Allāh has preferred the *Mujāhidīn* [who strive] with their wealth and lives over those who remain [behind] by degrees. And to all Allāh has promised the best [reward]. But Allāh has preferred the *Mujāhidīn* over those who remain [behind] with a great reward - degrees [of high position] from Him and forgiveness and mercy. And Allāh is ever Forgiving and Merciful.
>
> [*An-Nisā'* (4): 95-96]

=
base desires.'

Refer to: *'Ad-Durar al-Muntathirah'* [p. 157]; *'Kashf al-Khafā"* [1/511-512]; and *'Al-Asrār al-Marfū'ah'* [pp. 211-212].

{T} Considering that the ḥadīth was reported by al-Bayhaqī and al-Khaṭīb, both of whom were Ḥadīth Masters (*Ḥāfiẓ*), the words of ibn Taymiyyah, 'It has not been reported by anyone who has knowledge of the sayings and actions of the Prophet (ﷺ)' are not accurate.

۞ أَجَعَلْتُمْ سِقَايَةَ
ٱلْحَآجِّ وَعِمَارَةَ ٱلْمَسْجِدِ ٱلْحَرَامِ كَمَنْ ءَامَنَ بِٱللَّهِ وَٱلْيَوْمِ ٱلْءَاخِرِ
وَجَٰهَدَ فِى سَبِيلِ ٱللَّهِ ۚ لَا يَسْتَوُۥنَ عِندَ ٱللَّهِ ۗ وَٱللَّهُ لَا يَهْدِى ٱلْقَوْمَ
ٱلظَّٰلِمِينَ ﴿١٩﴾ ٱلَّذِينَ ءَامَنُوا۟ وَهَاجَرُوا۟ وَجَٰهَدُوا۟ فِى سَبِيلِ ٱللَّهِ
بِأَمْوَٰلِهِمْ وَأَنفُسِهِمْ أَعْظَمُ دَرَجَةً عِندَ ٱللَّهِ ۚ وَأُو۟لَٰٓئِكَ هُمُ ٱلْفَآئِزُونَ ﴿٢٠﴾
يُبَشِّرُهُمْ رَبُّهُم بِرَحْمَةٍ مِّنْهُ وَرِضْوَٰنٍ وَجَنَّٰتٍ لَّهُمْ فِيهَا
نَعِيمٌ مُّقِيمٌ ﴿٢١﴾ خَٰلِدِينَ فِيهَآ أَبَدًا ۚ إِنَّ ٱللَّهَ عِندَهُۥٓ أَجْرٌ
عَظِيمٌ ﴿٢٢﴾

Have you made the providing of water for the pilgrim and the maintenance of the *Masjid al-Ḥarām* equal to [the deeds of] one who believes in Allāh and the Last Day and strives in the cause of Allāh? They are not equal in the sight of Allāh and Allāh does not guide the wrongdoing people. The ones who have believed, emigrated and striven in the cause of Allāh with their wealth and their lives are greater in rank in the sight of Allāh. And it is those who are the attainers [of success]. Their Lord gives them glad tidings of Mercy from Him, His Pleasure and Gardens for them wherein is everlasting delight. They will dwell therein forever, indeed with Allāh is a great reward.

[*At-Tawbah* (9): 19-22]

It is established in Ṣaḥīḥ Muslim and others from Nu'mān bin Bashīr (*raḍiyAllāhu 'anhu*) who said,

"I was with the Prophet (ﷺ) when a person said, 'after Islām, I do not care to do anything except give water to the pilgrims.' Another said, 'After Islām, I do not care to do anything except look after the *Masjid al-Ḥarām*.' 'Alī bin Abī Ṭālib said, '*Jihād* in the Way of Allāh is better than what you two have mentioned.' Thereupon Umar said, 'Do not raise your voices near the pulpit of the Messenger of Allāh (ﷺ), but when the prayer is finished, I will ask him.' So he asked him and Allāh, the Exalted, revealed this verse." [10]

It is reported in the Two Ṣaḥīḥs from 'Abdullāh bin Mas'ūd (*raḍiyAllāhu 'anhu*) who said,

> "I asked, 'O Messenger of Allāh! Which action is the most superior in the Sight of Allāh, the Mighty and Magnificent?' He replied, *'prayer at its correct time.'* I asked, 'then which?' He replied, *'good treatment of parents.'* I asked, 'then which?' He replied, *'Jihād in the Way of Allāh.'* The Messenger of Allāh (ﷺ) told me about these and if I had asked further he would had added more." [11]

It is also reported in the Two Ṣaḥīḥs from him (ﷺ) that he was asked,

> أي الأعمال أفضل؟ قال: «إيمان بالله، وجهاد في سبيله»، قيل: ثم ماذا؟، قال: «حج مبرور»
>
> "Which action is the most superior?' He (ﷺ) replied, *'Faith in Allāh and Jihād in His Way.'* I asked, 'Then which?' He replied, *'An accepted Ḥajj [containing no element of sin].'"* [12]

It is reported in the Two Ṣaḥīḥs that,

---

[10] {F} Reported by Muslim [Eng. Trans. 3/1045 no. 4638] and Aḥmad [4/269].

[11] {F} Reported by Bukhārī [Eng. Trans. 1/300 no. 505, 4/35 no. 41, 8/1 no. 1, 9/471 no. 625] and Muslim [Eng. Trans. 1/49 no. 151].

[12] {F} Reported by Bukhārī [Eng. Trans. 1/26 no. 25, 2/347 no. 594] and Muslim [Eng. Trans. 1/49 no. 149].

يـا رسول الله! أخبـرني بعمل يعـدل
الجهاد في سبيل الله، قال: «لا تستطيعه ـ أو لا تطيقه ـ»
، قال: فأخبرني به، قال: «هل تستطيع إذا خرجت مجاهداً
أن تصوم ولا تفطر، وتقوم ولا تفتر؟»

"A man asked the Messenger of Allāh, 'O Messenger of Allāh! Inform me of an action that would equate to undertaking Jihād in the Way of Allāh?' He replied, *'You would not be able to perform it - or you would not be able to bear it.'* He said, 'Inform me of it.' He said, *'When you go out for Jihād are you able to fast continuously and to stand in prayer [continuously] without faltering?'*" [13]

It is reported in the *Sunan* from Muʿādh (*raḍiyAllāhu ʿanhu*) that the Prophet (ﷺ) advised him when he dispatched him to Yemen saying,

«يا معاذ، اتق الله حيثما كنت، وأتبع السيئة الحسنة تمحها،
وخالق الناس بخلق حسن»

"O Muʿādh! Fear Allāh wheresoever you may be, follow up an evil deed with a good deed for it will efface it and interact with people with good manners." [14]

He (ﷺ) also said,

---

[13] {F} Reported by Bukhārī [Eng. Trans. 4/36 no. 44] and Muslim [Eng. Trans. 3/1044 no. 4636].

{M} The wording of Bukhārī and Muslim however is, *"When the Mujāhid goes out [in the Way of Allāh] are you able to go to the Mosque and stand in prayer [continuously] without faltering and fast continuously?"*

[14] {F} Reported by at-Tirmidhī [no. 1987] and Aḥmad [5/228-236].

The ḥadīth is also reported from Abū Dharr by at-Tirmidhī [no. 1987] and Aḥmad [5/153, 158, 177]. I say: the ḥadīth is *ḥasan* due to witnesses.

«يا معاذ إني لأُحبك، فلا تدع أن تقول في دُبُرِ كلّ صلاة: اللهم أعني على ذكرك وشكرك، وحسن عبادتك»

"O Muʿādh! Indeed I love you, after every prayer never abandon saying, 'O Allāh! Aid me in performing Your dhikr, expressing gratitude to You and making good [my] worship of You.'" [15]

He (ﷺ) said to him while he was riding and Muʿādh was sitting behind him,

«يـا معاذ أتـدري ما حقّ الله على عبـاده؟»، قلت: الله ورسـولـه أعلم. قـال: «حقّـه عليهم أن يعبـدوه، ولا يشركوا به شيئاً. أتدري ما حقّ العباد على الله إذا فعلوا ذلك؟» قلت: الله ورسـوله أعلم. قال: «حقهم عليه ألّا يعذبهم»

"O Muʿādh! Do you know what the right of Allāh is over His servants?' I said, 'Allāh and His Messenger know best.' He said, *'His right over them is that they worship Him [Alone] without associating any partners with Him. Do you know what the [legislated] right of the servants upon Allāh is if they do this?'* I said, 'Allāh and His Messenger know best.' He said, *'Their right over Him is that He not punish them.'"* [16]

He (ﷺ) also said to Muʿādh,

«راس الامر الاسلام، وعموده الصلاة، وذروة سنامه الجهاد في سبيل الله»،

"The head of the matter is Islām, its supporting pillar is the prayer

[15] {F} Reported by Abū Dāwūd [Eng. Trans. 1/396 no. 1517], an-Nasāʾī [no. 109] and Aḥmad [5/244-247].
I say: its *isnād* is *ṣaḥīḥ*.

[16] {F} Reported by Bukhārī [Eng. Trans. 4/73 no. 108, 7/549 no. 850, 8/189 no. 283, 8/335 no. 507, 9/349 no. 470] and Muslim [Eng. Trans. 1/23 no. 47].

and its highest peak is undertaking Jihād in the Way of Allāh."

«يا معاذ ألا أُخبرك بأبواب البر؟ الصوم جُنّة، والصدقة تطفىءُ الخطيئة كما يطفىءُ الماءُ النار، وقيام الرجل في جوف الليل» ثم قرأ:

Then he said, *"O Muʿādh should I not inform you of the doors to righteousness? Fasting [which] is a shield, charity [which] extinguishes sins as water extinguishes fire, and the standing of a person [for prayer] in the depths of the night."* Then he recited,

تَتَجَافَىٰ جُنُوبُهُمْ
عَنِ ٱلْمَضَاجِعِ يَدْعُونَ رَبَّهُمْ خَوْفًا وَطَمَعًا وَمِمَّا رَزَقْنَٰهُمْ
يُنفِقُونَ ﴿١٦﴾ فَلَا تَعْلَمُ نَفْسٌ مَّآ أُخْفِىَ لَهُم مِّن قُرَّةِ أَعْيُنٍ جَزَآءًۢ
بِمَا كَانُوا۟ يَعْمَلُونَ ﴿١٧﴾

Their sides forsake their beds to invoke their Lord in fear and hope, and they spend out of what We have bestowed them. No person knows what is kept hidden for them of joy as reward for what they used to do.

[*As-Sajdah* (32): 16-17]

ثم قال: «يا معاذ ألا أُخبرك بما هو أملك لك من ذلك؟» فقال: «أمسك عليك لسانك هذا»، فأخذ بلسانه، قال: يا رسول الله، وإنا لمؤاخذون بما نتكلّم به؟ فقال: «ثكلتك أمّك يا معاذ، وهل يكبّ الناسَ في النار على مناخرهم إلا حصائدُ ألسنتهم»

Then he said, *"O Muʿādh! Should I not inform you of that which is more deserving of your care than that? Restrain your tongue,'* and he took hold of his tongue. He asked, 'O Messenger of Allāh! Are we to be taken to account for what we say?' He replied, *'May your mother be bereft of you O Muʿādh! What is it that throws the people into the Fire face first except for the harvest of the tongues!'"* [17]

[8.3 Praiseworthy and Blameworthy Silence]

The explanation to this ḥadīth is to be found in the ḥadīth reported in the Two Ṣaḥīḥs that the Prophet (ﷺ) said,

«من كـان يؤمن بالله واليـوم الآخر فليقل خيراً أو ليصـمت»

"Whosoever believes in Allāh and the Last Day then let him speak good or remain silent." [18]

Therefore speaking the good is better than remaining silent concerning it and refraining from speaking evil is better than speaking it. As for perpetual silence than this is a *bid'ah* that has been prohibited and the same applies to abstention from bread, meat and water for this is also a blameworthy *bid'ah*. It is established in Ṣaḥīḥ Bukhārī from ibn 'Abbās (*raḍiyAllāhu 'anhumā*) that,

أنّ النّبي - ﷺ - رأى رجـلاً قائمـاً في الشمس، فقال:
«ما هذا»؟ فقالوا: أبو إسرائيل نذر أن يقوم في الشمس،
ولا يستظلّ، ولا يتكلّم، ويصوم، فقال النبي ﷺ:

The Prophet (ﷺ) saw a person standing in the sun and asked, "*What is this?*" They replied, 'He is Abū Isrā'īl who has taken an oath to stand in the sun, not to seek the shade, not to speak and to fast.' Thereupon the Prophet

[17] {F} Reported by at-Tirmidhī [no. 2616], an-Nasā'ī , *'al-Kubrā'* [no. 11394], ibn Mājah [no. 3973] and Aḥmad [5/231, 241, 245-247].

I say: its *isnād* is *ḥasan inshaAllāh* when one gathers all the various routes of the ḥadīth from Mu'ādh.

[18] {F} Reported by Bukhārī [Eng. Trans. 8/29 no. 47, 8/99 no. 157, 8/321 no. 482] and Muslim [Eng. Trans. 1/32 no. 75-78].

(ﷺ) said,

«مروه فليجلس، وليستظل، وليتكلم، وليتم صومه»

"Order him to sit, seek the shade, speak and complete his fast." [19]

It is established in the Two Ṣaḥīḥs from Anas that,

> Some people asked about the worship of the Messenger of Allāh (ﷺ), [when they received the answer] it was as if they thought it to be little and said, 'Which of us is like the Messenger of Allāh (ﷺ).' Then one of them said, 'As for me, I will fast without ever breaking it.' Another said, 'As for for me, I will stand [for prayer by night] and not sleep.' Another said, 'As for me, I will not eat meat.' Another said, 'As for me, I will not marry.'

[19] {F} Reported by Bukhārī [Eng. Trans. 8/453 no. 695] and Abū Dāwūd [Eng. Trans. 2/934 no. 3284].

{T} Ibn Rajab al-Ḥanbalī says concerning this ḥadīth, "The Messenger (ﷺ) saw a person standing in the sun, and so he enquired about him and it was said in reply, 'He has taken an oath to stand and not to sit or take shade, and to fast.' So the Prophet (ﷺ) ordered him to sit and seek the shade and to complete his fast. So he (ﷺ) did not make his standing and exposure to the sun a means of getting close [to Allāh] such that it would require fulfilling the oath. It is reported that this event occurred on the day of *Jumu'ah* at the time of hearing the *khuṭbah* of the Prophet (ﷺ) while he was on the pulpit. So this man made the oath to stand and not sit or seek the shade for as long as the Prophet (ﷺ) gave his sermon, in glorification and respect of listening to the sermon of the Prophet (ﷺ), and yet the Messenger (ﷺ) did not make this a means of getting close to Allāh that would require fulfilment of his oath. This is despite the fact that standing is worship in other places such as prayer and *adhān* and offering supplication on Arafah. Exposure to the sun is also a means of getting closer to Allāh for the one in *iḥrām*, so this indicates that everything that is a means of getting close to Allāh on a particular occasion is not a means of getting close on every occasion, rather one follows what occurs in the *Sharī'ah* in its correct place for everything..." - *'Jāmi' al-'Ulum wal Ḥikam'* [1/120].

{T} It is known in the *Sharī'ah* that an oath which involves disobedience to Allāh does not require fulfilment.

فقال رسول الله ﷺ: «ما بال رجال يقول أحدهم: كذا وكذا، ولكني أصوم وأفطر، وأقوم وأنام، وآكل اللحم، وأتزوج النساء، فمن رغب عن سنتي فليس مني»

[When the Messenger of Allāh ((ﷺ) heard of this] he said, "*What is the matter with some people, one of whom says such-and-such. Indeed I fast and break my fast, I stand [for prayer] and I sleep, I eat meat and I marry women. So whosever turns away from my Sunnah is not of me.*" [20]

Meaning: whosoever turns away from my *Sunnah*, traversing another path thinking that it is better. Whosoever is like this is free of Allāh and His Messenger. Allāh, the Exalted says,

وَمَن يَرْغَبُ عَن مِّلَّةِ إِبْرَٰهِـۧمَ إِلَّا مَن سَفِهَ نَفْسَهُۥ

And who turns away from the religion of Abraham except one who befools himself?

[*Al-Baqarah* (2): 130]

Indeed it is obligatory upon every Muslim to believe that the best of speech is the speech of Allāh and the best of guidance is the guidance of Muḥammad (ﷺ) as is established in the Ṣaḥīḥ that he used to deliver his sermons commencing with these words every *Jumuʿah*. [21]

---

[20] {F} Reported by Bukhārī [Eng. Trans. 7/1 no. 1] and Muslim [Eng. Trans. 2/703 no. 3236].

[21] {F} Reported by Muslim [Eng. Trans. 2/410 no. 1885] and an-Nasāʿī [3/188].

In Summary

- There is nothing that differentiates the *Awliyā'* from others with respect to permissible matters.
- The *Awliyā'* are found amongst every section of the Muslim nation.
- The title given to the religious by the *Salaf* was *Qurrā'*.
- The title given to the religious by the later people was *Ṣufī* and *Faqīr*, and an analysis of these words.
- There are two types of *faqr*: poverty of wealth and the need for the Creator.
- The description of the *fuqarā'* amongst the *Muhājirīn*, who migrated from what Allāh forbade and strove in His Way, and their virtues.
- The virtue of *Jihād* and that the physical *Jihād* is the greatest form of *Jihād*.
- The regulations regarding silence containing a clarification of when it is better to remain silent and when it is better to speak.

CHAPTER NINE

[Being Sinless is not a Pre-Requisite of *Wilāyah*]

IT IS NOT A PRE-REQUISITE FOR A *Waliy* of Allāh that he be free of sin or error, instead it is possible that some knowledge of the *Sharīʿah* be unknown to him or some aspects of the religion confuse him to the extent that he think that some matters commanded by Allāh are actually prohibited by Him. It is possible that he think that some extraordinary occurrences are from the miracles of the *Awliyāʾ* of Allāh, the Exalted, when in reality they are from Shayṭān who has disguised them and [hence succeeded in fooling him] so that he is unaware that they are from him due to his lesser ranking. None of this ejects a person from being included amongst the ranks of the *Awliyāʾ* of Allāh, the Exalted. This is because Allāh, the Glorious and Exalted, has overlooked this nation's genuine errors, acts of forgetfulness and those things they were coerced into doing. Allāh, the Exalted says,

ءَامَنَ ٱلرَّسُولُ بِمَآ أُنزِلَ
إِلَيۡهِ مِن رَّبِّهِۦ وَٱلۡمُؤۡمِنُونَۚ كُلٌّ ءَامَنَ بِٱللَّهِ وَمَلَٰٓئِكَتِهِۦ وَكُتُبِهِۦ
وَرُسُلِهِۦ لَا نُفَرِّقُ بَيۡنَ أَحَدٖ مِّن رُّسُلِهِۦۚ وَقَالُواْ سَمِعۡنَا
وَأَطَعۡنَاۖ غُفۡرَانَكَ رَبَّنَا وَإِلَيۡكَ ٱلۡمَصِيرُ ﴿٢٨٥﴾ لَا يُكَلِّفُ
ٱللَّهُ نَفۡسًا إِلَّا وُسۡعَهَاۚ لَهَا مَا كَسَبَتۡ وَعَلَيۡهَا مَا ٱكۡتَسَبَتۡۗ
رَبَّنَا لَا تُؤَاخِذۡنَآ إِن نَّسِينَآ أَوۡ أَخۡطَأۡنَاۚ رَبَّنَا وَلَا تَحۡمِلۡ
عَلَيۡنَآ إِصۡرٗا كَمَا حَمَلۡتَهُۥ عَلَى ٱلَّذِينَ مِن قَبۡلِنَاۚ رَبَّنَا وَلَا
تُحَمِّلۡنَا مَا لَا طَاقَةَ لَنَا بِهِۦۖ وَٱعۡفُ عَنَّا وَٱغۡفِرۡ لَنَا وَٱرۡحَمۡنَآۚ
أَنتَ مَوۡلَىٰنَا فَٱنصُرۡنَا عَلَى ٱلۡقَوۡمِ ٱلۡكَٰفِرِينَ ﴿٢٨٦﴾

> The Messenger has believed in what was revealed to him from his Lord, and [so have] the believers. All of them have believed in Allāh and His Angels and His Books and His Messengers, [saying], 'We make no distinction between any of His Messengers.' And they say, 'We hear and we obey. [We seek] Your forgiveness, our Lord, and to You is the [final] destination.' Allāh does not charge a soul except [with that within] its capacity. It will have [the consequence of] what [good] it has gained, and it will bear [the consequence of] what [evil] it has earned. 'Our Lord, and lay not upon us a burden like that which You laid upon those before us. Our Lord, and burden us not with that which we have no ability to bear. Pardon us; forgive us; and have mercy upon us. You are our Protector, so give us victory over the disbelieving people.'
>
> [*Al-Baqarah* (2): 285-286]

It is established in the Ṣaḥīḥ that Allāh, the Glorious, has answered this supplication and said,

«قد فعلت»

"I have done so."

It is reported in Ṣaḥīḥ Muslim from ibn 'Abbās (*raḍiyAllāhu 'anhumā*) who said,

لما نزلت هذه الآية:

When this verse was revealed,

إِن تُبْدُوا مَا فِي أَنفُسِكُمْ أَوْ تُخْفُوهُ
يُحَاسِبْكُم بِهِ اللَّهُ فَيَغْفِرُ لِمَن يَشَاءُ وَيُعَذِّبُ مَن يَشَاءُ
وَاللَّهُ عَلَىٰ كُلِّ شَيْءٍ قَدِيرٌ ﴿٢٨٤﴾

Whether you disclose what is in yourselves or conceal it, Allāh will call you to account for it...

[*Al-Baqarah* (2): 284]

دخل قلوبهم منها شيء لم يدخلها قبل ذلك
شيء أشد منه، فقال النبي ﷺ: «قولوا: سمعنا وأطعنا وسلّمنا»
قال: فألقى الله الإيمان في قلوبهم، فأنزل الله تعالى:

Something entered the hearts of [the believers] and previously nothing more severe than this had entered them. The Prophet (ﷺ) said, *'Say: We hear, obey and submit.'* Thereupon Allāh placed faith in their hearts and revealed,

لَا يُكَلِّفُ
اللَّهُ نَفْسًا إِلَّا وُسْعَهَا لَهَا مَا كَسَبَتْ وَعَلَيْهَا مَا اكْتَسَبَتْ
رَبَّنَا لَا تُؤَاخِذْنَا إِن نَّسِينَا أَوْ أَخْطَأْنَا رَبَّنَا وَلَا تَحْمِلْ
عَلَيْنَا إِصْرًا كَمَا حَمَلْتَهُ عَلَى الَّذِينَ مِن قَبْلِنَا رَبَّنَا وَلَا
تُحَمِّلْنَا مَا لَا طَاقَةَ لَنَا بِهِ وَاعْفُ عَنَّا وَاغْفِرْ لَنَا وَارْحَمْنَا
أَنتَ مَوْلَانَا فَانصُرْنَا عَلَى الْقَوْمِ الْكَافِرِينَ ﴿٢٨٦﴾

Allāh does not charge a soul except [with that within] its capacity. It will have [the consequence of] what [good] it has gained, and it will bear [the consequence of] what [evil] it has earned. 'Our Lord, and lay not upon us a burden like that which You laid upon those before us. Our Lord, and burden us not with that which we have no ability to bear. Pardon us; forgive us; and have mercy upon us. You are our Protector, so give us victory over the disbelieving people.'

[*Al-Baqarah* (2): 286]

قال الله : «قد فعلت»

Allāh said, 'I have done so.'

رَبَّنَا وَلَا تَحْمِلْ
عَلَيْنَآ إِصْرًا كَمَا حَمَلْتَهُۥ عَلَى ٱلَّذِينَ مِن قَبْلِنَا ۚ

Our Lord, and lay not upon us a burden like that which You laid upon those before us.

قال الله : «قد فعلت»

Allāh said, 'I have done so.'

رَبَّنَا وَلَا
تُحَمِّلْنَا مَا لَا طَاقَةَ لَنَا بِهِۦ ۖ وَٱعْفُ عَنَّا وَٱغْفِرْ لَنَا وَٱرْحَمْنَآ ۚ
أَنتَ مَوْلَىٰنَا فَٱنصُرْنَا عَلَى ٱلْقَوْمِ ٱلْكَٰفِرِينَ ﴿٢٨٦﴾

Our Lord, and burden us not with that which we have no ability to bear. Pardon us; forgive us; and have mercy upon us. You are our Protector, so give us victory over the disbelieving people.

قال الله : «قد فعلت»

Allāh said, 'I have done so.' [1]

[1] {F} Reported by Muslim [Eng. Trans. 1/74 no. 229] and at-Tirmidhī [no. 2992].

Allāh, the Exalted says,

وَلَيْسَ عَلَيْكُمْ جُنَاحٌ فِيمَآ أَخْطَأْتُم
بِهِۦ وَلَٰكِن مَّا تَعَمَّدَتْ قُلُوبُكُمْ

> There is no sin upon you if you make a mistake except in regard to what your hearts deliberately intend.
>
> [*Al-Aḥzāb* (33): 5]

It is established in the Two Ṣaḥīḥs from Abū Hurayrah and ʿAmr bin al-ʿĀs that the Prophet (ﷺ) said,

«إذا اجتهد الحاكم فأصاب فله أجران، وإن أخطأ فله أجر»

> *"When the ruler strives to pass a verdict and is correct then he has two rewards, and [if he strives to pass a verdict and] is incorrect then he has one reward."*

Therefore the *Mujtahid* who made a mistake is not sinful, indeed Allāh rewards his *ijtihād* and forgives his error. On the other hand, the *Mujtahid* who is correct has two rewards and is therefore better than the one who was in error. When it is established that it is possible for the *Waliy* of Allāh to be mistaken then it is not obligatory to believe everything he says unless, of course, he is a Prophet. Furthermore it is not permissible for the *Waliy* to depend upon every feeling of inspiration that is placed in his heart which he believes to be from the Truth [Allāh], unless it first conforms to the *Sharīʿah.* Rather it is obligatory upon him to judge all of this according to what the Muḥammad (ﷺ) came with; if it is conformity to it he can accept it, if it is not he rejects it, and if cannot tell then he should refrain from accepting it or rejecting it.

[9.1 The Stances of People Regarding *Wilāyah*]

Concerning this topic, the people fall into three categories - two extremes and one balanced. So from amongst them are those who, when they believe that a particular individual is a *Waliy* of Allāh, accept everything that he thinks his heart has conveyed from his Lord and accept anything that he does. Others, when they see someone who they believe is a *Waliy* of Allāh, saying or doing something that does not conform to the *Sharīʿah*, eject him from being a *Waliy* of Allāh altogether, even if he be a *Mujtahid* who has made a genuine mistake. The best of ways is the middle, balanced way and this is not to believe the *Waliy* to be sinless or sinful in the case that he is a *Mujtahid* who has made a genuine mistake. He is not to be followed in everything that he says and neither is he given the verdict of disbelief or sin when he undertakes *ijtihād* [and is incorrect].

That which is obligatory upon the people is to follow all that Allāh sent His Messenger with. In the case that one were to disagree with the stances of some Legal Jurists and agree with the stances of others, then it is not allowable for anyone to force him to adhere to the stances of those Legal Jurists he disagrees with and to say, 'this person has opposed the *Sharīʿah*.'

It is established in the Two Ṣaḥīḥs from the Prophet (ﷺ) that he said,

«قد كان في الأمم قبلكم
محدَّثون فإن يكن من أمتي أحد فعمر منهم»

"Amongst the nations before you were those who were inspired [by Allāh].[2] If there is one of them amongst my nation then it is

[2] {T} Ar. *Muḥaddath*

'Umar." [3]

At-Tirmidhī and others report that the Prophet (ﷺ) said,

«لو لم أُبعث فيكم لبعث فيكم عمر»

"If I were not sent amongst you then 'Umar would have been sent instead." [4]

In another ḥadīth there occurs,

«إن الله ضرب الحق على لسان عمر وقلبه»

"Indeed Allāh has placed the truth upon the tongue of 'Umar and in his heart." [5]

In another ḥadīth there occurs,

«لو كان نبي بعدي لكان عمر»

"If there were to be a prophet after me it would have been 'Umar." [6]

'Alī bin Abī Ṭālib (*raḍiyAllāhu 'anhu*) used to say,

---

[3] {F} Reported by Bukhārī [Eng. Trans. 5/27 no. 38] and an-Nasā'ī, *'al-Kubrā'* [no. 8120] from Abū Hurayrah.

A similar ḥadīth has also been reported from 'Ā'ishah in Ṣaḥīḥ Muslim [Eng. Trans.4/1280 no. 5901] and at-Tirmidhī [no. 3693].

[4] {F} Reported by Aḥmad, *'Faḍā'il as-Ṣaḥābah'* [no. 676] and ibn 'Adī, *'al-Kāmil'* [3/144, 4/194].

I say: its *isnād* is *ḍa'īf.*

A similar ḥadīth has been reported from Bilāl by ibn 'Adī [3/216] and ibn al-Jawzī, *'Mawḍū'āt'* [1/320] with an *isnād* that is *ḍa'īf jiddan.*

[5] {F} Reported by Abū Dāwūd [Eng. Trans. 2/836 no. 2955] and Aḥmad [5/145, 165, 177].

I say: its *isnād* is *ḥasan.*

[6] {F} Reported by at-Tirmidhī [no. 3686] and Aḥmad [4/154].

I say: its *isnād* is *ḥasan.*

Similar *aḥādīth* have been reported from Usma and Abū Sa'īd al-Khudrī as per *'Majma' az-Zawā'id'* [9/68].

> We did not consider it far-fetched that *as-Sakīnah* would speak upon the tongue of 'Umar.[7]

This is established from him via the route of ash-Sha'bī. Ibn 'Umar used to say,

> 'Umar never said about something, 'I think it is like this' except that it turned out as he said.[8]

It is reported from Qais bin Muslim; from Ṭāriq bin Shihāb who said,

> We used to say that an Angel would speak upon the tongue of 'Umar.[9]

'Umar used to say,

> Gather close to the mouths of those who obey Allāh and pay attention to what they say for true matters are disclosed to them.[10]

These true matters that 'Umar (*raḍiyAllāhu 'anhu*) mentioned are those realities that Allāh, Mighty and Magnificent, unveils to them. It is established that the *Awliyā'* of Allāh have certain matters dis-

---

[7] {F} Reported by Aḥmad, *'Faḍā'il as-Ṣaḥābah'* [no.'s 310, 470, 522, 614, 627, 634, 707, 711] and *'al-Musnad'* [1/106].

{Y} Al-Haythamī, *'Majma' az-Zawā'id'* [9/67] said, 'Reported by at-Ṭabarānī, *'al-Awsaṭ'* with a *ḥasan isnād*.'

[8] {Y} Reported by at-Tirmidhī [no. 3765].

[9] {F} Reported by Aḥmad, *'Faḍā'il as-Ṣaḥābah'* [no. 341] and at-Ṭabarānī, *'al-Kabīr'* [no. 8202].

[10] {Y} Reported by ibn Abī Shaybah, *'Muṣannaf'* [13/272, 275] and ibn al-Mubārak, *'az-Zuhd'* [pp. 42, 49] with a different wording, but similar meaning.

closed to them or certain realities unveiled to them. The best of these *Awliyā'* amongst this nation after Abū Bakr (*raḍiyAllāhu 'anhu*) was 'Umar (*raḍiyAllāhu 'anhu*) for indeed,

فإن خير هذه الأمة بعد نبيها أبو بكر ثم عمر

> *"The best of this nation after its Prophet are Abū Bakr and then 'Umar."* [11]

[9.2 The Superiority of the *Ṣiddīq* to the *Muḥaddath*]

The specific mention of 'Umar as the *Muḥaddath* of this nation is established in the Ṣaḥīḥ. So if one were to take any *muḥaddath* or *mukhaaṭab* of this nation, 'Umar would be better than him; yet despite this he (*raḍiyAllāhu 'anhu*) would do all that was obligatory upon him and judge anything that was inspired to him according to what the Messenger (ﷺ) came with. Sometimes he would be in accordance to it, and this would be counted amongst his noble qualities, as occurred on more than one occasion with regards the revelation of the Qur'ān confirming what he said.[12] Other times he would be incorrect and he would retract what he said as occurred on the day of *Ḥudaybiyyah* when he thought that the polytheists should be fought.

The ḥadīth concerning this is well known and is recorded by al-Bukhārī and others.[13] The Prophet (ﷺ) went to perform *'Umrah* during the sixth year after *Hijrah* accompanied by about fourteen hundred Muslims - and these were the ones who gave him the Pledge of Allegiance under the tree. He (ﷺ) contracted a treaty between

---

[11] {F} Reported by Bukhārī [Eng. Trans. 5/6 no. 7, 5/33 no. 47] and Abū Dāwūd [Eng. Trans. 3/1299 no. 4610, 4611].

[12] {T} For many examples of this refer to the book, 'The *Khalifahs* Who Took the Right Way' [pp.119-123, trans. Abdassamad Clarke, Ta-Ha Publishers, 1415/1995].

[13] {F} Reported by Bukhārī [Eng. Trans. 3/560 no. 891].

himself and the polytheists, after a number of discussions, that the Muslims return from where they came in that year and perform *'Umrah* the following year. A number of conditions were set that outwardly seemed to humiliate the Muslims. This bore heavily on many of the Muslims but Allāh and His Messenger had the most knowledge and knew the underlying wisdom behind this treaty and the benefit it contained. 'Umar bin al-Khaṭṭāb was one of those who disliked what happened and objected, saying to the Prophet (ﷺ),

> "Are we not upon the truth and our enemies upon falsehood?' He replied, *'Certainly.'* He said, 'Are not our dead in Paradise while their dead are in the Fire?' He replied, *'certainly.'* He said, 'Then why are we humiliated in our religion in this way?' The Prophet (ﷺ) said to him, *'I am the Messenger of Allāh and He is my Helper and I will never disobey Him.'* He said, 'Did you not say that we would go to the House and perform *ṭawāf* around it?' He replied, *'Certainly, but did I tell you that you would come to it in this year?'* He replied, 'No.' The Prophet (ﷺ) said, *'Indeed you will come to the House and perform ṭawāf around it."*

Then 'Umar (*raḍiyAllāhu 'anhu*) went to Abū Bakr (*raḍiyAllāhu 'anhu*) and asked him the same things that he had asked the Prophet (ﷺ) and Abū Bakr gave the same replies that the Messenger of Allāh (ﷺ) had given even though he had not heard the replies of the Prophet (ﷺ). Therefore Abū Bakr (*raḍiyAllāhu 'anhu*) was greater and more complete with regards his conformity to Allāh and the Prophet (ﷺ) than 'Umar (*raḍiyAllāhu 'anhu*). He retracted his stance and said, 'So I did what needed to be done [in preparation] for that day.'

In a similar way, when the Prophet (ﷺ) passed away, 'Umar initially rejected the fact that he had actually died and when Abū Bakr confirmed that he had died, 'Umar retracted his stance.[14]

In a similar way, 'Umar asked Abū Bakr concerning fighting those who refused to pay the *zakāh* [after the death of the Prophet (ﷺ)],

> "How can we fight the people when the Messenger of Allāh (ﷺ) said, '*I have been commanded to fight the people until they testify that none has the right to be worshipped save Allāh and that I am the Messenger of Allāh. If they do this then their blood and property has become sacrosanct except by due right [demanded by Islām].*'
>
> Abū Bakr (*raḍiyAllāhu 'anhu*) replied, 'Did he not say, '*Except by due right [demanded by Islām]?*' and *zakāh* is from the rights [demanded by Islām]. By Allāh were they to refuse giving me a single horse-strap that they used to give the Messenger of Allāh (ﷺ), I would fight them for it.' Thereupon 'Umar said, 'So by Allāh, nothing led me to knowing that he was upon the truth except that I saw that Allāh had expanded the breast of Abū Bakr to fight."[15]

From these examples, the precedence of Abū Bakr over 'Umar becomes clear and this is despite that fact that 'Umar (*raḍiyAllāhu 'anhu*) was a *Muḥaddath*. The rank of *as-Ṣiddīq* is greater than the rank of *al-Muḥaddath* because the *Ṣiddīq* takes everything that he says and does from the Messenger who is sinless. On the other hand, the *Muḥaddath* takes some things from his heart which is not sinless and therefore he is in need of judging this according to what the Sinless

---

[14] {F} Reported by Bukhārī [Eng. Trans. 2/188 no. 333, 5/12 no. 19, 5/523 no. 733] and an-Nasā'ī [4/11].

[15] {F} Reported by Bukhārī [Eng. Trans. 2/274 no. 483, 2/309 no. 536, 9/46 no. 59, 9/286 no. 388] and Muslim [Eng. Trans. 1/15 no. 29].

Prophet came with.

Therefore ʿUmar (*raḍiyAllāhu ʿanhu*) used to consult the Companions (*raḍiyAllāhu ʿanhum*), debate with them and refer to them in some matters. They used to disagree with him concerning some issues and he would bring his proof and they theirs from the Book and *Sunnah*. He allowed them to do this and never said, 'I am a *muḥaddath*, one who is inspired and to whom realities are disclosed, therefore it is necessary for you to accept what I say and not argue with me.' Hence anyone who claims, or his followers claim on his behalf, that he is a *Waliy* of Allāh to whom certain realities are disclosed, and that it is necessary for his followers to accept everything he says without objection and to believe in his condition without referring back to the Book and *Sunnah*, are in grievous error. Indeed such a person is from amongst the most misguided of people for ʿUmar bin al-Khaṭṭāb (*raḍiyAllāhu ʿanhu*) was better than him, he was the Leader of the Believers, and the Muslims used to disagree with what he said that was erroneous, basing their arguments upon the Book and the *Sunnah*. The *Salaf* of this nation and their *Imāms* are agreed that every person's saying is taken or left except for the Messenger of Allāh (ﷺ).

[9.3 The Differences Between the Prophets and Others]

This then is one of the differences between the Prophets and other than them, for it is obligatory to believe everything that the Prophets *(ṣalwātullāhi ʿalayhim wa salāmuhu)* convey from Allāh, the Mighty and Magnificent, and it is also obligatory to obey them in everything they command. This is not the case for the *Awliyā* for it is not obligatory to obey them in everything they command and neither is it obligatory to believe everything they inform. Instead their command and information is judged in accordance to the Book and *Sunnah* and everything that agrees to them must be accepted and everything that contradicts them must be rejected. If the person who stated this contradictory information is a *Waliy* of Allāh and is a *mujtahid* who has made a mistake, he is rewarded for his *ijtihād* and his error is forgiven provided that he feared Allāh as much as he was able. Allāh, the Exalted says,

فَٱتَّقُوا۟ ٱللَّهَ مَا ٱسْتَطَعْتُمْ

> Keep your duty to Allāh and fear Him as much as you can.
>
> [*At-Taghābun* (64): 16]

This verse serves as an explanation to the saying of Allāh, the Exalted,

يَٰٓأَيُّهَا ٱلَّذِينَ ءَامَنُوا۟ ٱتَّقُوا۟ ٱللَّهَ حَقَّ تُقَاتِهِۦ

> O you who believe! Fear Allāh as He should be feared.
>
> [*Āli 'Imrān* (3): 102]

Ibn Mas'ud and others said concerning the words, *"as He should be feared"* -

> 'He should be obeyed and not disobeyed, he should be remembered and not forgotten and he should be shown gratitude and not ingratitude.' [16]

Meaning as much as one is able for Allāh, the Exalted, does not burden a soul beyond what it can bear, as He says,

لَا يُكَلِّفُ ٱللَّهُ نَفْسًا إِلَّا وُسْعَهَا ۚ لَهَا مَا كَسَبَتْ وَعَلَيْهَا مَا ٱكْتَسَبَتْ

> Allāh does not charge a soul except [with that within] its

[16] {M} It is *ṣaḥīḥ*. Ibn Kathīr referred it to ibn Abī Ḥātim, ibn Mardawiyyah and al-Ḥākim, *'al-Mustadrak'*

capacity. It will have [the consequence of] what [good] it has gained, and it will bear [the consequence of] what [evil] it has earned.

[*Al-Baqarah* (2): 286]

وَالَّذِينَ ءَامَنُوا۟ وَعَمِلُوا۟ ٱلصَّٰلِحَٰتِ لَا نُكَلِّفُ نَفْسًا إِلَّا وُسْعَهَآ أُو۟لَٰٓئِكَ أَصْحَٰبُ ٱلْجَنَّةِ ۖ هُمْ فِيهَا خَٰلِدُونَ ﴿٤٢﴾

As for those who believe and perform righteous deeds - the soul will not be charged except [with that within] its capacity - they are the Inhabitants of Paradise to abide therein forever.

[*Al-Aʿrāf* (7): 42]

وَأَوْفُوا۟ ٱلْكَيْلَ وَٱلْمِيزَانَ بِٱلْقِسْطِ ۖ لَا نُكَلِّفُ نَفْسًا إِلَّا وُسْعَهَا ۖ

Give full measure and full weight with justice. We do not charge a person except [with that within] his ability.

[*Al-Anʿām* (6): 152]

Allāh, the Exalted has mentioned the necessity of believing in what the Prophets came with in more than one place, as in His sayings,

قُولُوٓا۟ ءَامَنَّا بِٱللَّهِ وَمَآ أُنزِلَ إِلَيْنَا وَمَآ أُنزِلَ إِلَىٰٓ إِبْرَٰهِـۧمَ وَإِسْمَٰعِيلَ وَإِسْحَٰقَ وَيَعْقُوبَ وَٱلْأَسْبَاطِ وَمَآ أُوتِىَ مُوسَىٰ وَعِيسَىٰ وَمَآ أُوتِىَ ٱلنَّبِيُّونَ مِن رَّبِّهِمْ لَا نُفَرِّقُ بَيْنَ أَحَدٍ مِّنْهُمْ وَنَحْنُ لَهُۥ مُسْلِمُونَ ﴿١٣٦﴾

Say, 'We have believed in Allāh and what has been revealed to us and what has been revealed to Abraham and Ishmael and Isaac and Jacob and the Descendants and what was given to Moses and Jesus and what was given to the prophets from their Lord. We make no distinction between any of them, and we are Muslims [in submission] to Him.'

[*Al-Baqarah* (2): 136]

الٓمٓ ﴿١﴾ ذَٰلِكَ ٱلۡكِتَٰبُ لَا رَيۡبَۛ فِيهِۛ هُدٗى
لِّلۡمُتَّقِينَ ﴿٢﴾ ٱلَّذِينَ يُؤۡمِنُونَ بِٱلۡغَيۡبِ وَيُقِيمُونَ ٱلصَّلَوٰةَ
وَمِمَّا رَزَقۡنَٰهُمۡ يُنفِقُونَ ﴿٣﴾ وَٱلَّذِينَ يُؤۡمِنُونَ بِمَآ أُنزِلَ
إِلَيۡكَ وَمَآ أُنزِلَ مِن قَبۡلِكَ وَبِٱلۡأٓخِرَةِ هُمۡ يُوقِنُونَ ﴿٤﴾
أُوْلَٰٓئِكَ عَلَىٰ هُدٗى مِّن رَّبِّهِمۡۖ وَأُوْلَٰٓئِكَ
هُمُ ٱلۡمُفۡلِحُونَ ﴿٥﴾

Alif, Lām, Mīm. This is the Book about which there is no doubt, a guidance for those who fear Allāh - who believe in the unseen, establish the prayer and spend out of what We have provided for them. Who believe in what has been revealed to you and what was revealed before you, and of the Hereafter they are certain [in faith]. Those are upon [right] guidance from their Lord, and it is those who are successful.

[*Al-Baqarah* (2): 1-5]

۞ لَّيۡسَ ٱلۡبِرَّ أَن تُوَلُّواْ وُجُوهَكُمۡ قِبَلَ ٱلۡمَشۡرِقِ وَٱلۡمَغۡرِبِ وَلَٰكِنَّ
ٱلۡبِرَّ مَنۡ ءَامَنَ بِٱللَّهِ وَٱلۡيَوۡمِ ٱلۡأٓخِرِ وَٱلۡمَلَٰٓئِكَةِ وَٱلۡكِتَٰبِ
وَٱلنَّبِيِّـۧنَ وَءَاتَى ٱلۡمَالَ عَلَىٰ حُبِّهِۦ ذَوِي ٱلۡقُرۡبَىٰ وَٱلۡيَتَٰمَىٰ
وَٱلۡمَسَٰكِينَ وَٱبۡنَ ٱلسَّبِيلِ وَٱلسَّآئِلِينَ وَفِي ٱلرِّقَابِ وَأَقَامَ
ٱلصَّلَوٰةَ وَءَاتَى ٱلزَّكَوٰةَ وَٱلۡمُوفُونَ بِعَهۡدِهِمۡ إِذَا عَٰهَدُواْۖ
وَٱلصَّٰبِرِينَ فِي ٱلۡبَأۡسَآءِ وَٱلضَّرَّآءِ وَحِينَ ٱلۡبَأۡسِۗ أُوْلَٰٓئِكَ ٱلَّذِينَ
صَدَقُواْۖ وَأُوْلَٰٓئِكَ هُمُ ٱلۡمُتَّقُونَ ﴿١٧٧﴾

> It is not piety that you turn your faces towards the east or west [in prayers] but piety is [the quality of one] who believes in Allāh, the Last Day, the Angels, the Book, the Prophets and gives his wealth, in spite of love for it, to the kinsfolk, to the orphans, to the poor who beg, to the wayfarer, to those who ask, and to set slaves free and establish the prayers and give the *zakāh* and who fulfill their covenant when they make it, and who are patient in extreme poverty, ailment and at the time of fighting. Such are the people of truth and the pious and God-fearing.
>
> [*Al-Baqarah* (2): 177]

[9.4 A Point of Agreement]

What I have mentioned thusfar, that it is obligatory upon the *Awliyā'* of Allāh to cling firmly to the Book and the *Sunnah* and that there is none amongst them who is sinless such that it would allow him, or other than him, to follow what occurs in his heart without first taking into consideration the Book and the *Sunnah*, is something that the *Awliyā'* of Allāh, the Mighty and Magnificent, are agreed upon. Whosoever opposes this is not from the *Awliyā'* of Allāh, the Glorious, from those whom Allāh has ordered to be followed, instead such a person is either a disbeliever or steeped in ignorance. The scholars have frequently mentioned this fact, *Shaykh* Abū Sulaymān ad-Dārānī said,

> 'Indeed a word of wisdom occurs in my heart as it does to the nation [of the righteous] but I do not accept it until I first compare it to the Two Witnesses - the Book and the *Sunnah*.' [17]

Abū al-Qāsim al-Junaid, may Allāh have mercy upon him, said,

---

[17] {F} *'Al-Bidāyah wan Nihāyah'* [10/255]; *'Ṭabaqāt as-Ṣūfiyyah'* [pp. 77-78]; *'Siyar A'lām an-Nubulā'"* [10/183].

> 'This knowledge of ours is restricted and governed by the Book and the *Sunnah*. Therefore anyone who has not read the Qur'ān or written the *Sunnah* is not qualified to speak about our knowledge.' Or he said, 'should not be followed.' [18]

Abū 'Uthmān an-Naysābūrī said,

> 'Whosoever orders his self to the *Sunnah* in both speech and action shall speak with Wisdom, but whosoever orders his self to carnal desires in both speech and action shall speak with innovation. This is because Allāh, the Exalted, says in His Eternal Words,
>
> وَإِن تُطِيعُوهُ تَهْتَدُوا۟
>
> If you obey him then you will be rightly guided.
>
> [*An-Nūr* (24): 54]' [19]

Abū 'Amr bin Nujaid said,

> 'Every *wajd* (spiritual experience) that is not born testimony to by the Book and *Sunnah* is false.' [20]

---

[18] {F} Abū Nu'aym, *'al-Ḥilyah'* [10/255].

[19] {Y} Mentioned by Abū Nu'aym, *'al-Ḥilyah'* [10/244] and al-Qushayrī, *'ar-Risālah al-Qushayriyyah'* [p. 28].

[20] {Y} Mentioned by as-Sulamī, *'Ṭabaqāt as-Ṣūfiyyah'* [p. 455] and al-Qushayrī, *'ar-Risālah al-Qushayriyyah'* [1/139].

[9.5 An Erroneous and Dangerous Belief Concerning the *Awliyā'*]

Many people fall into error concerning this and think that if a particular individual is a *Waliy* of Allāh, then everything he says and does has to be accepted and believed, even if it contradicts the Book and *Sunnah*. Therefore they end up agreeing with this individual and contradicting that which Allāh sent His Messenger with! This Messenger with regards to whom Allāh made obligatory upon the whole of creation to believe what he said and obey what he ordered. Allāh appointed him as the criterion between His *Awliyā'* and His enemies, between the Inhabitants of Paradise and the denizens of Hell and between the Joyous and the wretched. So whosoever follows him is from the *Awliyā'* of Allāh, His party who have succeeded and His righteous servants. Whosoever does not follow him are His sinful enemies who have attained loss and anguish. Such people are first led to innovation and misguidance through their agreeing with this individual and opposing the Messenger and finally they end up in disbelief or hypocrisy and fall under the sayings of Allāh, the Exalted,

وَيَوْمَ يَعَضُّ ٱلظَّالِمُ عَلَىٰ يَدَيْهِ يَقُولُ
يَٰلَيْتَنِى ٱتَّخَذْتُ مَعَ ٱلرَّسُولِ سَبِيلًا ﴿٢٧﴾ يَٰوَيْلَتَىٰ لَيْتَنِى لَمْ أَتَّخِذْ
فُلَانًا خَلِيلًا ﴿٢٨﴾ لَّقَدْ أَضَلَّنِى عَنِ ٱلذِّكْرِ بَعْدَ إِذْ جَآءَنِى ۗ
وَكَانَ ٱلشَّيْطَٰنُ لِلْإِنسَٰنِ خَذُولًا ﴿٢٩﴾

> And [remember] the Day when the wrong-doer will bite his hands and say, 'Woe to me! Would that I had taken a path with the Messenger. Ah, woe to me! Would that I had never taken so-and-so as a friend. He indeed led me astray from the Remembrance after it had come to me and Shayṭān is ever a deserter to man in his hour of need.'
>
> [*Al-Furqān* (25): 27-29]

﴿٦٥﴾ يَوْمَ تُقَلَّبُ وُجُوهُهُمْ فِي النَّارِ يَقُولُونَ يَٰلَيْتَنَآ أَطَعْنَا اللَّهَ
وَأَطَعْنَا الرَّسُولَا۠ ﴿٦٦﴾ وَقَالُوا۟ رَبَّنَآ إِنَّآ أَطَعْنَا سَادَتَنَا وَكُبَرَآءَنَا
فَأَضَلُّونَا السَّبِيلَا۠ ﴿٦٧﴾ رَبَّنَآ ءَاتِهِمْ ضِعْفَيْنِ مِنَ الْعَذَابِ
وَالْعَنْهُمْ لَعْنًا كَبِيرًا ﴿٦٨﴾

On that Day when their faces will be turned over in the Fire, they will say, 'Woe to us, would that we had obeyed Allāh and obeyed the Messenger.' And they will say, 'Our Lord! Indeed we obeyed our chiefs and our great ones, and they misled us from the [Right] Way. Our Lord! Give them double torment and curse them with a mighty curse!'

[*Al-Aḥzāb* (33): 66-68]

وَمِنَ
النَّاسِ مَن يَتَّخِذُ مِن دُونِ اللَّهِ أَندَادًا يُحِبُّونَهُمْ كَحُبِّ اللَّهِ
وَالَّذِينَ ءَامَنُوٓا۟ أَشَدُّ حُبًّا لِّلَّهِ وَلَوْ يَرَى الَّذِينَ ظَلَمُوٓا۟ إِذْ يَرَوْنَ
الْعَذَابَ أَنَّ الْقُوَّةَ لِلَّهِ جَمِيعًا وَأَنَّ اللَّهَ شَدِيدُ الْعَذَابِ ﴿١٦٥﴾
إِذْ تَبَرَّأَ الَّذِينَ اتُّبِعُوا۟ مِنَ الَّذِينَ اتَّبَعُوا۟ وَرَأَوُا۟ الْعَذَابَ
وَتَقَطَّعَتْ بِهِمُ الْأَسْبَابُ ﴿١٦٦﴾ وَقَالَ الَّذِينَ اتَّبَعُوا۟ لَوْ أَنَّ
لَنَا كَرَّةً فَنَتَبَرَّأَ مِنْهُمْ كَمَا تَبَرَّءُوا۟ مِنَّا كَذَٰلِكَ يُرِيهِمُ اللَّهُ
أَعْمَٰلَهُمْ حَسَرَٰتٍ عَلَيْهِمْ وَمَا هُم بِخَٰرِجِينَ مِنَ النَّارِ ﴿١٦٧﴾

Of mankind are some who take partners [for worship] besides Allāh, loving them as they love Allāh whereas those who believe love Allāh [more than anything else]. If only those who do wrong could see, [as they will see] when they see the torment, that all power belongs to Allāh and that Allāh is Severe in punishment. When those who were followed, disown those who followed them, and they

> see the torment, then all their relations will be severed. When those who followed will say, 'If only we had one more chance to return [to the worldly life], we would disown them as they have disowned us.' Thus Allāh will show them their deeds as regrets for them and they will never leave the Fire.
>
> [*Al-Baqarah* (2): 165-167]

These people bear a resemblance to the Christians about whom Allāh, the Exalted says,

اتَّخَذُوٓا۟ أَحْبَارَهُمْ
وَرُهْبَـٰنَهُمْ أَرْبَابًا مِّن دُونِ ٱللَّهِ وَٱلْمَسِيحَ ٱبْنَ
مَرْيَمَ وَمَآ أُمِرُوٓا۟ إِلَّا لِيَعْبُدُوٓا۟ إِلَـٰهًا وَٰحِدًا

> They took their rabbis and monks to be lords besides Allāh, as well as the Messiah, son of Mary, while they were commanded to worship none save one God.
>
> [*At-Tawbah* (9): 31]

It is reported in the *Musnad* [of Aḥmad] and authenticated by at-Tirmidhī from 'Adī bin Ḥātim concerning the commentary to this verse that he asked the Prophet (ﷺ),

> 'But they did not worship them.' He replied, *'They made the unlawful lawful for them and the lawful unlawful and the people obeyed them in this. This was their worship of them.'* [21]

This is why it is said concerning these people, 'They have forbidden themselves from reaching the goal by neglecting the principles.' The most fundamental of principles is to actualise belief in what the Messenger (ﷺ) came with. Therefore it is necessary to have faith

[21] {F} Reported by at-Tirmidhī [no. 3095] and at-Ṭabarānī, *'al-Kabīr'* [no.'s 218-219].I say: its *isnād* is *ḍa'īf.*

in Allāh, His Messenger and all that the Messenger (ﷺ) came with. It is necessary to have faith that Muḥammad (ﷺ) is the Messenger of Allāh who was sent to the entirety of creation - man and Jinn, Arab and non-Arab, scholar and worshipper, king and subject. It is also necessary to have faith that there is no route to Allāh, Mighty and Magnificent, for anyone from amongst the creation except through following him (ﷺ) inwardly and outwardly. This is true to the point that had he met Moses, Jesus or any other Prophet, they too would have been obligated to follow him. Allāh, the Exalted says,

وَإِذْ أَخَذَ ٱللَّهُ مِيثَٰقَ ٱلنَّبِيِّـۧنَ لَمَآ ءَاتَيْتُكُم مِّن كِتَٰبٍ
وَحِكْمَةٍ ثُمَّ جَآءَكُمْ رَسُولٌ مُّصَدِّقٌ لِّمَا مَعَكُمْ لَتُؤْمِنُنَّ
بِهِۦ وَلَتَنصُرُنَّهُۥ ۚ قَالَ ءَأَقْرَرْتُمْ وَأَخَذْتُمْ عَلَىٰ ذَٰلِكُمْ إِصْرِى ۖ
قَالُوٓا۟ أَقْرَرْنَا ۚ قَالَ فَٱشْهَدُوا۟ وَأَنَا۠ مَعَكُم مِّنَ ٱلشَّٰهِدِينَ ﴿٨١﴾
فَمَن تَوَلَّىٰ بَعْدَ ذَٰلِكَ فَأُو۟لَٰٓئِكَ هُمُ ٱلْفَٰسِقُونَ ﴿٨٢﴾

> And [remember] when Allāh took the Covenant of the Prophets saying, 'Take whatever I give you from the Book and the Wisdom and afterwards there will come to you a Messenger [Muḥammad] confirming what is with you. You must then believe in him and help him.' Allāh said, 'Do you agree [to it and to] take up My Covenant?' They said, 'We agree.' He said, 'Then bear witness and I am with you among the witnesses.' Then whosoever turns away after this, they are the sinful.
>
> [*Āli 'Imrān* (3): 81-82]

Ibn 'Abbās (*raḍiyAllāhu 'anhumā*) said,

> 'Allāh did not sent a single Prophet except that He first took a covenant from them that if Muḥammad was to be sent while he was still living then he would believe in him

and aid him. Allāh also ordered that Prophet to take the same covenant from his nation that if Muḥammad was to be sent while they were alive then they would believe in him and aid him.'[22]

Allāh, the Exalted says,

أَلَمْ تَرَ إِلَى ٱلَّذِينَ يَزْعُمُونَ أَنَّهُمْ ءَامَنُوا۟ بِمَآ أُنزِلَ إِلَيْكَ
وَمَآ أُنزِلَ مِن قَبْلِكَ يُرِيدُونَ أَن يَتَحَاكَمُوٓا۟ إِلَى ٱلطَّٰغُوتِ
وَقَدْ أُمِرُوٓا۟ أَن يَكْفُرُوا۟ بِهِۦ وَيُرِيدُ ٱلشَّيْطَٰنُ أَن يُضِلَّهُمْ
ضَلَٰلًۢا بَعِيدًا ﴿٦٠﴾ وَإِذَا قِيلَ لَهُمْ تَعَالَوْا۟ إِلَىٰ مَآ أَنزَلَ
ٱللَّهُ وَإِلَى ٱلرَّسُولِ رَأَيْتَ ٱلْمُنَٰفِقِينَ يَصُدُّونَ عَنكَ
صُدُودًا ﴿٦١﴾ فَكَيْفَ إِذَآ أَصَٰبَتْهُم مُّصِيبَةٌۢ بِمَا
قَدَّمَتْ أَيْدِيهِمْ ثُمَّ جَآءُوكَ يَحْلِفُونَ بِٱللَّهِ إِنْ أَرَدْنَآ إِلَّآ
إِحْسَٰنًا وَتَوْفِيقًا ﴿٦٢﴾ أُو۟لَٰٓئِكَ ٱلَّذِينَ يَعْلَمُ ٱللَّهُ مَا
فِى قُلُوبِهِمْ فَأَعْرِضْ عَنْهُمْ وَعِظْهُمْ وَقُل لَّهُمْ فِىٓ
أَنفُسِهِمْ قَوْلًۢا بَلِيغًا ﴿٦٣﴾ وَمَآ أَرْسَلْنَا مِن رَّسُولٍ إِلَّا
لِيُطَاعَ بِإِذْنِ ٱللَّهِ ۚ وَلَوْ أَنَّهُمْ إِذ ظَّلَمُوٓا۟ أَنفُسَهُمْ
جَآءُوكَ فَٱسْتَغْفَرُوا۟ ٱللَّهَ وَٱسْتَغْفَرَ لَهُمُ ٱلرَّسُولُ
لَوَجَدُوا۟ ٱللَّهَ تَوَّابًا رَّحِيمًا ﴿٦٤﴾ فَلَا وَرَبِّكَ لَا يُؤْمِنُونَ
حَتَّىٰ يُحَكِّمُوكَ فِيمَا شَجَرَ بَيْنَهُمْ ثُمَّ لَا يَجِدُوا۟
فِىٓ أَنفُسِهِمْ حَرَجًا مِّمَّا قَضَيْتَ وَيُسَلِّمُوا۟ تَسْلِيمًا ﴿٦٥﴾

Have you not seen those who claim that they believe in that which was has been sent down to you, and that which was sent down before you, yet they wish to go for judg-

---

[22] {Y} Reported by ibn Jarīr [6/556] and ibn Kathīr [1/325].

> ment [in their disputes] to the *tāghut* despite being ordered to reject them? But Shayṭān wishes to lead them far astray. And when it is said to them, 'Come to what Allāh has sent down and to the Messenger,' you see the hypocrites turn away from you in aversion. How then, when a catastrophe befalls them because of what their hands have sent forth, do they come to you swearing by Allāh, 'We meant no more than goodwill and conciliation!' They are those whom Allāh knows what is in their hearts; so turn aside from them, admonish them and speak to them an effective word to [reach their inner selves]. We sent no Messenger, but to be obeyed by the permission of Allāh. If they had only, when they had been unjust to themselves, come to you [Muḥammad (ﷺ)] and begged Allāh's forgiveness, and the Messenger had begged Allāh's forgiveness for them; indeed they would have found Allāh all-Forgiving, Most Merciful. But no by your Lord! They can have no faith until they make you judge in all disputes between them, and find in themselves no resistance against your decisions, and accept them with full submission.
>
> [*An-Nisā'* (4): 60-65]

[9.6 The Obligation of Following the Messenger (ﷺ)]

So anyone who opposes something that the Messenger brought due to blind following of someone he thinks is a *Waliy* of Allāh, then such a person has built his affair upon the belief that the *Waliy* of Allāh is not to be opposed in anything. Know that if this person was to be one of the greatest of the Companions, or of those who followed them in good, even then anything that he said or did that contradicted the Book and *Sunnah* is not accepted, so what then of those less than them!

[9.7 Do not be Deceived by Miracles]

We find that many of these people merely depend upon the fact that a particular individual was able to unveil certain realities or perform some miraculous feats to prove that he is a *Waliy* of Allāh. Examples of such feats would be his pointing at a person who subsequently dies, or his flying through the air to Mecca or any other city, or his walking on water, or filling a pot from nothing, or his vanishing in front of people, or some people seeking relief and succour with him while he was absent or dead and they see him coming to them and fulfilling their need, or his telling people the whereabouts of their stolen property, or his telling them of the condition of one who is absent or sick, or other similar matters. None of these matters prove that the one doing them is a *Waliy* of Allāh, rather the *Awliyā'* of Allāh are agreed that if a person were to fly through the air or walk on water, none should be deceived by him until his following of the Messenger of Allāh (ﷺ) and his conforming to his order and prohibition are confirmed.

The miracles granted the *Awliyā'* are greater than the matters mentioned above, for even though these matters may be extraordinary, both the *Awliyā'* of Allāh and His enemies can perform them. They can be performed by many of the disbelievers, polytheists, People of the Book, hypocrites, People of Innovation and the devils. Hence it is not permissible to believe that whosoever performs such feats is a *Waliy* of Allāh, rather the standard for judging them to be the *Awliyā'* of Allāh is by comparing their attributes, actions and states to the Book and the *Sunnah*. They are known by the light of faith and the Qur'ān, by actualising the inner realities of faith and the outward laws of Islām.

[9.8 The Signs of the *Awliyā'* of Shayṭān]

For example, the matters mentioned above could be found in a certain person, yet this person does not perform ritual ablution (*wuḍū*) or perform the obligatory prayers, rather he wears garments covered in impurity, mixes amongst dogs and sleeps in toilets, refuse dumps, graves and dunghills. He smells disgusting and he does not clean himself as legislated by the *Sharī'ah*. The Prophet (ﷺ) said,

«لا تدخل الملائكة بيتاً فيه جنب ولا كلب»

"The Angels do not enter a house in which there is a junub or a dog." [23]

He (ﷺ) said concerning these places that are used for ones relieving himself,

«إن هذه الحشوش محتضرة»

"Indeed these privies are attended." [24]

Meaning attended by the devils. He (ﷺ) also said,

«من أكل من هاتين الشجرتين الخبيثتين، فلا يقربن مسجدنا، فإنّ الملائكة تتأذى بما يتأذى منه بنو آدم»

"Whosoever eats from these two foul plants then let him not come close to our Masjid, for indeed the Angels are harmed by that which

---

[23] {F} Reported by Bukhārī [Eng. Trans. 4/297 no. 448, 4/389 no. 539, 5/225 no. 338, 7/540 no. 833] and Muslim [Eng. Trans. 3/1157 no.'s 5246-5254].
{T} All with the wording *'picture'* in place of *'junub.'*
{Y} The mention of *'junub'* is found in Abū Dāwūd [Eng. Trans. 1/55 no. 227].

[24] {F} Reported by Abū Dāwūd [Eng. Trans. 1/2 no. 6] and ibn Mājah [no. 296].
I say: its *isnād* is *ṣaḥīḥ* and similar *aḥādīth* have been reported from Anas and ibn 'Abbās.

harms the Children of Ādam." [25]

«إن الله طيب لا يقبل إلا طيباً»

"Indeed Allāh is pure and accepts only that which is pure." [26]

«إن الله نظيف يحب النظافة»

"Indeed Allāh is clean and Loves cleanliness." [27]

«خمس من الفواسق يُقتَلْنَ في الحِلِّ والحَرَمِ : الحية والفأرة والحدأة والكلب العقور»

"There are five things that are amongst the harmful animals which should be killed regardless of whether one is in the state of iḥraam or not: the snake, rat, kite, crow and dog." [28]

In another report the wording is,

«الحية والعقرب»

"The snake and the scorpion."

---

[25] {F} Reported by Bukhārī [Eng. Trans. 1/451 no. 812, 7/263 no. 363] and Muslim [Eng. Trans. 1/279 no.'s 1141-1152] with wordings close to that mentioned above.

{T} The two foul plants refer to onion and garlic. In some narrations of Muslim the leek is also mentioned.

[26] {F} Reported by Muslim [Eng. Trans. 2/486 no. 2214] and at-Tirmidhī [no. 2989].

[27] {F} Reported by at-Tirmidhī [no. 2799] and Abu Ya'lā [no.'s 790-791].
I say: its *isnād* is *ḍa'īf jiddan.*

[28] {F} Reported by Bukhārī [Eng. Trans. 3/34 no.'s 54-55] and Muslim [Eng. Trans. 2/591 no.'s 2718-2731].

He (ﷺ) commanded the killing of dogs[29] and also said,

«من اقتنى كلباً لا يغني عنه زرعاً ولا ضـرعاً،
نقص من عمله كـلَّ يوم قيـراط»

"Whoever keeps a dog which he is no need of with respect to agriculture or protection then he loses one Qīrāṭ of his good actions every day." [30]

«لا تصحب الملائكة رفقة معهم كلب»

"The Angels do not accompany a party that has a dog with them."[31]

«إذا ولغ الكلب في إناء أحدكم
فليغسله، سبع مرات إحداهنَّ بالتراب»

"If the dog licks the vessel of any one of you then let him wash it seven times, employing earth on one of them." [32]

Allāh, the Exalted says,

---

[29] {F} Reported by ibn Mājah [no.'s 3200-3202] from 'Abdullāh bin Mughaffal and ibn 'Umar.

{T} and they are found in al-Albānī, *'Ṣaḥīḥ ibn Mājah.'*

[30] {F} Reported by Bukhārī [Eng. Trans. 7/283 no. 389] and Muslim [Eng. Trans. 3/826 no. 3821].

{T} *Qīrāṭ* = 1/20th of a *dīnār.*

[31] {F} Reported by Muslim [Eng. Trans. 3/1162 no. 5277] and Abū Dāwūd [Eng. Trans. 2/709 no. 2549].

[32] {F} Reported by Muslim [Eng. Trans. 1/167 no. 549] and Abū Dāwūd [Eng. Trans. 1/18 no.'s 71-73].

وَرَحْمَتِي
وَسِعَتْ كُلَّ شَيْءٍ فَسَأَكْتُبُهَا لِلَّذِينَ يَتَّقُونَ وَيُؤْتُونَ
ٱلزَّكَوٰةَ وَٱلَّذِينَ هُم بِـَٔايَٰتِنَا يُؤْمِنُونَ ﴿١٥٦﴾ ٱلَّذِينَ يَتَّبِعُونَ
ٱلرَّسُولَ ٱلنَّبِيَّ ٱلْأُمِّيَّ ٱلَّذِي يَجِدُونَهُۥ مَكْتُوبًا عِندَهُمْ
فِي ٱلتَّوْرَىٰةِ وَٱلْإِنجِيلِ يَأْمُرُهُم بِٱلْمَعْرُوفِ وَيَنْهَىٰهُمْ
عَنِ ٱلْمُنكَرِ وَيُحِلُّ لَهُمُ ٱلطَّيِّبَٰتِ وَيُحَرِّمُ عَلَيْهِمُ
ٱلْخَبَٰٓئِثَ وَيَضَعُ عَنْهُمْ إِصْرَهُمْ وَٱلْأَغْلَٰلَ ٱلَّتِي كَانَتْ
عَلَيْهِمْ فَٱلَّذِينَ ءَامَنُوا۟ بِهِۦ وَعَزَّرُوهُ وَنَصَرُوهُ وَٱتَّبَعُوا۟
ٱلنُّورَ ٱلَّذِيٓ أُنزِلَ مَعَهُۥٓ أُو۟لَٰٓئِكَ هُمُ ٱلْمُفْلِحُونَ ﴿١٥٧﴾

> My Mercy embraces all things. That [Mercy] I shall ordain for those who are the pious, who give the *zakāh* and believe in Our verses. Those who follow the Messenger, the Prophet who can neither read nor write whom they find mentioned in the Torah and Gospel with them. He commands them to good and forbids them from evil; he makes lawful for them all good things and makes unlawful all bad things. He releases them from their heavy burdens and from the fetters that were upon them. So those who believe in him, honour him, help him, and follow the Light which has been sent down with him, it is they who will be successful.
>
> [*Al-A'rāf* (7): 156-157]

So if a person is in constant contact with impurity and filth, both of which are loved by Shayṭān, or he sleeps in toilets and privies which are attended by devils, or he eats snakes, scorpions, hornets, or dogs ears all of which are filth and harmful animals, or drinks urine or similar things that are loved by Shayṭān, or he supplicates to other than Allāh, seeking relief and succour with the creation and directs his [worship] to them, or he prostrates towards his *shaykh* and does not make his religion sincerely for his Lord Alone, or he lives amongst dogs, or sleeps in dung heaps or impure places, or sleeps in graveyards especially the disbeliever's graveyards - such as the Jews, Christians or polytheists, or he dislikes listening to the *Qur'ān* and runs from it [when he hears it] and instead prefers listening to songs and recital of poetry, hence preferring the musical instruments of Shayṭān over the Speech of the Most Merciful, then all of these are the signs of the *awliyā'* of Shayṭān, not the *Awliyā'* of the Most Merciful.

[9.9 Those who can Differentiate the *Awliyā'* of Allāh from the *Awliyā'* of Shayṭān]

Ibn Mas'ūd (*raḍiyAllāhu 'anhu*) said,

> Let none of you ask about himself except concerning the *Qur'ān*. If he loves the *Qur'ān* then he loves Allāh, and if he hates the *Qur'ān* then he hates Allāh and His Messenger.[33]

'Uthmān bin 'Affān (*raḍiyAllāhu 'anhu*) said,

> If our hearts were pure then we would never become satisfied with the Speech of Allāh, the Mighty and Magnificent.[34]

Ibn Mas'ud (*raḍiyAllāhu 'anhu*) said,

> The remembrance of Allāh breeds faith in the heart just

---

[33] {F} Ibn Rajab al-Ḥanbalī, *'Istinshāq Nasīm al-Uns'* [pp. 67-69] and ibn 'Asākir, *'Tārīkh'* [p. 232].

[34] {F} Ibn al-Qayyim, *'Ighātha al-Lahfān'* [1/55].

as water causes onions to grow. Music breeds hypocrisy in the heart just as water causes onions to grow.[35]

If a person is fully aware of the inner realities of faith, able to distinguish between the states of those traversing the correct path of the Most Merciful and those traversing the path of Shayṭān then Allāh has placed some of His Light in his heart as He, the Exalted says,

يَٰٓأَيُّهَا ٱلَّذِينَ ءَامَنُوا۟ ٱتَّقُوا۟ ٱللَّهَ
وَءَامِنُوا۟ بِرَسُولِهِۦ يُؤْتِكُمْ كِفْلَيْنِ مِن رَّحْمَتِهِۦ وَيَجْعَل لَّكُمْ
نُورًا تَمْشُونَ بِهِۦ وَيَغْفِرْ لَكُمْ ۚ وَٱللَّهُ غَفُورٌ رَّحِيمٌ ﴿٢٨﴾

O you who believe! Fear Allāh and believe in His Messenger, He will give you a double portion of His Mercy and He will give you a light by which you shall walk [straight] and He will forgive you... [*Al-Ḥadīd* (57): 28]

وَكَذَٰلِكَ أَوْحَيْنَآ إِلَيْكَ رُوحًا مِّنْ أَمْرِنَا ۚ مَا كُنتَ تَدْرِى مَا ٱلْكِتَٰبُ
وَلَا ٱلْإِيمَٰنُ وَلَٰكِن جَعَلْنَٰهُ نُورًا نَّهْدِى بِهِۦ مَن نَّشَآءُ مِنْ عِبَادِنَا ۚ

And thus We have sent to you an inspiration and a mercy of Our Command. You knew not what is the Books nor what is faith, but we have made it [the Qur'ān] a light wherewith We guide whosoever of Our servants We Will. [*Ash-Shūrā* (42): 52]

Such a person is from amongst the believers that the ḥadīth reported by at-Tirmidhī from Abū Sa'īd al-Khuḍrī refers to,

"Beware of the insight and perception of the believer for indeed he

[35] {F} Ibn al-Qayyim, *'Ighātha al-Lahfān'* [1/225-268].

looks with the Light of Allāh." [36]

At-Tirmidhī ruled the ḥadīth to be *ḥasan ṣaḥīḥ*.

The authentic ḥadīth reported by Bukhārī and others has been previously mentioned in which the following words occur,

> *"My servant continues to draw near to Me by performing optional deeds such that I love him. And when I love him I am his hearing by which he hears, his sight by which he sees, his hand with which he strikes and his leg with which he walks. Were he to ask of Me, I would surely give him; and were he to ask Me for refuge, I would surely grant it to him. I am never so hesitant to do something as I am to take the soul of my believing servant, he dislikes death and I Dislike to harm him but he must die."*

So when the servant is one of these believers, he is able to differentiate between the state of the *Awliyā'* of the Most Merciful and the *awliyā'* of Shayṭān in the same way that the money exchanger can tell the difference between a good *dirham* and a forged *dirham*, or an expert in horses can tell the difference between a good horse and a bad horse, or one who understands chivalry can differentiate bravery from cowardice. In the same way it is obligatory to differentiate between a truthful Prophet and a lying imposter, hence he is able to differentiate Muḥammad, the Truthful and Trusted - the Messenger of the Lord of the universe, Moses, the Messiah and others from

---

[36] {F} Reported by at-Tirmidhī [no. 3127] and Bukhārī, *'Tārīkh al-Kabīr'* [4/2/354].

I say: its *isnād* is *ḍa'īf*.

Similar *aḥādīth* have been reported from Thawbān by Abū Nu'aym [4/81] with an *isnād* that is *ḍa'īf jiddan*; Abū Umāmah by at-Ṭabarānī, *'al-Kabīr'* [no. 7497] with an *isnād* that is *ḍa'īf*; ibn 'Umar by Abū Nu'aym, *'al-Ḥilyah'* [4/94] with an *isnād* that is *ḍa'īf. jiddan*; Abū Hurayrah by ibn al-Jawzī, *'al-Mawḍū'āt'* [3/147] with an *isnād* that is *ḍa'īf jiddan*.

Therefore the ḥadīth remains *ḍa'īf* having no witnesses that are appropriate to use in order to strengthen it. Allāh knows best.

Musaylamah the Liar, al-Aswad al-Ansī, Ṭalḥa al-Asadī, al-Ḥārith ad-Dimashqī, Bābā ar-Rumī and other such liars. In a similar way he is able to differentiate between the pious, *Awliyā'* of Allāh and the misguided *awliyā'* of Shayṭān.

In Summary

- Being sinless is not a pre-requisite to be *Awliyā'* and Allāh has overlooked genuine mistakes and things that people are coerced into doing. Therefore if the *Awliyā'* can be mistaken, it is not obligatory to follow them in all that they say.

- The errors that people fall into in this regard - they take to two extremes and often neglect the middle way.

- The principle obligation is to follow the Book and *Sunnah.*

- Contradicting a scholar does not mean contradicting the *Sharī'ah.*

- The example of 'Umar in this regard, he was one who received inspirations but he always judged them according to the Book and *Sunnah* and the Companions were never afraid to correct him.

- The early *Ṣūfīs a*re agreed that every feeling of inspiration must first be judged according to the Book and *Sunnah.*

- Reiteration of the errors that people fall into in this regard and the danger of putting anyone before the Messenger (ﷺ).

- The Messenger (ﷺ) was sent to the entirety of creation and there is no way to Allāh except through following him.

- Miracles do not prove a person to be a *Waliy* for they can be performed by both the believer and disbeliever.

- The condition for *wilāyah* is following the Book and *Sunnah.*

CHAPTER TEN

[The Reality Refers to the Religion of the Lord of the Universe]

THE *ḤAQĪQAH* (REALITY) IS THE reality of this religion, the religion of the Lord of the Universe and that is what the Prophets and Messengers agreed upon, even though each one among them may have had their own law (*shirʿah*) and way (*minhāj*). The word *shirʿah* means *sharīʿah*. Allāh, the Exalted says,

لِكُلٍّ جَعَلْنَا مِنكُمْ شِرْعَةً وَمِنْهَاجًا

> To each among you We have prescribed a law and a clear way.
>
> [*Al-Māʾidah* (5): 48]

ثُمَّ جَعَلْنَٰكَ عَلَىٰ شَرِيعَةٍ مِّنَ ٱلْأَمْرِ فَٱتَّبِعْهَا وَلَا تَتَّبِعْ
أَهْوَآءَ ٱلَّذِينَ لَا يَعْلَمُونَ ﴿١٨﴾ إِنَّهُمْ لَن يُغْنُوا۟ عَنكَ مِنَ ٱللَّهِ
شَيْـًٔا وَإِنَّ ٱلظَّٰلِمِينَ بَعْضُهُمْ أَوْلِيَآءُ بَعْضٍ وَٱللَّهُ وَلِىُّ ٱلْمُتَّقِينَ

> Then We have put you on a plain way of [Our] order so follow it and follow not the desires of those who know

> not. Verily they can avail you nothing against Allāh, indeed the wrong-doers are the *awliyā'* to one another but Allāh is the *Waliy* of the pious and God-fearing.
>
> [*Al-Jāthiyah* (45): 18-19]

The word *minhāj* means way or path. Allāh, the Exalted says,

وَأَلَّوِ ٱسْتَقَٰمُوا۟ عَلَى ٱلطَّرِيقَةِ لَأَسْقَيْنَٰهُم مَّآءً غَدَقًا ﴿١٦﴾ لِّنَفْتِنَهُمْ
فِيهِ ۚ وَمَن يُعْرِضْ عَن ذِكْرِ رَبِّهِۦ يَسْلُكْهُ عَذَابًا صَعَدًا ﴿١٧﴾

> If they had believed in Allāh and traversed the Right Way, We should surely have bestowed on them rain in abundance that We might try them thereby, and whosoever turns away from the Reminder of his Lord, He will cause him to enter a severe torment.
>
> [*Al-Jinn* (72): 16-17]

Therefore the *shir'ah* is comparable to the *sharī'ah* [linguistically: watering place for cattle found at a] river, the *minhāj* is the path that it takes, and the intended objective is the reality of the religion which is none other than to worship Allāh Alone without associating any partners with Him. This reality is that the servant submit to Allāh, the Lord of the universe, and not to anyone else. Whosoever submits to other than Allāh has committed *shirk* and Allāh does not forgive anyone committing *shirk* with Him. Whosoever does not submit to Allāh, being too arrogant to worship Allāh, then Allāh says about such a person,

إِنَّ ٱلَّذِينَ يَسْتَكْبِرُونَ عَنْ عِبَادَتِى سَيَدْخُلُونَ جَهَنَّمَ
دَاخِرِينَ ﴿٦٠﴾

> Indeed those who scorn My worship will surely enter Hell, utterly humiliated!
>
> [*Ghāfir* (40): 60]

[10.1 Islām is the Religion of all the Prophets]

The religion of Islām is the religion of the first and last Prophets and Messengers. Allāh, the Exalted says,

وَمَن يَبْتَغِ غَيْرَ ٱلْإِسْلَٰمِ دِينًا فَلَن يُقْبَلَ مِنْهُ

> Whosoever seeks a religion other than Islām, it will never be accepted of him.
>
> [*Āli 'Imrān* (3): 85]

This verse is general to all time and every place.

Therefore the religion of Noah, Abraham, Jacob, the Tribes, Moses, Jesus and his disciples was Islām, and Islām is to worship Allāh Alone without associating any partners with Him. Allāh, the Exalted relates the words of Noah,

۞ وَٱتْلُ عَلَيْهِمْ نَبَأَ نُوحٍ إِذْ قَالَ لِقَوْمِهِۦ يَٰقَوْمِ إِن كَانَ كَبُرَ عَلَيْكُم
مَّقَامِى وَتَذْكِيرِى بِـَٔايَٰتِ ٱللَّهِ فَعَلَى ٱللَّهِ تَوَكَّلْتُ فَأَجْمِعُوٓا۟
أَمْرَكُمْ وَشُرَكَآءَكُمْ ثُمَّ لَا يَكُنْ أَمْرُكُمْ عَلَيْكُمْ غُمَّةً ثُمَّ ٱقْضُوٓا۟
إِلَىَّ وَلَا تُنظِرُونِ ﴿٧١﴾ فَإِن تَوَلَّيْتُمْ فَمَا سَأَلْتُكُم مِّنْ أَجْرٍ ۖ إِنْ
أَجْرِىَ إِلَّا عَلَى ٱللَّهِ ۖ وَأُمِرْتُ أَنْ أَكُونَ مِنَ ٱلْمُسْلِمِينَ ﴿٧٢﴾

> ...O My people! If my staying [with you] and my reminding [you] of the signs of Allāh is hard on you, then I put my trust in Allāh. So devise your plot - you and your partners - and let not your plot be in doubt for you. Then pass your sentence on me and give me no respite. But if you turn away, then no reward have I asked of you, my reward is only from Allāh and I have been commanded to be one of the Muslims.
>
> [*Yūnus* (10): 71-72]

Allāh, the Exalted says,

وَمَن يَرْغَبُ عَن
مِّلَّةِ إِبْرَٰهِـۧمَ إِلَّا مَن سَفِهَ نَفْسَهُۥ ۚ وَلَقَدِ ٱصْطَفَيْنَـٰهُ فِى ٱلدُّنْيَا ۖ
وَإِنَّهُۥ فِى ٱلْـَٔاخِرَةِ لَمِنَ ٱلصَّـٰلِحِينَ ﴿١٣٠﴾ إِذْ قَالَ لَهُۥ رَبُّهُۥٓ أَسْلِمْ ۖ
قَالَ أَسْلَمْتُ لِرَبِّ ٱلْعَـٰلَمِينَ ﴿١٣١﴾ وَوَصَّىٰ بِهَآ إِبْرَٰهِـۧمُ بَنِيهِ
وَيَعْقُوبُ يَـٰبَنِىَّ إِنَّ ٱللَّهَ ٱصْطَفَىٰ لَكُمُ ٱلدِّينَ فَلَا تَمُوتُنَّ إِلَّا
وَأَنتُم مُّسْلِمُونَ ﴿١٣٢﴾ أَمْ كُنتُمْ شُهَدَآءَ إِذْ حَضَرَ يَعْقُوبَ
ٱلْمَوْتُ إِذْ قَالَ لِبَنِيهِ مَا تَعْبُدُونَ مِنۢ بَعْدِى قَالُوا۟ نَعْبُدُ
إِلَـٰهَكَ وَإِلَـٰهَ ءَابَآئِكَ إِبْرَٰهِـۧمَ وَإِسْمَـٰعِيلَ وَإِسْحَـٰقَ إِلَـٰهًا
وَٰحِدًا وَنَحْنُ لَهُۥ مُسْلِمُونَ ﴿١٣٣﴾

And who turns away from the religion of Abraham except he who befools himself? Truly We chose him in this world and verily, in the Hereafter he will be among the righteous. When his Lord said to him, 'Submit [in Islām]!' He said, 'I have submitted myself [as a Muslim] to the Lord of the universe.' This [submission] was enjoined by Abraham upon his sons and by Jacob [saying], 'O my sons! Allāh has chosen for you the [true] religion so die not except as Muslims.'

[*Al-Baqarah* (2): 130-132]

وَقَالَ مُوسَىٰ يَـٰقَوْمِ إِن كُنتُمْ
ءَامَنتُم بِٱللَّهِ فَعَلَيْهِ تَوَكَّلُوٓا۟ إِن كُنتُم مُّسْلِمِينَ ﴿٨٤﴾

Moses said, 'O my people! If you have believed in Allāh, put your trust in Him if you are [truly] Muslims.'

[*Yūnus* (10): 84]

The magicians [who came to believe] said,

رَبَّنَا لَمَّا جَاءَتْنَا رَبَّنَا أَفْرِغْ عَلَيْنَا صَبْرًا وَتَوَفَّنَا مُسْلِمِينَ

Our Lord! Pour out on us patience and cause us to die as Muslims.

[*Al-A'rāf* (7): 126]

Yūsuf (*'alayhi as-sallām*) said,

تَوَفَّنِي مُسْلِمًا وَأَلْحِقْنِي بِالصَّٰلِحِينَ ﴿١٠١﴾

Cause me to die as a Muslim and join me with the righteous.

[*Yūsuf* (12): 101]

Bilqīs said,

وَأَسْلَمْتُ مَعَ سُلَيْمَٰنَ لِلَّهِ رَبِّ ٱلْعَٰلَمِينَ ﴿٤٤﴾

I have submitted [in Islām] together with Solomon to Allāh, the Lord of the universe.

[*An-Naml* (27): 44]

Allāh, the Exalted says,

يَحْكُمُ بِهَا ٱلنَّبِيُّونَ ٱلَّذِينَ أَسْلَمُوا۟ لِلَّذِينَ
هَادُوا۟ وَٱلرَّبَّٰنِيُّونَ وَٱلْأَحْبَارُ

By it [the Torah] the Prophets who submitted [in Islām] judged the Jews, and the Rabbis and priests [also judged by the Torah].

[*Al-Mā'idah* (5): 44]

The disciples [of Jesus] said,

ءَامَنَّا بِٱللَّهِ وَٱشْهَدْ بِأَنَّا مُسْلِمُونَ ﴿٥٢﴾

We believe in Allāh, and bear witness that we are Muslims.

[*Āli 'Imrān* (3): 52]

In conclusion the religion of the Prophets is one and the same even though some specific legal laws may have differed from Prophet to Prophet as is mentioned in the Two Ṣaḥīḥs that the Prophet (ﷺ) said,

«إنّا معشرَ الأنبياءِ دِينُنا واحد»

"We, the gathering of Prophets, our religion is one." [1]

Allāh, the Exalted says,

﴿ شَرَعَ لَكُم مِّنَ ٱلدِّينِ مَا وَصَّىٰ بِهِۦ نُوحًا وَٱلَّذِىٓ أَوْحَيْنَآ إِلَيْكَ وَمَا وَصَّيْنَا بِهِۦٓ إِبْرَٰهِيمَ وَمُوسَىٰ وَعِيسَىٰٓ ۖ أَنْ أَقِيمُوا۟ ٱلدِّينَ وَلَا تَتَفَرَّقُوا۟ فِيهِ ۚ

He has ordained for you the same religion that He enjoined upon Noah and that which We revealed to you, and what We enjoined upon Abraham, Moses and Jesus - to establish the religion and not be divided therein. Intolerable for the polytheists is what you call them to...

[*Ash-Shūrā* (42): 13]

---

[1] {F} Reported by Bukhārī [Eng. Trans. 4/434 no.'s 651,652] and Ṣaḥīḥ Muslim [Eng. Trans. 4/1260 no.'s 5834-5836].

يَٰٓأَيُّهَا ٱلرُّسُلُ كُلُوا۟ مِنَ ٱلطَّيِّبَٰتِ وَٱعْمَلُوا۟ صَٰلِحًا ۖ إِنِّى بِمَا
تَعْمَلُونَ عَلِيمٌ ﴿٥١﴾ وَإِنَّ هَٰذِهِۦٓ أُمَّتُكُمْ أُمَّةً وَٰحِدَةً وَأَنَا۠ رَبُّكُمْ
فَٱتَّقُونِ ﴿٥٢﴾ فَتَقَطَّعُوٓا۟ أَمْرَهُم بَيْنَهُمْ زُبُرًا ۖ كُلُّ حِزْبٍۭ بِمَا لَدَيْهِمْ
فَرِحُونَ ﴿٥٣﴾

O Messengers! Eat of the good things and do righteous deeds, indeed I am Well-Acquainted with what you do. Verily, this religion of yours is one religion and I am your Lord, so keep your duty to Me. But they have broken their religion among them in sects, each group rejoicing in what it has.

[*Al-Mu'minūn* (23): 51-53]

In Summary

- The true meaning to the term *Ḥaqīqah* which is misused by some *Ṣūfīs*.

- The reality of this religion is to worship Allāh Alone, without associating any partners with him.

- The religion of all the Prophets was one - Islām, even though some of the laws may have differed.

CHAPTER ELEVEN

[The Prophets are Superior to the *Awliyā'* who are not Prophets]

THE *SALAF* OF THIS NATION, THEIR *Imāms* and all of the *Awliyā'* of Allāh, the Exalted, are agreed that the Prophets are better than, and more superior to those *Awliyā'* who are not Prophets. Allāh has categorised His joyous servants who have been favoured, into four divisions with His words,

وَمَن يُطِعِ ٱللَّهَ وَٱلرَّسُولَ فَأُو۟لَٰٓئِكَ مَعَ ٱلَّذِينَ أَنْعَمَ ٱللَّهُ عَلَيْهِم مِّنَ ٱلنَّبِيِّـۧنَ وَٱلصِّدِّيقِينَ وَٱلشُّهَدَآءِ وَٱلصَّٰلِحِينَ ۚ وَحَسُنَ أُو۟لَٰٓئِكَ رَفِيقًا ﴿٦٩﴾

> And whoever obeys Allāh and the Messenger -those will be with the ones upon whom Allāh has bestowed favour; the Prophets, the steadfast affirmers of the truth, the martyrs and the righteous...
>
> [*An-Nisā'* (4): 69]

In the ḥadīth there occurs,

«ما طلعت الشمسُ ولا غربت على أحد بعد النبيين
والمرسلين أفضل من أبي بكر»

"The sun has not risen or set on anyone after the Prophets and the Messengers who was better than Abū Bakr." [1]

[11.1 The Superiority of the Nation of Muḥammad (ﷺ)]

The best and most superior of nations is the nation of Muḥammad (ﷺ) as Allāh, the Exalted says,

كُنتُمْ خَيْرَ أُمَّةٍ أُخْرِجَتْ لِلنَّاسِ

You are the best nation brought forth for mankind.

[*Āli 'Imrān* (3): 110]

ثُمَّ أَوْرَثْنَا الْكِتَٰبَ الَّذِينَ اصْطَفَيْنَا مِنْ عِبَادِنَا

Then We caused to inherit the Book, those We have chosen of our servants.

[*Fāṭir* (35): 32]

The Prophet (ﷺ) said in the ḥadīth reported in *'al-Musnad'*,

«أَنتم توفون سبعين أمة، أنتم خيرها وأكرمها على الله»

---

[1] {F} Reported by Aḥmad, *'Faḍā'il as-Ṣaḥābah'* [no. 69, 137, 508] and Abū Nu'aym, *'al-Ḥilyah'* [3/325] from Abū ad-Dardā' (*raḍiyAllāhu 'anhu*).

I say: its *isnād* is *ḍa'īf*. {Y} The ḥadīth has also been reported from Jābir by at-Ṭabarānī; from Salama bin al-Akwa'; and from As'ad bin Zirāra as per *'Majma' az-Zawā'id'* [9/43]. All these *isnāds* are defective.

{T} Al-Albānī, *'ad-Ḍa'īfah'* [3/524 under no. 1356] mentions that some of the scholars have declared this ḥadīth *ḥasan*. 'Abdul-Qādir al-Arna'ūt, in his *taḥqīq* to *'al-Furqān'* [p. 89] declares the ḥadīth *ḥasan* due to witnesses.

"You are the fulfilment of seventy nations, you are the best of them and the most noble of them with Allāh." [2]

The best and most superior of the nation of Muḥammad were the first generation. It is established from the Prophet (ﷺ) via a number of different ways that he said,

«خير القـرون القرن الـذي بعثت
فيه، ثم الذين يلونهم، ثم الذين يلونهم»

"The best of generations is the generation that I was sent in, then the one that follows, then the one that follows." [3]

In the Two Ṣaḥīḥs it is reported that the Prophet (ﷺ) said,

«لا تسبوا أصحابي، فوالذي نفسي بيده،
لو أنفق أحدكم مثل أُحد ذهباً، ما بلـغ مُدَّ أحدهم ولا نصيفه»

"Do not abuse my Companions for by the One in Whose Hand is my soul if one of you were to give in charity the likes of [Mount] Uḥud in gold he would not attain [what they attained by giving] a handful - not even a half." [4]

The Forerunners from amongst the *Muhājirūn* and the *Anṣār* are better than and superior to the rest of the Companions. Allāh, the Exalted says,

---

[2] {F} Reported by at-Tirmidhī [no. 3001] and ibn Mājah [no. 3001]. I say: its *isnād* is *ḥasan.*

[3] {F} Reported by Bukhārī [Eng. Trans. 3/497 no.'s 819-820, 5/2 no.'s 2-3, 8/292 no.'s 436-437, 8/449 no. 686] and Muslim [Eng. Trans. 4/1345 no.'s 6150-6159].

[4] {F} Reported by Bukhārī [Eng. Trans. 5/17 no. 22] and Muslim [Eng. Trans. 4/1348 no. 6167].

لَا يَسْتَوِى مِنكُم مَّنْ أَنفَقَ مِن قَبْلِ ٱلْفَتْحِ
وَقَـٰتَلَ ۚ أُو۟لَـٰٓئِكَ أَعْظَمُ دَرَجَةً مِّنَ ٱلَّذِينَ أَنفَقُوا۟ مِنۢ بَعْدُ وَقَـٰتَلُوا۟ ۚ
وَكُلًّا وَعَدَ ٱللَّهُ ٱلْحُسْنَىٰ ۚ وَٱللَّهُ بِمَا تَعْمَلُونَ خَبِيرٌ ﴿١٠﴾

Not equal among you are those who spent before the conquest [of Mecca] and fought [and those who did so after it]. They are greater in degree than those who spent afterwards and fought. But to all Allāh has promised the best reward...

[*Al-Ḥadīd* (57): 10]

وَٱلسَّـٰبِقُونَ ٱلْأَوَّلُونَ مِنَ ٱلْمُهَـٰجِرِينَ وَٱلْأَنصَارِ وَٱلَّذِينَ
ٱتَّبَعُوهُم بِإِحْسَـٰنٍ رَّضِىَ ٱللَّهُ عَنْهُمْ وَرَضُوا۟ عَنْهُ

The Forerunners [in faith] and the *Muhājirūn* and the *Anṣār* and those who followed them in good - Allāh is Pleased with them and they are pleased with Him.

[*At-Tawbah* (9): 100]

The Forerunners are those who gave in charity and fought before the Conquest (*al-Fatḥ*) and the Conquest refers to the treaty of *Ḥudaybiyyah* for it was the first stage leading to the conquest of Mecca. It was concerning this treaty that Allāh, the Exalted revealed,

إِنَّا فَتَحْنَا لَكَ فَتْحًا مُّبِينًا ﴿١﴾ لِّيَغْفِرَ لَكَ ٱللَّهُ مَا تَقَدَّمَ مِن ذَنۢبِكَ
وَمَا تَأَخَّرَ

Indeed, We have given you a clear conquest. That Allāh may forgive you of your previous sin and what will follow.

[*Al-Fatḥ* (48): 1-2]

They asked, 'O Messenger of Allāh! Is this a conquest?' He replied, *'Yes.'* [5]

The best and most superior of the Forerunners were the Four *Khalīfs* - the best of these was Abū Bakr and then 'Umar. This fact was well known amongst the Companions, those who followed them in good, the *Imāms* of this nation and the majority of the Muslims. There are many proofs showing this and we have detailed them in [our book], *'Minhāj as-Sunnah an-Nabawiyya wa Naqd Kalām Ahl ash-Shī'ah wal Qadariyyah.'*

Generally speaking the adherents of the *Sunnah* and the *Shī'a* are agreed that the best of this nation after its Prophet is one of the Four *Khalīfs*. There is no one after the Companions who is better than and more superior to the Companions. The best of the *Awliyā'* of Allāh, the Exalted, are those who have the most knowledge of what the Messenger (ﷺ) came with and the most stringent in following him. An example of these *Awliyā'* lies with the Companions because from this nation they were the one who had the most complete knowledge of his religion and were the closest in following him. Abū Bakr *as-Ṣiddīq* had the most knowledge of what he came with and followed him most closely and therefore he is the best of the *Awliyā'*. In summary, the nation of Muḥammad (ﷺ) is the best of nations, the best of whom are the Companions of Muḥammad (ﷺ), the best of whom is Abū Bakr (*raḍiyAllāhu 'anhu*).

---

[5] {F} Reported by Abū Dāwūd [Eng. Trans. 2/762 no. 2730] and Aḥmad [3/420]. {T} It is *ḍa'īf* as per al-Albānī, *'Ḍa'īf Abū Dāwūd'* [no. 587].

[11.2 The Seal of the *Awliyā'*]

A group of people erroneously thought that the Seal of the *Awliyā'* was better than the rest of the *Awliyā'*, making analogy to the Seal of the Prophets, however none of the early generations ever made mention of the title 'Seal of the *Awliyā'*' with the exception of Muḥammad bin 'Alī al-Ḥakīm at-Tirmidhī. He authored a work in which he made a number of mistakes[6] and after him appeared a group of people each one of whom made claim to being the Seal of the *Awliyā'*. A group of these people went as far as to claim that the Seal of the *Awliyā'* was better than the Seal of the Prophets from the perspective of his knowledge of Allāh and that the Prophets derive their knowledge of Allāh from him. This was the presumption of ibn al-Arabī, the author of the works, *'Futuḥāt al-Makkiyyah'* and *'Fuṣūṣ al-Ḥikam.'*[7] By saying this he opposed the *Sharī'ah* as well as the intellect along with opposing all of the Prophets and *Awliyā'* of Allāh, indeed one says about him what one says about a person who says, 'The roof caved in on him from below' - neither the Qur'ān nor the intellect support him.[8]

---

[6] {Y} The name of the book is *'Khatm al-Wilāyah'* as mentioned by ibn Taymiyyah in his *'Ḥaqīqah Madhāhib al-Ittiḥādiyyīn'* wherein he mentioned examples of these errors.

{T} Two works of Ḥakīm at-Tirmidhī are available in English, published under the title, 'Concept of Sainthood in Early Islamic Mysticism: Two Works by al-Ḥakīm at-Tirmidhī' [trans. Bernd Radtke, Humanities Press International, 1996].

[7] {T} This book has been translated with the title 'The Wisdom of the Prophets' [tr. T. Burkhardt, Beshara Publications, 1975] and the quotes that the author mentions in the following pages are all to be found in the translation.

[8] {T} This is because a verse of the Qur'ān reads,

فَخَرَّ عَلَيْهِمُ ٱلسَّقْفُ مِن فَوْقِهِمْ

...so the roof fell upon them from above.

[*An-Naḥl* (16): 26].

This is because the Prophets of any particular time are better than the *Awliyā'* of this nation and the Prophets (*'alayhim afḍal as-ṣalāh was salām*) are better than the *Awliyā'* [unrestrictedly] so what then, when all of the Prophets are taken together? The *Awliyā'* only derive their knowledge of Allāh from those who came after the Prophets so how is it possible for one to claim that he is the Seal of the *Awliyā'*? The last of the *Awliyā'* is not the best of them as was the case for the last Prophet (ﷺ), for the nobility and excellence of Muḥammad (ﷺ) is established through textual evidences such as his sayings,

«أنا سيد ولد آدم ولا فخر»

"I am the master of the children of Ādam without boasting" [9]

«آتي باب الجنة فأستفتح، فيقول الخازن:
من أنت؟ فأقول: محمد، فيقول: بك أمرت،
أن لا أفتح لأحد قبلك»

"I will come to the door of paradise and attempt to open it. The guard will ask, 'Who are you?' I will reply, 'I am Muḥammad.' Thereupon he will say, 'You are the one for whom I was ordered to open and to no one else before you.'"

During the Ascent (*Mi'rāj*), Allāh raised his ranking above all of the other Prophets and hence he became the most deserving of being the one referred to in His saying,

﴿تِلْكَ ٱلرُّسُلُ فَضَّلْنَا بَعْضَهُمْ عَلَىٰ بَعْضٍ مِّنْهُم مَّن كَلَّمَ ٱللَّهُ
وَرَفَعَ بَعْضَهُمْ دَرَجَٰتٍ

Those Messengers - some of them We caused to exceed others. Among them were those to whom Allāh Spoke,

---

[9] {F} This is part of the ḥadīth of intercession previously mentioned on page 49

> and He raised some of them in degree.
>
> [*Al-Baqarah* (2): 253]

There are many other proofs establishing this fact. All of the Prophets received revelation, especially Muḥammad (ﷺ). He was not in need of anybody else and his *Sharī'ah* was not dependant upon a previous law or an ensuing law. This was not the case with the Messiah, for he referred his followers to the Torah and he came and merely completed it, this is why the Christians are dependent upon the Prophetic Books revealed before the Messiah such as the Torah, Zabur and the other twenty-four books. The nations before us were in need of *Muḥaddaths* but not so the nation of Muḥammad (ﷺ), for Allāh has sufficed them such that they are in no need of another Prophet or a *Muḥaddath*. Indeed Allāh combined in Muḥammad all of the virtues, knowledge and righteous actions that were previously only found scattered amongst the different Prophets. The blessings that Allāh bestowed upon him (ﷺ) by way of what He revealed to him and commissioned him to do did not come to him by the medium of any other human.

[11.3 *Wilāyah* is Dependant Upon Following the Messenger (ﷺ)]

This is not the case with the *Awliyā'*, for everyone who has the message of Muḥammad (ﷺ) conveyed to him cannot be a *Waliy* of Allāh except through following Muḥammad (ﷺ). Each time he attains some increase in guidance and the Religion of Truth then it is via the medium of Muḥammad (ﷺ). Similarly, the one who had the message of a Messenger [previous to Muḥammad (ﷺ)] conveyed to him cannot be a *Waliy* of Allāh except through following that Messenger who was sent to him.

Whosoever claims that there are amongst those who have received the Message of Muḥammad (ﷺ), *Awliyā'* who have a route to Allāh which is in no need of Muḥammad then such a person is a disbeliever and heretic (*mulḥid*). If such a person were to say, 'I am in need of Muḥammad for the outward knowledge but not the inner knowledge' or, 'The knowledge of the *Sharī'ah* but not the knowledge of the *Ḥaqīqah*' then he is more evil than those Jews and Christians who said, 'Indeed Muḥammad was sent to the illiterate people and not the People of the Book.' These people believed in some of the Book and disbelieved in some, just as this person who thinks that Muḥammad (ﷺ) was sent with the outward knowledge and not the inner knowledge has believed in some of what he brought and disbelieved in some. This person is a disbeliever and in fact he is a greater disbeliever than them. This is because the inner knowledge is the knowledge of the belief of the hearts, their affairs and their conditions - this is the knowledge of the inner realities of faith. This knowledge is better and nobler than having the mere knowledge of the outward actions required by Islām.

If someone were to claim that Muḥammad (ﷺ) only knew about these outward matters and knew nothing of the realities of faith and that he does not take these realities from the Book and *Sunnah* then he has in reality claimed that he believes in some of what the Messenger came with to the exception of the remainder. This saying is more evil than the saying of those who say, 'I believe in some and disbelieve in some,' [because such a person has accepted that the Messenger came with the remainder] and does not claim that the part he believes in is the lesser of the two.

[11.4 The Misguidance of those who believe that *Wilāyah* is Greater than Prophethood]

These heretics claim that the rank of a *Waliy* is better and more superior to Prophethood, they deceive the people and confuse them by claiming that the aspect of his (ﷺ) being a *Waliy* is superior to the aspect of his being a Prophet and proceed to recite the lines of poetry,

> The ranking of Prophethood in the *barzakh* [10]
> Slightly surpasses the rank of Messengership yet is less than
> the rank of the *Waliy*.

They then continue to say, 'We share with him in the aspect of his being a *Waliy* which is greater than his message.' This, in reality, is the greatest aspect of their misguidance for the *Wilāyah* of Muḥammad is not equalled by anyone, not Abraham or Moses, not to mention that he be equalled by the likes of these heretics!

Every Messenger is a Prophet and a *Waliy*, his messengership includes his prophethood and his prophethood necessarily includes his being a *Waliy*. So how is it possible that his *wilāyah*, which follows on from his being a Prophet, be superior to Prophethood?[11] If they assume that Allāh merely sent him as a Prophet without his being a *Waliy* of Allāh then this assumption is impossible. This is because it is impossible that at the time of his being commissioned a Prophet,

---

[10] {T} *Al-Barzakh*, refers to a barrier placed between a person who has deceased and this worldly life. It is a way of referring to the first stages of the life of the Hereafter. A very good treatment of *al-Barzakh* and the issues related to it can be found in Muḥammad al-Jibaly, 'Life in *al-Barzakh*' [*Al-Kitaab & As-Sunnah* publishing, 1998].

[11] {Y} This sentence does not occur in some of the texts of *al-Furqān*.

he be anything but a *Waliy* of Allāh. Therefore Prophethood and *wilāyah* go hand in hand, but if one were to assume that indeed his being a *Waliy* [was independent of his being a Prophet] then still nobody could be like the Messenger with regards his being a *Waliy*!

[11.5 The Deviations of ibn 'Arabī, ibn Sīnā and the Philosophers]

These people could say, as was said by ibn Arabī, the author of '*Fuṣūṣ*,' that they take from the same source as the Angel who revealed the message to the Messenger (ﷺ) took! This is because they took on board the beliefs of the philosophers and presented them in the guise of unveiling hidden realities. The philosophers[12] are those who said, 'Indeed the celestial spheres are eternal, without beginning and they have [an essential, eternal] cause which they seek to resemble,'[13] as was stated by Aristotle and his followers. Others said, 'Its beginning cause was the Necessary Existent,' such as the later philosophers like ibn Sīnā and his kind. They did not say that, 'It belongs to the Lord Who created the heavens and the earth and what is between them in Six Days.' In their view He did not create anything by His Will and Power and neither does He Know the details or particulars of the creation (*juz'iyyāt*). Rather, they either

---

[12] {T} At this point ibn Taymiyyah mentions a number of philosophical concepts briefly, stating that he has explained them in detail elsewhere. For a further explanation of these concepts in English, one can find an interesting discussion in Oliver Leaman, 'A Brief Introduction to Islamic Philosophy' [Polity Press, 1999]. Other references are 'ibn Taymiyyah Against the Greek Logicians' [tr. Wal B. Hallaq, Oxford University Press, 1993] and al-Ghazali's 'The Incoherence of the Philosophers' [tr. M. Marmura, Brigham Young University, 1998].

[13] {T} The early philosophers spoke of the First Cause and affirmed it as a Final Cause of celestial movement, where the heavenly bodies move according to its model. Therefore the First cause was not the Creator but rather a final cause to be imitated.

reject His Knowledge in totality as done by Aristotle, or they think that of those matters subject to change and alteration, He knows the generalities,[14] as said by ibn Sīnā. The reality of this saying of ibn Sīnā constitutes a rejection of His Knowledge of those matters for everything in existence is made up of smaller parts or particulars, and each of these parts are in turn made up of smaller parts. The same goes for every particle of existence, its attributes and actions. Therefore the one who knows nothing but the generalities in reality knows of nothing that is created. The generalities are only imagined to be so in ones mind, in reality, they are composite.

The discussion concerning this is detailed in [my work], *'Darr Ta'ārud al-'Aql wa an-Naql'* and other works.

The disbelief of these people is greater than the disbelief of the Jews and Christians, indeed it is greater than the disbelief of the polytheist Arabs. This is because all of them said, 'Allāh created the heavens and the earth and that He created the creation according to His Will and Power.'

Aristotle, those philosophers like him and the Greeks in general worshipped the stars and idols. They knew of the Angels and Prophets, however no mention of them is found in the books of Aristotle, instead their predominate concern was with the natural sciences.

With regards the affairs of revelation and Allāh then every single one of them was only rarely correct, frequently erring. The Jews and the Christians, even after the abrogation of their scriptures and their alteration of them, are more knowledgeable of such affairs than the

---

[14] {T} Ar. *Kulliyyāt.* A term referring to that which is possible to imagine as being divided or shared. For example, the term *insān* (mankind) is a global/general (*kulliy*) term [because the term refers to a set of individuals or composite parts]. This is because the generality of a thing is only considered so with respect to its composite parts (*juz'iy*). The composite parts make up the general. - *'at-Ta'rīfāt'* [pg. 239].

philosophers. However the later philosophers such as ibn Sīnā tried to combine and reconcile the words of the philosophers with that which the Messengers came with. They succeeded only in taking some of the principles of the *Jahmiyyah* and *Mu'tazilah* and inventing a school of thought that all the philosophers of the various religions could relate to. This school contains a great deal of corruption and self-contradiction that we have explained elsewhere.[15]

When this group of philosophers saw that the affair of the Messengers, such as Moses, Jesus and Muḥammad (ﷺ) had inundated the whole world, and they themselves acknowledged the message that Muḥammad (ﷺ) had been sent with, and they saw the Prophets talking of the Angels and Jinn, they tried to reconcile this with the statements of their Greek predecessors. These Greek philosophers who were the farthest removed of creation with respect to knowledge of Allāh, His Angels, His Books, His Messengers and the Last Day and instead affirmed ten forms of intellect[16] which they called

---

[15] {Y} For example in his work, *'Mukhtaṣar Naṣīḥah Ahl al-Īmān fi ar-Radd 'alā Manṭiq al-Yunān'*. Refer to *'Majmū' Fatāwā'* [9/133-135].

[16] {T} Their theory, taken on board by al-Farābī and others, can be summarised as follows: there is a First Being who is the first cause of other beings. All other beings proceed or emanate from him in successive stages. The first stage consists of ten different intellects which are absolutely incorporeal substances that do not reside in matter. With each of these intellects there is a celestial sphere - the first sphere, the sphere of stars, Saturn, Jupiter, Mars, the Sun, Venus, Mercury and the Moon. Each sphere is assigned a soul that has no need of matter in order to exist. The sphere of the Moon is the last of the heavenly bodies and from it comes the 'Active Intelligence,' which is the tenth intellect and bridges the gap between heaven and earth. The final stage of emanation consists of soul, form and matter. Ibn Sīnā identified these intellects and spheres to be Angels, the Active Intelligence being Jibrīl. - summarised from Soheil M. Afnan, 'Aviccenna' [pp. 31-32, 185-186, 198].

absolutes[17] and independents.[18]

The basis of this concept of theirs is derived from the soul separating from the body and they called this independent, due to its having separated from its substance. They affirmed the existence of celestial spheres (*aflāq*) of creation and ascribed a soul to each sphere. Most of them believed these souls to be incorporeal while others thought them to be essences (*jawāhir*).

These absolutes that they affirm, after research, one finds that they revolve around matters present in ones mind and imagination and not in reality. Examples of these are the imaginary or irrational numbers developed by the students of Pythagoras or the abstract Platonian theory developed by the students of Plato, the 'Theory of Forms.'[19] They affirmed primal substance or matter[20] as being something devoid of form and in the same way time and space as something eternal and unchangeable. The most skilled of philosophers

[17] {T} Ar. *Mujarradāt.* These are things that do not have an essence (*jawhar*), neither are they incarnated in another *jawhar* nor composed of the two. - *'at-Ta'rīfāt'* [pg. 260].

[18] {T} Ar. *Mufāraqāt.* These are essences (*jawāhir*) totally unrelated and independent of the substance/matter, existing in and of themselves. - *'at-Ta'rīfāt'* [pg. 286].

[19] {T}The theory proposes that objects in the physical world merely resemble perfect Forms in the ideal world, and that these perfect Forms are the objects of true knowledge. Everything in the world of space and time is what it is by virtue of its resemblance to its universal Form. The supreme Form is the Form of the Good, which illuminates all other Forms. Knowledge of this Form is the source of guidance in moral decision making. - 'Encarta Concise Encyclopedia'

[20] {T} Ar. *Hayūlā*, primal substance or material. It is a Greek word and technically refers to a *jawhar* in the body that is able to deal with those circumstances which are both connected to the body and divorced from it. It is the focal point of the two forms: bodily and subjective. - *'at-Ta'rīfāt'* [pg. 321].

are forced to acknowledge that such matters can only be imagined and never actually realised.

[11.5.1 Prophecy in the Eyes of the Philosophers]

Now, when the later philosophers such as ibn Sīnā tried to prove the matter of Prophethood based upon their false principles, they came to think that Prophethood has three specific qualities, whosoever has them is a Prophet:

1. That he possess a scholarly potential, which they called *'al-Quwā al-Qudusiyyah'* by which he could attain knowledge without the need to learn.

2. That he possess an imaginative potential such that he could imagine what he thought. Therefore he was able to see forms or hear voices [while awake] in the same way that the one dreaming sees and hears. These things he saw or heard have no reality to them - the forms he saw were the Angels of Allāh and the voices he heard was the Speech of Allāh, the Exalted.[21]

3. That he possess an active potential by which he could affect the very substance of creation. Hence they considered the miracles of the Prophets, *Awliyā'* and the extraordinary feats of the magicians to be the results of their own potential or strength. Therefore they accepted all that agreed to their principles, such as the staff changing to a snake, and rejected what did not, such as the moon being split in half.

We have a detailed discussion about these people in a number of

---

[21] {T} Refer to Soheil Afnan, 'Avicenna' [pp. 178-180].

places[22] and we have explained that these words of theirs are the most corrupt of words. We have explained that these qualities that they have specified for a Prophet have been surpassed by other individuals amongst normal people including some of the followers of the Prophets themselves. We have explained that the Angels of which the Prophets spoke are real, living beings which speak, are from the greatest of the creation of Allāh and they are many in number. Allāh, the Exalted says,

وَمَا يَعْلَمُ جُنُودَ رَبِّكَ إِلَّا هُوَ

And none knows the armies of your Lord except for He.
[*Muddaththir* (74): 31]

They are not ten in number and neither are they incorporeal, especially since these people believe that the beginning source was the First Intellect, and from this intellect emanated everything that was less than it. In their view, the Tenth Active Intellect is the lord of everything under the orbit of the moon.

All of this is known by necessity in the religion of the Messengers to be false. Not one of the Angels brought into being everything besides Allāh.

[11.5.2 The Aḥādīth Concerning the Intellect]

They think that the intellect has been spoken of in the ḥadīth,

«إن أول ما
خلق الله العقل، فقال له: أقبل، فأقبل، فقال له: أدبر،
فأدبر، فقال: وعزّتي ما خلقت خلقاً أكرم عليَّ منك، فبك
آخذ، وبك أُعطي، ولك الثواب وعليك العقاب»

[22] {Y} Such as his works *'an-Nubuwwāt'* [pp. 168+] and *'Radd 'alā al-Manṭiqiyyīn'* [p. 441].

> *"Indeed the first thing that Allāh created was the intellect. He said to it, 'come' so it came. Then He said, 'Go' and it went. Then He said, 'By My Might I have not created a creation which is more noble to Me than you. So for your sake I withhold and for your sake I give, the reward will be for you and the punishment will be for you.'"* [23]

They also call the intellect, 'the pen' due to the ḥadīth reported by at-Tirmidhī,

«إن أول ما خلق الله القلم»

"Indeed the first thing that Allāh created was the Pen." [24]

The ḥadīth that they mention concerning the intellect is a lie and a concoction in the view of the Scholars of Ḥadīth. This ruling was given by Abū Ḥātim al-Bustī, ad-Dāruquṭnī, ibn al-Jawzī and others. The ḥadīth is not recorded in any of the books that are depended upon, yet despite this its wording, were it to be authentic, constitutes evidence against them. This is because in one wording it reads,

«أول ما خلق الله تعالى العقل، قال له»

"Indeed the first thing that Allāh created was the intellect."

In another wording it reads,

«لما خلق الله العقل قال له...»

---

[23] {F} Reported by ibn 'Adī [2/390, 6/269] and ad-Daylamī, *'al-Firdaws'* [no. 4].
Ibn al-Qayyim said, 'All the *aḥādīth* concerning the intellect are lies.'
Refer to: ibn al-Jawzī, *'al-Mawḍū'āt'* [1/174-175]; *'Tanzīh ash-Sharī'ah'* [1/[illegible]]; as-Suyuṭī, *'al-Lā'ī al-Maṣnū'ah'* [1/129-132]; al-Qārī, *'al-Asrār al-Marfū'ah'* [pg. 154]; *'Fatḥ al-Bārī'* [13/346]; adh-Dhahabī, *'Mīzān al-I'tidāl'* [1/564, 3/356, 4/61]; *'ad-Ḍa'īfah'* [1/13].

[24] {F} Reported by at-Tirmidhī [no. 2155, 3319] and at-Ṭayālisī [no. 577].
Its *isnād* is *ṣaḥīḥ, inshaAllāh.*
Refer to: *'as-Ṣaḥīḥah'* [2/207] and *'Majma' az-Zawā'id'* [7/128].

"When Allāh created the intellect, He said to it...."

Therefore the meaning of the ḥadīth is that He addressed it immediately after creating it, the meaning is not that it is the first thing to be created. The word 'first' in the ḥadīth is grammatically in the place of an adjective denoting time or place and therefore carries the same meaning as the word 'when' mentioned in the variant wording. Also the remainder of the ḥadīth,

«ما خلقت خلقاً أكرم عليَّ منك»

"By My Might I have not created a creation which is more noble to Me than you."

Shows that there had been things created previously. Then the ḥadīth mentions,

«فبك آخذ، وبك أُعطي، ولك الثواب، وعليك العقاب»

"So for your sake I withhold and for your sake I give, the reward will be for you and the punishment will be for you."

So this ḥadīth mentions four types of contingents[25] yet in their view all essences in the upper and lower world emanate from this intellect, so how does the wording of the ḥadīth fit with this theory?

[11.5.3 The Actuality of the Intellect]

The reason for their erring is that the word intellect (*ʿaql*) in the language of the Muslims does not carry the same meaning as the word intellect in Greek. This is because in the language of the Muslims, the word *ʿaql* is the verbal noun derived from *ʿaqala*, *yaʿqilu*, *aqlan* as it occurs in the Qurʾān,

---

[25] {T} i.e. giving, withholding, rewarding and punishing.

وَقَالُوا لَوْ كُنَّا نَسْمَعُ أَوْ نَعْقِلُ مَا كُنَّا فِي أَصْحَٰبِ ٱلسَّعِيرِ ﴿١٠﴾

And they will say, 'If only we had been listening or reasoning, we would not be among the denizens of the Blaze.'
[*Al-Mulk* (67): 10]

إِنَّ فِي ذَٰلِكَ لَآيَٰتٍ لِّقَوْمٍ يَعْقِلُونَ ﴿٤﴾

Indeed in that are signs for a people who reason.
[*Ar-Ra`d* (13): 4]

أَفَلَمْ يَسِيرُوا فِي ٱلْأَرْضِ
فَتَكُونَ لَهُمْ قُلُوبٌ يَعْقِلُونَ بِهَآ أَوْ ءَاذَانٌ يَسْمَعُونَ بِهَا

So have they not travelled through the earth and have hearts by which to reason and ears by which to hear?
[*Al-Ḥajj* (22): 46]

The meaning of intellect is the instinctive faculty which Allāh, the Exalted, has placed in man by which he comprehends.

In the view of the Greek philosophers, the intellect was an essence existing in and of itself just like the intelligent. This definition does not concord to the language of the Messengers and the Qur'ān. The 'world of creation' in their view, as mentioned by Abū Ḥāmid, is the world of physical bodies. As for the intellect and souls then they referred to them as the 'world of order.' They also called the intellect, 'the world of omnipotence (*jabarūt*)'; the soul, 'the world of sovereignty (*malakūt*)'; and the bodies, 'the world of dominion (*mulk*).' Therefore those who were not cognisant of the language of the Messengers, and did not understand the meanings of the Qur'ān and *Sunnah*, thought that the words *mulk*, *malakūt* and *jabarūt* mentioned therein conformed to these definitions. This is not the case.

These philosophers perpetrate a great deception amongst the people such as their stating that the world is created, existential - meaning having a cause, this despite the fact that it is eternal in their view. Something that is created must first have been absent in order to be created. There is nowhere found, in the Arabic language or any other language for that matter, the usage of the word 'created' to mean 'eternal'. Allāh has informed us that He has created everything, and everything that is created is existential, and everything that is existential must have been brought about after once being absent.

The People of Theological Rhetoric including the *Jahmiyyah* and *Muʿtazilah* argued with these philosophers, but in a deficient way. This was because they did not fully understand what the Messenger brought and neither did they fully grasp the issues derived from sound reasoning. Therefore neither did they aid Islām, nor vanquish the enemies, instead they took on board some of their false principles and abandoned some of the issues derived from sound intellect. Therefore their deficiency spread to the realm of textual revelation and sound intellect due to the strong, compelling misguidance of the philosophers. This has been explained in another place.[26]

[11.5.4 The Angels in the Eyes of the Philosophers]

These philosophers considered Jibrīl to be a mere figment of imagination that took form in the soul of the Prophet (ﷺ). Imagination is a product the intellect. So these heretics[27] shared this concept with those heretical philosophers and came to think that they were the *Awliyā'* of Allāh, that the *Awliyā'* were better than the Prophets and that they could take directly from Allāh, the Exalted, with-

---

[26] {Y} Refer to his work, *'Bayān Talbīs al-Jahmiyyah'* [1/152+].

[27] {T} i.e. those discussed in sections 11.4 and 11.5

out the need of a medium. An example of such a person lies with ibn Arabī, the author of *'al-Futūḥāt'* and *'al-Fuṣūṣ'* who said that he took from the same source that the Angel who revealed the message to the Messenger took.[28] This source in his view was the intellect, the Angel was the figment of the imagination and the imagination is a product of the intellect. In his view, he took from the source of this imagination whereas the Messenger merely took from this imagination and therefore he thought himself to be above the Prophet! Now if the specific qualities of a Prophet were truly specific to him, as they mentioned, and one is not a Prophet let alone being above a Prophet, then how is what they mention possible to be found amongst another believer?!

The affair of Prophethood is something above and beyond what they think. Ibn Arabī and his likes only claimed to be a *Ṣūfī*, and they are in fact from the heretical *Ṣūfī* philosophers, not from the *Ṣūfīs* found amongst the People of Knowledge, let alone being scholars of the adherents to the Book and *Sunnah*! In no way were they the teachers of the likes of Fuḍayl bin 'Ayāḍ, Ibrāhīm bin Adham, Abū Sulaymān ad-Dārānī, Ma'rūf al-Karkhī, al-Junaid bin Muḥammad, Sahl bin 'Abdullāh at-Tustorī and their likes, may Allāh be pleased with them all.

[11.5.5 The Description of the Angels]

Allāh has described the Angels in His Book with attributes that clearly differ from what these people say. He says,

[28] {Y} ibn Arabī, *'Fuṣūṣ'* [1/62].

وَقَالُوا اتَّخَذَ الرَّحْمَٰنُ وَلَدًا ۗ سُبْحَانَهُ ۚ
بَلْ عِبَادٌ مُّكْرَمُونَ ﴿٢٦﴾ لَا يَسْبِقُونَهُ بِالْقَوْلِ وَهُم
بِأَمْرِهِ يَعْمَلُونَ ﴿٢٧﴾ يَعْلَمُ مَا بَيْنَ أَيْدِيهِمْ وَمَا خَلْفَهُمْ
وَلَا يَشْفَعُونَ إِلَّا لِمَنِ ارْتَضَىٰ وَهُم مِّنْ خَشْيَتِهِ مُشْفِقُونَ
﴿٢٨﴾ ۞ وَمَن يَقُلْ مِنْهُمْ إِنِّي إِلَٰهٌ مِّن دُونِهِ فَذَٰلِكَ نَجْزِيهِ
جَهَنَّمَ ۚ كَذَٰلِكَ نَجْزِي الظَّالِمِينَ ﴿٢٩﴾

And they say, 'The Most Merciful has taken a son.' Exalted is He! Rather, they [the Angels] are honoured servants. They cannot precede Him in word and they act by His Command. He Knows what is [presently] before them and what will be after them and they cannot intercede except on behalf of one whom He approves. And they are, from fear of Him, apprehensive. And whoever of them should say, 'Indeed I am a god besides Him' - such a one We would recompense with Hell; thus do We recompense the wrongdoers.

[*Al-Anbiyā'* (21): 26-29]

۞ وَكَم مِّن مَّلَكٍ فِي السَّمَاوَاتِ لَا تُغْنِي
شَفَاعَتُهُمْ شَيْئًا إِلَّا مِن بَعْدِ أَن يَأْذَنَ اللَّهُ لِمَن يَشَاءُ وَيَرْضَىٰ ﴿٢٦﴾

And how many Angels are there in the heavens whose intercession will not avail at all except [only] after Allāh has permitted [it] to whom He wills and approves.

[*An-Najm* (53): 26]

قُلِ ادْعُوا الَّذِينَ زَعَمْتُم مِّن دُونِ
اللَّهِ ۖ لَا يَمْلِكُونَ مِثْقَالَ ذَرَّةٍ فِي السَّمَاوَاتِ وَلَا فِي
الْأَرْضِ وَمَا لَهُمْ فِيهِمَا مِن شِرْكٍ وَمَا لَهُ مِنْهُم مِّن ظَهِيرٍ ﴿٢٢﴾
وَلَا تَنفَعُ الشَّفَاعَةُ عِندَهُ إِلَّا لِمَنْ أَذِنَ لَهُ

> Say: 'Supplicate to those you claim [as deities] besides Allāh.' They do not possess an atoms weight [of ability] in the heavens or on the earth, and they do not have therein any partnership [with Him], nor is there for Him from among them any assistant. And intercession does not benefit with Him except for one whom He permits.
>
> [*Saba'* (34): 22-23]

﴿١٨﴾ وَلَهُۥ مَن فِي ٱلسَّمَٰوَٰتِ وَٱلۡأَرۡضِۚ وَمَنۡ عِندَهُۥ لَا يَسۡتَكۡبِرُونَ
عَنۡ عِبَادَتِهِۦ وَلَا يَسۡتَحۡسِرُونَ ﴿١٩﴾ يُسَبِّحُونَ ٱلَّيۡلَ وَٱلنَّهَارَ
لَا يَفۡتُرُونَ ﴿٢٠﴾

> To Him belongs whoever is in the heavens and the earth. Those near Him [the Angels] are not prevented by arrogance from His worship and nor do they tire. They exalt [His praises] night and day and do not slacken.
>
> [*Al-Anbiyā'* (21): 19-20]

He informs us that the Angels came to Abraham in the guise of humans, and that the Angel came in the form of a well-proportioned man to Mary. Jibrīl used to come to the Prophet (ﷺ) in the guise of Diḥya al-Kalbī[29] and in the form of a Bedouin Arab who was seen by the people in general. Allāh has described Jibrīl as one who possesses might with His words,

ذِي قُوَّةٍ عِندَ ذِي ٱلۡعَرۡشِ مَكِينٖ ﴿٢٠﴾ مُّطَاعٖ ثَمَّ أَمِينٖ ﴿٢١﴾

> [Who] possesses power, secure [in position] with the Owner of the Throne. Obeyed there [in the heavens] and trustworthy.
>
> [*At-Takwīr* (81): 20-21]

---

[29] {Y} Aḥmad [2.107, 4/17] reports that, *'Jibrīl used to come to the Prophet (ﷺ) in the form of Diḥya.'*

{T} Al-Albānī, *'as-Ṣaḥīḥah'* [3/104 under no. 1111] declares the ḥadīth *ṣaḥīḥ* according to the criteria of Muslim.

Muḥammad (ﷺ),

وَلَقَدْ رَءَاهُ بِٱلْأُفُقِ ٱلْمُبِينِ

Saw him [Jibrīl] on the clear horizon.

[*At-Takwīr* (81): 23]

He described Jibrīl as being,

شَدِيدُ ٱلْقُوَىٰ ﴿٥﴾

ذُو مِرَّةٍ فَٱسْتَوَىٰ ﴿٦﴾ وَهُوَ بِٱلْأُفُقِ ٱلْأَعْلَىٰ ﴿٧﴾ ثُمَّ دَنَا فَتَدَلَّىٰ ﴿٨﴾
فَكَانَ قَابَ قَوْسَيْنِ أَوْ أَدْنَىٰ ﴿٩﴾ فَأَوْحَىٰٓ إِلَىٰ عَبْدِهِۦ مَآ أَوْحَىٰ ﴿١٠﴾
مَا كَذَبَ ٱلْفُؤَادُ مَا رَأَىٰٓ ﴿١١﴾ أَفَتُمَٰرُونَهُۥ عَلَىٰ مَا يَرَىٰ ﴿١٢﴾ وَلَقَدْ رَءَاهُ
نَزْلَةً أُخْرَىٰ ﴿١٣﴾ عِندَ سِدْرَةِ ٱلْمُنتَهَىٰ ﴿١٤﴾ عِندَهَا جَنَّةُ ٱلْمَأْوَىٰٓ ﴿١٥﴾
إِذْ يَغْشَى ٱلسِّدْرَةَ مَا يَغْشَىٰ ﴿١٦﴾ مَا زَاغَ ٱلْبَصَرُ وَمَا طَغَىٰ ﴿١٧﴾ لَقَدْ رَأَىٰ
مِنْ ءَايَٰتِ رَبِّهِ ٱلْكُبْرَىٰٓ ﴿١٨﴾

...One intense in strength - one of soundness [in body and mind]. He rose to [his] true form while he was in the higher [part of the] horizon. Then he approached and descended and was at a distance of two bow lengths or nearer. And he revealed to His servant what he revealed. The heart did not lie about what it saw. So will you dispute with him over what he saw? And he certainly saw him in another descent. At the Lote Tree of the Utmost Boundary - near it is the Garden of Refuge [Paradise]. When there covered the Lote Tree that which covered [it]. The sight [of the Prophet (ﷺ)] did not swerve, nor did it transgress [its limit]. He certainly saw one of the greatest signs of his Lord.

[*An-Najm* (53): 5-18]

It is established in the Two Ṣaḥīḥs from ʿĀʾishah (*raḍiyAllāhu ʿanhā*) that

أنه لم يرَ جبريل في صورته التي خلق
عليها غير مرتين - يعني: المرة الأولى بالأفق الأعلى،
والنزلة الاخرى عند سدرة المنتهى

> The Prophet (ﷺ) did not see Jibrīl in his original form except on two occasions - the first on the Highest Horizon and the second at the Lote Tree at the Utmost Boundary. [30]

In another place Allāh described Jibrīl as being the Trustworthy Spirit, the Spirit of the Holy and other such descriptions which make clear that he is from the greatest, living, intelligent creatures of Allāh, the Exalted. He is an existing essence and is not a figment of imagination realising itself in the soul of the Prophet as claimed by those heretical philosophers and those claimants to *wilāyah* and more knowledge than the Prophets.

[11.6 The Deviancy of those who Believe in the Unity of Existence]

The reality of these people ends up in rejection of the foundations of faith, these being to believe in Allāh, His Angels, His Books, His Messengers and the Last Day. In reality they reject the Creator for they consider the existence of the creation to be the existence of the Creator. They said, 'Existence is one and the same' and hence failed to distinguish between oneness in actuality and oneness in genus. All of creation shares the fact that it is in existence just as all of mankind share the fact that they are humans and all animals share the fact that they belong to the animal kingdom. However, this general sharing is only so in ones mind for in reality the animalness to

[30] {F} A portion of a lengthy ḥadīth reported by Bukhārī [Eng. Trans. 6/359 no. 378] and Muslim [Eng. Trans. 1/111 no. 337].

be found in mankind is not the same as the animalness of animals. Similarly, the existence of the heavens is not one and the same thing as the existence of mankind. Therefore the existence of the Creator, Mighty and Magnificent, is not the same thing as the existence of the creation.

The reality of their saying is the same as the saying of Pharaoh who denied the Maker. Pharaoh never denied the existence of this creation and all that is physically witnessed, however he thought that he came into existence by himself and that nobody made him. These philosophers agreed with him in this but they thought that the creation was Allāh and therefore ended up in a misguidance greater and more severe than his, even though his position may outwardly seem to be more severe. It is for this reason that they considered those who worshiped idols to be, in reality, worshipping Allāh. They said, 'Because Pharaoh was in the position of leadership, having military backing, he said, 'I am your lord most high.' Meaning that if one considers that each and everyone of you are lords over what you possess, then I am the above all of you with respect to this due to what I have been granted, outwardly, of ruling amongst you.

They went on to say, 'When the magicians came to know of the truth that Pharaoh spoke, they affirmed it and said,

فَاقْضِ مَا أَنتَ قَاضٍ إِنَّمَا تَقْضِي هَٰذِهِ الْحَيَاةَ الدُّنْيَا ﴿٧٢﴾

So decree whatever you are to decree. You can only decree for this worldly life.

[*Ṭā Hā* (20): 72]'

They said, 'therefore the saying of Pharaoh,

فَقَالَ أَنَا رَبُّكُمُ الْأَعْلَىٰ ﴿٢٤﴾

I am your lord most high.

[*An-Nāzi'āt* (79): 24]

Was correct and he was the actual manifestation of the Truth.'[31]

Then they proceeded to reject the reality of the Last Day, they stated that the denizens of the Fire would be in bliss just as the People of the Fire would be in bliss. Therefore they ended up disbelieving in Allāh, the Last Day, His Angels, His Books and His Messengers. Their claim of being the elite of the elite, the *Awliyā'* of Allāh, that they were better than the Prophets, that the Prophets only came to know Allāh by way of their niche was rendered meaningless and false.

[11.6.1 The Source of the Heretical Ṣūfis]

This is not the place to detail the heresy of these people.[32] We have only mentioned them here because the discussion is concerning the *Awliyā* of Allāh and their distinction from the *awliyā'* of Shayṭān, and these people are the most frequent claimants whereas in reality they are the greatest *awliyā'* of Shayṭān. This is why the generality of their words arise from satanic states and conditions. They say, as was stated by the author of *'al-Futūḥāt'*, 'Chapter: the land of reality' and they meant by this the land of imagination.

So it becomes known that the reality that he spoke of was nothing more than imaginations, which is the arena in which Shayṭān does his work, for he makes man imagine things that are contrary to their true state. Allāh, the Exalted says,

---

[31] {Y} ibn Arabī, *'Fuṣūṣ'* [1/210-211].

[32] {Y} Refer to ibn Taymiyyah, *'Majmū' Fatawā'* [2/134-185]; *'ar-Radd 'alā ibn 'Arabī fī Da'wā īmān Fir'awn'* [pp. 203-216].

وَمَن يَعْشُ عَن ذِكْرِ ٱلرَّحْمَٰنِ نُقَيِّضْ لَهُۥ شَيْطَٰنًا
فَهُوَ لَهُۥ قَرِينٌ ﴿٣٦﴾ وَإِنَّهُمْ لَيَصُدُّونَهُمْ عَنِ ٱلسَّبِيلِ وَيَحْسَبُونَ
أَنَّهُم مُّهْتَدُونَ ﴿٣٧﴾ حَتَّىٰٓ إِذَا جَآءَنَا قَالَ يَٰلَيْتَ بَيْنِى وَبَيْنَكَ
بُعْدَ ٱلْمَشْرِقَيْنِ فَبِئْسَ ٱلْقَرِينُ ﴿٣٨﴾ وَلَن يَنفَعَكُمُ ٱلْيَوْمَ
إِذ ظَّلَمْتُمْ أَنَّكُمْ فِى ٱلْعَذَابِ مُشْتَرِكُونَ ﴿٣٩﴾

And whoever is blinded from the remembrance of the Most Merciful - We appoint for him a devil and he is to him a companion. And indeed, they [the devils] divert them from the way [of guidance] while they think that they are rightly guided. Until, when he comes to Us, he says, 'Oh, I wish there was between me and you a distance [like that] between the east and west - how wretched a companion!' Never will it benefit you that Day, when you have [already previously] wronged, and you are [all] sharing in the punishment.

[*Az-Zukhruf* (43): 36-39]

إِنَّ ٱللَّهَ لَا يَغْفِرُ أَن يُشْرَكَ بِهِۦ وَيَغْفِرُ مَا دُونَ
ذَٰلِكَ لِمَن يَشَآءُ ۚ وَمَن يُشْرِكْ بِٱللَّهِ فَقَدْ ضَلَّ ضَلَٰلًۢا بَعِيدًا
﴿١١٦﴾ إِن يَدْعُونَ مِن دُونِهِۦٓ إِلَّآ إِنَٰثًا وَإِن يَدْعُونَ
إِلَّا شَيْطَٰنًا مَّرِيدًا ﴿١١٧﴾ لَّعَنَهُ ٱللَّهُ ۘ وَقَالَ لَأَتَّخِذَنَّ
مِنْ عِبَادِكَ نَصِيبًا مَّفْرُوضًا ﴿١١٨﴾ وَلَأُضِلَّنَّهُمْ وَلَأُمَنِّيَنَّهُمْ
وَلَءَامُرَنَّهُمْ فَلَيُبَتِّكُنَّ ءَاذَانَ ٱلْأَنْعَٰمِ وَلَءَامُرَنَّهُمْ
فَلَيُغَيِّرُنَّ خَلْقَ ٱللَّهِ ۚ وَمَن يَتَّخِذِ ٱلشَّيْطَٰنَ وَلِيًّا
مِّن دُونِ ٱللَّهِ فَقَدْ خَسِرَ خُسْرَانًا مُّبِينًا ﴿١١٩﴾
يَعِدُهُمْ وَيُمَنِّيهِمْ ۖ وَمَا يَعِدُهُمُ ٱلشَّيْطَٰنُ إِلَّا غُرُورًا ﴿١٢٠﴾

Indeed, Allāh does not forgive association with Him, but He forgives what is less than that for whom He Wills. Whoever associates others with Allāh has certainly gone far astray... He [Shayṭān] promises them and arouses desire in them. But Shayṭān does not promise them except delusion.

[*An-Nisā'* (4): 116-120]

وَقَالَ الشَّيْطَٰنُ
لَمَّا قُضِيَ الْأَمْرُ إِنَّ اللَّهَ وَعَدَكُمْ وَعْدَ الْحَقِّ وَوَعَدتُّكُمْ
فَأَخْلَفْتُكُمْ ۖ وَمَا كَانَ لِيَ عَلَيْكُم مِّن سُلْطَٰنٍ إِلَّا أَن دَعَوْتُكُمْ
فَاسْتَجَبْتُمْ لِي ۖ فَلَا تَلُومُونِي وَلُومُوا أَنفُسَكُم ۖ مَّا أَنَا۠
بِمُصْرِخِكُمْ وَمَا أَنتُم بِمُصْرِخِيَّ ۖ إِنِّي كَفَرْتُ بِمَا
أَشْرَكْتُمُونِ مِن قَبْلُ ۗ إِنَّ الظَّٰلِمِينَ لَهُمْ عَذَابٌ أَلِيمٌ

And Shayṭān will say when the matter has been concluded, 'Indeed Allāh had promised you the promise of truth. I promised you, but I betrayed you, I had no authority over you except that I invited you and you responded to me. So do not blame me; but blame yourselves. I cannot be called to your aid, nor can you be called to my aid. Indeed I deny your prior association of me [with Allāh]. Indeed for the wrongdoers is a painful punishment.'

[*Ibrāhīm* (14): 22]

وَإِذْ زَيَّنَ لَهُمُ
الشَّيْطَٰنُ أَعْمَٰلَهُمْ وَقَالَ لَا غَالِبَ لَكُمُ الْيَوْمَ مِنَ
النَّاسِ وَإِنِّي جَارٌ لَّكُمْ ۖ فَلَمَّا تَرَاءَتِ الْفِئَتَانِ نَكَصَ
عَلَىٰ عَقِبَيْهِ وَقَالَ إِنِّي بَرِيءٌ مِّنكُمْ إِنِّي أَرَىٰ مَا لَا تَرَوْنَ
إِنِّي أَخَافُ اللَّهَ ۚ وَاللَّهُ شَدِيدُ الْعِقَابِ ﴿٤٨﴾

> And [remember] when Shayṭān made their deeds pleasing to them and said, 'None can overcome you today from among the people, and indeed I am your protector.' But when the two armies sighted each other, he turned on his heels and said, 'Indeed I am free of you; indeed I see what you do not see; indeed I fear Allāh and Allāh is severe in punishment.
>
> [*Al-Anfāl* (8): 48]

In the authentic ḥadīth it is reported that the Prophet (ﷺ) saw Jibrīl arraying the Angels in ranks.[33]

When the devils see the Angels of Allāh who have been commissioned to aid His servants, they flee from them. Indeed Allāh Aids His believing servants through the Angels. Allāh, the Exalted says,

إِذْ يُوحِي رَبُّكَ إِلَى ٱلْمَلَٰٓئِكَةِ أَنِّي مَعَكُمْ فَثَبِّتُوا۟ ٱلَّذِينَ ءَامَنُوا۟ۚ

> [Remember] when your Lord inspired to the Angels, 'I am with you, so strengthen those who have believed.'
>
> [*Al-Anfāl* (8): 12]

يَٰٓأَيُّهَا ٱلَّذِينَ ءَامَنُوا۟ ٱذْكُرُوا۟ نِعْمَةَ ٱللَّهِ عَلَيْكُمْ إِذْ جَآءَتْكُمْ
جُنُودٌ فَأَرْسَلْنَا عَلَيْهِمْ رِيحًا وَجُنُودًا لَّمْ تَرَوْهَاۚ

> O you who have believed! Remember the favour of Allāh upon you when the armies came to [attack] you and We sent upon them a wind and armies [of Angels] you did not see.
>
> [*Al-Aḥzāb* (33): 9]

---

[33] {F} Reported by Mālik [Eng. Trans. p. 195 no. 937] and 'Abdur-Razzāq, *'Muṣannaf'* [no. 8832].

I say: it is *mursal ṣaḥīḥ*.

إِذْ يَقُولُ لِصَٰحِبِهِۦ لَا تَحْزَنْ إِنَّ ٱللَّهَ مَعَنَا ۖ فَأَنزَلَ ٱللَّهُ سَكِينَتَهُۥ عَلَيْهِ وَأَيَّدَهُۥ بِجُنُودٍ لَّمْ تَرَوْهَا

When he [Muḥammad] said to his companion [Abū Bakr], 'Do not despair, indeed Allāh is with us.' And Allāh sent down his tranquillity upon him and supported him with soldiers [the Angels] that you did not see.

[*At-Tawbah* (9): 40]

إِذْ تَقُولُ لِلْمُؤْمِنِينَ أَلَن يَكْفِيَكُمْ أَن يُمِدَّكُمْ رَبُّكُم بِثَلَٰثَةِ ءَالَٰفٍ مِّنَ ٱلْمَلَٰٓئِكَةِ مُنزَلِينَ ﴿١٢٤﴾ بَلَىٰٓ ۚ إِن تَصْبِرُوا۟ وَتَتَّقُوا۟ وَيَأْتُوكُم مِّن فَوْرِهِمْ هَٰذَا يُمْدِدْكُمْ رَبُّكُم بِخَمْسَةِ ءَالَٰفٍ مِّنَ ٱلْمَلَٰٓئِكَةِ مُسَوِّمِينَ

[Remember] when you said to the believers, 'is it not sufficient for you that your Lord should reinforce you with three thousand Angels sent down? Yes, if you remain patient and conscious of Allāh and they [the enemy] come upon you [attacking] in rage, your Lord will reinforce you with five thousand Angels having marks [of distinction].'

[*Āli 'Imrān* (3): 124-125]

However, certain spirits come to and address these people and take certain forms for them, these spirits are none other than the Jinn and devils which they believe to be Angels. These are the same types of spirits that address those who worship idols and stars.

Their first spokesman amongst the followers of Islām was al-Mukhtār bin Abū 'Ubaid, the Prophet (ﷺ) spoke of him in the ḥadīth reported by Muslim,

«سيكون في ثقيف كذّاب ومبير»

"There will arise a great liar and a wreaker of havoc from Thaqīf."[34]

The great liar was this Mukhtār bin Abū 'Ubaid and the wreaker of havoc was al-Ḥajjāj bin Yūsuf. It was said to ibn 'Umar and ibn 'Abbās, 'al-Mukhtār thinks that he has [inspiration] sent to him.' They said, 'Allāh, the Exalted, spoke truthfully when he said,

هَلۡ أُنَبِّئُكُمۡ عَلَىٰ مَن تَنَزَّلُ ٱلشَّيَٰطِينُ ﴿٢٢١﴾ تَنَزَّلُ عَلَىٰ كُلِّ أَفَّاكٍ أَثِيمٖ ﴿٢٢٢﴾

> Shall I inform you upon whom the devils descend? They descend upon every sinful liar.
>
> [*Ash-Shu'arā'* (26): 221-222][35]

Another person was asked, 'al-Mukhtār thinks that he is inspired.' He replied, 'Allāh, the Exalted says,

وَإِنَّ ٱلشَّيَٰطِينَ لَيُوحُونَ إِلَىٰٓ
أَوۡلِيَآئِهِمۡ لِيُجَٰدِلُوكُمۡۖ وَإِنۡ أَطَعۡتُمُوهُمۡ إِنَّكُمۡ لَمُشۡرِكُونَ ﴿١٢١﴾

> Indeed the devils inspire their allies [among men] to dispute with you...
>
> [*Al-An'ām* (6): 121]'[36]

These satanic spirits are the same spirits that the author of *'al-Futūḥāt'* thought dictated his book to him. This is why he mentioned different methods of seclusion, eating only specific types of food

---

[34] {F} Reported by Muslim [Eng. Trans. 4/1351 no. 6176] and Aḥmad [6/351-352].

[35] {Y} Reported by at-Ṭabarī from 'Abdullāh bin Zubair [19/126] and ibn 'Abbās [12/86]. I have not come across a narration from ibn 'Umar concerning this.

[36] {Y} Reported from ibn 'Abbās by at-Ṭabarī [12/86].

and undertaking specific activities. Such matters open the door to contact with the Jinn and devils although the people performing them come to think that these are the miracles accorded to the *Awliyā'*, when in reality they are just satanic states. I know a number of these types of people, some of them are carried through the air to a distant place and then returned, others are given stolen property - stolen by the devils and given to them, yet others direct the people to find their stolen property in return for some reward or wage and the likes.

Because the states of these people are satanic, they are in open contravention to the Messengers (ﷺ) as can be seen in the words of the author of *'al-Futūḥāt'* and *'al-Fuṣūṣ.'* For example, one finds that he praises the disbelievers such as the people of Noah, Hud, Pharaoh and others. He opposes the Prophets such as Noah, Abraham, Moses and Aaron. He censures the praiseworthy *shaykhs* of the Muslims such as al-Junaid bin Muḥammad, Sahl bin 'Abdullāh at-Tustorī and their likes. He commends those who have been censured by the Muslims such as al-Ḥallāj and others. All of this has been mentioned by him in his imaginary, satanic visions.

[11.6.2 Between ibn al-Arabī and al-Junaid]

Indeed al-Junaid, may Allāh sanctify his soul, was from the *Imāms* of true guidance, he was asked about *Tawḥīd* to which he replied, '*Tawḥīd* is to single out the created from the Eternal.'[37] Therefore he explained that *Tawḥīd* was to differentiate between that which is brought into being and the Eternal, between the Creator and created.

The author of *'al-Fuṣūṣ'* rejected this reality and said during one of his imaginary, satanic discourses,

[37] {F} Abū Nu'aym, *'al-Ḥilyah'* [10/256-291].

> O Junaid! Who can differentiate between that brought into being and the Eternal except one who is neither of the two?

Therefore he declared the statement of al-Junaid to be erroneous based upon his premise that the existence of that brought into being is one and the same as the existence of the Eternal. He said in his *'al-Fuṣūṣ,'*

> One of His Beautiful and Perfect Names is the Most High (*Al-'Aliy*). The Most High over whom? What is there but Him? The Most High from what? There is no he but He! So His Highness is for Himself, He is all that is in existence. [These] named existences are ephemeral, they are exalted in their essence for they are none but He...
>
> He is actually all that is hidden, He is actually all that is apparent, it is not possible to see other than Him, and there is none to speak for Him other than him. He is the one called Abū Sa'īd al-Kharrāz and other such names of ephemeral beings.[38]

It is said to this heretic, 'Who puts the conditions that the one to differentiate between two things must be a third person?' Every single person is able to differentiate between himself and other than him, yet he is not some third person! The servant knows that he is a servant and hence differentiates between himself and his Creator. The Creator, Mighty and Magnificent, differentiates between Himself and other than Him, knowing that He is their Lord and they are His servants. This has been spoken of by the Qur'ān in more than one place, and for the believers who believe in it inwardly and outwardly, it is the place to look for proof.

---

[38] {Y} ibn Arabī, *'al-Fuṣūṣ'* [1/76-77].

As for these heretics, they think as thought by at-Talmasānī, who was one of the most skilled of them in this incarnationist theory. When *'al-Fuṣūṣ'* was read to him and it was said to him,

> "'The Qur'ān contradicts this book [that you read].' He replied, 'the whole of the Qur'ān, in its entirety is *shirk* and *Tawḥīd* is only to be found in our words.' It was then asked of him, 'If all of existence is one and the same then why is ones wife lawful [for him] but his sister not?' He replied, 'It is all lawful in our view, however those people who have been veiled [from the 'true reality'] say that it is unlawful so we say, 'It is unlawful for you.'"

This stance, alongside its serious disbelief, is obviously self-contradictory. If all of existence is one and the same, then who is the veiled and who is the veiler? This is why when one of their *shaykhs* said to his disciple, 'Whosoever tells you that there is something in existence apart from Allāh has lied,' the disciple replied, 'So who is the one who lies?'

They said to another [disciple], 'These are merely outward forms,' he asked, 'Are these outward forms other than what they seem to be or are they the same? If they are other, you have spoken in relative terms and if they are the same, there is no difference [between the forms and the reality].'

We have a detailed discussion unveiling the truth about these people in another place wherein we have explained the true imports of the saying of each of them.[39] [For example] the author of *'al-Fuṣūṣ'* said, 'That which is not in existence is something, and the existence

[39] {Y} Refer to his works, *'Ḥaqīqah Madhāhib al-Ittiḥādiyyah', 'al-Ḥujaj al-'Aqaliyyah wa an-Naqaliyyah fīmā Yūnāfī al-Islām min Bida' al-Jahmiyyah wa as-Ṣūfiyyah', 'ar-Radd al-Aqwam 'alā mā fī Fuṣūṣ al-Ḥikam'* all contained in his *'Majmū' Fatāwā'* [2/134-451]. Also refer to his, *'Bayān Talbīs al-Jahmiyyah'* [2/537].

of the Truth [Allāh] engulfs both [that which is present and absent],' and hence is forced to distinguish between actual existence (*wujūd*) and presence (*thubūt*).[40]

The *Mu'tazilah* who say, 'That which is not in existence is something present in reality,' are better than him, despite their also being misguided. They say, 'The Lord has created an existence for those things that are present in non-existence, an existence which is not the same as the existence of the Lord,' whereas he believes the actual existence of the Lord engulfs both the existing and non-existing. So in his view there is nothing that is created in existence that is separate from the existence of the Creator. His student, ad-Durr al-Qunawī differentiated between the absolute existence and actual existence because he was closer to philosophy than his teacher and therefore did not accept that which was not in existence was something. However he considered the Truth to be the absolute and total existence and authored a work entitled, *'Miftāḥ Ghayb al-Jam' wa al-Wujūd.'* [41]

This opinion enters the realms of negating the Creator and affirming his non-existence. This is because the absolute, when taken with the condition that it is unrestricted, and this is what is known as the rational universal, only exists in ones mind and thoughts and not in reality. As for the absolute that does not have this condition, it is known as the physical universal.[42] If they say, 'He is in existence in

---

[40] {T} Meaning by this the affirmation of that which is not in existence. For example if it is said that A did not kill B, then this is provable although it did not actually occur.

[41] {Y} Mentioned by Ḥājī Khalīfah, *'Kashf adh-Ẓunūn'* [2/1768] under the name *'Miftāḥ al-Ghayb'*

[42] {T} Which refers to individual existing things in reality. Here the author is using =

reality [outside of ones mind]' then in reality one finds only specific, existing objects. Therefore He is a part of these specific, existing objects in the view of those who affirm His existence in reality [outside of mere thoughts and imagination]. Hence it is necessary that the existence of the Lord either be non-existent in reality, or it be a part of the existence of the creation, or it be the very same existence as that of the creation. So can a portion of the whole create the whole, or can something create itself? Can that which is non-existent create the existent? Can a portion of something create the whole thing?

These people flee from the word incarnation (*ḥulūl*) because it necessitates a subsistent (*ḥāl*) and a substratum (*maḥall*),[43] and from the word unification (*ittiḥād*) because it necessitates that there be two things, one of which unifies with the other. In their view, the existence is one and the same and the Christians disbelieved because they specified divinity to the Messiah, saying that he was Allāh, but had they generalised [to the whole of creation] then they would not have disbelieved.

They said the same thing concerning the worshippers of idols, they erred by worshipping only some of these outward forms, had they worshipped everything then they would not have been in error. The Gnostic who has actualised the reality, in their view, is one who is not harmed by the worship of idols.

This stance, alongside its serious disbelief, is self-contradictory from

=

their theory which states that things either exist as an imaginable reality in ones mind and/or they exist as actual objects in the real world. Therefore the theory necessitates that either Allāh only exists in ones imagination or He is a definable object in the real world. He then proceeds to point out the logical inconsistencies in this theory.

[43] {T} Refer to *'at-Ta'rīfāt'* [pg. 125] for a more detailed definition of these terms.

beginning to end. It is asked of them, 'Who is the one who has erred?' However they say, 'The Lord is described with all the defects that the creation are described with and that the creation are described with all of the perfect attributes that the Lord is described with.' They state, as was said by the author of *'al-Fuṣūṣ'*,

> The Most High for Himself is the One Who possesses perfection which encompasses every description in existence and every non-existent relation, regardless of whether this is praiseworthy according to custom, intellect, or legislation, or it is blameworthy according to custom, intellect, or legislation. All of this is for He Who is called Allāh, exclusively.[44]

This stance, alongside its serious disbelief, can never be free of self-contradiction. It is known through physical experience and intellect that the praiseworthy characteristics are not the same as the blameworthy, but they say as was stated by at-Talmasānī, 'That which contradicts reason becomes established in our view by way of unveiling of the realities (*kashf*).' They also say, 'Whosoever desires to actualise the realities - meaning their realities - then let him abandon the intellect and the *Sharī'ah*.'

I said to one of them, in the course of a discussion with him,

> It is known that the unveiling of the Prophets is greater and more complete than the unveiling of other than them. The information they give us is more truthful than the information presented by other than them. The Prophets (ﷺ) inform us of that which the intellects of man are incapable of coming to know, they do not inform us of that which the intellects of man know is impossible. Therefore they inform mankind of that which there in-

[44] {Y} Ibn Arabī, *'al-Fuṣūṣ'* [1/76-77].

> tellects can comprehend, not that which is impossible for them to comprehend. It is not possible that the information that the Messenger gives contradict sound intellects and it is not possible that two definitive evidences contradict each other, regardless if they both be intellectual or textual, or one be intellectual and the other be textual. So what is the case of someone who claims unveiling which contradicts both the sound intellect and the *Sharīʿah*?!

It is possible that these people not deliberately lie but rather they imagine certain things that [represent] pre-existing notions in themselves and they think that these imaginations are in fact real. It is also possible that they see other things that do really exist but believe them to be the miracles of the righteous when in fact they arise due to the deceptions of the devils.

[11.6.3 The Stages of Gnosis with the Heretical *Ṣūfis*]

These people who believe in the Unity of Existence possibly place the *Awliyāʾ* before the Prophets and mention that prophecy has not come to an end as was mentioned by ibn Sabʿīn and others. They believe [that the Gnostic passes through] three stages, saying:

1. The servant first witnesses obedience and disobedience.

2. Then there is obedience without disobedience.

3. Then there is no obedience or disobedience.

As for the first stage then this is correct for it differentiates between obedience and disobedience.

As for the second stage then what they mean is that the servant witnesses the Decree [to such an extent that he no longer sees himself as having any freewill whatsoever]. This was further articulated by some of them when they said, 'I disbelieve in a Lord Who is disobeyed.' Such a person thinks that disobedience is to oppose the Desire [of Allāh] which is the same as [His] Will and that the whole of creation is subject to His Will [and therefore He cannot be disobeyed]. Their poet says,

I awoke doing whatsoever You Willed of me
Therefore everything I do is obedience to You

It is known that this contradicts that which Allāh sent His Messengers with and revealed in His Books. This is because the disobedience that makes its perpetrator deserve blame and punishment is that which opposes the command of Allāh and His Messenger. Allāh, the Exalted says,

تِلْكَ حُدُودُ ٱللَّهِ ۚ وَمَن يُطِعِ ٱللَّهَ وَرَسُولَهُۥ
يُدْخِلْهُ جَنَّـٰتٍ تَجْرِى مِن تَحْتِهَا ٱلْأَنْهَـٰرُ
خَـٰلِدِينَ فِيهَا ۚ وَذَٰلِكَ ٱلْفَوْزُ ٱلْعَظِيمُ ﴿١٣﴾
وَمَن يَعْصِ ٱللَّهَ وَرَسُولَهُۥ وَيَتَعَدَّ حُدُودَهُۥ يُدْخِلْهُ
نَارًا خَـٰلِدًا فِيهَا وَلَهُۥ عَذَابٌ مُّهِينٌ ﴿١٤﴾

These are the limits set by Allāh, and whoever obeys Allāh and His Messenger will be admitted by Him to Gardens beneath which rivers flow, abiding eternally therein; and that is the great achievement. And whoever disobeys Allāh and His Messenger and transgresses his limits - He will make him to enter the Fire, to abide therein for eternity; and he will have a humiliating punishment.

[*An-Nisā'* (4): 13-14]

We shall soon mention the difference between the Universal Will and the Religious Will and the difference between the Universal Command and the Religious Command.[45]

This issue [of Decree] has confused a group of the *Ṣūfis* and al-Junaid, may Allāh have mercy upon him, explained it for them. Therefore whosoever follows al-Junaid is firmly upon the Straight Path but whosoever opposes him has been misguided. This is because they went to extremes in the belief that everything occurs by the Will and Decree of Allāh just as they went to extremes in their witnessing of this *Tawḥīd* which they called the First Union. Al-Junaid explained to them that it was necessary to witness a second matter, this was that along with witnessing the fact that everything falls under the Will, Decree and creation of Allāh it is necessary to differentiate between that which He Commands, Loves, and is Pleased with and between that which He Prohibits, Hates and Angers Him. Therefore one has to differentiate between His *Awliyā'* and His enemies as He says,

أَفَنَجْعَلُ ٱلْمُسْلِمِينَ كَٱلْمُجْرِمِينَ ﴿٣٥﴾ مَا لَكُمْ كَيْفَ تَحْكُمُونَ ﴿٣٦﴾

> Then should We treat the Muslims like the criminals? What is [the matter] with you? How do you judge?
>
> [*Al-Qalam* (68): 35-36]

أَمْ نَجْعَلُ ٱلَّذِينَ ءَامَنُوا۟ وَعَمِلُوا۟
ٱلصَّٰلِحَٰتِ كَٱلْمُفْسِدِينَ فِى ٱلْأَرْضِ أَمْ نَجْعَلُ ٱلْمُتَّقِينَ كَٱلْفُجَّارِ

> Or should We treat those who believe and do righteous deeds like corrupters in the land? Or should We treat those who fear Allāh like the wicked.
>
> [*Ṣād* (38): 28]

---

[45] {T} In the following chapters.

أَمْ حَسِبَ ٱلَّذِينَ ٱجْتَرَحُوا۟ ٱلسَّيِّـَٔاتِ أَن نَّجْعَلَهُمْ كَٱلَّذِينَ ءَامَنُوا۟ وَعَمِلُوا۟ ٱلصَّـٰلِحَـٰتِ سَوَآءً مَّحْيَاهُمْ وَمَمَاتُهُمْ ۚ سَآءَ مَا يَحْكُمُونَ ﴿٢١﴾

Or do those who commit evil deeds think that We will make them like those who have believed and done righteous deeds - [make them] equal in their life and their death. Evil is that which they judge.

[*Al-Jāthiyah* (45): 21]

وَمَا يَسْتَوِى ٱلْأَعْمَىٰ وَٱلْبَصِيرُ وَٱلَّذِينَ ءَامَنُوا۟ وَعَمِلُوا۟ ٱلصَّـٰلِحَـٰتِ وَلَا ٱلْمُسِىٓءُ ۚ قَلِيلًا مَّا تَتَذَكَّرُونَ ﴿٥٨﴾

Not equal are the blind and the seeing, nor are those who believe and do righteous deeds and the evil doer. Little do you remember.

[*Ghāfir* (40): 58]

It is for this reason that the belief of the *Salaf* of this nation and their *Imāms* was that Allāh is the Creator of everything, its Lord and its Owner. Whatsoever He Wills is and Whatsoever He does not Will is not. There is no Lord other than Him yet despite this He has enjoined obedience and forbidden disobedience. He does not Love corruption and is not Pleased with disbelief for His servants. He does not enjoin shameful and indecent deeds even though they occur by His Will, but He does not Love them and is not Pleased with them, instead He Hates them and censures those who commit them and punishes them.

As for the third stage which is neither to witness obedience nor disobedience then this is because the servant now thinks the whole of existence to be one and the same. In their view, this is the peak of realisation and the height of closeness and allegiance to Allāh! In reality however, this view is the pinnacle of incarnation with regards to the Names of Allāh and His signs and the height of enmity to Allāh. This is because the witnesser of this stage considers the Jews, Christians and the entirety of the disbelievers to be from the *Awliyā'* of Allāh. Allāh, the Exalted says,

وَمَن يَتَوَلَّهُم مِّنكُمْ فَإِنَّهُۥ مِنْهُمْ

> And whoever among you is an ally to them - then indeed he is [one] of them.
>
> [*Al-Mā'idah* (5): 51]

Such a person does not declare himself free of *shirk* and the worship of idols and thereby ejects himself from the religion of Abraham, the Beloved of Allāh (*'alayhi as-salām*). Allāh, the Exalted says,

قَدْ كَانَتْ لَكُمْ أُسْوَةٌ حَسَنَةٌ فِىٓ إِبْرَٰهِيمَ وَٱلَّذِينَ مَعَهُۥٓ إِذْ قَالُوا۟ لِقَوْمِهِمْ إِنَّا بُرَءَٰٓؤُا۟ مِنكُمْ وَمِمَّا تَعْبُدُونَ مِن دُونِ ٱللَّهِ كَفَرْنَا بِكُمْ وَبَدَا بَيْنَنَا وَبَيْنَكُمُ ٱلْعَدَٰوَةُ وَٱلْبَغْضَآءُ أَبَدًا حَتَّىٰ تُؤْمِنُوا۟ بِٱللَّهِ وَحْدَهُۥٓ

> There has already been an excellent example for you in Abraham and those with him; when they said to their people, 'Indeed we are free of you and whatever you worship besides Allāh. We have denied you and there has appeared between us and you hatred and animosity until you believe in Allāh Alone.'
>
> [*Al-Mumtaḥinah* (60): 4]

The Beloved of Allāh (*'alayhi as-salām*) said to his polytheistic people,

أَنتُمْ
وَءَابَآؤُكُمُ ٱلْأَقْدَمُونَ ﴿٧٦﴾ فَإِنَّهُمْ عَدُوٌّ لِّىٓ إِلَّا رَبَّ ٱلْعَٰلَمِينَ

He said, 'Then do you see what you have been worshipping, you and your ancient forefathers? Indeed they are enemies to me, except the Lord of the worlds.'

[*Ash-Shu'arā'* (26): 75-77]

Allāh, the Exalted says,

لَّا تَجِدُ قَوْمًا يُؤْمِنُونَ بِٱللَّهِ وَٱلْيَوْمِ ٱلْآخِرِ يُوَآدُّونَ مَنْ حَآدَّ ٱللَّهَ وَرَسُولَهُۥ وَلَوْ كَانُوٓا۟ ءَابَآءَهُمْ أَوْ أَبْنَآءَهُمْ أَوْ إِخْوَٰنَهُمْ أَوْ عَشِيرَتَهُمْ ۚ أُو۟لَٰٓئِكَ كَتَبَ فِى قُلُوبِهِمُ ٱلْإِيمَٰنَ وَأَيَّدَهُم بِرُوحٍ مِّنْهُ

You will not find a people who believe in Allāh and the Last Day having affection for those who oppose Allāh and His Messenger, even if they were their fathers or their sons or their brothers or their kindred. Those - He has decreed faith within their hearts and supported them with spirit from Him.

[*Al-Mujādilah* (58): 22]

Some of these people authored books and poems promoting their beliefs such as the poem of ibn al-Fāriḍ entitled, *'Nadham as-Sulūk'* in which he writes,

I establish my prayers at my station to her [46]
I bear witness in them that she also prayed to me.
Both of us are the ones performing prayer,

[46] {T} It is known that in the poetry of ibn al-Fāriḍ, the feminine pronoun refers to Allāh, and refuge is sought with Allāh!

as one prostrating to his reality,
Every prostration performed in union
It is not for me to pray to other than me
Not a single *rakʿah* of prayer was performed
to other than me...
I am still her and she is still me
There is no difference, rather my self prayed to my self
To me as a messenger, I was sent from myself [47]
My self used my signs to prove my existence
If someone called upon me,
I would be the one who responded
If I was the one supplicated to,
she would answer whosoever called me
with acceptance [48]

And other similar statements. This is why this person spoke the following lines of poetry at his death,

If my rank in love amongst you
Is what I have suffered from you then
I have certainly wasted my days
A vain wish which my soul lived for, for a time
Today I believe that they were but false dreams [49]

He thought that he was Allāh but when the Angels of Allāh came to take his soul, he realised the fallacy of what he believed.

[47] {T} i.e. he is the messenger and he is the one who sent the messenger.

[48] {Y} ibn Fāriḍ, *'Dīwān'* [p. 97].

[49] {Y} Ibid. [p. 81].

[11.6.4 Some Evidences Refuting those who Believe in the Unity of Existence]

Allāh, the Exalted says,

سَبَّحَ لِلَّهِ مَا فِي ٱلسَّمَٰوَٰتِ وَٱلْأَرْضِ ۖ وَهُوَ ٱلْعَزِيزُ ٱلْحَكِيمُ ﴿١﴾

> Whatever is in the heavens and earth exalts [the praises of] Allāh; and He is the Exalted in Might, the Wise.
>
> [*Al-Ḥadīd* (57): 1]

Therefore everything in the heavens and the earth glorifies the praises of Allāh. It is not Allāh. Then Allāh proceeds to say,

لَهُۥ مُلْكُ
ٱلسَّمَٰوَٰتِ وَٱلْأَرْضِ ۖ يُحْيِۦ وَيُمِيتُ ۖ وَهُوَ عَلَىٰ كُلِّ شَيْءٍ قَدِيرٌ ﴿٢﴾
هُوَ ٱلْأَوَّلُ وَٱلْءَاخِرُ وَٱلظَّٰهِرُ وَٱلْبَاطِنُ ۖ وَهُوَ بِكُلِّ شَيْءٍ عَلِيمٌ ﴿٣﴾

> His is the dominion of the heavens and earth. He gives life and causes death, and He is over all things powerful. He is the First and the Last, the Ascendant and the Intimate; and He Knows all things.
>
> [*Al-Ḥadīd* (57): 2-3]

In Ṣaḥīḥ Muslim it is reported that the Prophet (ﷺ) used to say in his supplication,

اللَّهُمَّ رَبَّ السَّمَوَاتِ السَّبْعِ، وَرَبَّ الْعَرْشِ الْعَظِيمِ، رَبَّنَا وَرَبَّ كُلِّ شَيْءٍ، فَالِقَ الْحَبِّ وَالنَّوَى وَمُنَزِّلَ التَّوْرَاةِ وَالإِنْجِيلِ، وَالْفُرْقَانِ، أَعُوذُ بِكَ مِنْ شَرِّ كُلِّ شَيْءٍ أَنْتَ آخِذٌ بِنَاصِيَتِهِ. اللَّهُمَّ أَنْتَ الأَوَّلُ فَلَيْسَ قَبْلَكَ شَيْءٌ، وَأَنْتَ الآخِرُ فَلَيْسَ بَعْدَكَ شَيْءٌ، وَأَنْتَ الظَّاهِرُ فَلَيْسَ فَوْقَكَ شَيْءٌ، وَأَنْتَ الْبَاطِنُ فَلَيْسَ دُونَكَ شَيْءٌ. اقْضِ عَنَّا الدَّيْنَ وَأَغْنِنَا مِنَ الْفَقْرِ.

> *"O Allāh! The Lord of the seven heavens and the lord of the Great Throne; our Lord and the Lord of everything. The Splitter of the grain and seed, the One Who revealed the Torah, Injeel and Qur'ān. I take refuge with You from every creature whose forelock You hold. You are the First, there was nothing before You; You are the Last, there is nothing after You; You are the Manifest, there is nothing above You; You are the Inward, there is nothing beyond You. Remove the burden of debt from me and relieve me from poverty."* [50]

Then He says,

هُوَ ٱلَّذِى خَلَقَ ٱلسَّمَٰوَٰتِ وَٱلْأَرْضَ فِى سِتَّةِ أَيَّامٍ ثُمَّ ٱسْتَوَىٰ
عَلَى ٱلْعَرْشِ ۚ يَعْلَمُ مَا يَلِجُ فِى ٱلْأَرْضِ وَمَا يَخْرُجُ مِنْهَا وَمَا يَنزِلُ مِنَ
ٱلسَّمَآءِ وَمَا يَعْرُجُ فِيهَا ۖ وَهُوَ مَعَكُمْ أَيْنَ مَا كُنتُمْ ۚ

> It is He Who created the heavens and earth in Six Days and then Rose over the Throne. He knows what penetrates into the earth and what emerges from it and what descends from the heaven and what ascends therein; and He is with you wherever you are.
>
> [*Al-Ḥadīd* (57): 4]

Hence He mentions that the Heavens and the earth, and in another places He adds, *"and everything between them,"* is created and praising Him. He also informs us that He Knows everything.

As for His saying,

وَهُوَ مَعَكُمْ

And He is with you

[*Al-Ḥadīd* (57): 4]

---

[50] {F} Reported by Muslim [Eng. Trans. 4/1422 no. 6551] and Abū Dāwūd [Eng. Trans. 3/1403 no. 5033].

Then the word *maʿa* (with) does not necessitate that one of two things be mixed with the other according to the rules of the Arabic language. This is like His, the Exalted's saying,

اتَّقُوا اللَّهَ وَكُونُوا مَعَ الصَّادِقِينَ

Fear Allāh and be with those who are true.

[*At-Tawbah* (9): 119]

مُحَمَّدٌ رَسُولُ اللَّهِ وَالَّذِينَ مَعَهُ أَشِدَّاءُ عَلَى الْكُفَّارِ

Muḥammad (ﷺ) is the Messenger of Allāh; those who are with him are severe against the disbelievers...

[*Al-Fatḥ* (48): 29]

وَالَّذِينَ آمَنُوا مِن بَعْدُ وَهَاجَرُوا وَجَاهَدُوا مَعَكُمْ فَأُولَٰئِكَ مِنكُمْ

And those who believed after [the first emigration] and emigrated and fought with you - they are of you.

[*Al-Anfāl* (8): 75]

The word *maʿa* has been used in the Qur'ān in a general and specific sense.

The general usage can be seen in the previously quoted verse and in the verse of *Sūrah Mujādilah*,

أَلَمْ تَرَ أَنَّ اللَّهَ يَعْلَمُ مَا فِي السَّمَاوَاتِ وَمَا فِي الْأَرْضِ مَا يَكُونُ مِن نَّجْوَىٰ ثَلَاثَةٍ إِلَّا هُوَ رَابِعُهُمْ وَلَا خَمْسَةٍ إِلَّا هُوَ سَادِسُهُمْ وَلَا أَدْنَىٰ مِن ذَٰلِكَ وَلَا أَكْثَرَ إِلَّا هُوَ مَعَهُمْ أَيْنَ مَا كَانُوا ثُمَّ يُنَبِّئُهُم بِمَا عَمِلُوا يَوْمَ الْقِيَامَةِ إِنَّ اللَّهَ بِكُلِّ شَيْءٍ عَلِيمٌ ﴿٧﴾

Have you not considered that Allāh knows what is in the heavens and what is on earth? There is no private conversation of three but that He is the fourth; nor five but that He is the sixth; and no less than that or more than that except that He is with them wherever they are. Then He will inform them of what they did on the Day of Resurrection. Indeed Allāh knows all things.

[*Al-Mujādilah* (58): 7]

The context opens by mentioning knowledge and closes by mentioning knowledge and this is why ibn 'Abbās,[51] ad-Daḥḥāk,[52] Sufyān ath-Thawrī [53] and Aḥmad bin Ḥanbal [54] said, 'He is with them with His Knowledge.'

The specific usage can be seen in His, the Exalted's saying,

إِنَّ ٱللَّهَ مَعَ ٱلَّذِينَ ٱتَّقَوا۟ وَّٱلَّذِينَ هُم مُّحْسِنُونَ ﴿١٢٨﴾

Indeed Allāh is with those who fear Him and those who do good.

[*An-Naḥl* (16): 128]

And His saying to Moses,

---

[51] {F} Reported by 'Abdullāh, *'as-Sunnah'* [pp. 80-81] with a *ḥasan isnād.* As-Suyuṭī, *'ad-Durr al-Manthūr'* [6/171] referred it to ibn Abī Ḥātim.

[52] {F} Reported by al-Lālikā'ī, *'Uṣūl I'tiqād Ahl as-Sunnah'* [3/401]; 'Abdullāh, *'as-Sunnah'* [p. 80]; al-Bayhaqī, *'al-Asmā' was Ṣifāt'* [2/172] with a *ṣaḥīḥ isnād.*

[53] {F} Reported by al-Lālikā'ī, *'Uṣūl I'tiqād Ahl as-Sunnah'*[3/401]; 'Abdullāh, *'as-Sunnah'* [p. 81]; al-Bayhaqī, *'al-Asmā' was Ṣifāt'* [2/172] with a *ṣaḥīḥ isnād.*

[54] {F} Refer to *'ar-Radd 'alā al-Jahmiyyah'* [pp. 92-94]; *'al-'Uluww'* [p. 130]; *'Mukhtaṣar al-'Uluww'* [p. 190]; *'Ijtimā' al-Juyūsh al-Islāmiyyah.'*

قَالَ لَا تَخَافَآ إِنَّنِي مَعَكُمَآ أَسْمَعُ وَأَرَىٰ

...Indeed I am with you both; I Hear and I See.

[*Tā Hā* (20): 46]

And He, the Exalted says,

إِذْ
يَقُولُ لِصَٰحِبِهِۦ لَا تَحْزَنْ إِنَّ ٱللَّهَ مَعَنَا

When he [Muḥammad (ﷺ)] said to his companion [Abū Bakr], 'Do not despair, indeed Allāh is with us.'

[*At-Tawbah* (9): 40]

Meaning the Prophet (ﷺ) and Abū Bakr (*raḍiyAllāhu 'anhu*). So in this sense He is with Moses and Aaron but not Pharaoh. He is with Muḥammad (ﷺ) and his companion but not with Abū Jahl and His other enemies. He is with those who fear Allāh and those who do good but not with the wrongdoers and oppressors.

If the meaning was that he was with them with His Essence in every place, the specific sense would contradict the general sense. Rather the meaning is that He is with them, in this specific sense, by way of His Aid and support. As for the saying of the Exalted,

وَهُوَ ٱلَّذِي فِي ٱلسَّمَآءِ إِلَٰهٌ وَفِي ٱلْأَرْضِ
إِلَٰهٌ وَهُوَ ٱلْحَكِيمُ ٱلْعَلِيمُ ﴿٨٤﴾

And it is He Who is the [only] deity in the heaven and the [only] deity in the earth.

[*Az-Zukhruf* (43): 84]

Then this means that He is the deity of whoever is in the heavens and whoever is on the earth as He, the Exalted says,

وَلَهُ الْمَثَلُ الْأَعْلَىٰ فِي السَّمَاوَاتِ
وَالْأَرْضِ ۚ وَهُوَ الْعَزِيزُ الْحَكِيمُ ﴿٢٧﴾

To Him belongs the highest description in the heavens and the earth. He is the Mighty and Wise.

[*Ar-Rūm* (30): 27]

In a similar vein one understands His saying,

وَهُوَ الَّذِي فِي السَّمَاءِ إِلَٰهٌ وَفِي الْأَرْضِ
إِلَٰهٌ ۚ وَهُوَ الْحَكِيمُ الْعَلِيمُ ﴿٨٤﴾

And it is He Who is the [only] deity in the heaven and the [only] deity in the earth.

[*Az-Zukhruf* (43): 84]

That He is the One worshipped in the heavens and the earth. This is how it was explained by the *Imāms* of knowledge such as *Imām* Aḥmad[55] and others.[56]

The *Salaf* of this nation and their *Imāms* are unanimously agreed that the Lord is separate from His creation, he is described with what He described Himself with and what His Messenger described Him with without distortion or denial and without enquiring how or likening to creation. He is described with Attributes of perfection and not with deficient attributes just as Allāh, the Exalted says,

قُلْ هُوَ اللَّهُ أَحَدٌ ﴿١﴾ اللَّهُ الصَّمَدُ ﴿٢﴾ لَمْ يَلِدْ
وَلَمْ يُولَدْ ﴿٣﴾ وَلَمْ يَكُن لَّهُ كُفُوًا أَحَدٌ ﴿٤﴾

[55] {F} Refer to *Imām* Aḥmad, *'Ar-Radd 'alā al-Jahmiyyah'* [p. 93] and *'Ijtimā' al-Juyūsh al-Islāmiyyah'* [pp. 190-191].

[56] {F} As is reported from Qatādah and others.
Refer to *'al-Asmā' was Ṣifāt'* [2/174] and *'ad-Durr al-Manthūr'* [6/24].

> Say: 'He is Allāh, the One. Allāh, the Eternal Refuge. He neither begets nor is born. There is nothing equivalent to Him.'
>
> [*Al-Ikhlāṣ* (112): 1-4]

Ibn ʿAbbās (*raḍiyAllāhu ʿanhumā*) said,

> *As-Ṣamad* means *al-ʿAlīm*, whose Knowledge is perfect, *al-Adhīm* whose greatness is perfect, *al-Qadīr* whose ability is perfect, *al-Ḥakīm* whose wisdom is perfect and *as-Sayyid* whose mastery is perfect.[57]

Ibn Masʿud (*raḍiyAllāhu ʿanhu*) and others said,

> He is the One Who about whom there is nothing pointless and meaningless. *Al-Aḥad* meaning that there is nothing comparable to Him.[58]

Therefore the Name *as-Ṣamad* includes describing Him with perfect Attributes and negating any deficiency from Him. The Name *al-Aḥad* means that there is nothing like Him. We have explained this at length in the commentary to this *Sūrah* and we have explained why it is equivalent to one third of the Qur'ān.[59]

---

[57] {F} Reported by as-Suyuṭī, *'ad-Durr al-Manthūr'* [6/415] who refers it to ibn al-Mundhir, ibn Abī Ḥātim, Abū ash-Shaykh, *'al-ʿAdhamah'* and al-Bayhaqī, *'al-Asmā' was Ṣifāt'* [1/108].

[58] {F} This is reported from ibn ʿAbbās, ibn Masʿud, Saʿīd bin al-Musayyab, ʿAṭā' bin Abī Rabāḥ, al-Ḥasan, Mujāhid, ibn Jubair, ʿIkrimah, ad-Ḍaḥḥāk, Qatādah and as-Suddī.

Refer to: *'Zād al-Masīr'* [9/268]; *'al-Asmā' was Ṣifāt'* [1/69]; *'Sunan al-Bayhaqī'* [1/109]; ibn Kathīr [4/570]; al-Baghawī, [4/554-545].

[59] {F} Refer to ibn Taymiyyah, *'Jawāb Ahl al-ʿIlm wa al-Īmān'* and *'Tafsīr Sūrah al-Ikhlāṣ.'*

In Summary

- The nation is agreed that the Prophets are better than the *Awliyā'*.
- The best of this nation are the first generation and therefore the greatest of the *Awliyā'* after the Prophets is Abū Bakr.
- The issue of the Seal of the *Awliyā'* and that this term was not spoken of by early Muslims.
- The belief of the extreme *Ṣūfīs* that the Seal of the *Awliyā'* is better than the Seal of the Prophets and its refutation.
- Clarification that the source of the belief of the extreme *Ṣufis* was philosophy and its refutation.
- Refutation of their belief in the Unity of Existence and that this belief actually ends up in disbelieving in Allāh. The source of these beliefs is none other than Shayṭān.
- The three stages that the Gnostic passes through and an explanation that all but the first are incorrect because of their misunderstanding the issue of *Qadr*.
- Proof that Allāh is separate and distinct from His creation and not everywhere with His Essence.

CHAPTER TWELVE

[The Confusion Between the Universal Reality and the Religious Reality]

MOST PEOPLE CONFUSE THE realities of this religion and faith that has been ordered with the realities of the creation that occur by the Universal Decree for indeed to Allāh belongs both creation and command. Allāh, the Exalted says,

إِنَّ رَبَّكُمُ ٱللَّهُ ٱلَّذِى خَلَقَ ٱلسَّمَٰوَٰتِ وَٱلْأَرْضَ فِى سِتَّةِ
أَيَّامٍ ثُمَّ ٱسْتَوَىٰ عَلَى ٱلْعَرْشِ يُغْشِى ٱلَّيْلَ ٱلنَّهَارَ يَطْلُبُهُۥ حَثِيثًا
وَٱلشَّمْسَ وَٱلْقَمَرَ وَٱلنُّجُومَ مُسَخَّرَٰتٍۭ بِأَمْرِهِۦٓ ۗ أَلَا لَهُ ٱلْخَلْقُ
وَٱلْأَمْرُ ۗ تَبَارَكَ ٱللَّهُ رَبُّ ٱلْعَٰلَمِينَ ﴿٥٤﴾

> Indeed your Lord is Allāh Who created the heavens and the earth in six days and then Rose over the Throne. He covers the night with the day [with another night] chasing it rapidly; [He created] the sun, the moon and the stars - all subjected by His command. Unquestionably His is the creation and the command, so Blessed is Allāh, Lord of the creation.
>
> [*Al-A'rāf* (7): 54]

Therefore He, the Glorious and Exalted, is the creator of everything, its Lord and Master. There is no creator other than Him and no Lord besides Him. Whatsoever He Wills is and whatsoever He does not Will is not. Hence every motion or stillness in creation occurs by His Decree, Destiny, Will, Ability and creation. He, the Glorious, has ordered that He and His Messengers be obeyed and prohibited that He and His Messengers be disobeyed. He has ordered *Tawḥīd* and sincerity and prohibited *shirk* for the greatest of good deeds is *Tawḥīd* and the gravest of sins is *shirk*. Allāh, the Exalted says,

إِنَّ ٱللَّهَ لَا يَغْفِرُ أَن يُشْرَكَ بِهِۦ وَيَغْفِرُ مَا دُونَ ذَٰلِكَ لِمَن يَشَآءُ

> Indeed Allāh does not forgive committing *shirk* with Him, but He forgives what is less than that for whomsoever He Wills.
>
> [*An-Nisā'* (4): 48, 116]

وَمِنَ ٱلنَّاسِ مَن يَتَّخِذُ مِن دُونِ ٱللَّهِ أَندَادًا يُحِبُّونَهُمْ كَحُبِّ ٱللَّهِ وَٱلَّذِينَ ءَامَنُوٓا۟ أَشَدُّ حُبًّا لِّلَّهِ

> Of mankind are some who take partners [for worship] besides Allāh, loving them as they love Allāh whereas those who believe love Allāh [more than anything else].
>
> [*Al-Baqarah* (2): 165]

It is reported in the Two Ṣaḥīḥs from ibn Masʿūd (*raḍiyAllāhu ʿanhu*) that he asked,

> 'O Messenger of Allāh! Which sin is the most grave?' He replied, *'That you set up a partner with Allāh even though He created you.'* I asked, 'Then what?' He replied, *'That you kill your child fearing that you have to feed him in addition to yourself.'*

> I asked, 'Then what?' He replied, *'That you commit illegal sexual intercourse with your neighbours wife.'* [1]

Then Allāh confirmed this by revealing,

وَالَّذِينَ لَا يَدْعُونَ مَعَ اللَّهِ إِلَٰهًا آخَرَ وَلَا يَقْتُلُونَ النَّفْسَ
الَّتِي حَرَّمَ اللَّهُ إِلَّا بِالْحَقِّ وَلَا يَزْنُونَ ۚ وَمَن يَفْعَلْ ذَٰلِكَ يَلْقَ
أَثَامًا ﴿٦٨﴾ يُضَاعَفْ لَهُ الْعَذَابُ يَوْمَ الْقِيَامَةِ وَيَخْلُدْ فِيهِ
مُهَانًا ﴿٦٩﴾ إِلَّا مَن تَابَ وَآمَنَ وَعَمِلَ عَمَلًا صَالِحًا
فَأُولَٰئِكَ يُبَدِّلُ اللَّهُ سَيِّئَاتِهِمْ حَسَنَاتٍ ۗ وَكَانَ اللَّهُ غَفُورًا
رَّحِيمًا ﴿٧٠﴾

> And those who do not invoke another deity alongside Allāh, or kill the soul which Allāh has forbidden - except by due right, and do not commit unlawful sexual intercourse. Whoever should do that will meet a [grievous] penalty - multiplied for him is the punishment on the Day of Resurrection, and he will abide therein humiliated. Except for those who repent, believe and do righteous work, for them Allāh will replace their evil deeds with good, and ever is Allāh Forgiving and Merciful.
>
> [*Al-Furqān* (25): 68-70]

He, the Glorious, has ordered justice, benevolence and giving to those near of kin. He has prohibited all indecent deeds, evil and transgression. He informs us that He Loves the pious and God-fearing, those who do good, the just, the penitent, those who purify themselves and those who fight in His Way in ranks as if they were a single structure, firmly built. [He also informs us that] He Dislikes everything that He has prohibited as He says,

---

[1] {F} Reported by Bukhārī [Eng. Trans. 6/6 no. 4, 8/20 no. 30, 8/525 no. 802, 9/1 no. 1, 9/458 no. 611] and Muslim [Eng. Trans. 1/50 no.'s 156-157].

كُلُّ ذَٰلِكَ كَانَ سَيِّئُهُۥ عِندَ رَبِّكَ مَكْرُوهًا ﴿٣٨﴾

All that is evil is ever detested in the sight of your Lord.
[*Al-Isrā'* (17): 38]

He has prohibited *shirk* and disobedience to parents and ordered that those near of kin be given their rights. He has also prohibited squandering and stinginess, He has prohibited that ones hand be tied [like a miser] to his neck or that it be stretched forth to its utmost reach [like a spendthrift].[2] He has prohibited killing a soul without due right, from fornication and from approaching the wealth of the orphan except in the way that is best. Then He concluded by saying,

كُلُّ ذَٰلِكَ كَانَ سَيِّئُهُۥ عِندَ رَبِّكَ مَكْرُوهًا ﴿٣٨﴾

All that is evil is ever detested in the sight of your Lord.
[*Al-Isrā'* (17): 38]

He, the Glorious, does not Love corruption and is not Pleased with disbelief for His servants.

[12.1 Inducement to Repentance]

The servant is ordered to turn to Allāh in repentance all the time. Allāh, the Exalted says,

وَتُوبُوٓا۟ إِلَى ٱللَّهِ جَمِيعًا أَيُّهَ ٱلْمُؤْمِنُونَ لَعَلَّكُمْ تُفْلِحُونَ ﴿٣١﴾

And turn to Allāh in repentance all of you, O believers that you may be successful.
[*An-Nūr* (24): 31]

---

[2] {T} Refer to *al-Isrā'* (17): 29

In Ṣaḥīḥ Bukhārī it is reported that the Prophet (ﷺ) said,

«أَيُّهـا النَّاسُ تُـوبُوا إلى رَبِّكُمْ فوالذي نفسي بيده
إني لأستغفر الله وأتوب إليه في اليوم أكثر من سبعين مرة»

"O People! Turn in repentance to your Lord for indeed I seek His forgiveness and turn to Him more than seventy times in one day." [3]

In Ṣaḥīḥ Muslim it is reported that he (ﷺ) said,

«إنـه ليغان على قلبي، وإني لأستغفـر الله في اليوم مائة مرة»

"Indeed there is [at times] a darkness upon my heart [4] *and I seek the forgiveness of Allāh one hundred times in one day."* [5]

In the *Sunan* it is reported from ibn Umar that he said,

> 'We used to count the Messenger of Allāh (ﷺ) saying,
>
> «رب اغفـر لي وتب عليَّ إنك أنت التـواب الرحيم، مـائة مـرة»
>
> *"My Lord! Forgive me and turn to me in forgiveness for You are the Oft-Returning, the Most Merciful!"* one hundred times in one sitting.' [6]

---

[3] {F} Reported by Bukhārī [Eng. Trans. 8/213 no. 319] and at-Tirmidhī [no. 3259].

[4] {Y} Meaning by this a time where he was not busy remembering Allāh, calling to Him or working for the benefit of the Muslims. Sometimes he (ﷺ) would be distracted to undertaking only the mundane affairs of life and would see this as a deficiency and hence seek forgiveness from Allāh. - *'Majma' Biḥār al-Anwār'* [4/85].

[5] {F} Reported by Muslim [Eng. Trans. 4/1418 no. 6522] and Abū Dāwūd [Eng. Trans. 1/395 no. 1510].

[6] {F} Reported by Abū Dāwūd [Eng. Trans. 1/395 no. 1511] and at-Tirmidhī [no. 3434].

I say: its *isnād* is *ṣaḥīḥ*

[12.1.1 Ending Good Actions with Repentance]

Allāh, the Glorious, has ordered that righteous actions be sealed with seeking forgiveness, therefore when the Prophet (ﷺ) said the *taslīm* in prayer he would seek the forgiveness of Allāh three times and then say,

اللّٰهُـمَّ أَنْـتَ السَّـلامُ
ومِنْـكَ السَّـــلامُ تَبارَكْـتَ يَاذا الجَلالِ وَالإِكْرامِ.

"O Allāh! You are the Source of Peace and from You comes peace. Blessed are You O Possessor of Magnificence and Honour!" [7]

Allāh, the Exalted says,

وَٱلْمُسْتَغْفِرِينَ بِٱلْأَسْحَارِ ﴿١٧﴾

...and those who seek forgiveness before dawn.

[*Āli 'Imrān* (3): 17]

And therefore ordered them to pray by night and seek forgiveness at the first appearance of dawn. He also concluded *Sūrah Muzzammil* - which deals with praying by night - by saying,

وَٱسْتَغْفِرُوا۟ ٱللَّهَ ۖ إِنَّ ٱللَّهَ غَفُورٌ رَّحِيمٌۢ ﴿٢٠﴾

...and seek forgiveness of Allāh, indeed Allāh is Forgiving and Merciful.

[*Al-Muzzammil* (73): 20]

Similarly He says regarding the *Ḥajj*,

---

[7] {F} Reported by Muslim [Eng. Trans. 1/292 no. 1227] and Abū Dāwūd [Eng. Trans. 1/394 no. 1507].

فَإِذَآ أَفَضۡتُم مِّنۡ
عَرَفَٰتٖ فَٱذۡكُرُواْ ٱللَّهَ عِندَ ٱلۡمَشۡعَرِ ٱلۡحَرَامِۖ
وَٱذۡكُرُوهُ كَمَا هَدَىٰكُمۡ وَإِن كُنتُم مِّن قَبۡلِهِۦ
لَمِنَ ٱلضَّآلِّينَ ١٩٨ ثُمَّ أَفِيضُواْ مِنۡ حَيۡثُ أَفَاضَ
ٱلنَّاسُ وَٱسۡتَغۡفِرُواْ ٱللَّهَۚ إِنَّ ٱللَّهَ غَفُورٞ رَّحِيمٞ ١٩٩

When you depart from *'Arafāt*, remember Allāh at the Sacred Monument (*Muzdalifah*) and remember Him, as He has guided you, for indeed you were amongst those astray before that. Then depart from the place from where [all] the people depart and ask the forgiveness of Allāh, indeed Allāh is Forgiving and Merciful.

[*Al-Baqarah* (2): 198-199]

Indeed He, the Glorious and Exalted, revealed the following verses at the end of the military expedition of *Tabūk* - which was the last expedition undertaken by the Prophet (ﷺ),

لَّقَد تَّابَ ٱللَّهُ عَلَى
ٱلنَّبِيِّ وَٱلۡمُهَٰجِرِينَ وَٱلۡأَنصَارِ ٱلَّذِينَ ٱتَّبَعُوهُ فِي
سَاعَةِ ٱلۡعُسۡرَةِ مِنۢ بَعۡدِ مَا كَادَ يَزِيغُ قُلُوبُ فَرِيقٖ
مِّنۡهُمۡ ثُمَّ تَابَ عَلَيۡهِمۡۚ إِنَّهُۥ بِهِمۡ رَءُوفٞ رَّحِيمٞ ١١٧
وَعَلَى ٱلثَّلَٰثَةِ ٱلَّذِينَ خُلِّفُواْ حَتَّىٰٓ إِذَا ضَاقَتۡ عَلَيۡهِمُ ٱلۡأَرۡضُ
بِمَا رَحُبَتۡ وَضَاقَتۡ عَلَيۡهِمۡ أَنفُسُهُمۡ وَظَنُّوٓاْ أَن لَّا مَلۡجَأَ
مِنَ ٱللَّهِ إِلَّآ إِلَيۡهِ ثُمَّ تَابَ عَلَيۡهِمۡ لِيَتُوبُوٓاْۚ إِنَّ ٱللَّهَ هُوَ ٱلتَّوَّابُ
ٱلرَّحِيمُ ١١٨

Allāh has already forgiven the Prophet, the *Muhājirīn* and the *Anṣār* who followed him in the hour of difficulty af-

> ter the hearts of a party of them had almost inclined [to doubt], and then He forgave them. Indeed He was Kind and Merciful to them. [He also forgave] the three who were left behind [and regretted their error] to the point that the earth seemed restricted to them despite its vastness, and their [very] souls seemed straitened to them and they were certain that there is no refuge from Allāh except in Him. Then He turned to them so they could repent, indeed Allāh is the Oft-Returning, the Merciful.
>
> [*At-Tawbah* (9): 117-118]

These are some of the last verses revealed of the Qur'ān. It is also stated that the last *Sūrah* revealed was His saying,

إِذَا جَآءَ نَصۡرُ ٱللَّهِ وَٱلۡفَتۡحُ ﴿١﴾ وَرَأَيۡتَ ٱلنَّاسَ يَدۡخُلُونَ فِي دِينِ ٱللَّهِ أَفۡوَاجٗا ﴿٢﴾ فَسَبِّحۡ بِحَمۡدِ رَبِّكَ وَٱسۡتَغۡفِرۡهُۚ إِنَّهُۥ كَانَ تَوَّابَۢا ﴿٣﴾

> When the victory of Allāh comes and the conquest, and you see the people entering into the religion of Allāh in multitudes - exalt [Him] with the praise of your Lord and ask forgiveness of Him. Indeed He is the Oft-Returning.
>
> [*An-Naṣr* (110): 1-3][8]

In the Two Ṣaḥīḥs it is reported from 'Ā'ishah (*raḍiyAllāhu 'anhā*) that, 'He (ﷺ) used to say in his bowings and prostrations,

سُبْحَانَكَ اللَّهُمَّ رَبَّنَا وَبِحَمْدِكَ اللَّهُمَّ اغْفِرْ لِي.

> *"Glory be to You, O Allāh, our Lord and all praise. O Allāh forgive me!"* implementing the Qur'ān.' [9]

[8] {F} As is reported from ibn 'Abbās by Bukhārī [Eng. Trans. 6/465 no.'s 493-494] and an-Nasā'ī, *'al-Kubrā'* [no. 11713].

[9] {F} Reported by Bukhārī [Eng. Trans. 1/434 no. 781, 4/409 chpt. 50, 6/464 no's 491-493] and Muslim [Eng. Trans. 1/254 no's 981-984].

[12.1.2 Everyone is in Need of Repentance]

It is reported in the Two Ṣaḥīḥs that he (ﷺ) used to say,

«اللهم اغفـر لي خـطيئتي، وجهلي،
وإسـرافي في أمري، ومـا أنت أعلم به مني،
اللهم اغفـر لي هـزلي وجـدي، وخـطئي،
وعمـدي، وكل ذلـك عندي، اللهم اغفـر لي
ما قـدمت ومـا أخـرت، ومـا أسـررت ومـا
أعلنت، لا إله إلا أنت»

"O Allāh! Forgive me my errors, my ignorance and my going to excesses in my affairs, and all that of which You Know better than me. O Allāh! Forgive me my [errors done when] joking and in seriousness, what I unintentionally and intentionally did for all of them are from me. O Allāh! Forgive me what I have done in the past and what is to come, that which I did secretly and that which I did openly. There is none worthy of worship save You." [10]

It is reported in the Two Ṣaḥīḥs that Abū Bakr *as-Ṣiddīq* (*raḍiyAllāhu ʿanhu*) asked, 'O Messenger of Allāh! Teach me a supplication that I may employ in my prayer.' He said,

اللَّهُمَّ إِنِّي ظَلَمْتُ نَفْسِي ظُلْماً كَثِيراً وَلاَ يَغْفِرُ الذُّنوبَ إلاَّ أَنْتَ فَاغْفِرْ لِي
مَغْفِرَةً مِنْ عِنْدِكَ وَارْحَمْنِي، إِنَّكَ أَنْتَ الْغَفُورُ الرَّحِيمُ.

"Say: O Allāh! Indeed I have wronged myself greatly and none can forgive sins except You, so forgive me with a forgiveness from Yourself and bestow Mercy upon me; indeed You are the Forgiving, the

[10] {F} Reported by Bukhārī [Eng. Trans. 8/271 no. 407] and Muslim [Eng. Trans. 4/1424 no. 6563].

Most Merciful." [11]

In the *Sunan* it is reported that Abū Bakr (*raḍiyAllāhu ʿanhu*) said, 'O Messenger of Allāh! Teach me a supplication that I may say when I go to sleep and wake up.' He said,

اللَّهُمَّ عَالِمَ الْغَيْبِ وَالشَّهَادَةِ فَاطِرَ السَّمَوَاتِ وَالأَرْضِ رَبَّ كُلِّ شَيْءٍ وَمَلِيكَهُ ، أَشْهَدُ أَنْ لاَ إِلَهَ إِلاَّ أَنْتَ أَعُوْذُ بِكَ مِنْ شَرِّ نَفْسِي وَمِنْ شَرِّ الشَّيْطَانِ وَشِرْكِهِ ، وَأَنْ أَقْتَرِفَ عَلَى نَفْسِي سُوءاً أَوْ أَجُرَّهُ إِلَى مُسْلِمٍ.

"Say, 'O Allāh! Originator of the heavens and the earth, the Knower of the unseen and seen, the Lord of everything and its Owner, I bear witness that none has the right to be worshipped save you, I take refuge with You from the evil of my self, from the evil of Shayṭān and his shirk, that I perpetrate a sin against myself or I spread it to another Muslim.' Say this when you wake up, when you go to sleep and when you lie down on your bed." [12]

So it is not for anyone to think that he is no need of repentance from sins and turning to Allāh, rather every single person is continuously in need of this. Allāh, the Blessed and Exalted says,

أَن يَحْمِلْنَهَا وَأَشْفَقْنَ مِنْهَا وَحَمَلَهَا
ٱلْإِنسَٰنُ إِنَّهُۥ كَانَ ظَلُومًا جَهُولًا ﴿٧٢﴾ لِّيُعَذِّبَ ٱللَّهُ ٱلْمُنَٰفِقِينَ
وَٱلْمُنَٰفِقَٰتِ وَٱلْمُشْرِكِينَ وَٱلْمُشْرِكَٰتِ وَيَتُوبَ ٱللَّهُ
عَلَى ٱلْمُؤْمِنِينَ وَٱلْمُؤْمِنَٰتِ وَكَانَ ٱللَّهُ غَفُورًا رَّحِيمًا ﴿٧٣﴾

[11] {F} Reported by Bukhārī [Eng. Trans. 1/442 no. 796, 8/227 no. 338, 9/360 no. 485] and Muslim [Eng. Trans. 4/1419 no. 6533].

[12] {F} Reported by Abū Dāwūd [Eng. Trans. 3/1406 no. 5049] and at-Tirmidhī [no. 3392].
I say: its *isnād* is *ṣaḥīḥ*.

> ...but man [undertook to] bear it, indeed he was unjust and ignorant. [It was] so that Allāh may punish the hypocrites - male and female, the polytheists - male and female, and that Allāh may turn in forgiveness to the believers - male and female. And ever is Allāh Forgiving and Merciful.
>
> [*Al-Aḥzāb* (33): 72-73]

Therefore man is an oppressor and ignorant, the objective of the believers - male and female, is to turn to Allāh in repentance. Allāh has informed us of the repentance of His righteous servants and His forgiveness of them in His Book.

[12.1.3 None shall Enter Paradise by Virtue of his Actions]

It is established in the Ṣaḥīḥ that the Prophet (ﷺ) said,

«لن يدخل الجنةَ أحدٌ بعمله»، قالوا: ولا أنت، يا رسول الله؟ قال:
«ولا أنا إلاّ أن يتغمّدني الله برحمة منه وفضل»

> "*None shall enter Paradise by virtue of his actions.*' They asked, 'Not even you O Messenger of Allāh?' He replied, '*Not even me, unless Allāh envelop me with Mercy from Him and Beneficence.*" [13]

This does not negate His saying,

كُلُوا وَاشْرَبُوا هَنِيٓـًٔا بِمَآ أَسْلَفْتُمْ فِى ٱلْأَيَّامِ ٱلْخَالِيَةِ ﴿٢٤﴾

> [They will be told], 'eat and drink in satisfaction for what you put forth in the days past.'
>
> [*Al-Ḥāqqah* (69): 24]

[13] {F} Reported by Bukhārī [Eng. Trans. 7/391 no. 577, 8/313 no. 470] and Muslim [Eng. Trans. 4/1472 no.' s 6760-6771].

Because the Messenger (ﷺ) negated the meanings of recompense and equality [of good actions and their reward] whereas the Qur'ān affirms [actions as] the cause [for entering Paradise].

As for the saying of someone that, 'When Allāh Loves a servant, sins no longer harm him' then its meaning is that when Allāh Loves a servant, He inspires him with returning to Him and seeking His forgiveness, therefore he does not persist in committing sins. Whosoever thinks that sins are not harmful to one who persists in committing them is misguided and standing in open contravention to the Book, *Sunnah* and the consensus of the *Salaf* and the *Imāms*. Rather, whosoever does an atoms weight of good shall see it and whosoever commits an atoms weight of evil shall see it.

His servants who have been praised are only those mentioned in His saying,

۞ وَسَارِعُوٓا۟ إِلَىٰ مَغْفِرَةٍ مِّن رَّبِّكُمْ وَجَنَّةٍ عَرْضُهَا
ٱلسَّمَٰوَٰتُ وَٱلْأَرْضُ أُعِدَّتْ لِلْمُتَّقِينَ ﴿١٣٣﴾ ٱلَّذِينَ يُنفِقُونَ
فِى ٱلسَّرَّآءِ وَٱلضَّرَّآءِ وَٱلْكَٰظِمِينَ ٱلْغَيْظَ وَٱلْعَافِينَ
عَنِ ٱلنَّاسِ ۗ وَٱللَّهُ يُحِبُّ ٱلْمُحْسِنِينَ ﴿١٣٤﴾ وَٱلَّذِينَ إِذَا
فَعَلُوا۟ فَٰحِشَةً أَوْ ظَلَمُوٓا۟ أَنفُسَهُمْ ذَكَرُوا۟ ٱللَّهَ فَٱسْتَغْفَرُوا۟
لِذُنُوبِهِمْ وَمَن يَغْفِرُ ٱلذُّنُوبَ إِلَّا ٱللَّهُ وَلَمْ يُصِرُّوا۟ عَلَىٰ
مَا فَعَلُوا۟ وَهُمْ يَعْلَمُونَ ﴿١٣٥﴾ أُو۟لَٰٓئِكَ جَزَآؤُهُم مَّغْفِرَةٌ
مِّن رَّبِّهِمْ وَجَنَّٰتٌ تَجْرِى مِن تَحْتِهَا ٱلْأَنْهَٰرُ خَٰلِدِينَ
فِيهَا ۚ وَنِعْمَ أَجْرُ ٱلْعَٰمِلِينَ ﴿١٣٦﴾

And hasten to forgiveness from your Lord and a Garden as wide as the heavens and the earth, prepared for the righteous. Those who spend [in the cause of Allāh] dur-

> ing ease and hardship, who restrain anger and pardon the people - and Allāh Loves those who do good. And those who, if they commit an immoral deed or wrong themselves, remember Allāh and seek forgiveness for their sins - and who is there who can forgive sins except Allāh? - those [who] do not persist in what they have done while they know. Those - their reward is forgiveness from their Lord and gardens beneath which rivers flow wherein they will abide forever. Excellent indeed is the reward of the [righteous] workers.
>
> [*Āli 'Imrān* (3): 133-136]

[12.2 Refuting those who use Decree as an Excuse to Commit Sins]

Whosoever surmises that the decree is a proof [that grants license] to those who commit sins, [14] is like the polytheists in this regard about whom Allāh, the Exalted relates,

سَيَقُولُ ٱلَّذِينَ أَشْرَكُوا۟ لَوْ شَآءَ ٱللَّهُ مَآ أَشْرَكْنَا وَلَآ ءَابَآؤُنَا وَلَا حَرَّمْنَا مِن شَىْءٍ

> Those who committed *shirk* will say, 'If Allāh had Willed we would not have committed *shirk* and neither would our fore-fathers, nor would we have prohibited anything.'
>
> [*Al-An'ām* (6): 148]

Allāh, the Exalted refutes them by saying,

كَذَٰلِكَ كَذَّبَ ٱلَّذِينَ مِن قَبْلِهِمْ حَتَّىٰ ذَاقُوا۟ بَأْسَنَا ۗ قُلْ هَلْ عِندَكُم مِّنْ عِلْمٍ فَتُخْرِجُوهُ لَنَآ ۖ إِن تَتَّبِعُونَ إِلَّا ٱلظَّنَّ وَإِنْ أَنتُمْ إِلَّا تَخْرُصُونَ ﴿١٤٨﴾ قُلْ فَلِلَّهِ ٱلْحُجَّةُ ٱلْبَٰلِغَةُ ۖ فَلَوْ شَآءَ لَهَدَىٰكُمْ أَجْمَعِينَ ﴿١٤٩﴾

[14] {F} Refer to ibn Taymiyyah, '*al-Iḥtijāj bi al-Qadr*'.

> Likewise did those before deny until they tasted Our punishment. Say, 'Do you have any knowledge that you can produce for us? You follow only conjecture and you are not but falsifying.' Say, 'With Allāh is the conclusive argument. If He had Willed, He would have guided you all.'
>
> [*Al-Anʿām* (6): 148-149]

If decree was indeed a proof for them, Allāh would not have punished those who denied the Messengers, such as the people of Noah, ʿĀd, Thamūd, the cities overthrown [the people of Lūt] and the people of Pharaoh. Similarly, the establishment of prescribed punishment (*ḥudūd*) would not have been enjoined upon the transgressors. Indeed nobody depends upon the decree [to justify his sins] except one who is following his base desires, devoid of any guidance from Allāh. Whosoever thinks that decree is a proof for those who commit sins such that it removes any blame or punishment from them, then it is upon him not to blame or punish anyone who oppresses him, indeed in his eyes all that leads to delight should be equivalent to all that leads to pain! He should not differentiate between one who behaves with him in a good manner or one who behaves with him in an imprudent, evil manner. However this is impossible according to human nature, intellect and the *Sharīʿah*. Allāh, the Exalted says,

أَمْ نَجْعَلُ ٱلَّذِينَ ءَامَنُوا۟ وَعَمِلُوا۟
ٱلصَّٰلِحَٰتِ كَٱلْمُفْسِدِينَ فِى ٱلْأَرْضِ أَمْ نَجْعَلُ ٱلْمُتَّقِينَ كَٱلْفُجَّارِ

> Or should We treat those who believe and do righteous deeds like corrupters in the land? Or should We treat those who have *taqwā* like the wicked?
>
> [*Ṣād* (38): 28]

أَفَنَجْعَلُ ٱلْمُسْلِمِينَ كَٱلْمُجْرِمِينَ ﴿٣٥﴾ مَا لَكُمْ كَيْفَ تَحْكُمُونَ ﴿٣٦﴾

> Then should We treat the Muslims like the criminals?...
>
> [*Al-Qalam* (68): 35]

أَمْ حَسِبَ ٱلَّذِينَ ٱجْتَرَحُوا۟ ٱلسَّيِّـَٔاتِ أَن نَّجْعَلَهُمْ كَٱلَّذِينَ ءَامَنُوا۟ وَعَمِلُوا۟ ٱلصَّـٰلِحَـٰتِ سَوَآءً مَّحْيَاهُمْ وَمَمَاتُهُمْ ۚ سَآءَ مَا يَحْكُمُونَ ﴿٢١﴾

Or do those who commit evil think that We will make them like those who have believed and done righteous deeds - [make them] equal in their life and their death? Evil is what they assume!

[*Al-Jāthiyah* (45): 21]

أَفَحَسِبْتُمْ أَنَّمَا خَلَقْنَـٰكُمْ عَبَثًا وَأَنَّكُمْ إِلَيْنَا لَا تُرْجَعُونَ ﴿١١٥﴾

Then do you think that We created you uselessly and that you would not be returned to Us?

[*Al-Mu'minūn* (23): 115]

أَفَنَجْعَلُ ٱلْمُسْلِمِينَ كَٱلْمُجْرِمِينَ ﴿٣٥﴾ مَا لَكُمْ كَيْفَ تَحْكُمُونَ ﴿٣٦﴾

Does man think that he will be left neglected?

[*Al-Qiyāmah* (75): 36]

meaning: without purpose, not being commanded or forbidden.

[12.2.1 Between Ādam and Moses]

It is established in the Two Ṣaḥīḥs that the Prophet (ﷺ) said,

«احتجَّ آدم وموسى، قال موسى:
يا آدم! أنت أبو البشر، خلقك الله بيده، ونفخ فيك من
روحه، وأسجد لك ملائكته، أخرجتنا ونفسك من الجنة؟ فقال
له آدم: أنت موسى الذي اصطفاك الله بكلامه، وكتب
لك التوراة بيده؟ فبكم وجدت مكتوباً عليَّ قبل أن أخلق

"Ādam debated with Moses. Moses said, 'You are Ādam, the father of mankind. Allāh created you with His Hand, breathed the soul [He created for you] into you and made the Angels prostrate to you. So why have you expelled yourself and us from Paradise?' Ādam replied, 'You are Moses whom Allāh favoured with His Speech and wrote the Torah for with His Hand. How long before I was created did you find [these words] written for me,

وَعَصَىٰٓ ءَادَمُ رَبَّهُۥ فَغَوَىٰ ١٢١

Ādam disobeyed his lord and erred.

[*Ṭā Hā* (20): 121]

قال: بأربعين سنة؟ قال: فَلِمَ تلومني على أمر قدّره الله
عليّ قبل أنْ أُخلق بأربعين سنة؟ قال: فحجّ آدم موسى»

He replied, 'Forty years.' Ādam said, 'Then why do you blame me for a matter that Allāh has decreed to occur forty years before I was created?' Thus Adam got the better of Moses." [15]

meaning: he overcame him by virtue of the strength of his proofs.

Two groups of people have gone astray concerning [their interpretation of] this ḥadīth.[16] One group denied this ḥadīth altogether because they thought it entailed the removal of blame and punishment from whosoever disobeyed Allāh by excuse of the decree. Another group, worse than the first, used this ḥadīth as a proof [for committing sins]. It is possible that this latter group says, 'The de-

---

[15] {F} Reported by Bukhārī [Eng. Trans. 4/410 no. 621, 6/232 no. 260, 8/399 no. 611, 9/448 no. 606] and Muslim [Eng. Trans. 4/1395 no.'s 6409-6412].

[16] {F} Refer to: ibn Taymiyyah, *'al-Iḥtijāj bi al-Qadr'* and ibn al-Qayyim, *'Shifā' al-'Alīl'*, *'Ṭarīq al-Hijratayn'* [pp. 115-172].

{T} Ibn al-Qayyim's, *'Shifā' al-'Alīl'* has been translated into English by Dr. Ṣāliḥ as-Ṣāleḥ as 'Fate in Islām' [Dar al-Bukhari].

cree is a proof for those who have actualised the Reality and have witnessed it' or 'For those who do not believe that they have any action [arising from free will].' Some people said [in explanation to this ḥadīth], 'Ādam got the better of Moses because he was his father,' or 'Because he had repented,' or 'Because the sin was considered so in one *Sharīʿah* and censured in another', or 'This was [only considered a sin] in the world and not the Hereafter.' All of these opinions are false.

However the correct opinion is that Moses (*ʿalayhi as-salāam*) only censured his father with regards the calamity that occurred as a result of his eating from the tree, saying *'So why have you expelled yourself and us from Paradise?'* He did not censure him for his actually committing a sin and subsequently repenting from it. This is because Moses knew that the one who has repented from a sin is not to be censured, and he too had also repented. Now if Ādam had believed that there was no blame attached to what he did, using the excuse of decree, he would not have said,

رَبَّنَا ظَلَمْنَآ أَنفُسَنَا وَإِن لَّمْ تَغْفِرْ لَنَا وَتَرْحَمْنَا لَنَكُونَنَّ مِنَ
ٱلْخَٰسِرِينَ ﴿٢٣﴾

> Our Lord! We have wronged ourselves and if You do not forgive us and have mercy upon us, we will surely be amongst the losers.
>
> [*Al-Aʿrāf* (7): 23]

[12.3 Inducement to Patience and Acceptance of Calamity]

At the onset of calamity, the believer is ordered with patience and acceptance. When he commits sins he is ordered to seek forgiveness and to return to Allāh. Allāh, the Exalted says,

فَٱصْبِرْ إِنَّ وَعْدَ ٱللَّهِ حَقٌّ وَٱسْتَغْفِرْ لِذَنۢبِكَ

> So be patient, indeed the promise of Allāh is true, and ask forgiveness for your sin...
>
> [*Ghāfir* (40): 55]

Therefore He ordered him with patience at the onset of calamities, and repentance for any shortcomings and faults.

Allāh, the Exalted says,

مَآ أَصَابَ مِن مُّصِيبَةٍ إِلَّا بِإِذْنِ ٱللَّهِ ۗ وَمَن يُؤْمِنۢ بِٱللَّهِ يَهْدِ قَلْبَهُۥ ۚ

> No calamity strikes except by the permission of Allāh and whosoever believes in Allāh, He will guide his heart.
>
> [*At-Taghābun* (64): 11]

Ibn Mas'ūd (*raḍiyAllāhu 'anhu*) said,

> This refers to a person who has been afflicted with a calamity and he knows that it is from Allāh and therefore he is pleased with it and accepts it. [17]

When the believers are afflicted by a calamity such as sickness, poverty or humiliation, they should be patient at the verdict of Allāh,

[17] {F} As-Suyuṭī, *'ad-Durr al-Manthūr'* [6/227] refers it to 'Abd bin Ḥumaid, ibn al-Mundhir and al-Bayhaqī, *'Shu'ab al-Īmān'* from Alqamah. He also refers it to Sa'īd bin Manṣūr from ibn Mas'ūd. Refer also to ibn Kathīr [4/375].

even if this calamity occurs due to the sins of those other than them. An example of this would be a father spending his wealth in disobedience and his children being afflicted with poverty as a result, it is upon them to bear with patience that which they have been tried with. When these children complain to their father that they are not receiving their due right he mentions the decree to them!

Patience is obligatory by agreement of the scholars, a higher level than patience is to be pleased with the verdict of Allāh. Of this latter case it is postulated that this too is obligatory and it is postulated that it is recommended - and this is the correct opinion. An even higher level is that the servant thank Allāh for the calamity that has afflicted him because he sees this to be from His beneficence to him. This is because it is a means for the expiation of his sins, the raising of his rank, his repenting to Allāh, humbling himself before Him, and making his reliance (*tawakkul*) and reverential hope (*rajā'*) sincerely for Him Alone and not the creation.

As for those who have transgressed and gone astray, you will find them depending upon the decree when they sin and follow their base desires and they attribute any good actions that they do to themselves when He favours them with them. It is as one scholar said, 'when you do actions of obedience, you are a *Qadarī,*[18] and when you commit a sin, you are a *Jabarī.*[19] You take on board any way of thinking that agrees with your base desires.'

When the people upon guidance and clear direction perform a good deed they acknowledge the beneficence of Allāh upon them and that He is the One Who favoured them and made them Muslims, made them establish the prayer, inspired them with *taqwā* and

[18] {T} Meaning one who believes he has a total, unrestricted free will.

[19] {T} Meaning one who believes that he has no free will and is in fact coerced.

that there is no might or movement except with Him. Therefore their witnessing of the decree removes self-amazement, the desire for some form of reward and harm from them. When they commit a sin they seek the forgiveness of Allāh and return to Him.

It is reported in Ṣaḥīḥ Bukhārī from Shaddād bin Aws that the Messenger of Allāh (ﷺ) said, 'The master of seeking forgiveness is that the servant says,

اللَّهُمَّ أَنْتَ رَبِّي لاَ إِلَهَ إِلاَّ أَنْتَ خَلَقْتَنِي وَأَنَا عَبْدُكَ، وَأَنَا عَلَى عَهْدِكَ وَوَعْدِكَ مَا اسْتَطَعْتُ أَعُوذُ بِكَ مِنْ شَرِّ مَا صَنَعْتُ، أَبُوءُ لَكَ بِنِعْمَتِكَ عَلَيَّ، وَأَبُوءُ بِذَنْبِي، فَاغْفِرْ لِي فَإِنَّهُ لاَيَغْفِرُ الذُّنُوبَ إِلاَّ أَنْتَ.

> *"O Allāh! You are my Lord, none deserves worship save You. You created me and I am Your servant, and I am doing all I can to keep to Your covenant and fulfil my promise to You. I take refuge with You from the evil that I have committed. I acknowledge Your favours upon me and I confess my sins to You so forgive me, indeed there is none who can forgive sins save You." Whosoever says this with certainty when he awakes and then dies at night, he will enter Paradise.'* [20]

In the authentic ḥadīth, reported from Abū Dharr (*raḍiyAllāhu 'anhu*), that the Prophet (ﷺ) said, in that which he conveyed from his Lord, the Blessed and Exalted,

[20] {F} Reported by Bukhārī [Eng. Trans. 8/212 no. 318, 8/226 no. 335] and at-Tirmidhī [no. 3393].

يَا عِبَادِي إِنِّي
حَرَّمْتُ الظُّلْمَ عَلَى نَفْسِي وَجَعَلْتُهُ بَيْنَكُمْ مُحَرَّمًا فَلَا تَظَالَمُوا يَا
عِبَادِي كُلُّكُمْ ضَالٌّ إِلَّا مَنْ هَدَيْتُهُ فَاسْتَهْدُونِي أَهْدِكُمْ يَا
عِبَادِي كُلُّكُمْ جَائِعٌ إِلَّا مَنْ أَطْعَمْتُهُ فَاسْتَطْعِمُونِي أُطْعِمْكُمْ يَا
عِبَادِي كُلُّكُمْ عَارٍ إِلَّا مَنْ كَسَوْتُهُ فَاسْتَكْسُونِي أَكْسُكُمْ يَا
عِبَادِي إِنَّكُمْ تُخْطِئُونَ بِاللَّيْلِ وَالنَّهَارِ وَأَنَا أَغْفِرُ الذُّنُوبَ جَمِيعًا
فَاسْتَغْفِرُونِي أَغْفِرْ لَكُمْ يَا عِبَادِي إِنَّكُمْ لَنْ تَبْلُغُوا ضَرِّي
فَتَضُرُّونِي وَلَنْ تَبْلُغُوا نَفْعِي فَتَنْفَعُونِي يَا عِبَادِي لَوْ أَنَّ أَوَّلَكُمْ
وَآخِرَكُمْ وَإِنْسَكُمْ وَجِنَّكُمْ كَانُوا عَلَى أَتْقَى قَلْبِ رَجُلٍ وَاحِدٍ
مِنْكُمْ مَا زَادَ ذَلِكَ فِي مُلْكِي شَيْئًا يَا عِبَادِي لَوْ أَنَّ أَوَّلَكُمْ
وَآخِرَكُمْ وَإِنْسَكُمْ وَجِنَّكُمْ كَانُوا عَلَى أَفْجَرِ قَلْبِ رَجُلٍ وَاحِدٍ
مَا نَقَصَ ذَلِكَ مِنْ مُلْكِي شَيْئًا يَا عِبَادِي لَوْ أَنَّ أَوَّلَكُمْ
وَآخِرَكُمْ وَإِنْسَكُمْ وَجِنَّكُمْ قَامُوا فِي صَعِيدٍ وَاحِدٍ فَسَأَلُونِي
فَأَعْطَيْتُ كُلَّ وَاحِدٍ مَسْأَلَتَهُ مَا نَقَصَ ذَلِكَ مِمَّا عِنْدِي إِلَّا كَمَا
يَنْقُصُ الْمِخْيَطُ إِذَا أُدْخِلَ الْبَحْرَ يَا عِبَادِي إِنَّمَا هِيَ أَعْمَالُكُمْ
أُحْصِيهَا لَكُمْ ثُمَّ أُوَفِّيكُمْ إِيَّاهَا فَمَنْ وَجَدَ خَيْرًا فَلْيَحْمَدِ اللَّهَ
وَمَنْ وَجَدَ غَيْرَ ذَلِكَ فَلَا يَلُومَنَّ إِلَّا نَفْسَهُ

"O My servants! I have forbidden oppression for Myself and I have made it forbidden for you, therefore do not oppress one another. O My servants! All of you are lost except for those whom I have guided, therefore seek guidance from Me and I will guide you. O My servants! All of you are hungry except for those whom I have fed, therefore seek sustenance from Me and I will sustain you. O My servants! All of you are naked except for those whom I have clothed, therefore seek clothing from Me and I will clothe you. O My servants! You sin by night and day and I forgive all sins, therefore seek forgiveness from Me and I will forgive you. O My servants! You will not be able to harm Me so as to bring about any

harm to Me and you will not be able to benefit Me so as to bring about any benefit to Me. O My servants! If the first and last of you, the human and jinn of you, were as pious as the most pious heart of anyone amongst you, it would not add anything to My dominion. O My servants! If the first and last of you, the human and jinn of you, were as wicked as the most wicked heart of anyone amongst you, it would not decrease anything from My dominion. O My servants! If the first and last of you, the human and jinn of you, were to gather together at one place and all asked of Me, and if I were to give everyone of them what he asked, that would not decrease what I have any more than a needle decreases what is in the ocean when it is pulled out. O My servants! It is but your deeds that I judge for you, then I recompense you for them. The one who finds good is to praise and thank Allāh, the one who finds other than this has no one to blame but himself."[21]

Hence Allāh ordered the servant to praise and thank Him if he finds good and to blame only himself if he finds evil.

[12.4 Between the Universal Reality and Religious Reality]

Many people speak under the guise of speaking about the Reality, yet do not differentiate between the Universal Reality and Decree which is linked to His act of creation and Will and between the Religious Reality and Command which is linked to His Pleasure and Love. They do not differentiate between the one who established the Religious Reality in conformity to that which Allāh ordered upon the tongues of His Messengers, and between the one who lives by his spiritual ecstasy and experience, not taking into consideration what the Book and *Sunnah* have to say.

[21] {F} Reported by Muslim [Eng. Trans. 4/1365 no. 6246] and at-Tirmidhī [no. 2495].

[12.4.1 The Different Applications of the Word *Sharīʿah*]

In the same way many people mention the word *sharīʿah* yet fail to distinguish between the *Sharīʿah* that Allāh, the Exalted, revealed - which is the Book and *Sunnah* that Allāh sent His Messenger with - and between the *sharīʿah* that arose due to the verdicts of a ruler. The first type is that which is not permissible for anyone amongst the creation to leave, and in fact only the disbeliever leaves it whereas the ruler can be correct on occasion and incorrect on another. This is assuming that he is a just scholar and if not then the Messenger of Allāh (ﷺ) said,

«القضاة ثلاثة: قاضيان في النار، وقاض في
الجنة، رجل علم الحق وقضى به فهو في الجنة،
ورجل قضى للناس على جهل فهو في النار،
ورجل علم الحق فقضى بغيره فهو في النار»

> *"The judges are of three types: two are in the Fire and one in Paradise. The judge who knows the truth and judges according to it is in Paradise. The judge who judges the people based upon ignorance is in the Fire as is the judge who knows the truth yet judges by other than it."* [22]

The most noble of just, scholarly judges is the Master of the children of Ādam, Muḥammad (ﷺ). It is established from him in the Two Ṣaḥīḥs that he said,

> *"Indeed you come to me for arbitration in your disputes. It is possible that some of you express his proof more eloquently and convinc-*

---

[22] {F} Reported by Abū Dāwūd [Eng. Trans. 3/1013 no. 3566] and ibn Mājah [no. 2315].

I say: its *isnād* is *ṣaḥīḥ* and similar *aḥādīth* have been reported by ʿAlī and ibn ʿUmar.

> *ingly than others and I only judge in accordance to what I hear. So when I judge on behalf of someone at the expense of the due right of his brother then let him not take to that judgement - for it only amounts to taking a portion of the Fire."* [23]

Therefore he (ﷺ) informed us that were he to pass a judgement based upon what he heard, and the reality was the opposite to what he judged, it is not permissible for the one in whose favour he ruled to take the ruling for it would only be taking a portion of the Fire.

This is something that the scholars have agreed upon with regards all types of property unrestrictedly. When the ruler passes a judgement based upon what he thinks to be a valid proof such as clear evidence and testimony, and the reality is opposite to what he judged, it is not permissible for the person in whose favour he ruled to take that ruling by consensus. If however he judges on issues of covenants and the revocation [of contracts] and the likes, the majority of scholars state that the same applies, this is the opinion of Mālik, ash-Shāfiʿī and Aḥmad. However Abu Ḥanīfah, may Allāh be pleased with him, differentiated between the two categories. [24]

[12.4.2 Between Moses and al-Khiḍr]

When the words *'sharʿ'* and *'sharīʿah'* are employed to refer to the Book and *Sunnah*, it is not permissible for any of the *Awliyā'* of Allāh to leave it. Whosoever thinks that any of the *Awliyā'* have a route to Allāh other than through following Muḥammad (ﷺ) inwardly and

---

[23] {F} Reported by Bukhārī [Eng. Trans. 3/381 no. 638, 3/523 no. 845, 9/212 no. 281] and Muslim [Eng. Trans. 3/972 no.'s 4247-4249].

[24] {T} Meaning that in the case of property in general he agreed with the majority, but in the case of contracts and revocations he was of the opinion that the verdict of the ruler was to be applied unrestrictedly. Refer to al-Baghawī, *'Sharḥ as-Sunnah'* [10/111].

outwardly, and does not follow him inwardly or outwardly is a disbeliever.

Whosoever uses the story of Moses and al-Khiḍr to prove this stance is wrong for two reasons:

1. Moses was not sent to al-Khiḍr and therefore it was not upon al-Khiḍr to follow him. Moses was sent to the Children of Israel whereas the message of Muḥammad (ﷺ) was universal and applied to both mankind and jinn. If one who was more noble than al-Khiḍr were to have met him (ﷺ) such as Abraham, Moses or Jesus, it would have been obligatory upon them to follow him, so what then of al-Khiḍr - irrespective of whether he was a *Waliy* or a Prophet? This is why al-Khiḍr said to Moses,

   > *"I have knowledge, from the Knowledge of Allāh that He taught me but did not teach you. You have knowledge, from the Knowledge of Allāh that He taught you but did not teach me."* [25]

2. That which al-Khiḍr did, did not contradict the *Sharīʿah* of Moses (*ʿalayhi as-salām*), Moses just did not know the causes behind his actions that rendered them permissible and when al-Khiḍr explained these causes to him, he agreed with him.

Making a hole in the boat and then later fixing it to bring about benefit for its owners, when their exists the fear of an oppressor seizing it, actually constitutes good treatment to its owners and that is permissible. Killing a tyrant is permissible, even if he be young, and whosoever would make his parents into disbelievers, and there is no way to stop this from happening except by killing that person

[25] {F} Reported by Bukhārī [Eng. Trans. 1/90 no. 124, 4/402 no. 613, 6/211 no. 249, 6/215 no. 250, 6/220 no. 251] and Muslim [Eng. Trans. 4/1267 no.'s 5864-5865].

- then it is permissible to kill him.

Ibn ʿAbbās said to Najdah al-Ḥarūrī, when he asked him about killing young boys,

> If you know about them what al-Khiḍr knew about that boy then kill them, otherwise do not kill them.[26]

Reported by Bukhārī.

As for good treatment of the orphan without asking for anything in return, and bearing hunger with patience then this is one of the righteous actions and contains no element of opposition to the Law of Allāh.

[When the word] *sharʿ* is employed to refer to the verdict of a ruler then he could be an oppressor, or just, or correct or wrong. It is possible that the word *sharʿ* also be employed to refer to the opinions of the *Imāms* of *Fiqh* such as Abū Ḥanīfah, ath-Thawrī, Mālik bin Anas, al-Awzāʿī, al-Layth bin Saʿd, ash-Shāfiʿī, Aḥmad, Isḥāq, Dāwūd and others. These scholars based their opinions upon the Book and *Sunnah* and if one were to follow another scholar, in the case that this is possible, then this is permissible. This means that it is not obligatory upon the whole Muslim nation to follow one of these *Imāms* as is the case with the Messenger (ﷺ). It is also not forbidden to follow (*taqlīd*) any one of these *Imāms* as is the case with following one who speaks without knowledge.

As for the case where someone adds something to the *Sharīʿah* which is not part of it, such as fabricated *aḥādīth*, or interpretation

[26] {F} Reported by Muslim [Eng. Trans. 3/1003 no.'s 4457-4461] and an-Nasāʾī [no's 4435-4437, 8617].

The ḥadīth has not been reported by Bukhārī as *Shaykh al-Islām* said, may Allāh have mercy upon him.

of texts that contradicts the intent of Allāh and the likes then this is a type of altering and replacing the *Sharīʿah*. It is obligatory to differentiate between the *Sharīʿah* that has been revealed, the *sharīʿah* that has come to existence by means of incorrect interpretation, and the *sharīʿah* that has been altered. It is also obligatory to differentiate between the Universal Reality and The Religious Reality that has been ordered, between that which is supported by the Book and *Sunnah* and that which has only spiritual ecstasy and experience to support it.

In Summary

- The Confusion between the Universal Reality and the Religious Reality.
- The Decree is not an excuse to commit sins.
- The servant is enjoined to repentance.
- Everybody is in need of repentance.
- The argument between Ādam and Moses and its correct understanding. It is not a proof granting license to commit sins.
- The obligation of the servants at the onset of calamity, which itself occurs by the Decree, is to be patient and accept it. The best possible response is to be pleased with it.
- Most people do not differentiate between the Universal Reality and the Religious reality, or between the revealed law and the law imposed by a ruler.
- It is not permissible to go outside the bounds of the revealed law.

CHAPTER THIRTEEN

[The Difference Between the Universal and the Religious]

IN HIS BOOK, ALLĀH HAS mentioned the Will (*irādah*), Command (*amr*), Decree (*qaḍā*), Permission (*al-idhn*), Prohibition (*taḥrīm*), sending (*al-baʿth*), dispatching (*irsāl*), speech (*kalām*) and appointing (*al-jaʿl*). In each case, He has mentioned the difference between the Universal [aspect] and the Religious [aspect]. The Universal aspect is that which He has created and decreed - even though He has not ordered it, legislated it, rewarded and honoured the one who does it, and made him to be one of the pious, God-fearing *Awliyā*ʾ. The Religious aspect is that which He has ordered, legislated, rewarded and honoured the one who does it and made to be one of the pious, God-fearing *Awliyā*ʾ, His successful party and victorious group. This is one of the greatest matters that differentiate the *Awliyā*ʾ of Allāh from His enemies. So whosoever the Lord, Glorious and Exalted is He, allows to do that which He Loves and is Pleased with and he dies upon this, he is one of His *Awliyā*ʾ. Whosoever does that which Angers and Displeases the Lord and dies upon this, he is one of His enemies.

[13.1 The Universal and Religious Will]

The Universal Will refers to His Intent to create all that He created. The whole of creation falls under his Intent and Universal Will.

The Religious Will refers to all that He Loves and is Pleased with, this being all that He has ordered and appointed to be *Sharī'ah* and religion and is specific to faith and righteous actions. Allāh, the Exalted says,

فَمَن يُرِدِ ٱللَّهُ أَن يَهْدِيَهُۥ يَشْرَحْ صَدْرَهُۥ لِلْإِسْلَٰمِ ۖ وَمَن يُرِدْ
أَن يُضِلَّهُۥ يَجْعَلْ صَدْرَهُۥ ضَيِّقًا حَرَجًا كَأَنَّمَا يَصَّعَّدُ
فِى ٱلسَّمَآءِ ۚ

> So whoever Allāh wants to guide, He expands his breast to [contain] Islām; and whoever He wants to misguide, He makes his breast tight and constricted as though he were climbing into the sky.
>
> [*Al-An'ām* (6): 125]

Noah (*'alayhi as-salām*) said to his people,

وَلَا يَنفَعُكُمْ
نُصْحِىٓ إِنْ أَرَدتُّ أَنْ أَنصَحَ لَكُمْ إِن كَانَ ٱللَّهُ يُرِيدُ أَن يُغْوِيَكُمْ ۚ

> My advice will not benefit you - although I wished to advise you - if Allāh should intend to put you in error.
>
> [*Hūd* (11): 34]

Allāh, the Exalted says,

وَإِذَآ أَرَادَ ٱللَّهُ بِقَوْمٍ سُوٓءًا فَلَا مَرَدَّ لَهُۥ ۚ وَمَا لَهُم مِّن دُونِهِۦ مِن
وَالٍ ﴿١١﴾

> When Allāh intends ill for a people, there is no repelling it and there is no Patron for them besides Him.
> [*Ar-Ra'd* (13): 11]

Allāh says, concerning the second type of Will,

وَمَن كَانَ مَرِيضًا أَوْ عَلَىٰ سَفَرٍ فَعِدَّةٌ مِّنْ
أَيَّامٍ أُخَرَ ۗ يُرِيدُ اللَّهُ بِكُمُ الْيُسْرَ وَلَا يُرِيدُ بِكُمُ
الْعُسْرَ

> ...and whoever is ill or on a journey, then an equal number of other days. Allāh intends ease for you and does not intend hardship for you.
> [*Al-Baqarah* (2): 185]

مَا يُرِيدُ اللَّهُ
لِيَجْعَلَ عَلَيْكُم مِّنْ حَرَجٍ وَلَٰكِن يُرِيدُ لِيُطَهِّرَكُمْ
وَلِيُتِمَّ نِعْمَتَهُ عَلَيْكُمْ لَعَلَّكُمْ تَشْكُرُونَ ﴿٦﴾

> Allāh does not intend to make difficulty for you, but He intends to purify you and complete His favour upon you so that you may be grateful.
> [*Al-Mā'idah* (5): 6]

After Allāh mentions what He has allowed and forbidden with regards to marriage, He says,

يُرِيدُ اللَّهُ لِيُبَيِّنَ لَكُمْ وَيَهْدِيَكُمْ سُنَنَ الَّذِينَ
مِن قَبْلِكُمْ وَيَتُوبَ عَلَيْكُمْ ۗ وَاللَّهُ عَلِيمٌ حَكِيمٌ ﴿٢٦﴾
وَاللَّهُ يُرِيدُ أَن يَتُوبَ عَلَيْكُمْ وَيُرِيدُ الَّذِينَ يَتَّبِعُونَ
الشَّهَوَاتِ أَن تَمِيلُوا مَيْلًا عَظِيمًا ﴿٢٧﴾ يُرِيدُ اللَّهُ أَن يُخَفِّفَ
عَنكُمْ ۚ وَخُلِقَ الْإِنسَانُ ضَعِيفًا ﴿٢٨﴾

> Allāh wants to make clear to you [the lawful from the unlawful] and guide you to the [good] practices of those before you and to accept your repentance. Allāh is the Knowing and Wise. Allāh wants to accept your repentance, but those who follow their lusts want you to digress [into] a great deviation. And Allāh wants to lighten [your difficulties] for you; and mankind was created weak.
>
> [*An-Nisā'* (4): 26-28]

After mentioning what He has ordered and forbidden the wives of the Prophet (ﷺ), He says,

إِنَّمَا
يُرِيدُ ٱللَّهُ لِيُذْهِبَ عَنكُمُ ٱلرِّجْسَ أَهْلَ ٱلْبَيْتِ وَيُطَهِّرَكُمْ
تَطْهِيرًا ﴿٣٣﴾

> Allāh intends only to remove the impurity [of sin] from you, O people of the [Prophet's(ﷺ)] household and to purify you with extensive purification.
>
> [*Al-Aḥzāb* (33): 33]

The meaning is that He has ordered you with that which would remove any impurity from you O People of the House [of the Prophet] and to purify you completely. Therefore whosoever obeys His command becomes pure and the impurity has left him. The opposite applies to the one who disobeys Him.

[13.2 The Universal and Religious Command]

As for the Command, Allāh says with regards the Universal Command,

إِنَّمَا قَوْلُنَا لِشَيْءٍ إِذَآ أَرَدْنَٰهُ أَن نَّقُولَ لَهُۥ كُن فَيَكُونُ ﴿٤٠﴾

> Indeed Our word to a thing when We intend it to be is

that We say, 'Be!' and it is.

[*An-Naḥl* (16): 40]

وَمَآ أَمْرُنَآ إِلَّا وَٰحِدَةٌ كَلَمْحٍۭ بِٱلْبَصَرِ ﴿٥٠﴾

And Our command is but one, like a glance of the eye.

[*Al-Qamar* (54): 50]

أَتَىٰهَآ أَمْرُنَا لَيْلًا أَوْ نَهَارًا فَجَعَلْنَٰهَا حَصِيدًا كَأَن لَّمْ تَغْنَ
بِٱلْأَمْسِ ۚ كَذَٰلِكَ نُفَصِّلُ ٱلْءَايَٰتِ لِقَوْمٍ يَتَفَكَّرُونَ ﴿٢٤﴾

...there comes to it Our command by night or day, and We make it as a harvest as if it had not flourished yesterday...

[*Yūnus* (10): 24]

As for the Religious Command, Allāh says,

﴿ إِنَّ ٱللَّهَ يَأْمُرُ بِٱلْعَدْلِ
وَٱلْإِحْسَٰنِ وَإِيتَآئِ ذِى ٱلْقُرْبَىٰ وَيَنْهَىٰ عَنِ ٱلْفَحْشَآءِ
وَٱلْمُنكَرِ وَٱلْبَغْىِ ۚ يَعِظُكُمْ لَعَلَّكُمْ تَذَكَّرُونَ

Indeed Allāh orders justice, good conduct and giving to relatives. He forbids immorality, bad conduct and oppression. He admonishes you so that perhaps you will be reminded.

[*An-Naḥl* (16): 90]

﴿ إِنَّ
ٱللَّهَ يَأْمُرُكُمْ أَن تُؤَدُّوا۟ ٱلْأَمَٰنَٰتِ إِلَىٰٓ أَهْلِهَا وَإِذَا حَكَمْتُم بَيْنَ
ٱلنَّاسِ أَن تَحْكُمُوا۟ بِٱلْعَدْلِ ۚ إِنَّ ٱللَّهَ نِعِمَّا يَعِظُكُم بِهِۦٓ ۗ إِنَّ ٱللَّهَ كَانَ سَمِيعًۢا
بَصِيرًا ﴿٥٨﴾

> Indeed Allāh orders you to render trusts to whom they are due and when you judge between people to judge with justice. Excellent indeed is that which Allāh instructs you and Allāh is ever Hearing and Seeing.
>
> [*An-Nisā'* (4): 58]

[13.3 The Universal and Religious Permission]

As for the Universal Permission, Allāh says when He mentions magic,

وَمَا هُم بِضَآرِّينَ بِهِۦ مِنْ أَحَدٍ إِلَّا بِإِذْنِ ٱللَّهِ

> But they do not harm anyone through it except by permission of Allāh.
>
> [*Al-Baqarah* (2): 102]

Meaning by His Will and Power, otherwise Allāh, the Mighty and Magnificent, has not allowed the use of magic.

He says with regards the Religious Permission,

أَمْ لَهُمْ شُرَكَـٰٓؤُا۟ شَرَعُوا۟ لَهُم مِّنَ ٱلدِّينِ
مَا لَمْ يَأْذَنۢ بِهِ ٱللَّهُ

> Or have they partners who have ordained for them a religion to which Allāh has not consented?
>
> [*Ash-Shūrā* (42): 21]

إِنَّآ أَرْسَلْنَـٰكَ شَـٰهِدًا وَمُبَشِّرًا وَنَذِيرًا ﴿٤٥﴾ وَدَاعِيًا
إِلَى ٱللَّهِ بِإِذْنِهِۦ وَسِرَاجًا مُّنِيرًا ﴿٤٦﴾

> Indeed We have sent you as a witness and a bringer of good tidings and a warner. And one who invites to Allāh, by His permission and an illuminating lamp.
>
> [*Al-Aḥzāb* (33): 45-46]

وَمَآ أَرْسَلْنَا مِن رَّسُولٍ إِلَّا لِيُطَاعَ بِإِذْنِ ٱللَّهِ

And We did not send any Messenger except to be obeyed by the permission of Allāh.

[*An-Nisā'* (4): 64]

مَا قَطَعْتُم مِّن لِّينَةٍ أَوْ تَرَكْتُمُوهَا قَآئِمَةً
عَلَىٰٓ أُصُولِهَا فَبِإِذْنِ ٱللَّهِ

Whatever you have cut down of [their] palm trees or left standing upon their trunks - it was by the permission of Allāh...

[*Al-Ḥashr* (59): 5]

[13.4 The Universal and Religious Decree]

As for the Universal Decree, Allāh says,

فَقَضَىٰهُنَّ سَبْعَ سَمَٰوَاتٍ فِى يَوْمَيْنِ

And He completed them as seven heavens in two days...

[*Fuṣṣilat* (41): 12]

وَإِذَا قَضَىٰٓ أَمْرًا فَإِنَّمَا يَقُولُ لَهُۥ كُن فَيَكُونُ ﴿١١٧﴾

When He decrees a matter, He only says to it, 'Be!' and it is.

[*Al-Baqarah* (2): 117]

As for the Religious Decree, Allāh says,

۞ وَقَضَىٰ رَبُّكَ أَلَّا تَعْبُدُوٓا۟ إِلَّآ إِيَّاهُ

And your Lord has decreed that you not worship anyone save Him...

[*Al-Isrā'* (17): 23]

Al-Khalīl (*'alayhi as-salām*) said to his people,

قَالَ أَفَرَءَيْتُم مَّا كُنتُمْ تَعْبُدُونَ ﴿٧٥﴾ أَنتُمْ
وَءَابَآؤُكُمُ ٱلْأَقْدَمُونَ ﴿٧٦﴾ فَإِنَّهُمْ عَدُوٌّ لِّىٓ إِلَّا رَبَّ ٱلْعَٰلَمِينَ

> Then do you see what you have been worshipping, you and your forefathers of old? Indeed you are enemies to me except the Lord of the universe.
>
> [*Ash-Shu'arā'* (26): 75-77]

Allāh, the Exalted says,

قَدْ
كَانَتْ لَكُمْ أُسْوَةٌ حَسَنَةٌ فِىٓ إِبْرَٰهِيمَ وَٱلَّذِينَ مَعَهُۥٓ إِذْ قَالُوا۟ لِقَوْمِهِمْ
إِنَّا بُرَءَٰٓؤُا۟ مِنكُمْ وَمِمَّا تَعْبُدُونَ مِن دُونِ ٱللَّهِ كَفَرْنَا بِكُمْ وَبَدَا بَيْنَنَا
وَبَيْنَكُمُ ٱلْعَدَٰوَةُ وَٱلْبَغْضَآءُ أَبَدًا حَتَّىٰ تُؤْمِنُوا۟ بِٱللَّهِ وَحْدَهُۥٓ إِلَّا
قَوْلَ إِبْرَٰهِيمَ لِأَبِيهِ لَأَسْتَغْفِرَنَّ لَكَ وَمَآ أَمْلِكُ لَكَ مِنَ ٱللَّهِ مِن شَىْءٍ

> There has already been an excellent example for you in Abraham and those with him; when they said to their people, 'Indeed we are free of you and whatever you worship besides Allāh. We have denied you and there has appeared between us and you hatred and animosity until you believe in Allāh Alone,' except for the saying of Abraham to his father, 'I will surely ask forgiveness for you, but I have not [power to do] for you anything against Allāh...'
>
> [*Al-Mumtaḥinah* (60): 4]

قُلْ يَٰٓأَيُّهَا ٱلْكَٰفِرُونَ ﴿١﴾ لَآ أَعْبُدُ مَا تَعْبُدُونَ ﴿٢﴾
وَلَآ أَنتُمْ عَٰبِدُونَ مَآ أَعْبُدُ ﴿٣﴾ وَلَآ أَنَا۠ عَابِدٌ مَّا عَبَدتُّمْ ﴿٤﴾
وَلَآ أَنتُمْ عَٰبِدُونَ مَآ أَعْبُدُ ﴿٥﴾ لَكُمْ دِينُكُمْ وَلِىَ دِينِ ﴿٦﴾

> Say: 'O you disbelievers! I do not worship what you wor-

ship. Nor do you worship what I worship. Nor will I worship what you worship. Nor will you worship what I worship. For you is your religion and for me is my religion.'

[*Al-Kāfirūn* (109): 1-6]

These words necessitate complete disassociation from their religion, they do not necessitate his being Pleased with their religion as He says,

وَإِن كَذَّبُوكَ فَقُل لِّي عَمَلِي وَلَكُمْ عَمَلُكُمْ
أَنتُم بَرِيٓـُٔونَ مِمَّآ أَعْمَلُ وَأَنَا۠ بَرِىٓءٌ مِّمَّا تَعْمَلُونَ ﴿٤١﴾

And if they deny you [O Muḥammad (ﷺ)], say, 'For me are my deeds and for you are your deeds. Your are disassociated from what I do and I am disassociated from what you do.'

[*Yūnus* (10): 41]

As for those amongst the heretics who think that these verses imply that He is Pleased with the religion of the disbelievers, then such people are from the worst liars and greatest disbelievers to be found amongst mankind. For example the one who thinks that His words,

۞ وَقَضَىٰ رَبُّكَ أَلَّا تَعْبُدُوٓا۟ إِلَّآ إِيَّاهُ

Your Lord has decreed that you worship none save Him...

[*Al-Isrā'* (17): 23]

actually means that your Lord has planned and actualised [this] and that everything that Allāh has decreed must occur, therefore he went on to say that the idol worshippers in reality worshipped Allāh. This person is the greatest of disbelievers in the [Heavenly] Books.[1]

---

[1] {T} The author is referring to ibn 'Arabī who said, for example, concerning the worshippers of the cow at the time of Moses (*'alayhis as-salām*), 'Moses (*'alayhis as-salām*) was more knowledgeable of this matter than Aaron because he knew what =

[13.5 The Universal and Religious Sending]

With regards the Universal Sending, Allāh says,

فَإِذَا جَآءَ وَعْدُ أُولَىٰهُمَا بَعَثْنَا
عَلَيْكُمْ عِبَادًا لَّنَآ أُو۟لِى بَأْسٍ شَدِيدٍ فَجَاسُوا۟ خِلَـٰلَ ٱلدِّيَارِ ۚ
وَكَانَ وَعْدًا مَّفْعُولًا ﴿٥﴾

So when the [time of] promise came for the first of them, We sent against you servants of Ours - those of great military might and they probed [even] into the homes, and it was a promise fulfilled.

[*Al-Isrā'* (17): 5]

With regards the Religious Sending, Allāh says,

هُوَ ٱلَّذِى بَعَثَ فِى ٱلْأُمِّيِّـۧنَ رَسُولًا مِّنْهُمْ يَتْلُوا۟
عَلَيْهِمْ ءَايَـٰتِهِۦ وَيُزَكِّيهِمْ وَيُعَلِّمُهُمُ ٱلْكِتَـٰبَ وَٱلْحِكْمَةَ

It is He Who sent among the unlettered a Messenger from amongst themselves, reciting to them His verses, purifying them and teaching them the Book and Wisdom...

[*Al-Jumu'ah* (62): 2]

وَلَقَدْ بَعَثْنَا فِى كُلِّ أُمَّةٍ رَّسُولًا أَنِ ٱعْبُدُوا۟ ٱللَّهَ
وَٱجْتَنِبُوا۟ ٱلطَّـٰغُوتَ ۖ

=
the Companions of the Cow [truly] worshipped. This is because he knew that Allāh had decreed that none was to be worshipped save Him Alone and that when Allāh decrees a thing it must occur. Therefore when Moses censured his brother Aaron it was because of Aaron rejecting [what the Companions of the Cow did] and his inability to truly comprehend it. For the Gnostic is the one who sees the Truth [Allāh] in everything, indeed he sees the Truth to be everything.' - as quoted in Burhān ad-Dīn al-Baqā'ī, *'Tanbīh al-Ghabbī ilā Takfīr ibn 'Arabī.'* The *muḥaqqiq* to that book refers the quote to *'Fuṣūṣ'* [p. 192].

And We certainly sent to every nation a Messenger [saying], 'Worship Allāh and avoid *ṭāghūt*.'

[*An-Naḥl* (16): 36]

[13.6 The Universal and Religious Dispatching]

With regards the Universal Dispatching, Allāh says,

أَلَمْ تَرَ أَنَّآ أَرْسَلْنَا ٱلشَّيَـٰطِينَ عَلَى ٱلْكَـٰفِرِينَ تَؤُزُّهُمْ أَزًّا ﴿٨٣﴾

Do you not see that We have dispatched the devils upon the disbelievers, inciting them [to evil] constantly?

[*Maryam* (19): 83]

وَهُوَ ٱلَّذِىٓ أَرْسَلَ ٱلرِّيَـٰحَ بُشْرًۢا بَيْنَ يَدَىْ رَحْمَتِهِۦ

And it is He Who dispatches the winds as good tidings before His Mercy...

[*Al-Furqān* (25): 48]

He says with regards the Religious Dispatching,

إِنَّآ أَرْسَلْنَـٰكَ شَـٰهِدًا وَمُبَشِّرًا وَنَذِيرًا ﴿٤٥﴾

Indeed We have sent you as a witness and a bringer of good tidings and a warner.

[*Al-Aḥzāb* (33): 45]

إِنَّآ أَرْسَلْنَا نُوحًا إِلَىٰ قَوْمِهِۦٓ

Indeed We sent Noah to his people...

[*Nūḥ* (71): 1]

إِنَّآ أَرْسَلْنَآ إِلَيْكُمْ رَسُولًا شَـٰهِدًا عَلَيْكُمْ كَمَآ أَرْسَلْنَآ إِلَىٰ فِرْعَوْنَ رَسُولًا

Indeed We sent you a Messenger as a witness upon you just as We sent to Pharaoh a Messenger.

[*Al-Muzzammil* (73): 15]

ٱللَّهُ يَصْطَفِى مِنَ ٱلْمَلَٰٓئِكَةِ رُسُلًا وَمِنَ ٱلنَّاسِ

Allāh chooses from the Angels, Messengers and from the people.

[*Al-Ḥajj* (22): 75]

[13.7 The Universal and Religious Appointing]

With regards the Universal Appointing, Allāh says,

وَجَعَلْنَٰهُمْ أَئِمَّةً يَدْعُونَ إِلَى ٱلنَّارِ

And We made them leaders inviting to the Fire...

[*Al-Qaṣaṣ* (28): 41]

He says with regards the Religious Appointing,

لِكُلٍّ جَعَلْنَا مِنكُمْ شِرْعَةً وَمِنْهَاجًا

To each of you We have prescribed a law and a way.

[*Al-Mā'idah* (5): 48]

مَا جَعَلَ ٱللَّهُ مِنۢ بَحِيرَةٍ وَلَا سَآئِبَةٍ وَلَا وَصِيلَةٍ وَلَا حَامٍ

Allāh has not appointed [such innovations] as the *baḥīrah*, *sā'ibah*, *waṣīlah* or *ḥām*.

[*Al-Mā'idah* (5): 103]

[13.8 The Universal and Religious Prohibition]

With regards the Universal Prohibition, Allāh says,

﴿وَحَرَّمْنَا عَلَيْهِ ٱلْمَرَاضِعَ مِن قَبْلُ

And We had prevented from him [all] wet nurses from before...

[*Al-Qaṣaṣ* (28): 12]

قَالَ فَإِنَّهَا مُحَرَّمَةٌ عَلَيْهِمْ أَرْبَعِينَ سَنَةً يَتِيهُونَ فِي الْأَرْضِ

[Allāh] said, 'Then indeed it is forbidden to them for forty years [in which] they will wander throughout the land.'

[*Al-Mā'idah* (5): 26]

He says with regards the Religious Prohibition,

حُرِّمَتْ عَلَيْكُمُ الْمَيْتَةُ وَالدَّمُ وَلَحْمُ الْخِنزِيرِ وَمَا أُهِلَّ لِغَيْرِ اللَّهِ بِهِ

Prohibited to you are dead animals, blood, the flesh of swine and that which has been dedicated to other than Allāh...

[*Al-Mā'idah* (5): 3]

حُرِّمَتْ عَلَيْكُمْ أُمَّهَاتُكُمْ وَبَنَاتُكُمْ وَأَخَوَاتُكُمْ وَعَمَّاتُكُمْ وَخَالَاتُكُمْ وَبَنَاتُ الْأَخِ

Prohibited to you [for marriage] are your mothers, your daughters, your sisters, your father's sisters, your mother's sisters, your brother's sisters...

[*An-Nisā'* (4): 23]

[13.9 The Universal and Religious Words]

With regards the Universal Words, Allāh says,

وَصَدَّقَتْ بِكَلِمَاتِ رَبِّهَا وَكُتُبِهِ وَكَانَتْ مِنَ الْقَانِتِينَ ﴿١٢﴾

...and she believed in the words of her Lord and His scriptures and was devoutly obedient.

[*At-Taḥrīm* (66): 12]

It is established in the Ṣaḥīḥ that the Prophet (ﷺ) used to say,

«أعوذ بكلمات الله التامّة كلّها
من شر ما خلق، ومن غضبه وعقابه وشر عباده،
ومن همزات الشياطين وأن يحضرون»

"I take refuge with all of the perfect Words of Allāh from the evil of what He has created; from His Anger, punishment and the evil of His servants; from the whisperings of the devils and that they should accompany [me]." [2]

He (ﷺ) said,

«من نزل منزلاً فقال: أعوذ بكلمات الله التامات من شر ما
خلق، لم يضره شيءٌ حتى يرتحل من منزله ذلك»

"Whosoever takes sojourn in a place and says, 'I take refuge with the perfect Words of Allāh from the evil of what He created', he will not be harmed by anything until he travels on from that place."[3]

He (ﷺ) also used to say,

«أعوذ بكلمات الله التامّة
التي لا يجاوزهن برّ ولا فاجر، ومن شر ما ذرأ في الأرض ومن
شر ما يخرج منها ومن شر فتن الليل والنهار، ومن شر كل
طارق، إلا طارقاً يطرق بخير يا رحمن»

"I take refuge with the perfect Words of Allāh that cannot be

---

[2] {F} Reported by Abū Dāwūd [Eng. Trans. 3/1091 no. 3884] and at-Tirmidhī [no. 3528]

I say: the *isnād* is *ḍaʿīf.*

You saw that *Shaykh al-Islām* attributed this ḥadīth to the Ṣaḥīḥ when it is not there and perhaps he intended his comments to precede the following ḥadīth.

[3] {F} Reported by Muslim [Eng. Trans. 4/1421 no.'s 6541-6543] and at-Tirmidhī [no. 3437].

> *overstepped by the pious or sinner; from the evil of all that crawls on the land; from the evil of everything that comes out of it; from the evil of the trials of the night and day; and from the evil of every bright star except for those that portend of good, O Most Merciful!"*[4]

The perfect Words of Allāh that neither the pious or sinner can overstep are those that He employed to create the creation and therefore neither the pious or sinner is excluded from His creation, Will and Ability.

As for His Religious Words then they refer to His Revealed Books and what they contain of command and prohibition. Therefore the pious obeys them and the sinner disobeys them.

The pious, God-fearing *Awliyā'* of Allāh are those who obey his Religious Words, Religious Appointing, Religious Permission and Religious Will. As for the Universal Words that neither the pious or sinner can overstep then the entirety of creation is included - all of the disbelievers and everyone who shall enter the Fire, even Iblīs and his armies.

Therefore the creation, even though they share in falling under the Creation, Will, Ability and that which Allāh has decreed for them, they separate when it comes to His Command, Prohibition, Love, Pleasure and Anger. The pious, God-Fearing *Awliyā'* of Allāh are those who enact the obligatory, leave the prohibited and bear the decree with patience, hence He Loves them and they love Him, He is Pleased with them and they are pleased with Him. On the other hand with regards His enemies, the *awliyā'* of Shayṭān, He Hates them, is Angry at them, Curses them and displays enmity to them even though they fall under His Ability.

---

[4] {F} Reported by an-Nasā'ī, *"Amal al-Yawm wa al-Layla'* [no. 956] {Y} and *'al-Muwaṭṭa'* [Eng. Trans. p. 401 no. 1711].

I say: the ḥadīth is *ḥasan* due to witnesses.

[13.10 The Fundamental Scale for Differentiating the *Awliyā'* of Allāh from the *awliyā'* of Shayṭān]

The detailed explanation of what we have briefly mentioned above is done in another place. I have only written it here to make one aware of the general differences between the *Awliyā'* of the Most Merciful and the *awliyā'* of Shayṭān. These differences can be reduced to considering how a person conforms to the Messenger of Allāh (ﷺ) for it is by him that Allāh differentiates His Joyous *Awliyā'* from His wretched enemies; His *Awliyā'* who are the People of Paradise from His enemies who are the denizens of the Fire; His *Awliyā'* who are the People of Guidance and clear direction from His enemies who are the People of deviancy, misguidance and corruption. His *Awliyā'* are those in whose hearts He has written faith and aided them with a spirit from Him. Allāh, the Exalted says,

لَّا تَجِدُ قَوْمًا يُؤْمِنُونَ بِٱللَّهِ وَٱلْيَوْمِ ٱلْـَٔاخِرِ يُوَآدُّونَ مَنْ
حَآدَّ ٱللَّهَ وَرَسُولَهُۥ

> You will not find a people who believe in Allāh and the Last Day having affection for those who oppose Allāh and His Messenger...
>
> [*Al-Mujādilah* (58): 22]

إِذْ يُوحِى رَبُّكَ إِلَى ٱلْمَلَٰٓئِكَةِ أَنِّى مَعَكُمْ فَثَبِّتُوا۟ ٱلَّذِينَ ءَامَنُوا۟ۚ
سَأُلْقِى فِى قُلُوبِ ٱلَّذِينَ كَفَرُوا۟ ٱلرُّعْبَ فَٱضْرِبُوا۟ فَوْقَ
ٱلْأَعْنَاقِ وَٱضْرِبُوا۟ مِنْهُمْ كُلَّ بَنَانٍ ﴿١٢﴾

> [Remember] when your Lord inspired to the Angels, 'I am with you, so strengthen those who have believed. I will cast terror into the hearts of the disbelievers, so strike [them] upon the necks and strike them at every fingertip.'
>
> [*Al-Anfāl* (8): 12]

He says concerning His enemies,

وَإِنَّ ٱلشَّيَٰطِينَ لَيُوحُونَ إِلَىٰٓ
أَوْلِيَآئِهِمْ لِيُجَٰدِلُوكُمْ ۖ وَإِنْ أَطَعْتُمُوهُمْ إِنَّكُمْ لَمُشْرِكُونَ ﴿١٢١﴾

Indeed the devils inspire their *awliyā'* [among men] to dispute with you...

[*Al-An'ām* (6): 121]

وَكَذَٰلِكَ جَعَلْنَا لِكُلِّ نَبِىٍّ عَدُوًّا
شَيَٰطِينَ ٱلْإِنسِ وَٱلْجِنِّ يُوحِى بَعْضُهُمْ إِلَىٰ بَعْضٍ زُخْرُفَ
ٱلْقَوْلِ غُرُورًا ۚ

And thus have We made for every Prophet an enemy - devils from mankind and Jinn, inspiring one another with decorative speech in delusion.

[*Al-An'ām* (6): 112]

هَلْ أُنَبِّئُكُمْ عَلَىٰ مَن تَنَزَّلُ ٱلشَّيَٰطِينُ ﴿٢٢١﴾ تَنَزَّلُ عَلَىٰ
كُلِّ أَفَّاكٍ أَثِيمٍ ﴿٢٢٢﴾ يُلْقُونَ ٱلسَّمْعَ وَأَكْثَرُهُمْ كَٰذِبُونَ ﴿٢٢٣﴾
وَٱلشُّعَرَآءُ يَتَّبِعُهُمُ ٱلْغَاوُۥنَ ﴿٢٢٤﴾ أَلَمْ تَرَ أَنَّهُمْ فِى كُلِّ وَادٍ
يَهِيمُونَ ﴿٢٢٥﴾ وَأَنَّهُمْ يَقُولُونَ مَا لَا يَفْعَلُونَ ﴿٢٢٦﴾ إِلَّا ٱلَّذِينَ
ءَامَنُوا۟ وَعَمِلُوا۟ ٱلصَّٰلِحَٰتِ وَذَكَرُوا۟ ٱللَّهَ كَثِيرًا وَٱنتَصَرُوا۟ مِنۢ
بَعْدِ مَا ظُلِمُوا۟ ۗ وَسَيَعْلَمُ ٱلَّذِينَ ظَلَمُوٓا۟ أَىَّ مُنقَلَبٍ يَنقَلِبُونَ ﴿٢٢٧﴾

Shall I inform you upon whom the devils descend? They descend upon every sinful liar. They pass on what is heard and most of them are liars. And the poets - [only] the deviators follow them. Do you not see that in every valley they roam [speaking lies indiscriminately] and that they say what they do not do? Except those [poets] who believe and do righteous deeds, remember Allāh and assist

> [the Muslims] after they were wronged. And those who have wronged will soon know what [kind of] return they will receive.
>
> [*Ash-Shu'arā'* (26): 221-227]

[13.11 The Messenger (ﷺ) and Jibrīl have been Absolved of all Falsehood]

Allāh, the Exalted says,

فَلَآ أُقۡسِمُ بِمَا تُبۡصِرُونَ ﴿٣٨﴾ وَمَا لَا تُبۡصِرُونَ ﴿٣٩﴾
إِنَّهُۥ لَقَوۡلُ رَسُولٖ كَرِيمٖ ﴿٤٠﴾ وَمَا هُوَ بِقَوۡلِ شَاعِرٖۚ قَلِيلٗا مَّا تُؤۡمِنُونَ ﴿٤١﴾
وَلَا بِقَوۡلِ كَاهِنٖۚ قَلِيلٗا مَّا تَذَكَّرُونَ ﴿٤٢﴾ تَنزِيلٞ مِّن رَّبِّ ٱلۡعَٰلَمِينَ ﴿٤٣﴾ وَلَوۡ
تَقَوَّلَ عَلَيۡنَا بَعۡضَ ٱلۡأَقَاوِيلِ ﴿٤٤﴾ لَأَخَذۡنَا مِنۡهُ بِٱلۡيَمِينِ ﴿٤٥﴾ ثُمَّ لَقَطَعۡنَا
مِنۡهُ ٱلۡوَتِينَ ﴿٤٦﴾ فَمَا مِنكُم مِّنۡ أَحَدٍ عَنۡهُ حَٰجِزِينَ ﴿٤٧﴾ وَإِنَّهُۥ لَتَذۡكِرَةٞ
لِّلۡمُتَّقِينَ ﴿٤٨﴾ وَإِنَّا لَنَعۡلَمُ أَنَّ مِنكُم مُّكَذِّبِينَ ﴿٤٩﴾ وَإِنَّهُۥ لَحَسۡرَةٌ عَلَى
ٱلۡكَٰفِرِينَ ﴿٥٠﴾ وَإِنَّهُۥ لَحَقُّ ٱلۡيَقِينِ ﴿٥١﴾ فَسَبِّحۡ بِٱسۡمِ رَبِّكَ ٱلۡعَظِيمِ ﴿٥٢﴾

> So I swear by what you see and what you do not see that indeed it [the Qur'ān] is the word of a noble Messenger. It is not the word of a poet; little do you believe. Nor the word of a soothsayer; little do you take heed. [It is] a revelation from the Lord of the universe. And if he [Muḥammad (ﷺ)] had made up about Us some [false] sayings, We would have seized him by the right hand; then We would have cut from him the life-vein and there is no one of you who could prevent [Us] from him. And indeed it is a reminder for the righteous and indeed We know that among you are deniers. Indeed it will be [a cause of] regret upon the disbelievers and indeed it is the truth of certainty. So exalt the Name of your Lord, the Most Great.

[*Al-Ḥāqqah* (69): 38-52]

فذكر فما أنت بنعمت
ربك بكاهن ولا مجنون ﴿٢٩﴾ أم يقولون شاعر نتربص به ريب
المنون ﴿٣٠﴾ قل تربصوا فإني معكم من المتربصين ﴿٣١﴾
أم تأمرهم أحلامهم بهذا أم هم قوم طاغون ﴿٣٢﴾ أم يقولون تقوله
بل لا يؤمنون ﴿٣٣﴾ فليأتوا بحديث مثله إن كانوا صادقين

So remind [O Muḥammad (ﷺ)], for you are not by the favour of your Lord a soothsayer or a madman. Or do they say [of you], 'A poet for whom we await the misfortune of time'? Say, 'Wait, for indeed I am, with you, among the waiters.' Or do their minds command them to [say] this, or are they a transgressing people? Or do they say, 'He has made it up'? Rather, they do not believe. Then let them produce a statement like it, if they are truthful.

[*At-Ṭūr* (52): 29-34]

Therefore Allāh, the Glorious and Exalted, absolved our Prophet, Muḥammad (ﷺ), from those whom the devils accompany such as the soothsayers, poets and insane. He made clear that the one who came with the Qur'ān was a noble Angel that He chose. Allāh, the Exalted says,

الله يصطفي من الملائكة رسلا ومن الناس

Allāh chooses from the Angels, Messengers and from the people.

[*Al-Ḥajj* (22): 75]

وإنه لتنزيل رب العالمين ﴿١٩٢﴾ نزل به الروح
الأمين ﴿١٩٣﴾ على قلبك لتكون من المنذرين ﴿١٩٤﴾ بلسان عربي
مبين ﴿١٩٥﴾

And indeed it [the Qur'ān] is the revelation of the Lord of the universe. The Trustworthy Spirit brought it down upon your heart that you may be of the warners - in a clear Arabic tongue.

[*Ash-Shu'arā'* (26): 192-195]

مَن كَانَ عَدُوًّا لِّجِبْرِيلَ فَإِنَّهُۥ نَزَّلَهُۥ عَلَىٰ قَلْبِكَ بِإِذْنِ ٱللَّهِ

Say: 'Whoever is an enemy to Jibrīl for it is none but he who has brought it [the Qur'ān] down upon your heart by the permission of Allāh...'

[*Al-Baqarah* (2): 97]

فَإِذَا قَرَأْتَ ٱلْقُرْءَانَ
فَٱسْتَعِذْ بِٱللَّهِ مِنَ ٱلشَّيْطَـٰنِ ٱلرَّجِيمِ ﴿٩٨﴾ إِنَّهُۥ لَيْسَ لَهُۥ سُلْطَـٰنٌ
عَلَى ٱلَّذِينَ ءَامَنُوا۟ وَعَلَىٰ رَبِّهِمْ يَتَوَكَّلُونَ ﴿٩٩﴾ إِنَّمَا
سُلْطَـٰنُهُۥ عَلَى ٱلَّذِينَ يَتَوَلَّوْنَهُۥ وَٱلَّذِينَ هُم بِهِۦ مُشْرِكُونَ
﴿١٠٠﴾ وَإِذَا بَدَّلْنَآ ءَايَةً مَّكَانَ ءَايَةٍ ۙ وَٱللَّهُ أَعْلَمُ
بِمَا يُنَزِّلُ قَالُوٓا۟ إِنَّمَآ أَنتَ مُفْتَرٍۭ ۚ بَلْ أَكْثَرُهُمْ لَا يَعْلَمُونَ
﴿١٠١﴾ قُلْ نَزَّلَهُۥ رُوحُ ٱلْقُدُسِ مِن رَّبِّكَ بِٱلْحَقِّ لِيُثَبِّتَ
ٱلَّذِينَ ءَامَنُوا۟ وَهُدًى وَبُشْرَىٰ لِلْمُسْلِمِينَ ﴿١٠٢﴾

So when you recite the Qur'ān, [first] seek refuge with Allāh from the Accursed Shayṭān. Indeed there is for him no authority over those who have believed and rely upon their Lord. His authority is only over those who take him as an ally and those who associate others with Allāh. And when We substitute a verse in place of a verse - and Allāh is most Knowing of what He sends down - they say, 'You [O Muḥammad (ﷺ)] are but an inventor [of lies].' But most of them do not know. Say, 'The Spirit of the Holy has brought it down from your Lord in truth to make firm those who believe and as guidance and good tidings to the Muslims.'

[*An-Naḥl* (16): 98-102]

Hence He called him the Trustworthy Spirit and the Spirit of the Holy. Allāh, the Exalted says,

فَلَآ أُقْسِمُ بِٱلْخُنَّسِ ﴿١٥﴾ ٱلْجَوَارِ ٱلْكُنَّسِ ﴿١٦﴾

So I swear by the retreating stars, those that run [their courses] and disappear.

[*At-Takwīr* (81): 15-16]

Meaning the stars that are in the heaven, hidden before their appearance. When they appear, the people see them running their course through the heaven and when they set, they disappear to the place of setting that veils them.

وَٱلَّيْلِ إِذَا عَسْعَسَ ﴿١٧﴾

And by the night as it closes in.

[*At-Takwīr* (81): 17]

Meaning when it goes and the morning arrives.

وَٱلصُّبْحِ إِذَا تَنَفَّسَ ﴿١٨﴾

And by the dawn when it breathes.

[*At-Takwīr* (81): 18]

Meaning arrives.

إِنَّهُۥ لَقَوْلُ رَسُولٍ كَرِيمٍ ﴿١٩﴾

[That] indeed it [the Qur'ān] is a word [conveyed by] a noble Messenger.

[*At-Takwīr* (81): 19]

Meaning Jibrīl (*ʿalayhi as-salām*).

ذِى قُوَّةٍ عِندَ ذِى ٱلْعَرْشِ مَكِينٍ ۝٢٠ مُّطَاعٍ ثَمَّ أَمِينٍ ۝٢١

> [Who is] possessed of power and with the Owner of the Throne, secure [in position], obeyed there and trustworthy.
>
> [*At-Takwīr* (81): 20-21]

Meaning obeyed in the heaven and trusted. Then He says,

وَمَا صَاحِبُكُم بِمَجْنُونٍ ۝٢٢

> And your companion [Muḥammad (ﷺ)] is not mad.
>
> [*At-Takwīr* (81): 22]

Meaning your companion through whom Allāh has favoured you, since He sent him as a Messenger to you, being of the same species as you and living amongst you because you would not have been able to bear seeing the Angels. This is as Allāh, the Exalted says,

وَقَالُوا۟ لَوْلَآ أُنزِلَ
عَلَيْهِ مَلَكٌ ۖ وَلَوْ أَنزَلْنَا مَلَكًا لَّقُضِىَ ٱلْأَمْرُ ثُمَّ لَا يُنظَرُونَ ۝٨
وَلَوْ جَعَلْنَٰهُ مَلَكًا لَّجَعَلْنَٰهُ رَجُلًا

> And they say, 'Why was there not sent to him an Angel?' But if We had sent down an Angel, the matter would have been decided; then they would not be reprieved. And if We had made him [the Messenger] an Angel, We would have made him [appear as] a man...
>
> [*Al-Anʿām* (6): 8-9]

Allāh says,

وَلَقَدْ رَءَاهُ بِٱلْأُفُقِ ٱلْمُبِينِ

> And he has already seen him in the clear horizon.

[*At-Takwīr* (81): 23]

Meaning he saw Jibrīl (*ʿalayhi as-salām*).

وَمَا هُوَ عَلَى ٱلْغَيْبِ بِظَنِينٍ ﴿٢٤﴾

And he [Muḥammad (ﷺ)] is not untrustworthy with regards the unseen.

[*At-Takwīr* (81): 24]

Meaning dishonest and suspect. In another recitation the wording is,

وَمَا هُوَ عَلَى ٱلْغَيْبِ بِضَنِينٍ ﴿٢٤﴾

And he [Muḥammad (ﷺ)] is not a withholder of [knowledge of] the unseen.

[*At-Takwīr* (81): 24]

Meaning miserly such that he hides knowledge and does not distribute it unless it be for a fee, as is done by those who conceal knowledge unless they are given something in return.

وَمَا هُوَ بِقَوْلِ شَيْطَٰنٍ رَّجِيمٍ ﴿٢٥﴾

And it [the Qur'ān] is not the word of an accursed Shayṭān.

[*At-Takwīr* (81): 25]

Therefore He absolved Jibrīl (*ʿalayhi as-salām*) from being a devil just as He absolved Muḥammad (ﷺ) from being a poet or soothsayer.

[13.12 The Miracles of the *Awliyā'* are only Attained Through Following the Messenger (ﷺ)]

Hence the pious, God-fearing *Awliyā'* of Allāh are those who follow Muḥammad (ﷺ), doing what he ordered and refraining from what he warned against. They follow him in that which He told them that they should follow him in and hence He aids them with His Angels and a spirit from Him. Allāh places His light in their hearts and honours them with miracles. The miracles of the choicest of these *Awliyā'* are performed for the benefit of the Religion or to fulfil the needs of the Muslims just as the miracles of their Prophet (ﷺ) were performed for this end.

The miracles of the *Awliyā'* are only attained due to the blessing that lies in following His Messenger, hence, in reality, they are included amongst the miracles of the Messenger (ﷺ). Such miracles as splitting the moon in two[5], the glorification of stones held in his palm,[6] the tree leaning to him,[7] the trunk of the palm tree yearning for him,[8] his narrating the description of *Bayt al-Maqdis* on the Nights Journey,[9] his narrating that which was and will be,[10] his coming with

---

[5] {Y} Refer to *al-Qamar* (54): 1. Refer also to Ṣaḥīḥ Bukhārī [Eng. Trans. 4/533 no. 830].

[6] {Y} Abū Nu'aym, *'Dalā'il an-Nubuwwah'* [p. 214] and refer to *'Majma' az-Zawā'id'* [8/299].

[7] {F} Refer to: Abū Ya'lā [no. 2350] and Abū Nu'aym, *'ad-Dalā'il'* [no. 297].
{Y} Reported by Muslim [Eng. Trans. 4/1547 under no. 7149].

[8] {F} Reported by Bukhārī [Eng. Trans. 4/505 no. 783] and at-Tirmidhī [no. 505].

[9] {Y} Reported by Bukhārī [Eng. Trans. 5/142 no. 226].

[10] {Y} Refer to Bukhārī [Eng. Trans. 4/278 no. 414].

the Great Book and his increasing the quantity of food and drink on many occasions. During the Battle of *al-Khandaq* he satisfied the hunger of an army from a small amount of food that never diminished as is reported in the famous ḥadīth of Umm Sulaym,[11] he quenched the thirst of the army during the military expedition of *Khaybar* from a water-skin that did not diminish[12] and he filled the vessels of the army during the year of *Tabūk* from a small amount of food that did not diminish despite the fact that they numbered thirty thousand.[13] Water flowed from his fingertips on more than one occasion such that it sufficed all of the people who were with him at that time, for example during the expedition of *Ḥudaybiyyah* wherein they numbered fourteen or fifteen hundred.[14]

Other examples are his returning the eye of Qatādah to its socket when it slipped out onto his cheek and it ended being the better of his eyes.[15] When he sent Muḥammad bin Muslimah to kill Ka'b bin al-Ashraf, he fell and broke his leg and he (ﷺ) wiped his hand over it and he was cured.[16] From a single sheep he fed one hundred and thirty people, he cut a piece for each person, served it on two large trays and they all partook of it, afterwards there was still some left

---

[11] {F} Reported by Bukhārī [Eng. Trans. 4/500 no. 500, 7/223 no. 293, 8/443 no. 679] and Muslim [Eng. Trans. 3/1124 no. 5058].

[12] {Y} Reported by Bukhārī [Eng. Trans. 1/204 no. 340].

[13] {Y} Reported by Muslim [Eng. Trans. 1/20 no.'s 41-42].

[14] {F} Reported by Bukhārī [Eng. Trans. 4/499 no. 776]. Refer to Muslim [Eng. Trans. 4/1231-1232] for more examples of this category of miracles.

[15] {Y} Reported by al-Bayhaqī, *'ad-Dalā'il'* [2/30] and refer to *'Majma' az-Zawā'id'* [8/297].

[16] {Y} Reported by Bukhārī [Eng. Trans. 5/251 no. 371].

over.[17] He paid off the debt that 'Abdullāh Abū Jābir owed the Jew which amounted to thirty *wasq*. Jābir narrated,

> "So he ordered the person to whom the debt was owed to take all the dates [off the trees] as would pay off the debt but he refused to accept the offer [because the dates were not enough]. So the Messenger of Allāh (ﷺ) walked amongst them and then said to Jābir, *'Pick what is owed him.'* Hence the thirty *wasq* was paid off and there still remained the equivalent of seventeen *wasq*." [18]

There are many more examples, indeed about one thousand have been collected.[19]

[13.13 Mention of Some of the Miracles Performed by the Companions and Successors]

The miracles performed by the Companions, the Successors (*Tābi'īn*) and the generality of the righteous are many.

Usayd bin Huḍair used to recite *Sūrah al-Kahf* and the likes of a cloud would descend from the sky containing what seemed to be lit lamps, these were the Angels that descended for his recitation.[20]

The Angels used to extend the *salām* to 'Imrān bin Ḥusain.[21]

---

[17] {Y} Reported by Bukhārī [Eng. Trans. 7/225 no. 294].

[18] {F} Reported by Bukhārī [Eng. Trans. 4/502 no. 780] and Aḥmad [3/397-398].

[19] {F} Refer to: as-Suyūṭī, *'al-Khaṣā'iṣ al-Kubrā'*; al-Bayhaqī, *'Dalā'il an-Nubuwwah'*; Abū Nu'aym, *'Dalā'il an-Nubuwwah'*.

[20] {F} Reported by Bukhārī [Eng. Trans. 6/496 no. 536].

[21] {F} Reported by Aḥmad [4/427] and ibn Sa'd, *'Ṭabaqāt'* [4/290].

Salmān and Abū ad-Dardā' used to eat from a single plate and the plate or what it contained used to glorify Allāh.[22]

'Abbād bin Bishr and Usayd bin Huḍair went out after having been with the Messenger of Allāh (ﷺ) during a dark night, a light resembling the end of a whip illuminated the way for them and when they separated, the light also separated with them. Reported by Bukhārī and others.[23]

The story of *as-Ṣiddīq* is reported in the Two Ṣaḥīḥs when he went to his house accompanied by three guests. They commenced eating and they did not eat a morsel of food except that more than they had eaten appeared beneath it. They ate to their fill, yet more food remained than when they had started. When Abū Bakr and his wife saw that there was more than they had started with, they gave it to the Messenger of Allāh (ﷺ) and a group of people came to him and ate their fill. [24]

Khubaib bin 'Adī was captured by the polytheists in Mecca, may Allāh the Exalted ennoble it, and grapes would be brought to him and he would eat them except that there were no grapes to be found in Mecca. [25]

Āmir bin Fuhairah was killed as a martyr and when they went looking for his body they were unable to find it, because when he was

[22] {F} Refer to *'Siyar A'lām an-Nubulā'* [2/348] {Y} and Abū Nu'aym [1/224].

[23] {F} Reported by Bukhārī [Eng. Trans. 5/95 no. 149] and Aḥmad [3/138, 190, 272].

[24] {Y} Reported by Bukhārī [no. 537] and Muslim [Eng. Trans. 3/1134 no. 5106].

[25] {F} Refer to Bukhārī [Eng. Trans. 4/176 no. 282, 5/216 no. 325, 5/283 no. 412] and *'al-Iṣābah'* [4/392].

killed he was raised up as witnessed by Āmir bin at-Tufail. 'Urwah reports, 'They saw the Angels raising him up.' [26]

Umm Ayman left in order to undertake migration without taking any food or drink, [During the journey] she almost died of thirst, when it was time to break fast - she was fasting - she heard something above her head and looked up and behold there was a pail of water hanging there. She drank from it until her thirst was quenched and never did she become thirsty again for the remainder of her life.[27]

Safīnah, the slave of the Messenger of Allāh (ﷺ) informed a lion that he was the messenger of the Messenger of Allāh (ﷺ), so the lion walked with him until he reached his intended destination. [28]

When al-Barā'a bin Mālik took an oath by Allāh, the Exalted, his oath was always fulfilled.[29] When the Muslims were fighting *Jihād* and the fighting became fierce they would cry out, 'O Barā'a! Make an oath by your Lord!' he would say, 'O my Lord! I take an oath by You that You confer victory upon us' and the enemy would be vanquished. On the day of *at-Tustar* [30] he said, 'O my Lord! I take an

[26] {F} Refer to *'al-Iṣābah'* [4/247] {Y} and refer to Bukhārī [Eng. Trans. 5/290 no. 419].

[27] {F} Refer to: *'Siyar'* [2/224] and ibn Sa'd, *'Ṭabaqāt'* [8/224] {Y} and it is reported by Abū Nu'aym [2/67].

[28] {F} Reported by at-Ṭabarānī [no. 6432] and al-Ḥākim [3/606].

[29] {F} Reported by al-Ḥākim [3/292] who declared it *ṣaḥīḥ* and adh-Dhahabī agreed. Refer also to at-Tirmidhī [no. 3853].

[30] {Y} In some editions the wording is *al-Qādisiyyah* or *al-Yamāmah* or *al-Yarmuk*, but what I have established is correct as this is what occurs in the books of biographies.

oath by You that You confer victory upon us and that you make me the first martyr.' So they were granted victory and al-Barā'a was killed as a martyr. [31]

Khālid bin al-Walīd besieged an impenetrable fortress and the besieged said, 'We will not accept Islām until you first drink poison.' So he drank it and it did not harm him. [32]

The supplications of Sa'd bin Abī Waqqās would be answered, not a single supplication of his would go unanswered. [33] He was the one who vanquished the armies of Chosroes and conquered Iraq. [34]

When 'Umar bin al-Khattāb sent out an army, he appointed a man named Sāriyah as their leader. Then while 'Umar was delivering the *Khuṭbah* he started shouting, 'O Sāriyah, the mountain! O Sāriyah, the mountain, the mountain!' Then a messenger from the army came and he questioned him [concerning the army], he said, 'O Leader of the Believers! We met with the enemy and they had [almost] defeated us, then a voice proclaimed, 'O Sāriyah, the mountain! O Sāriyah, the mountain!' So we put our backs against the mountain and Allāh vanquished them.' [35]

[31] {F} Refer to: *'Majma' az-Zawā'id'* [9/350] and *'al-Iṣābah'* [3/73].

[32] {F} Refer to: 'at-Tirmidhī' [no. 3751] and ibn Ḥibbān [no. 2215].
I say: its *isnād* is *ṣaḥīḥ*.

[33] {Y} Tirmidhī [no. 3835] reports that the Prophet (ﷺ) said, *"O Allāh! Respond to Sa'd when he supplicates to You."*

[34] {Y} Ibn Kathīr, *'al-Bidāyah wa an-Nihāyah'* [7/33] mentions the conquests of Sa`d.

[35] {F} Reported by al-Lālikā'ī, *'Karāmāt al-Awliyā'* [no. 67] and al-Bayhaqī, *'ad-Dalā'il.'*
I say: the narration is *ḥasan* due to witnesses. Allāh Knows best.
Refer to: *'al-Maqāṣid'* [p. 474] and *'as-Ṣaḥīḥah'* [no. 1110].

When az-Zanīrah was tortured due to her professing Islām, she absolutely refused to renounce Islām and then her eyesight went. The polytheists said, '*al-Lāt* and *al-'Uzzah* have afflicted her sight.' She said, 'No, by Allāh!' and Allāh returned her sight to her. [36]

Sa'īd bin Zayd supplicated against Arwā bint al-Hakam when she lied against him and as a result she became blind. He said, 'O Allāh! If she is lying then make her blind and kill her in her land.' She became blind and fell in a pit on her land and died. [37]

Al-'Alā' bin al-Khadramī was given the position of governor over Bahrain by the Messenger of Allāh (ﷺ). He used to say in his supplication, 'O the All-Knowing! O the Forbearing! O the Exalted One! O the Great One!' and his supplication would be answered. He supplicated to Allāh that they be given water to drink and perform ritual ablution when they found no water, and water for those after them and his supplication was answered. He also supplicated to Allāh when the sea prevented them from crossing with their horses and they could find no way to do so, and every single person crossed the water and not a single saddle got wet. He supplicated to Allāh that no one see his body when he died and they did not find him in his grave. [38]

A similar thing happened to Abu Muslim al-Khawlānī who was

---

[36] {F} Refer to ibn Ḥajr, *'al-Iṣābah'* [4/305] {Y} who referred the report to ibn Abī Shaybah and ibn 'Abdul Barr, *'al-Istī'āb'*

[37] {F} Reported by Bukhārī [Eng. Trans. 4/281 no. 420] and Muslim [Eng. Trans. 3/847 no.'s 3921-3922].

[38] {F} Reported by al-Lālikā'ī, *'Karāmāt al-Awliyā'"* [p. 149] and ibn Abī ad-Dunyā, *'Majābu ad-Du'ā'* [p. 75].

I say: its *isnād* contains weakness as per *'Majma' az-Zawā'id'* [9/376] and al-Bayhaqī, *'Dalā'il an-Nubuwwah'* [6/51].

thrown in a fire. He, and those with him, set out from the military camp upon the river Tigris which was ejecting pieces of wood due to its overflowing. Then he turned to those with him and said, 'Have any of you lost some of your belongings so that I may supplicate to Allāh, the Mighty and Magnificent, for them?' Some people said, 'I have lost a nosebag.' He said, 'Follow me' and they followed him and they found it hanging on something and they took it. [39] Al-Asad al-Ansī sought him out when he claimed Prophethood and asked, 'Do you bear witness that I am the Messenger of Allāh?' He replied, ' I did not hear you.' He asked, 'Do you bear witness that Muḥammad is the Messenger of Allāh?' He replied, 'Yes,' so al-Asad ordered that a fire be kindled and he be thrown in it. After he was thrown in, they found him therein standing and praying, enveloped with coolness and peace. [40]

He went to Madīnah after the death of the Prophet (ﷺ) and 'Umar made him sit between himself and Abū Bakr *as-Ṣiddīq* (*raḍiyAllāhu 'anhumā*). He said, 'All praise and thanks are due to Allāh who did not cause me to die before seeing some of the nation of Muḥammad (ﷺ), who Allāh treated the same as Abraham, the Beloved of Allāh.[41] His slave-girl once put poison in his food but it caused him no harm. His wife had another woman pretend to be his wife and so he supplicated against her, as a result she became blind and came to him and sought his forgiveness. He supplicated for her and Allāh returned her sight to her. [42]

---

[39] {F} Refer to *'Siyar'* [4/8-11] {Y} and *'al-Bidāyah wa an-Nihāyah'* [6/295].

[40] {Y} Reported by Abū Nu'aym [2/128].

[41] {F} Refer to *'Siyar'* [4/8-9] {Y} and Abū Nu'aym [2/127].

[42] {F} Refer to *'Siyar'* [4/18] and *'al-Ḥilya'* [2/91]. It was reported by Aḥmad, *'az-Zuhd'* [no. 274] and ibn al-Mubārak, *'az-Zuhd'* [no. 295].

'Āmir bin 'Abd Qais used to take his wages of two thousand *dirhams* and place them in his sleeve and not a single beggar did he meet on his way except that he gave to him without counting how much he gave. Then he would arrive home and the number and weight of the *dirhams* would be exactly the same as he started with. [43] He came across a caravan that had been besieged by a lion, he went up to the lion until his clothes touched it and put his leg upon its neck saying, 'Indeed you are a dog from amongst the dogs belonging to Allāh, and I am ashamed to fear anything else besides Him,' [44] the caravan then passed by. He supplicated to Allāh that He make purification easy for him in the winter and water used to be brought to him while steaming. [45] He also supplicated to Allāh that He prevent his heart from [being enticed] by Shayṭān while in prayer and hence Shayṭān was never able to [entice him]. [46]

Al-Ḥasan al-Basrī could not be found by al-Ḥajjāj, [his men] entered his house six times [while he was there] and he supplicated to Allāh, the Mighty and Magnificent, and they did not see him. He supplicated against one of the *Khawārij* who used to harm him and he immediately died. [47]

The horse of Silah bin Ashīm died in battle upon which he said, 'O Allāh! Do not bestow [Your] favour on a creature over me,' so

---

[43] {F} Reported by al-Lālikā'ī [p. 206] and Abū Nu'aym, *'al-Ḥilya'* [2/96] with a *ḍa'īf isnād.* Refer to *'Siyar'* [4/17].

[44] {F} Reported by al-Lālikā'ī [p. 204] and ibn Abī ad-Dunyā, *'Majābu ad-Du'ā'* [no. 117] with a *ḍa'īf isnād.*

[45] {Y} Reported by ibn al-Mubārak, *'az-Zuhd'* [p. 295].

[46] {Y} Ibid.

[47] {F} Reported by al-Lālikā'ī [p. 204] and ibn Abī ad-Dunyā, *'Majābu ad-Du'ā'* [no. 117].

Allāh brought his horse back to life. When he reached his house he said, 'O my son, take the saddle of the horse for it is only on loan,' when he removed its saddle, it died. [48] One time he felt hungry at *al-Ahwāz* and supplicated to Allāh, the Mighty and Magnificent, that He feed him and a pile of moist dates fell behind him wrapped in palm leaves. He ate the dates and the palm leaves remained with his wife for some time. [49] Another time he was praying in a jungle at night when a lion came up to him, when he had performed the *taslīm* he said to it, 'Seek your sustenance elsewhere,' and the lion retreated, roaring at the same time. [50]

During the days of *al-Ḥurra*, [51] Saʿīd bin al-Musayyab used to hear the call to prayer coming from the grave of the Messenger of Allāh (ﷺ) at the times of prayer while the *Masjid* was empty, there being nobody there but him. [52]

A person from *an-Nakhʿ* had his donkey die while he was travelling, his companions said to him, 'Come we shall distribute your belongings on our animals.' He said to them, 'Leave me for a time.' He performed ritual ablution in the best of ways and prayed two *rakʿāhs* of prayer, then he supplicated to Allāh, the Exalted, and He brought his donkey back to life and it carried his belongings. [53]

---

[48] {Y} Reported by al-Munāwī, *'al-Kawākib ad-Durriyyah'* [1/125].

[49] {Y} Reported by Abū Nuʿaym [2/239].

[50] {F} Refer to al-Lālikā'ī[p. 218].

[51] {Y} Meaning the days when Madīnah was besieged by people from *al-Ḥurra*, led by Yazīd bin Muʿāwiyah.

[52] {F} Reported by al-Lālikā'ī [p. 165] and ibn Saʿd, *'at-Ṭabaqāt'* [5/132].

[53] {Y} Reported in *'al-Bidāyah wa an-Nihāyah'* [6/175].

When Awais al-Qarnī died they found the white burial sheets amongst his clothes that had previously not been there, they also found a grave already dug for him in the desert containing the *laḥd*, they buried him there in those burial sheets. [54]

ʿAmr bin ʿUtbah bin Farqad prayed one day in extreme heat and he was shaded by a cloud. The predatory animals used to protect him while he was tending to the animals of his companions because he used to set a condition upon them that he serve them while on a military expedition. [55]

Whenever Muṭarraf bin ʿAbdullāh bin ash-Shakhayyir used to enter his house, his utensils used to glorify Allāh along with him.[56] One time he and a companion were travelling in the dark and a beam of light like the end of a whip alighted their way for them.[57]

When al-Aḥnaf bin Qais[58] died, a hat of a person fell in his grave so he descended to retrieve it and found that the grave had expanded as far as the eye could see.

Ibrāhīm at-Taimī[59] used to go a month or two months without eating anything, [60] one time he left to find food for his family and

[54] {Y} Reported by Abū Nuʿaym [2/83].

[55] {Y} Reported by Abū Nuʿaym [2/157] and ibn al-Mubārak [p. 301].

[56] {F} Refer to *'as-Siyar'* [4/194] and al-Lālikā'ī [p. 208].

[57] {F} Refer to *'Siyar'* [4/86].

[58] {F} Refer to *'Siyar'* [5/60].

[59] {F} Refer to *'Siyar'* [7/62]. It is reported by al-Lālikā'ī [p. 225] and ibn Abī ad-Dunyā, *'Majābu ad-Duʿā'* [no. 133].

[60] {Y} Reported by Aḥmad, *'az-Zuhd'* [p. 362].

was unable to find any. He passed by flat ground containing soft red mud and took some of it, when he returned to his family he opened it and found it to contain red wheat and when he planted it, the wheat grew with ears full of grain.

'Utbah al-Ghulām asked his Lord for three qualities: a beautiful voice, plentiful tears and food without undue difficulty. When he used to recite he would cry and cause others to cry and his tears remained flowing for the whole of his life. When he lay down to sleep in his house, he would find his nourishment their and not know where it came from. [61]

'Abdul-Wāḥid bin Zayd was afflicted by semi-paralysis of his limbs and so he asked his Lord that He relieve his limbs at the time of performing ritual ablution. During the time of his performing ritual ablution his limbs would become active and then return to their state. [62]

This topic is vast and we have a detailed discussion concerning this in another place. As for what we ourselves know due to having witnessed it or being informed of it, then it is a great deal.

It is necessary to know that these miracles could occur in accordance to the need of the person, so if one who has weak faith or one who is needy is in need of these miracles, he is given that which would strengthen his faith and fulfil his need. It is possible that a person who has greater allegiance to, and love of, Allāh not require this, and so the same type of miracles not occur for him. This is due to his exalted ranking and not due to some deficiency in his allegiance to and love of Allāh, this is why such miracles occurred more

[61] {Y} Reported by Abū Nu'aym [6/236].

[62] {Y} Reported by Abū Nu'aym [6/155].

frequently for the Successors than they did for the Companions. A greater level then this are those miracles that occur at the hands of someone for the guidance of the creation or to fulfil their needs [and not ones own].

[13.14 Those Subject to Satanic States]

The satanic states oppose what has previously been mentioned, such as the state of the 'Abdullāh bin Sayyād who appeared during the time of the Prophet (ﷺ), who was thought to be the Dajjāl by some of the Companions. The Prophet (ﷺ), however, refrained from passing a verdict on him until it later became clear to him that he was not the Dajjāl but rather a type of soothsayer. The Prophet (ﷺ) said to him,

«قد خَبَّأْتُ لك خبئاً» قال: الدَّخ الدَّخ. وقد كان خبَّأ له سورة الدخان، فقال له النبي ﷺ «إخسأ فلن تعدوَ قدرك»

> *"I have hidden something from you."* He said, *'ad-Dukh, ad-Dukh,'* the Prophet (ﷺ) had hidden *Sūrah Dukhān* from him. The Prophet (ﷺ) then remarked, *"Be in ignominy for you will not exceed your capabilities."* [63]

Meaning that you are only a brother of the soothsayers. It is possible that the soothsayer be accompanied by a devil who informs him of much that is unseen which he stole by listening [to the discourse of the Angels] and at the same time mixes truth with falsehood. In the authentic ḥadīth reported by Bukhārī and others that the Prophet (ﷺ) said,

---

[63] {F} Reported by Bukhārī [Eng. Trans. 2/244 no. 437, 4/184 no. 290, 8/124 no.'s 193-194, 8/401 no. 615,] and Muslim [Eng. Trans. 4/1511 no. 6991, 7000].

«إن الملائكة
تنزل في العنان - وهو السحاب - فتذكر الأمر قضي في
السماء، فتسترق الشياطين السمع فتوحيه إلى الكهان،
فيكذبون معها مائة كذبة من عند أنفسهم»

"Indeed the Angels descend to the clouds and mention the matters decreed in the heaven. The devils stealthily listen to these matters and then descend to inspire the soothsayers adding one hundred lies of their own." [64]

In the ḥadīth reported by Muslim from ibn ʿAbbās who said,

> 'While the Prophet (ﷺ) was amongst a group of the Anṣār, a shooting star was seen that lit up [the sky]. The Prophet (ﷺ) asked, *"What did you say when you saw the likes of this occurrence in the days of Pre-Islāmic ignorance?"* They replied, 'we would say that a great man has died or a great person has been born.' The Messenger of Allāh said, *"Indeed it is not shot at the death or birth of anyone, however when our Lord, the Blessed and Exalted, decrees a matter the carriers of the Throne glorify Him, then the inhabitants of the heaven beneath them glorify Him, then those beneath them until the glorification reaches the inhabitants of this heaven. Then the inhabitants of the seventh heaven ask the carriers of the Throne, 'What has our Lord said?' They inform them, then the inhabitants of each heaven ask until the matter is relayed to the inhabitants of this, the lowest heaven. The devils then manage to steal a hearing and carry the information to their allies, that which they narrate in this way is the truth but they add to it [their own falsehood].'"*

And in another report, Māʿmar said,

> 'I asked az-Zuhrī, 'Were they flung at them during the

[64] {F} Reported by Bukhārī [Eng. Trans. 4/291 no. 432].

pre-Islāmic ignorance?' He replied, "Yes, but they were increased after the sending of Muḥammad (ﷺ).'" [65]

Another example lies with al-Aswad al-Ansī who claimed Prophethood.[66] He was accompanied by devils who would inform him of some of the unseen affairs and when the Muslims fought him they used to fear that the devils would inform him of what they planned, until his wife aided them against him, when his disbelief became clear to her, and they killed him.

Likewise Musaylamah, the Liar, used to be accompanied by devils of who would inform him of some of the unseen affairs and aid him in some matters.

Examples of these people are many, such as al-Ḥārith ad-Dimashqī who left Syria during the rule of al-Malik bin Marwān and made claim to Prophethood. The devils used to remove his legs from the shackles that bound them and prevent swords from piercing him. Marble slabs used to glorify [Allāh] when he touched them with his hand and the people used to see men and legions of riders upon horses in the air which he claimed were Angels whereas in reality they were Jinn. When the Muslims captured him with the intent of killing him, a spear-thrower threw a spear at him but it did not penetrate his body. 'Abdul-Malik said to the thrower, 'You did not mention the Name of Allāh [before throwing]' so he mentioned the Name of Allāh and threw, and the spear killed him.

This is the case with all of the satanic states, the devils retreat when something that would drive them away is mentioned in their presence such as the *Āyah al-Kursī*. It is established in the Ṣaḥīḥ from

[65] {F} Reported by Muslim [Eng. Trans. 4/1210 no. 5538] and Aḥmad [1/218, 274, 323].

the Prophet (ﷺ), in the ḥadīth of Abū Hurayrah (*raḍiyAllāhu ʿanhu*) wherein the Prophet (ﷺ) appointed him to guard the *Zakāh al-Fiṭr* and Shayṭān kept trying to steal it night after night, each time he would catch him and Shayṭān would repent and so Abū Hurayrah would let him go. The Prophet (ﷺ) would ask him,

> "*What did your prisoner do yesterday?*" He replied, 'He promised that he would not return.' He said, "*He has lied to you for he will certainly return.*" On the third occasion, [Shayṭān said to Abū Hurayrah], 'Release me and I will teach you that which would bring you benefit: when you lie down on your bed, recite *Āyah al-Kursī*, for Allāh will appoint a guard over you who will stay with you and Shayṭān will not be able to come close to you until you awake in the morning.' When he informed the Prophet (ﷺ) about this, he said, *"He has told the truth even though he is a great liar."* [67]

This is why if a person were to recite this at the onset of satanic states, with truthfulness and sincerity, it would render those states obsolete. Examples of such states lie with a person entering the fire whilst in a satanic state, or his being present to listen to singing and dancing and therefore the devils descend upon him and speak on his tongue while he is unaware, or even not understand what is being said, or his unveiling what is in the hearts of some of those present with him, or his speaking in numerous tongues just as the Jinn speak upon the tongue of one who is possessed. A person who has been afflicted with such a condition is not aware just like the one possessed, who Shayṭān has driven mad with his touch, confused him and spoken upon his tongue. When such a person regains his

---

[66] {T} Refer to Bukhārī [Eng. Trans. 5/468 no. 662] concerning mention of him.

[67] {F} Reported by Bukhārī [Eng. Trans. 3/289 no. 505, 4/319 no. 495, 6/491 no. 530] as a *taʿlīq* report and it was quoted with its full *isnād* by an-Nasāʾī, *'ʿAmal al-Yawm wa al-Laylah'* [no.'s 958-959].

sanity, he is not aware of what he previously said.

This is why the one who is possessed can sometimes take a severe beating, such as would have killed a normal person or at least made him ill, without being harmed. This is because this beating did not harm the actual person but the Jinn who had possessed him, this is why when he regains sanity, he is not aware of the previous beating he undertook.

From these people are those who are approached by the devils with food, fruits and sweets and other such things that may not have previously been present at that place. Some of these are flown by the Jinns through the air to Mecca, or *Bait al-Maqdis* or other places. Some of these are carried to *ʿArafah* on the eve of the Day of *ʿArafah* and subsequently returned in the same night. Such people do not perform a valid *Ḥajj* as required by the *Sharīʿah*, rather they go with their clothes and do not enter the state of *iḥrām* when at the *mīqāt*, they do not say the *talbiyyah*, they do not stop at *Muzdalifah*, they do not perform the *ṭawāf* of the House, they do not run between *Ṣafā* and *al-Marwā* and nor do they throw pebbles at the *Jimār*. Instead they merely stand on *ʿArafah* in their clothes, to return on the same night. In no way can this be considered to be a *Ḥajj* that is legislated by the *Sharīʿah* by agreement of the Muslims. Rather this case is comparable to one who goes to the *Jumuʿah* prayer and prays without performing ritual ablution and without facing the *Qiblah*. One such person was carried to *ʿArafah* and subsequently returned, in a dream he saw the Angels writing down [the names of] the pilgrims and he asked them, 'Will you not write my name?' They replied, 'You are not one of the pilgrims,' meaning: you have not performed a *Ḥajj* as required by the *Sharīʿah*.

[13.15 The Differences Between Miracles and Satanic States]

There are many differences between the miracles performed by the *Awliyā'* and those satanic states that resemble these miracles. From amongst these is that the cause of the miracles of the *Awliyā'* is their faith and *taqwā* whereas the cause for these satanic states lies in undertaking what Allāh and His Messenger have prohibited. Allāh, the Exalted says,

قُلْ إِنَّمَا حَرَّمَ رَبِّيَ ٱلْفَوَٰحِشَ مَا ظَهَرَ مِنْهَا وَمَا
بَطَنَ وَٱلْإِثْمَ وَٱلْبَغْيَ بِغَيْرِ ٱلْحَقِّ وَأَن تُشْرِكُوا۟ بِٱللَّهِ مَا لَمْ يُنَزِّلْ بِهِۦ
سُلْطَٰنًا وَأَن تَقُولُوا۟ عَلَى ٱللَّهِ مَا لَا تَعْلَمُونَ ﴿٣٣﴾

> Say: 'My Lord has only forbidden immoralities - what is apparent of them and what is concealed - sin, oppression without due right, that you associate with Allāh that which He has not sent down authority for and that you say about Allāh that which you do not know.'
>
> [*Al-A'rāf* (7): 33]

Therefore speaking about Allāh without knowledge, oppression and indecent deeds have been prohibited by Allāh, the Exalted, and His Messenger, hence they cannot be a cause for Allāh ennobling a person [who commits them] with miracles. So if these miracles are not attained through *ṣalāh*, *dhikr* and the recitation of the Qur'ān, and are instead attained by doing that which Shayṭān loves and through enacting matters that contain *shirk* such as seeking succour with the created, or these 'miracles' aid one in oppressing the created and committing indecent deeds, then these are satanic states and not from the miracles granted by the Most Merciful.

From amongst these people are those who, when they attend sessions of singing and dancing, his devil approaches him and carries him in the air and he leaves the place he was in. Then, when he comes into the presence of one of the *Awliyā'* of Allāh, his devil retreats and as a result the person falls. This has happened to more than one person.

From amongst these people are those who seek succour from a created being - either dead or alive, regardless of whether he is a Muslim, Christian or polytheist. Shayṭān takes on the form of the person with whom succour is sought and fulfils some of the requester's need. The requester in turn believes the one with whom he had sought succour had appeared to him or that an Angel who had taken his form had come to him. In reality it was Shayṭān who had come to him in order to misguide him [further] due to his having committed *shirk* with Allāh. In the same way the devils enter the idols and speak to the polytheists.

From amongst these people are those to whom Shayṭān comes in a [human] form and claims to be Khiḍr, possibly informing him of some [hidden] matters and even aiding him in fulfilling some of his needs. A common event that has happened to the Muslim, Jew, Christian and in the lands of the disbelievers - east and west - is that when one of their own dies, Shayṭān comes to them in his form after his death and they believe that he is the deceased. He may pay off the deceased debts, return things entrusted to him and do other things connected to the deceased such as entering upon his wife and then leaving. It is possible that they may even have burned the deceased as is done by the disbelievers of India, yet are still lulled into believing that he continues to live after his death.

From amongst these was an old man in Egypt who enjoined his servant in a will not to let anyone wash him after his death because he himself would come and wash himself. When he died, his servant saw somebody having his masters' form and believed that it was he and that he had washed himself. When this person had finished washing the deceased, he disappeared. This was none other than Shayṭān who had misguided the deceased into believing that he would wash himself after his death. Then when he died, he appeared in his form in order to misguide the living, just as he had previously misguided the deceased.

From amongst these are those who see a throne suspended in the air above which is light, he hears someone addressing him with the words, 'I am your Lord.' If this person is from the People of Cognisance, he knows that this is none other than Shayṭān, so he avoids him and takes refuge with Allāh from him and as a result he disappears.

From amongst these are those who see a personage while awake who claims to be a prophet, *ṣiddīq* or some righteous *shaykh*. This has happened to more than one person and from amongst these were those who saw this personage by the grave of one whom they were visiting - they saw the grave split open and a form emerge from it and therefore believed that it was the deceased. In reality it was a Jinn who had appeared in that form. Also from amongst these are those who see a knight leaving or entering his grave and in reality it was none other than Shayṭān.

Therefore everyone who claims to have a seen a Prophet with the eyes of his head, has only imagined it.

From amongst these are those who see some senior personage in his dream such as *as-Ṣiddīq* (*raḍiyAllāhu 'anhu*) cutting or shaving his hair, or giving him his hat or clothes to wear. When he awakes, he sees that the hat is upon his head and his hair has been shortened or shaved, again this was done by none other than the Jinn.

These satanic states occur to those who leave the bounds of the Book and *Sunnah* and such people are of varying levels [as per their degree of leaving the Book and *Sunnah*]. The Jinn who associate themselves with them are of the same type and of a similar belief. Amongst the Jinn there is found the disbeliever, sinner and the mistaken. If the human is a disbeliever, sinner or ignorant, the Jinn will join him in his disbelief, sin or misguidance. It is possible that they then proceed to aid him if he conforms to the type of disbelief that they themselves have chosen such as swearing by the names of those Jinn, and others, who they exalt and glorify. Or such as his writing the Names of Allāh, or some of His Speech with filth, or reversing the order of *al-Fātiḥah*, or *Sūrah al-Ikhlāṣ* or *Āyah al-Kursī* or others and writing them with filth. As a result the Jinn will transport him across water due to his doing those actions of disbelief that please them. It is possible that they bring to him someone he lusts after such as a woman or child - either through the air or by driving them in his direction.

There are many more example of this and mentioning them would only lengthen the discussion.

To believe in these is to believe in *al-Jabt* and all that is falsely worshipped besides Allāh (*ṭāghut*). *Al-Jabt* means magic and *ṭāghut* refers to the devils and the idols. If a person is obedient to Allāh and His Messenger, both inwardly and outwardly, then it is not possible for the devils to accompany him or make him accept them.

[13.16 The Prohibition of Exalting Graves]

This is why the worship of the Muslims is legislated to be carried out in the *Masjids*, which are the houses of Allāh and those who regularly attend the *Masjids* are the furthest removed of people from these satanic states.

As for the people of *shirk* and innovation, they exalt the graves and memorials of the dead, supplicating to the dead or via the dead, or believing that supplication by the graves will be answered. Due to this they are much closer and more prone to satanic states. It is established in the Two Ṣaḥīḥs that the Prophet (ﷺ) said,

«لعن الله اليهود والنصارى اتخذوا قبور أنبيائهم مساجد»

"Allāh cursed the Jews and Christians for they took the graves of their Prophets as Masjids." [68]

It is established in Ṣaḥīḥ Muslim that he (ﷺ) said, five days before his death,

> *"Indeed the person who has favoured me most with his company and property is Abū Bakr. If I were to have taken a beloved friend from the inhabitants of this earth, I would have taken Abū Bakr as a beloved friend, however your companion [i.e. the Prophet] is the beloved of Allāh. Let all the gates to the Masjid be closed except for the gate of Abū Bakr. Indeed those who came before you took the graves as Masjids, do not take the graves as Masjids for I prohibit you from that."* [69]

---

[68] {F} Reported by Bukhārī [Eng. Trans. 1/255 no.'s 427-428, 2/232 no. 414, 2/267 no. 472, 4/439 no. 660, 5/516 no. 725, 7/474 no. 706] and Muslim [Eng. Trans. 1/268 no. 1079].

[69] {F} Reported by Bukhārī [Eng. Trans. 1/270 no. 455, 5/5 no. 6, 5/156 no. 244] and Muslim [Eng. Trans. 4/1274 no. 5869].

It is reported in the Two Ṣaḥīḥs that the beauty and pictures of the churches in Abysinnia were mentioned to him during the illness [from which he died]. He said,

«إن أولئك إذا مات فيهم الرجل الصالح بنوا على قبره
مسجداً وصوّروا فيها تلك التصاوير، أولئك شرار الخلق
عند الله يوم القيامة»

"Indeed those people, when a righteous person amongst them died, they built a Masjid over him and drew those picture. They are the worst of people in the Sight of Allāh on the Day of Judgement."[70]

It is reported in *'Musnad'* of Aḥmad and *'Ṣaḥīḥ Abū Ḥātim'*[71] that he (ﷺ) said,

«إن من شرار الخلق من تدركهم الساعة
وهم أحياء، والذين اتخذوا القبور مساجد»

"Indeed the worst of creation are those who will be alive when the Last Hour will fall and those who take the graves as Masjids."[72]

It is reported in the Ṣaḥīḥ from him (ﷺ) that he said,

«لا تجلسوا على القبور ولا تصلوا إليها»

"Do not sit upon graves and do not perform prayer towards them."[73]

---

[70] {F} Reported by Bukhārī [Eng. Trans. 1/251 no. 419, 1/255 no. 426, 2/237 no. 425, 5/136 no. 213] and Muslim [Eng. Trans. 1/268 no. 1076].

[71] {Y} Which is famously known as *'Ṣaḥīḥ ibn Ḥibbān.'*

[72] {F} Reported by Bukhārī [Eng. Trans. 9/151 no. 187] and Aḥmad [1/405, 430, 454].

[73] {F} Reported by Muslim [Eng. Trans. 2/460 no. 2121] and Abū Dāwūd [Eng. Trans. 2/917 no. 3223].

It is reported in the *Muwaṭṭa* that he (ﷺ) said,

«اللهم لا تجعل قبـري وثناً يُعبـد، اشتدَّ غضب الله
على قوم اتخذوا قبور أنبيائهم مساجد»

"O Allāh! Do not make my grave an idol that is worshipped, indeed the Anger of Allāh was severe upon a people who took the graves of their Prophets as Masjids." [74]

In the *Sunan* it is reported that he (ﷺ) said,

قال: بأربعين سنة؟ قال: فَلِمَ تلومني على أمر قدَّره الله
عليَّ قبل أنْ أُخلق بأربعين سنة؟قال: فحجَّ آدم موسى»

"Do not take my grave as a place of festivities, send ṣalāh upon me from wherever you may be for indeed your ṣalāh is conveyed to me."[75]

He (ﷺ) said,

«مـا من رجـل يسـلِّم عليَّ إلا ردَّ الله عـليَّ روحي حـتى
أردَّ عـليـه السلام»

"There is not a single person who extends the salām to me except that Allāh returns my soul to me so that I may reply to his salām."[76]

He (ﷺ) said,

«إن الله وكَّل بقبري ملائكة يُبلغونني عن أُمتي السلام»

"Indeed Allāh has appointed Angels for my grave who convey the

---

[74] {F} Reported by Mālik [Eng. Trans. p. 82 no. 409] and Aḥmad [2/246] with a *ṣaḥīḥ isnād.*

[75] {F} Reported by Abū Dāwūd [Eng. Trans. 2/542 no. 2037] and Aḥmad [2/367] with a *ṣaḥīḥ isnād.*

[76] {F} Reported by Abū Dāwūd [Eng. Trans. 2/542 no. 2036] with a *ḥasan isnād.*

salām of my nation to me." [77]

He (ﷺ) said,

> *"Frequent the ṣalāh upon me on the day and night of Jumu'ah for indeed your ṣalāh is presented to me."* They asked, 'O Messenger of Allāh! How can our *ṣalāh* be presented to you when you have decayed?' He replied, *"Indeed Allāh has prohibited the earth from consuming the flesh of the Prophets."* [78]

Allāh, the Exalted, says in His Book concerning the polytheists of the nation of Noah (*'alayhi as-salām*),

> وَقَالُوا۟
> لَا تَذَرُنَّ ءَالِهَتَكُمْ وَلَا تَذَرُنَّ وَدًّا وَلَا سُوَاعًا وَلَا يَغُوثَ وَيَعُوقَ
> وَنَسْرًا ﴿٢٣﴾
>
> And they said, 'Never leave your gods and never leave *Wadd* or *Suwā'* or *Yaghuth* or *Ya'ūq* or *Naṣr*.'
>
> [*Nūḥ* (71): 23]

Ibn 'Abbās and others from the *Salaf* said,

> "These were a people who were righteous amongst the nation of Noah, when they died the people secluded themselves upon their graves [in devotion]. Then they depicted forms and pictures of them and worshipped

---

[77] {F} Reported by Bukhārī, *'Tārīkh al-Kabīr'* [3/2/416] from Ammār with similar meaning. I say the *isnād* is *ḍa'īf*, refer to *'Majma' az-Zawā'id'* [10/162].

However the following ḥadīth is *ṣaḥīḥ*, *'Indeed Allāh has Angels roaming the earth who convey to me the salām of my nation.'*

[78] {F} Reported by Abū Dāwūd [Eng. Trans. 1/269 no. 1042] and an-Nasā'ī [3/91] with a *ṣaḥīḥ isnād*.

them. This was the first occurrence of idol worship." [79]

So the Prophet (ﷺ) prohibited the taking of graves as *Masjids* in order to close the avenue to *shirk*. It was for this same reason that he prohibited praying at the rising and setting of the sun for the polytheists used to prostrate to the sun at these times and Shayṭān accompanies it at these times. Therefore praying at these times would bear a resemblance to the prayers of the polytheists and hence this possible avenue [to committing *shirk*] was shut.

Shayṭān expends all of his efforts to lead the children of Ādam astray. Therefore he descends to those who worship the sun, moon and stars and supplicate to them - as is done by those who worship stars - and informs them of some [hidden] matters. These people in turn call this [being who talks to them] 'The spirit of the stars' whereas in reality he is Shayṭān. Shayṭān, even though he may aid and support man in fulfilling some of his needs and goals, the harm he afflicts is many times greater than this benefit. The end of one who obeys him is evil unless that person was to turn in repentance to Allāh.

Similarly the worshippers of idols are addressed by the devils, the same applies to those who seek relief and succour from the dead or absent, to those who supplicate to the dead or via the dead and to those who think that supplication by a grave is better than supplicating in houses or *Masjids*. They report a ḥadīth which is a lie by agreement of the People of Cognisance,

"When cognisance fails you then go to the inhabitants of the grave." [80]

---

[79] {F} Reported by Bukhārī [Eng. Trans. 6/414 no. 442].

[80] {F} *'Kashf al-Khafā"* [1/88] and *'Ighātha al-Lahfān'* [1/215] with the words, *'When matters fail you...'*

'Taḥdhīr al-Muslimīn' [p. 133] with the words, *'When matters confuse you then seek aid with the inhabitants of the grave.'*

This ḥadīth was fabricated by those who opened the door to *shirk*.

The People of Innovation, the People of *Shirk* who resemble them [in certain acts] such as the worshippers of the stars and the Christians, and the misguided Muslims experience certain things and events at memorials which they think are miracles when in fact they come about by way of the devils. Examples of this are someone putting trousers by a grave and later finding it having been tied in a knot or people leaving a possessed person by it and seeing his Shayṭān leaving him - this being done by Shayṭān in order to misguide the people. When *Āyatul Kursī* is recited on such occasions truthfully and sincerely, [this ploy of Shayṭān] is nullified for *Tawḥīd* makes Shayṭān turn on his heels. This is why, when some of them are carried through the air, and says, 'There is none worthy of worship save Allāh,' he falls down. Another example of such events is a person seeing the grave split open and a person coming out of it who he believes to be the deceased when in reality it is a Shayṭān.

Examples of this are many and space does not allow mention of all of them.

Now, because isolation in caves and desolate lands is an innovation that has not been legislated by Allāh or His Messenger, the devils frequent these caves and mountains. Examples of this lie with the Cave of Blood on mount *Qāsiyūn*, mount Lebanon which is on the Syrian coast, mount *al-Fatḥ* which is at *Aswān* in Egypt, the mountains to be found in *Rūm* and *Khurasān*, the mountains in the Arabian peninsula, mount *al-Lukām*, mount *al-Aḥyash*, mount *Sabalān*[81] which is close to *Ardabīl*, mount *Sahl*[82] at *Tabrīz*, mount *Māshku* at *Atshwān*, mount *Nahāwund* and other such mountains at which people think

[81] {Y} In some texts the word is *Sulān* but what we have established is correct.

[82] {Y} In some texts the word is *Shahank*.

righteous people live. They call these people, 'The unseen men' but the only residents there are men from amongst the Jinn. The Jinn are men just as humans are men. Allāh, the Exalted says,

وَأَنَّهُۥ كَانَ رِجَالٌ مِّنَ ٱلْإِنسِ يَعُوذُونَ بِرِجَالٍ مِّنَ ٱلْجِنِّ فَزَادُوهُمْ رَهَقًا ۝٦

> And there were men from mankind who sought refuge with men from the Jinn, so they increased them only in the burden [of sin].
>
> [*Al-Jinn* (72): 6]

From amongst these [Jinn] are those who appear in the guise of a man covered in hair, whose skin resembles that of a goat. Anyone who does not know him would think that he is a human when in reality he is a Jinn. It is said that at each of these mountains are forty *Abdāl*, whereas these people at these places who are thought to be the *Abdāl* are actually Jinn, this fact is known via many methods [of investigation].

Again, examples of this are many and space does not allow mention of all of them, not even just those that we know of and have heard of. This brief book has only been written in response to one who asked that we mention the most important points concerning the *Awliyā'* of Allāh, the Exalted.

[13.17 The Stances of People Towards Miracles]

The people fall into three categories with regards miraculous occurrences:

1. Those who deny the existence of miracles for anyone other than the Prophets. It is also possible that such a person believe in miracles in principle, but reject what many people mention to

him of them because the person from whom they emanate is not a *Waliy* in his view.

2. Those who believe that anyone who performs a miraculous feat is a *Waliy* of Allāh. Both these stances are erroneous. This is why you will find people [who fall in this second category] saying that the polytheists and People of the Book have helpers who aid them in fighting the Muslims, and that these helpers are from amongst the *Awliyā'* of Allāh. The people of the first category would deny that [those disbelievers] can perform miracles altogether.

3. The correct position is that those disbelievers have helpers who are of the same nature and type as them. They are not from the *Awliyā'* of Allāh, the Mighty and Magnificent. Allāh, the Exalted says,

﴿ يَٰٓأَيُّهَا ٱلَّذِينَ ءَامَنُواْ لَا تَتَّخِذُواْ ٱلْيَهُودَ وَٱلنَّصَٰرَىٰٓ أَوْلِيَآءَ بَعْضُهُمْ أَوْلِيَآءُ بَعْضٍۚ وَمَن يَتَوَلَّهُم مِّنكُمْ فَإِنَّهُۥ مِنْهُمْۗ

> O you who have believed! Do not take the Jews and Christians as allies. They are [in fact] allies of one another, and whoever is an ally to them among you - then indeed he is one of them.
>
> [*Al-Mā'idah* (5): 51]

So those worshippers and ascetics who are not from the pious, God-fearing *Awliyā'* of Allāh who follow the Book and *Sunnah* are accompanied by the devils. Hence it is possible that they perform such miracles as befit their state and condition, but the miracles performed by these people contradict each other. When one who is established and firm amongst the *Awliyā'* of Allāh, the Exalted, is present, he nullifies [their so-called miracles]. It is necessary that these people be guilty of some form of lying - either due to ignorance or deliberately - and some type of sin that is appropriate to the devils who accompany them. It is in this way that Allāh differentiates between his pious, God-fearing *Awliyā'* and those who seek to resemble them from the *awliyā'* of Shayṭān. Allāh, the Exalted says,

هَلْ أُنَبِّئُكُمْ عَلَىٰ مَن تَنَزَّلُ ٱلشَّيَٰطِينُ ﴿٢٢١﴾ تَنَزَّلُ عَلَىٰ كُلِّ أَفَّاكٍ أَثِيمٍ ﴿٢٢٢﴾

> Shall I inform you upon whom the devils descend? They descend upon every sinful liar.
>
> [*Ash-Shu'arā'* (26): 221-222]

The word *affāq* means habitual liar and the word *athīm* means sinner.

[13.18 Music Strengthens Satanic States just as the Qur'ān Strengthen Faith]

From the greatest things that strengthen satanic states is listening to song and music, this is none other than the listening of the polytheists about which Allāh, the Exalted says,

وَمَا كَانَ صَلَاتُهُمْ
عِندَ ٱلْبَيْتِ إِلَّا مُكَآءً وَتَصْدِيَةً

> And their prayer at the House was nothing save whistling and clapping.
>
> [*Al-Anfāl* (8): 35]

Ibn 'Abbās and ibn 'Umar (*raḍiyAllāhu 'anhu*), and others from the *Salaf* said,

> "At-Taṣdiya *is clapping with the hands and* al-Mukā' *is like*

whistling. The polytheists used to do this as an act of worship." [83]

As for the Prophet (ﷺ) and his Companions, their worship consisted entirely of that which was ordered by Allāh such as *ṣalāh*, recitation of the Qur'ān, *dhikr* and the likes. They gathered together for those actions of worship legislated in a gathering and therefore they never gathered to listen to song - not that done by clapping nor with drums. Never once did he (ﷺ) become overcome with spiritual ecstasy and never did his cloak fall off him - all [narrations that mention this] are lies by agreement of the Scholars of Ḥadīth.

When the Companions of the Prophet (ﷺ) used to gather, he would order one of them to recite and the rest would listen.[84] 'Umar bin al-Khattāb (*raḍiyAllāhu 'anhu*) used to say to Abū Mūsā al-Ash'arī,

> 'Remind us of our Lord.' So he would recite and they would listen.[85]

The Prophet (ﷺ) passed by Abū Musā while he was reciting and he said to him,

> «مررت بك البارحة وأنت تقرأ، فجعلت أستمع لقراءتك»
>
> *"I passed by you last night while you were reciting, so I stood listening to your recitation."*

---

[83] {F} As-Suyuṭī, *'ad-Durr al-Manthūr'* [3/183] referred it to al-Faryābī, 'Abd bin Ḥumaid, ibn Jarīr, ibn al-Mundhir and ibn Abī Shaybah from ibn 'Abbās (*raḍiyAllāhu 'anhumā*).

He also referred it to ibn Abī Shaybah, 'Abd bin Ḥumaid, ibn Jarīr and others from ibn 'Umar (*raḍiyAllāhu 'anhumā*).The narration is also reported from Mujāhid, as-Suddī, ibn Jubair and others.

[84] {F} Refer to at-Ṭurṭushī, *'al-Ḥawādith wal Bida'a'* [pp. 161-167].

[85] {F} Reported by ad-Dārimī [no.'s 3493-3496] and 'Abdur-Razzāq, *'al-Muṣannaf'* [no.'s 4179-4182] with a *ṣaḥīḥ isnād.*

> He replied, 'If I knew that you were listening, I would have embellished it for you in the best of ways.' [86]

Meaning that I would have beautified my recitation for you. This is as the Prophet (ﷺ) said,

«زينـوا القـرآن بأصواتكم»

"Beautify the Qur'ān with your voices." [87]

He (ﷺ) said,

«لله أشد أذنـاً - أي استماعـاً - إلى الرجـل الحسن الصوت بـالقـرآن من صاحب القينة إلى قينته»

"Allāh Listens more attentively to a man who recites the Qur'ān with a beautiful voice than the owner of a songstress listens to her [sing]." [88]

He (ﷺ) said to ibn Mas'ūd,

«إقرأ عليَّ القرآن»

"Recite the Qur'ān to me."

> He said, 'should I recite to you when it was revealed to you?' He replied,

«إني أحب أن أسمعه من غيري»

---

[86] {F} Reported by Abū Ya'lā [no. 7279] with a *ḍa'īf isnād*. Refer to *'Majma' az-Zawā'id'* [/171].
The basis of the ḥadīth is ṣaḥīḥ and is found in Muslim.

[87] {F} Reported by Abū Dāwūd [Eng. Trans. 1/384 no. 1463] and an-Nasā'ī [no. 1468] with a *ṣaḥīḥ isnād.*

[88] {F} Reported by ibn Mājah [no. 1340] and Aḥmad [6/19-20] with a *ḍa'īf isnād.*

"Indeed I love that I hear it from other than me."

So I recited *Sūrah an-Nisā'* to him until I reached this verse,

فَكَيْفَ إِذَا جِئْنَا مِن كُلِّ أُمَّةٍۭ بِشَهِيدٍ
وَجِئْنَا بِكَ عَلَىٰ هَٰٓؤُلَآءِ شَهِيدًا ﴿٤١﴾

So how [will it be] when We bring from every nation a witness and We bring you [O Muḥammad (ﷺ)] against these [people] as a witness?

[*An-Nisā'* (4): 41]

He said,

«حسبك»،

"That is sufficient for you,"

and his eyes were overflowing with tears.[89]

The likes of this listening is the listening of the Prophets and their followers as has been mentioned by Allāh in the Qur'ān,

أُولَٰٓئِكَ ٱلَّذِينَ
أَنْعَمَ ٱللَّهُ عَلَيْهِم مِّنَ ٱلنَّبِيِّـۧنَ مِن ذُرِّيَّةِ ءَادَمَ وَمِمَّنْ حَمَلْنَا مَعَ نُوحٍ
وَمِن ذُرِّيَّةِ إِبْرَٰهِيمَ وَإِسْرَٰٓءِيلَ وَمِمَّنْ هَدَيْنَا وَٱجْتَبَيْنَآ ۚ إِذَا تُتْلَىٰ عَلَيْهِمْ
ءَايَٰتُ ٱلرَّحْمَٰنِ خَرُّوا۟ سُجَّدًا وَبُكِيًّا ۩

Those were the ones upon whom Allāh bestowed favour from among the Prophets of the descendants of Adam and of those We carried [in the ship] with Noah, and of the descendants of Abraham and Israel [Jacob], and of

[89] {F} Reported by Bukhārī [Eng. Trans. 6/514 no. 569, 6/515 no. 570, 6/518 no. 575] and Muslim [Eng. Trans. 1/383 no. 1750].

> those whom We guided and chose. When the verses of the Most Merciful were recited to them, they fell in prostration weeping.
>
> [*Maryam* (19): 58]

He said concerning the People of Cognisance,

وَإِذَا سَمِعُوا مَا أُنزِلَ إِلَى الرَّسُولِ تَرَىٰ أَعْيُنَهُمْ تَفِيضُ مِنَ الدَّمْعِ مِمَّا عَرَفُوا مِنَ الْحَقِّ

> And when they hear what has been revealed to the Messenger, you see their eyes overflowing with tears because of what they have recognised of the truth.
>
> [*Al-Mā'idah* (5): 83]

He, Glorious is He, commended those who listen in this way due to what they attain of increase in faith, the trembling of their skins and the tears in their eyes. He, the Exalted says,

اللَّهُ نَزَّلَ أَحْسَنَ الْحَدِيثِ كِتَابًا مُّتَشَابِهًا مَّثَانِيَ تَقْشَعِرُّ مِنْهُ جُلُودُ الَّذِينَ يَخْشَوْنَ رَبَّهُمْ ثُمَّ تَلِينُ جُلُودُهُمْ وَقُلُوبُهُمْ إِلَىٰ ذِكْرِ اللَّهِ

> Allāh has sent down the best statement; a consistent Book wherein is reiteration. The skins shiver therefrom of those who fear their Lord; then their skins and their hearts relax at the remembrance of Allāh.
>
> [*Az-Zumar* (39): 23]

إِنَّمَا ٱلْمُؤْمِنُونَ ٱلَّذِينَ إِذَا ذُكِرَ ٱللَّهُ وَجِلَتْ قُلُوبُهُمْ وَإِذَا تُلِيَتْ عَلَيْهِمْ ءَايَٰتُهُۥ زَادَتْهُمْ إِيمَٰنًا وَعَلَىٰ رَبِّهِمْ يَتَوَكَّلُونَ ﴿٢﴾ ٱلَّذِينَ يُقِيمُونَ ٱلصَّلَوٰةَ وَمِمَّا رَزَقْنَٰهُمْ يُنفِقُونَ ﴿٣﴾ أُوْلَٰٓئِكَ هُمُ ٱلْمُؤْمِنُونَ حَقًّا لَّهُمْ دَرَجَٰتٌ عِندَ رَبِّهِمْ وَمَغْفِرَةٌ وَرِزْقٌ كَرِيمٌ ﴿٤﴾

> The believers are only those who, when Allāh is mentioned, their hearts become fearful, and when His verses are recited to them, it increases them in faith; and upon their Lord do they rely - the ones who establish prayer and spend from what We have provided them. Those are the believers truly. For them are degrees [of position] with their Lord, forgiveness and noble provision.
>
> [*Al-Anfāl* (8): 2-4]

As for the innovated listening which is the listening to clapping, drums and wind instruments, none of the Companions, the Successors and any of the great *Imāms* of this religion took this to be a route to Allāh, the Blessed and Exalted. Not one of them considered it to be a means of drawing close to Allāh and an action of obedience, instead they considered this to be a blameworthy innovation.[90] Ash-Shāfiʿī said,

> 'I have left behind me in Baghdād something that was innovated by the heretics that they called *at-taghbīr*,[91] which

[90] {F} Refer to ibn al-Qayyim, *'Mas'alah as-Samāʿ'* and *'Talbīs Iblīs'* [pp. 288-327 - the summary of Alī Ḥasan].

[91] {F} Ibn al-Qayyim, *'Mas'alah as-Samāʿ'* [pp. 119-120] said, '*Taghbīr* was where they struck stretched leather with stick or a cushion which gave off a particular sound to which they would recite moving poetry that would incite one to asceti- =

they used to distract people from the Qur'ān.' [92]

The Gnostic *Awliyā'* of Allāh know this fact well and know that Shayṭān has a major role to play in it and this is why the best of them who used to attend such sessions later repented.

The further a person is from cognisance and completion in his closeness to and love of Allāh, the greater the role that Shayṭān has to play [in misguiding him]. This [innovated listening] is comparable to alcohol, rather its affect upon the soul is greater than the affect of alcohol. This is why when the intoxication of the listeners becomes strong the devils descend to them, speaking upon the tongues of some and carrying others through the air. It is also possible that enmity arise between the listeners in the same way that enmity appears amongst the drunk, the devils accompanying one person could be stronger than the devils accompanying another and therefore when they fight, they kill the opponent. The ignorant would think that all of this is from the miracles granted the pious, God-fearing *Awliyā'* of Allāh when in reality [such sessions] take the person further away from Allāh and are actually satanic states. Killing a Muslim is not allowed except in those cases that Allāh has allowed, so how is it possible that killing an innocent person be a way of Allāh ennobling his *Awliyā'*?! The objective of miracles is to make a person more steadfast and firm [in obedience to Allāh], therefore Allāh has not bestowed a greater honour upon His servant than aiding him to do that which He Loves and is Pleased with and increasing him in that

=

cism. Now if this is what ash-Shāfi'ī, may Allāh sanctify his soul, thought of *taghbīr* then what would he have said concerning listening to the types of poetry and singing that contains mention of the belover, the excellence of meeting him, the sweetness of his reprimand, communion in love, coming close to him, the bitterness of leaving him.... '

[92] {F} Refer to *al-Ḥāfiẓ* Diyā' ad-Dīn al-Maqdisī, *'Juz Ittibā' as-Sunan'* [pp. 28-29] and *'Talbīs Iblīs'* [p. 301 of the summary].

which would bring him closer to Him and raise his ranks.

This is because miracles either fall into the category of knowledge such as the unveiling of certain realities, or the category of ability and possession such as miraculous feats, or the category of wealth such as those things that people are granted including knowledge, authority, wealth and property. Now if any of these things which Allāh grants His servant are used by the servant to aid in him in doing that which Allāh Loves and is Pleased with, in doing that which would take him closer to Allāh and raise his ranks, in doing that which Allāh and His Messenger have commanded, he will increase in ranking and closeness to Allāh and His Messenger. If the servant employs them to aid him in doing that which Allāh and His Messenger have prohibited such as *shirk*, oppression and indecent acts, he then deserves censure and punishment. If the Grace of Allāh does not reach him such as would allow him to turn in repentance to Him or do righteous deeds that would serve as an expiation for his sins, then he is counted amongst the ranks of the sinners.

This is why the people who have performed these miracles are frequently punished, sometimes by having the miracle taken away such as the owner having his property taken away or the scholar losing his knowledge, and other times by having his optional deeds taken away such that he moves from the rank of the special *Awliyā'* to the rank of the general *Awliyā'*, he could even join the ranks of the sinner or apostate. This occurs to many who perform satanic miracles, for many of them apostate from the religion and many of them never understand that what they were doing was satanic and instead believe them to be the miracles of the *Awliyā'* of Allāh.

Some people think that when Allāh grants them a miracle, He will not bring them to account over it. Some people think that if Allāh grants them a servant, wealth, property or authority, He will not judge them concerning it [and hence they are free to dispose of it as they wish]. Some people use miracles to aid them in doing affairs that are merely permissible, not commanded or prohibited, these people are counted amongst the general *Awliyā'* - the righteous who take a medium path. As for the Foremost, those brought near, then they are of a higher ranking just as the Servant-Messenger is higher than the Prophet-King.

Because miracles frequently serve to decrease a persons' rank, many of the righteous would repent and seek forgiveness of Allāh from the likes of this occurring in the same way that one repents from sins such as fornication and stealing. Sometimes one of them would be offered a miracle and he would ask Allāh to remove it and all of them would enjoin their disciples who were traversing the path, not to stop when they attained a miracle and not to make miracles their goal or boast about them. This advice was given despite the fact that they believed that these miracles were from Allāh, so what then of those miracles that are in reality from Shayṭān who tries to misguide people through them?!

[13.19 From the Whisperings of the Devils]

I know people who have beneficial discourses with plants when in reality it is none other than Shayṯān who has entered the plant and talks to them. I know people who are spoken to by stones and trees that say, 'glad tidings to you, O *Waliy* of Allāh,' and when they recite *Āyah al-Kursī*, Shayṭān goes away. I know people who hunt birds and sparrows talk to them saying, 'Take me so that the poor can eat me.' All that has happened is that Shayṭān has entered them just as he enters humans and speaks to them.

Some people are in their homes and the door is closed, then he sees himself outside the house without having opened the door.

The opposite also happens. The same applies to the gates of a city, a Jinn has taken him in or out at great speed. Sometimes they show him lights or bring a person he sought into his presence, again this is done by the devils who take on the form of the person he was looking for and when he repeatedly recites *Āyah al-Kursī* all such occurrences disappear.

I know people who are spoken to by someone who claims, 'I am from the command of Allāh' and therefore thinks that he is the *Mahdī* about whom the Prophet (ﷺ) foretold. This personage shows him miracles such as his imagining that he has control over the movements of birds and locusts in the air, hence if he imagines them veering to the left or right, he sees them go in that direction. If he imagines that some cattle are about to stand up, or he wishes to go to sleep, or go somewhere, he finds that this happens without any external activity on his part. He is carried to Mecca and back and the personage brings people having a beautiful external form and says, 'These are the best of the Angels who wished to visit you.' He says to himself, 'How is it that they have taken the form of beardless youth?' and then raises his head and sees them all having a beard. He says to the personage, 'The sign of your being the *Mahdī* is that a birthmark will appear on your body' and it appears for him to see. All of these are the ploys of Shayṭān.

There are many more examples, and if I were to mention all that I know of, it would take a large volume to record them. Allāh, the Exalted says,

فَأَمَّا
ٱلْإِنسَٰنُ إِذَا مَا ٱبْتَلَىٰهُ رَبُّهُۥ فَأَكْرَمَهُۥ وَنَعَّمَهُۥ فَيَقُولُ رَبِّىٓ أَكْرَمَنِ ﴿١٥﴾ وَأَمَّآ إِذَا مَا ٱبْتَلَىٰهُ فَقَدَرَ عَلَيْهِ رِزْقَهُۥ فَيَقُولُ رَبِّىٓ أَهَٰنَنِ ﴿١٦﴾

And as for man, when his Lord tries him and [thus] is generous to him and favours him, he says, 'My Lord has

> honoured me.' But when He tries him and restricts his provision, he says, 'My Lord has humiliated me.'
>
> [*Al-Fajr* (89): 15-16]

Then Allāh, the Blessed and Exalted says, 'nay' (*kallā*). The word *kallā* contains the meaning of rebuke and warning, rebuke for saying the likes of what has preceded and warning for the consequences and His orders that follow [in the ensuing verses]. This is because not every worldly blessing is counted as a honour bestowed by Allāh, the Mighty and Magnificent. Likewise, whosoever is restricted from some worldly blessing is not necessarily humiliated, rather He, Glorious is He, tries His servant with both ease and difficulty. It is possible that He give worldly blessings to those who He does not Love, to those who have no nobility in His Sight, so that He may gradually lead them to their punishment. It is also possible that He restrict them from those He does Love in order to shelter them so that perchance they do not decrease in rank in His Sight or fall into something that He Dislikes.

Also, it is necessary that the cause of the miracles bestowed to the *Awliyā'* be *taqwā* and faith. Therefore any miracle whose cause is disbelief, sin and transgression, is from the miracles of the enemies of Allāh and not the miracles of the *Awliyā'* of Allāh. Whoever's miracle has not been attained by way of prayer, recitation of the Qur'ān, *dhikr*, praying by night and supplication and instead has been attained by way of *shirk* such as supplicating to the dead or absent, or by way of sin, transgression and eating the unlawful such as snakes, hornets, beetles or blood or by way of listening to music and dancing, especially dancing with women, strangers and youth and the strength of his miracle decreases when he hears the Qur'ān and increases when he hears the musical instruments of Shayṭān, he dances through the night and when the time for prayer comes he prays while sitting, or prays so quickly that he resembles the pecking of a crow [when in prostration], or he hates listening to the Qur'ān and flees from it, or finds it difficult and burdensome, or he has no love of it or delight when reciting it, or he loves listening to song and music and feels delight when he does so, then all of these are satanic states and are included in His saying,

وَمَن يَعْشُ عَن ذِكْرِ ٱلرَّحْمَٰنِ نُقَيِّضْ لَهُۥ شَيْطَٰنًا فَهُوَ لَهُۥ قَرِينٌ ﴿٣٦﴾

> And whoever is blinded from the remembrance of the Most Merciful - We appoint for him a devil, and he is to him a companion.
>
> [*Az-Zukhruf* (43): 36]

The Qur'ān is the remembrance of the Most Merciful. Allāh, the Exalted says,

وَمَنْ أَعْرَضَ عَن ذِكْرِى فَإِنَّ لَهُۥ مَعِيشَةً ضَنكًا وَنَحْشُرُهُۥ يَوْمَ ٱلْقِيَٰمَةِ أَعْمَىٰ ﴿١٢٤﴾ قَالَ رَبِّ لِمَ حَشَرْتَنِىٓ أَعْمَىٰ وَقَدْ كُنتُ بَصِيرًا ﴿١٢٥﴾ قَالَ كَذَٰلِكَ أَتَتْكَ ءَايَٰتُنَا فَنَسِيتَهَا ۖ وَكَذَٰلِكَ ٱلْيَوْمَ تُنسَىٰ ﴿١٢٦﴾

> And whoever turns away from My remembrance - indeed, he will have a depressed life, and We will gather him on the Day of Resurrection blind. He will say, 'My Lord, why have You raised me blind while I was [once] seeing?' [Allāh] will say, 'Thus did Our signs come to you, and you forgot them; thus will you this Day be forgotten.'
>
> [*Ṭā Hā* (20): 124-126]

Meaning: you left acting by it.

Ibn 'Abbās said,

> 'Allāh has undertaken not to misguide in this world, or

make miserable in the Hereafter, whosoever recites His Book and acts by it.'

Then he recited the above verse. [93]

In Summary

- The difference between the Universal and the Religious.

- The differences between the *Awliyā'* of Allāh and the *awliyā'* of Shayṭān, these can be summarised into investigating how they conform to the Prophet (ﷺ).

- The purpose behind the miracles performed by the Prophet (ﷺ) was to bring benefit to others and examples of them.

- The purpose behind the miracles performed by the *Awliyā'* of Allāh is to aid them in their faith and religion or to aid others and examples of them. These miracles are only attained by virtue of them following the Prophet (ﷺ) and hence they come under the category of his miracles.

- The satanic miracles and examples of them.

- The stances of people with regards miracles and the correct position.

- Music and other forbidden matters strengthen the influence of Shayṭān over a person.

- The fundamental obligation is to follow the Messenger (ﷺ).

- Miracles could be granted by Allāh as a trial.

[93] {F} As-Suyūṭī, *'ad-Durr al-Manthūr'* [4/311] referred it to al-Faryābī, Sa'īd bin Mansūr, ibn Abī Shaybah and others.

CHAPTER FOURTEEN

[The Prophet (ﷺ) was Sent to the Entirety of Man and Jinn]

From amongst the things that are obligatory to know is that Allāh sent Muḥammad (ﷺ) to the whole of mankind and the Jinn. Therefore there is not a single man or Jinn except that it is obligatory upon him to have faith in Muḥammad (ﷺ) and follow him. It is upon him to believe all that he informs and obey him in all that he commands. So whosoever has the evidence established upon him, yet does not believe in his Message is a disbeliever regardless of whether he be man or Jinn.

Muḥammad (ﷺ) has been sent to both the worlds of man and Jinn by agreement of the Muslims. A group of the Jinn listened to the Qur'ān, [believed] and returned to their people as warners. This happened when the Prophet (ﷺ) prayed with his Companions at Baṭn Nakhla [1] when he had returned from *Ṭā'if*. Allāh informs of this in His Book,

[1] {Y} A place between Mecca and Ṭā'if as mentioned in *'Fatḥ al-Bārī'* [18/320].

وَإِذْ صَرَفْنَآ إِلَيْكَ نَفَرًا مِّنَ ٱلْجِنِّ يَسْتَمِعُونَ ٱلْقُرْءَانَ فَلَمَّا
حَضَرُوهُ قَالُوٓا۟ أَنصِتُوا۟ ۖ فَلَمَّا قُضِىَ وَلَّوْا۟ إِلَىٰ قَوْمِهِم مُّنذِرِينَ
﴿٢٩﴾ قَالُوا۟ يَٰقَوْمَنَآ إِنَّا سَمِعْنَا كِتَٰبًا أُنزِلَ مِنۢ بَعْدِ مُوسَىٰ
مُصَدِّقًا لِّمَا بَيْنَ يَدَيْهِ يَهْدِىٓ إِلَى ٱلْحَقِّ وَإِلَىٰ طَرِيقٍ مُّسْتَقِيمٍ
﴿٣٠﴾ يَٰقَوْمَنَآ أَجِيبُوا۟ دَاعِىَ ٱللَّهِ وَءَامِنُوا۟ بِهِۦ يَغْفِرْ لَكُم مِّن
ذُنُوبِكُمْ وَيُجِرْكُم مِّنْ عَذَابٍ أَلِيمٍ ﴿٣١﴾ وَمَن لَّا يُجِبْ دَاعِىَ ٱللَّهِ
فَلَيْسَ بِمُعْجِزٍ فِى ٱلْأَرْضِ وَلَيْسَ لَهُۥ مِن دُونِهِۦٓ أَوْلِيَآءُ ۚ أُو۟لَٰٓئِكَ
فِى ضَلَٰلٍ مُّبِينٍ ﴿٣٢﴾

And [remember] when We sent to you a group of the Jinn, listening to the Qur'ān. When they stood in the presence thereof, they said, 'Listen in silence!' When it had finished, they returned to their people as warners. They said, 'O our people! Indeed we have heard a Book sent down after Moses, confirming what came before it, it guides to the truth and to a Straight Path. O our people! Respond to the caller of Allāh and believe in him. He will forgive you your sins and will save you from a painful torment. And whoever does not respond to the caller of Allāh, he cannot escape on the earth and there will be no protectors for him besides Allāh. They are those in manifest error.'

[*Al-Aḥqāf* (46): 29-32]

After this, Allāh, the Exalted revealed,

قُلْ أُوحِيَ إِلَيَّ أَنَّهُ اسْتَمَعَ نَفَرٌ مِّنَ الْجِنِّ فَقَالُوا إِنَّا سَمِعْنَا قُرْآنًا
عَجَبًا ﴿١﴾ يَهْدِي إِلَى الرُّشْدِ فَآمَنَّا بِهِ ۖ وَلَن نُّشْرِكَ بِرَبِّنَا أَحَدًا ﴿٢﴾
وَأَنَّهُ تَعَالَىٰ جَدُّ رَبِّنَا مَا اتَّخَذَ صَاحِبَةً وَلَا وَلَدًا ﴿٣﴾ وَأَنَّهُ كَانَ
يَقُولُ سَفِيهُنَا عَلَى اللَّهِ شَطَطًا ﴿٤﴾ وَأَنَّا ظَنَنَّا أَن لَّن تَقُولَ الْإِنسُ
وَالْجِنُّ عَلَى اللَّهِ كَذِبًا ﴿٥﴾ وَأَنَّهُ كَانَ رِجَالٌ مِّنَ الْإِنسِ يَعُوذُونَ بِرِجَالٍ
مِّنَ الْجِنِّ فَزَادُوهُمْ رَهَقًا ﴿٦﴾

Say: it has been revealed to me that a group of the Jinn listened to the Qur'ān and said, 'Verily we have heard a wonderful Recital! It guides to the Right Path and we have believed in it, we shall never associate any partners with our Lord. And exalted be the Majesty of our Lord, He has taken neither a wife nor a son. The foolish amongst us used to utter against Allāh that which was wrong and indeed we thought that man and Jinn would not utter a lie against Allāh. And there were men from mankind who sought refuge with men from the Jinn, so they increased them only in the burden [of sin].'

[*Al-Jinn* (72): 1-6]

More than one of the *Salaf* said,

كان الرجل من الإنس إذا نزل بالوادي قال: أعوذ
بعظيم هذا الوادي من شر سفهاءِ قومه، فلما استغاثت
الإنس والجن، ازدادت الجن طغياناً وكفراً،

"*When a man would take sojourn at a valley, he would say, 'I take refuge with the great one of the valley from the evil of the fools amongst his people.' Therefore when the human and Jinn sought succour [with the Jinn of that valley] it increased the Jinn in transgression and disbelief.*" [2]

---

[2] {F} Refer to *'ad-Durr al-Manthūr'* [6/271] and *'Fatḥ al-Bārī'* [8/672].

This is as Allāh, the Exalted says,

وَأَنَّهُۥ كَانَ رِجَالٌ مِّنَ ٱلْإِنسِ يَعُوذُونَ بِرِجَالٍ
مِّنَ ٱلْجِنِّ فَزَادُوهُمْ رَهَقًا ﴿٦﴾ وَأَنَّهُمْ ظَنُّوا۟ كَمَا ظَنَنتُمْ أَن لَّن يَبْعَثَ
ٱللَّهُ أَحَدًا ﴿٧﴾ وَأَنَّا لَمَسْنَا ٱلسَّمَآءَ فَوَجَدْنَٰهَا مُلِئَتْ حَرَسًا
شَدِيدًا وَشُهُبًا ﴿٨﴾

> ...And there were men from mankind who sought refuge with men from the Jinn, so they increased them only in the burden [of sin]. And they thought as you thought, that Allāh will not send any Messenger. And we have sought to reach the heaven but found it filled with stern guards and flaming fire.
>
> [*Al-Jinn* (72): 6-8]

The devils used to be bombarded with flaming fires before the revelation of the Qur'ān and sometimes they were able to steal some information [that they had heard from the discourse of the Angels] before the flames reached them. Then, when Muḥammad (ﷺ) was sent, the heaven became filled with stern guards and flaming fires and the fires would be flung at them before they could [steal] a hearing. This is as they said,

وَأَنَّا كُنَّا نَقْعُدُ مِنْهَا مَقَٰعِدَ لِلسَّمْعِ ۖ فَمَن
يَسْتَمِعِ ٱلْـَٔانَ يَجِدْ لَهُۥ شِهَابًا رَّصَدًا ﴿٩﴾

> And verily we used to sit there in stations to [steal] a hearing, but any who listens now will find a flaming fire watching him in ambush.
>
> [*Al-Jinn* (72): 9]

Allāh, the Exalted says in another verse,

وَمَا تَنَزَّلَتْ بِهِ
ٱلشَّيَٰطِينُ ﴿٢١٠﴾ وَمَا يَنۢبَغِى لَهُمْ وَمَا يَسْتَطِيعُونَ ﴿٢١١﴾ إِنَّهُمْ
عَنِ ٱلسَّمْعِ لَمَعْزُولُونَ ﴿٢١٢﴾

And it is not the devils who have brought it [the Qur'ān] and neither would it suit them, nor can they [produce the likes of it]. Verily they have been removed far from hearing it.

[*Ash-Shu'arā'* (26): 210-212]

The Jinn said,

وَأَنَّا لَا نَدْرِىٓ أَشَرٌّ أُرِيدَ
بِمَن فِى ٱلْأَرْضِ أَمْ أَرَادَ بِهِمْ رَبُّهُمْ رَشَدًا ﴿١٠﴾ وَأَنَّا مِنَّا ٱلصَّٰلِحُونَ
وَمِنَّا دُونَ ذَٰلِكَ كُنَّا طَرَآئِقَ قِدَدًا ﴿١١﴾

And we know not whether evil is intended for those on earth, or whether their Lord intends for them a Right Path. There are among us some that are righteous and some the contrary; we are groups each following a different way.

[*Al-Jinn* (72): 10-11]

Meaning upon many different beliefs. The scholars have said that amongst them are found the Muslim, the polytheist, the Christian, the Jew, the sunni and the innovator.

وَأَنَّا ظَنَنَّآ أَن لَّن نُّعْجِزَ
ٱللَّهَ فِى ٱلْأَرْضِ وَلَن نُّعْجِزَهُۥ هَرَبًا ﴿١٢﴾

And we think that we cannot escape Allāh in the earth nor can we escape by flight.

[*Al-Jinn* (72): 12]

They informed us that they were not capable of escape, not if they remained on earth nor if they fled.

وَأَنَّا لَمَّا سَمِعْنَا ٱلْهُدَىٰٓ
ءَامَنَّا بِهِۦ ۖ فَمَن يُؤْمِنۢ بِرَبِّهِۦ فَلَا يَخَافُ بَخْسًا وَلَا رَهَقًا ﴿١٣﴾
وَأَنَّا مِنَّا ٱلْمُسْلِمُونَ وَمِنَّا ٱلْقَـٰسِطُونَ ۖ

And indeed when we heard the Guidance, we believed therein. Whoever believes in his Lord shall have no fear - either of decrease in reward or increase in punishment. And some of us are Muslims and some of us are deviators (*qāsitūn*).

[*Al-Jinn* (72): 13-14].

Meaning [by *qāsitūn*], oppressors. It is said *aqsata* when one is just and *qasata* when one oppresses and coerces.

وَأَنَّا مِنَّا ٱلْمُسْلِمُونَ وَمِنَّا ٱلْقَـٰسِطُونَ ۖ فَمَنْ أَسْلَمَ فَأُو۟لَـٰٓئِكَ
تَحَرَّوْا۟ رَشَدًا ﴿١٤﴾ وَأَمَّا ٱلْقَـٰسِطُونَ فَكَانُوا۟ لِجَهَنَّمَ حَطَبًا ﴿١٥﴾
وَأَلَّوِ ٱسْتَقَـٰمُوا۟ عَلَى ٱلطَّرِيقَةِ لَأَسْقَيْنَـٰهُم مَّآءً غَدَقًا ﴿١٦﴾ لِّنَفْتِنَهُمْ
فِيهِ ۚ وَمَن يُعْرِضْ عَن ذِكْرِ رَبِّهِۦ يَسْلُكْهُ عَذَابًا صَعَدًا ﴿١٧﴾ وَأَنَّ
ٱلْمَسَـٰجِدَ لِلَّهِ فَلَا تَدْعُوا۟ مَعَ ٱللَّهِ أَحَدًا ﴿١٨﴾ وَأَنَّهُۥ لَمَّا قَامَ عَبْدُ ٱللَّهِ
يَدْعُوهُ كَادُوا۟ يَكُونُونَ عَلَيْهِ لِبَدًا ﴿١٩﴾ قُلْ إِنَّمَآ أَدْعُوا۟ رَبِّى وَلَآ أُشْرِكُ
بِهِۦٓ أَحَدًا ﴿٢٠﴾ قُلْ إِنِّى لَآ أَمْلِكُ لَكُمْ ضَرًّا وَلَا رَشَدًا ﴿٢١﴾ قُلْ إِنِّى
لَن يُجِيرَنِى مِنَ ٱللَّهِ أَحَدٌ وَلَنْ أَجِدَ مِن دُونِهِۦ مُلْتَحَدًا ﴿٢٢﴾

'...And whoever has embraced Islām, then such have sought the Right Path. And as for the *qāsitūn*, they shall be firewood for Hell.' If they had believed in Allāh and traversed the Right Way, We should surely have bestowed

> on them rain in abundance that We might try them thereby. And whoever turns away from the Reminder of his Lord, He will cause him to enter a severe torment. And the *Masjids* are for Allāh [Alone], so invoke not anything along with Allāh. [And] when the servant of Allāh stood up, supplicating to Him they made a dense crowd around him. Say, 'I invoke only my Lord and I associate none as partners with Him.' Say, 'It is not in my power to cause you harm or bring you to the Right Path.' Say, 'None can protect me from the punishment of Allāh [if were to disobey him], nor should I find refuge except in Him.'
>
> [*Al-Jinn* (72): 14-22]

Meaning [by *multaḥda*] a source of recourse and refuge.

إِلَّا بَلَٰغًا

مِّنَ ٱللَّهِ وَرِسَٰلَٰتِهِۦۚ وَمَن يَعْصِ ٱللَّهَ وَرَسُولَهُۥ فَإِنَّ لَهُۥ نَارَ جَهَنَّمَ

خَٰلِدِينَ فِيهَآ أَبَدًا ﴿٢٣﴾ حَتَّىٰٓ إِذَا رَأَوْا۟ مَا يُوعَدُونَ فَسَيَعْلَمُونَ

مَنْ أَضْعَفُ نَاصِرًا وَأَقَلُّ عَدَدًا ﴿٢٤﴾

> '...[mine is] but the conveyance [of the truth] from Allāh and His messages, and whoever disobeys Allāh and His Messenger, for him is the Fire of Hell wherein he shall dwell forever.' Till, when they see that which they are promised, they will know who it is that is weaker with respect to helping and less important with respect to number.
>
> [*Al-Jinn* (72): 23-24]

[14.1 The Jinn who Believed in him (ﷺ)]

Then when the Jinn heard the Qur'ān, they came to the Prophet (ﷺ) and believed in him. These Jinn were from Naṣībayn[3] as is reported in the Ṣaḥīḥ from ibn Mas'ūd.[4] It is also reported that he recited *Sūrah ar-Raḥmān* to them and when he reached,

فَبِأَيِّ ءَالَآءِ رَبِّكُمَا تُكَذِّبَانِ ﴿١٣﴾

> Then which of the favours of your Lord will you two deny?
>
> [*Ar-Raḥmān* (55): 13]

They said, 'O our Lord! Not one of Your favours do we deny and to You belongs all praise and thanks.'[5]

When they assembled with the Prophet (ﷺ) they asked him for provision for themselves and their animals. He said

«لكم كل عظم ذكر
اسم الله عليه تجدونه أوفر ما يكون لحماً،
وكل بعرة علف لدوابكم»

> "For you is every bone that you find which has had the Name of Allāh mentioned upon it, you will find it fully laden with meat and every piece of dung is fodder for your animals."

---

[3] {Y} A city falling between Damascus and Mosul, it was conquered by the Muslim in 18H.

[4] {F} Reported by Bukhārī [Eng. Trans. 6/415 no. 443] and Muslim [Eng. Trans. 1/243 no.'s 902-907] both from ibn 'Abbās.

[5] {F} Reported by at-Tirmidhī [no. 3291] and al-Ḥākim [2/473].
I say: the ḥadīth is *ḥasan* due to witnesses. Refer to *'as-Ṣaḥīḥah'* [5/183].

The Prophet (ﷺ) went on to say,

«فلا تستنجوا بهما فإنهما زاد إخوانكم من الجن»

"So do not perform *istinjā'* with these two because they are provision for your brothers amongst the Jinn." [6]

This prohibition is established from him, [being reported via] many different routes [7] and it was upon this ḥadīth that the scholars depended in order to prohibit performing *istinjā'* with them. The scholars went on to say, 'Because we have been prohibited from using the [provision] of the Jinn and their animals for *istinjā'*, then using the food that has been prepared for man, or the fodder of their animals is more deserving not to be used.'

Muḥammad (ﷺ) has been sent to the entirety of mankind and the Jinn. This fact has greater standing in the Sight of Allāh, the Exalted, then the Jinn being made subservient to Solomon (*'alayhi as-ṣalām*). This is because they were put under his authority to do whatever he wished with them as a King. Muḥammad (ﷺ), on the other hand, was sent to them to enjoin them to what Allāh and His Messenger commanded. This is because he was the servant of Allāh and His Messenger and the ranking of the Servant-Messenger is above the Prophet-King.

The disbelievers amongst the Jinn will enter the Fire by consensus. As for the believers amongst them then the majority of scholars hold the position that they shall enter Paradise. [8] The majority of scholars also hold that the Messengers can only be human and that

---

[6] {F} Reported by Muslim [Eng. Tran. 1/244 no. 903] and at-Tirmidhī [no. 18].

[7] {Y} Refer to az-Zayla'i, *'Naṣb ar-Rāyah'* [1/137-148].

[8] {F} For a discussion on this refer to ibn al-Qayyim, *'Ṭarīq al-Hijratayn'* [pp. 286-297] and ash-Shawkānī, *'Fatḥ al-Qadīr'* [5/350].

a Messenger has not been sent who was a Jinn. However they do have warners amongst them, the discussion of these issues is better done in another place. [9]

[14.2 The Relationships of Jinn to Man]

The purpose of this discussion is to show that the Jinn have different relationships with man. So if a man enjoins the Jinn to that which Allāh and His Messenger (ﷺ) have commanded which comprises worship of Him Alone and obedience to His Prophet, and he also enjoins the people to this, then such a person is from the most noble of the *Awliyā'* of Allāh, the Exalted. In this respect he is like a successor to the Messenger (ﷺ) and one of his representatives.

Whoever uses the Jinn to do matters that are permissible is like one who uses man to do matters that are permissible. Such a person enjoins them to do which is obligatory upon them and prohibits them from committing that which is unlawful and uses them to carry out permissible matters, in this respect he is comparable to kings. Such a person, if we were to assume that he is from the *Awliyā'* of Allāh, the Exalted, then the most he can be is one of the general *Awliyā'*. His comparison is that of the Prophet-King to the Servant-Messenger such as Solomon and Joseph to Abraham, Moses, Jesus and Muḥammad (*ṣalawātu Allāh ʿalayhim ajmaʿīn*).

Whoever used the Jinn to do that which Allāh and His Messenger have prohibited, either by committing *shirk*, or by killing one whose blood is sacrosanct, or by showing enmity to innocent Muslims without actually killing them such as making them ill or making them forget knowledge and other such things, or by committing indecent deeds such as promoting that from which indecency is sought then

---

[9] {Y} Refer to ibn Taymiyyah, *'Kitāb an-Nubuwwāt.'*

such a person has sought aid from them in committing sin and transgression. If he seeks aid from them in committing disbelief, then he is a disbeliever, if seeks aid from them in committing sin then he is a sinner - either a *fāsiq* or merely a sinner.

[14.3 Examples of the Ploys Employed by Shayṭān]

If a person is lacking in his knowledge of *Sharīʿah*, and seeks their aid in doing something which he believes to be a miracle such as his seeking their aid in performing *Ḥajj*, or that they make him fly while he is listening to the innovated form of listening [such as listening to music and song], or that they carry him to *ʿArafah* and hence he does not perform the *Ḥajj* as legislated by the *Sharīʿah*, or that they convey him from city to city, then such a person has been fooled and deceived and the Jinn are merely plotting against him.

It is possible that many of these people not know that all those matters are done by the Jinn, rather such a person could just merely have heard that the *Awliyā'* of Allāh can perform miracles. However, he does not have a level of faith and knowledge of the Qur'ān that would allow him to differentiate the miracles bestowed by the Most Merciful from satanic deceptions. Because of this the Jinn plot against him in accordance to his belief, so if he is a polytheist - worshipping stars and idols - they make him think that he is benefiting from his worship. The intention of this polytheist is to seek intercession from the person depicted by the idol be he an Angel, Prophet or righteous *shaykh*, he thinks that he is worshipping that Prophet or righteous person when in reality his worship is of Shayṭān. Allāh, the Exalted says,

وَيَوْمَ يَحْشُرُهُمْ جَمِيعًا ثُمَّ يَقُولُ لِلْمَلَٰٓئِكَةِ أَهَٰٓؤُلَآءِ إِيَّاكُمْ كَانُوا۟ يَعْبُدُونَ ﴿٤٠﴾ قَالُوا۟ سُبْحَٰنَكَ أَنتَ وَلِيُّنَا مِن دُونِهِم ۖ بَلْ كَانُوا۟ يَعْبُدُونَ ٱلْجِنَّ ۖ أَكْثَرُهُم بِهِم مُّؤْمِنُونَ ﴿٤١﴾

> [Remember] the Day when He will gather them all together and then will say to the Angels, 'Was it you that these people used to worship?' They will say, 'Glory be to You! You are our Lord rather than they. Nay, they used to worship the Jinn; most of them were believers in them.'
> [*Saba'* (34): 40-41]

This is why those who prostrate to the sun, moon and stars intend thereby to prostrate to those actual things, therefore at the time of their prostrating to them, Shayṭān accompanies them so that they end up prostrating to him. This is why Shayṭān takes on the form of those with whom the polytheists seek succour and relief, if the person is a Christian seeking succour with George (*Jarjis*), Shayṭān comes to him in the form of George. If the person is one of those attributed to Islām and seeks succour with a *shaykh* that he has a good opinion of, Shayṭān comes to him in the form of that *shaykh*. If the person is a polytheist from India, Shayṭān comes to him in the form of the person he exalts and magnifies.

Furthermore, if the *shaykh* who has been sought succour with has some knowledge of the *Sharī'ah* then Shayṭān will not inform him that he took his form for those who sought succour with him. If the *shaykh* has no knowledge of the *Sharī'ah*, Shayṭān will inform him of their words and those people will in turn believe that the *shaykh* heard their words from afar and responded to them, whereas in reality the go between was Shayṭān.

Some of the *shaykhs* to whom this has occurred by way of unveiling and disclosure [of hidden realities] said that, 'The Jinn showed me something that glitters in the same way that water or glass glitters.' Therein they depicted for him whatever information he sought and he informed the people of it. He continued, 'the Jinn convey to me the speech of those who seek succour with me and I respond to them and they convey my words back to them.'

When people who do not recognise miracles say to many of these *shaykhs* who perform miracles, 'You are lying, all you do is trickery as is done by those who enter the fire, previously having coated themselves in finely ground rock, or the skin of bitter oranges, or frogs oil,' the *shaykhs* are taken aback and say, 'By Allāh we know nothing of this trickery!' When one who is knowledgeable says to them, 'You are telling the truth, however what you do arises from satanic states,' they accept this. From amongst these are those who proceed to turn to Allāh in repentance when the truth becomes clear to them and it becomes clear to them via many ways that what they previously did was from Shayṭān. They understand that they are from the devils when they see that they arise due to committing blameworthy innovations and acts of disobedience to Allāh. They see that what they did not arise by performing that which Allāh and His Messenger love which comprises the legislated actions of worship and hence come to know that they were the miracles that Shayṭān grants his *awliyā'* and not the miracles that the Most Merciful grants His *Awliyā'*.

And Allāh, the Glorious and Exalted, Knows best as to what is correct and to Him is the return and final judgement. Peace and blessing be upon Muḥammad, the Master of His Messengers and Prophets, upon his family, his Companions, those who aid him, those follow him and his successors - a peace and blessings that would lead to his intercession for us. *Āmīn.*

In Summary

- The Prophet (ﷺ) was sent to the whole of mankind and Jinn, therefore it is obligatory upon them to follow him.

- Mention of some Jinn who accepted Islām and the fact that they used to steal information from the Angels and give it to the soothsayers, mixing their own lies with it.

- The possible relationships that Jinn and man can have and their consequences.

- Mention of various satanic states and the ploys that Shayṭān uses to misguide the people such as his fulfilling some of their requests.

INDEX OF PROPER NAMES

The Companions

'Ā'ishah: bint Abū Bakr *as-Ṣiddīq*, the Mother of the Believers and most beloved wife of the Prophet (ﷺ). She reported many *aḥādīth* from the Prophet and many Companions and Successors reported from her. She died in the year 58H.

'Āmir bin Fuhairah: at-Taimī, the servant of Abū Bakr. He migrated along with the Prophet and Abū Bakr and witnessed *Badr* and *Uḥud*. He was martyred in the year 4H.

'Abbād bin Bishr: bin Waqsh al-Anṣārī Abū Bishr. He witnessed *Badr* and the following battles and was one of those who killed Ka'b al-Ashraf. He was martyred on the Day of *al-Yamāmah* in the year 12H.

'Abdullāh bin 'Abbās: bin 'Abdul-Muṭṭalib bin Hāshim bin 'Abd Munāf al-Qurashī al-Hāshimī, the cousin of the Prophet (ﷺ) and the interpreter of the Qur'ān. He was born three years before the *Hijrah* and was called the 'Ocean of knowledge' due to his vast knowledge. He took part in the *Jihād* in North Africa in the year 27H and died in the year 68H.

'Abdullāh bin 'Amr: bin al-'Ās bin Wā'il bin Hāshim bin Su'ayd bin Sa'd bin Sahm as-Sahmī. He and his father were Companions. He was literate and attained permission from the Prophet (ﷺ) to write everything he said. He died in the year 65H.

'Abdullāh Abū Jābir: bin 'Amr bin Ḥazzām bin Thalabah al-Anṣārī al-Khazrajī as-Sulamī, amongst those who gave the pledge of *'Uqbah*. He witnessed *Badr* and was martyred at *Uḥud*.

'Abdullāh bin Mas'ūd: bin Ghāfil bin Ḥabīb al-Hadhlī Abū 'Abdur-Raḥmān. One of the scholars amongst the Companions and he witnessed *Badr* and the following battles. He had many virtues and died in the year 32H.

'Abdullāh bin 'Umar: bin al-Khaṭṭāb al-'Adawī, Abū 'Abdur-Raḥmān, the noble Companion and scholar. He reported many *aḥādīth* from the Messenger (ﷺ) and died in the year 73H.

'Abdur-Raḥmān bin Auf: bin Awf bin Abd Awf bin al-Ḥārith al-Qurashī az-Zuhrī, Abū Muḥammad, one of the ten promised Paradise. He migrated to Abysinnia on both occasions and witnessed every battle with the Prophet (ﷺ). He was very rich and very generous when giving in the Way of Allāh. He died in the year 32H.

Abū Bakr as-Ṣiddīq: 'Abdullāh bin 'Uthmān bin Āmir al-Qurashī. The first *Khalīfah* of the Messenger (ﷺ), his companion in the cave, his closest friend and one of the ten promised Paradise. He was the first man to accept Islām and died in the year 13H.

Abū ad-Dardā': Uwaymir bin Mālik bin Zayd bin Qays al-Khazrajī al-Anṣārī. There is a difference of opinion concerning his name. He accepted Islām on the day of *Badr* and witnessed *Uḥud*. He was from the Legal Jurists and ascetics of the Companions. He died in the year 32H.

Abū Dharr al-Ghifārī: Jundub bin Junādah bin Sakn, he was of those who accepted Islām early on but delayed his migration and hence did not witness *Badr*. His virtues are many and he died in the year 32H.

Abū Hurayrah: 'Abdur-Raḥmān bin Ṣakhr ad-Dusī. His name is greatly differed over. He accepted Islām in the year 7H and reported the most ḥadīth from the Prophet (ﷺ). He died in the year 59H.

Abū Isrā'īl: There is a difference of opinion concerning his name, but it is known that he is Qurashī, then Āmirī.

Abū Mūsā al-Ash'arī: 'Abdullāh bin Qays bin Salīm. He had a beautiful recitation and was one of the scholars amongst the Companions. He died in the year 42H or 44H.

Abū Sa'īd al-Khudrī: Sa'd bin Mālik bin Sinān bin 'Ubaid al-Anṣārī al-Khazrajī. He and his father were both Companions and he witnessed all the battles that followed *Uḥud*. He was one of the scholars amongst the Companions and reported many *aḥādīth* from the Messenger (ﷺ). He died in the year 74H.

Abū 'Ubaidah bin al-Jarrāḥ: 'Āmir bin 'Abdullāh bin al-Jarrāḥ bin Hilāl al-Qurashī al-Fahrī, one of the ten promised Paradise. He accepted Islām early on and witnessed the battle of *Badr* and the following battles. He is the trustworthy one of this nation and died as a martyr due to a plague in the year 18H at the age of fifty-eight.

'Adī bin Ḥātim: bin 'Abdullāh bin Sa'd bin al-Ḥashraj bin 'Amr al-

Qays at-Ṭā'ī, Abu Ṭarīf. He was a Christian who accepted Islām and witnessed the battles of *al-Jamal*, *Ṣiffīn* and *an-Nahrawān* with ʿAlī. He died in the year 68H.

Al-ʿAlā' bin al-Khaḍramī: al-Khazrajī. His supplications would be answered and he died in the year 21H.

ʿAlī bin Abī Ṭālib: bin ʿAbdul-Muṭṭalib bin Hāshim al-Qurashī al-Hāshimī, the fourth Rightly Guided *Khalīfah* and one of ten promised Paradise. He accepted Islām at the age of thirteen and was famous for his chivalry, bravery and knowledge. He married Fāṭimah, the daughter of the Prophet (ﷺ) and was martyred in the year 40H.

ʿAmr bin al-ʿĀs: bin Wā'il al-Qurashī as-Sahmī. He accepted Islām during the year of *Ḥudaybiyyah* and was the one who conquered Egypt. He died in the year 43H.

Anas bin Mālik: bin an-Naḍar bin Ḍamḍam al-Anṣārī al-Khazrajī, the servant of the Messenger (ﷺ). He witnessed *Badr* but was not of age to actually participate. He died in the year 93H.

Al-Barā'a bin Mālik: bin an-Naḍr al-Anṣārī. He witnessed *Uḥud* and gave the pledge of allegiance under the tree. He was martyred in the year 20H on the Day of *Tustor*.

Diḥya al-Kalbī: bin Khalīfah bin Farwa bin Faḍālah al-Kalbī, the messenger that the Prophet (ﷺ) sent to Qaisar. He witnessed the battle of *al-Khandaq* and lived to see the reign of Muʿāwiyah.

ʿImrān bin Ḥusain: al-Khuzā'ī al-Kaʿbī Abū Nujaid. He accepted Islām during the year of *Khaybar* and reported some *aḥādīth* from the Prophet (ﷺ). He died in the year 52H.

Jābir bin 'Abdullāh: bin 'Amr bin Ḥarrām al-Anṣārī as-Sulamī, he witnessed the second pledge at *'Uqbah* while he was still a child. It is said that he witnessed *Badr* and *Uḥud* and he reported many *aḥādīth* from the Messenger (ﷺ). He died in the year 74H.

Khālid bin al-Walīd: bin al-Mughīrah al-Makhzūmī al-Qurashī Abū Sulaymān. He was a great warrior and military leader and was given the nickname, 'Sword of Allāh.' He died in the year 21H.

Khubaib bin 'Adī: bin Mālik bin 'Āmir al-Awsī al-Anṣārī. He witnessed *Badr* and was martyred during the lifetime of the Prophet (ﷺ) when he was captured by the polytheists in Mecca.

Mu'ādh bin Jabal: bin 'Amr bin Aws al-Anṣārī al-Khazrajī, Abū 'Abdur-Raḥmān, one of the foremost Companions known for his knowledge of legal rulings and the Qur'ān. He was present at the pledge of *'Uqbah* and witnessed *Badr* and the following battles and was martyred due to a plague in the year 17H or 18H.

Mu'āwiyah: bin Abū Sufyān bin Ṣakhr bin Ḥarb bin Umayyah bin 'Abd Shams al-Qurashī al-Amawī. He accepted Islām in the year of the Conquest and witnessed *Ḥunain* and *al-Yamāmah*. He was one of the scribes who would write the revelation and died in the year 60H.

Al-Mughīrah bin Shu'bah: bin Abū 'Āmir bin Mas'ūd ath-Thaqafī, Abū 'Abdullāh. He witnessed *Hudaybiyyah*, *al-Yamāmah* and the conquests of Syria and Iraq. He died in the year 50H.

Muḥammad bin Muslimah: bin Salamah al-Anṣārī, he witnessed *Badr* and all the following battles except *Tabuk*. He died in the year 43H.

Nu'mān bin Bashīr: bin Sa'd al-Anṣārī al-Khazrajī Abū 'Abdullāh. He was a poet and lecturer and died in the year 65H.

Qatādah: ibn an-Nu'mān bin Zayd al-Anṣārī al-Awsī, Abū 'Amr, he witnessed the pledge of *'Uqbah*, *Badr* and every other battle that the Prophet (ﷺ) fought. He died in the year 23H.

Sāriyah: bin Zanīm bin 'Amr al-Kanānī. He was responsible for a number of conquests such as Aṣbahān and died in the year 30H.

Sa'd bin Abī Waqqās: Sa'd bin Mālik bin Ahīb bin 'Abd Munāf al-Qurashī az-Zuhrī Abū Isḥāq bin Abī Waqqās. One of the ten who were promised Paradise and one whose supplications were answered. He was the last of the ten to pass away in the year 55H.

Sa'īd bin Zayd: bin 'Amr al-Adawī al-Qurashī. He witnessed all the battles except for *Badr* and was one of the ten promised Paradise. He died in the year 51H.

Safinah: He was a Persian slave who was bought by Umm Salamah and subsequently freed. He then devoted himself to serving the Prophet (ﷺ).

Salmān: al-Fārisī Abū 'Abdullāh, the servant of the Messenger (ﷺ). The first battle he witnessed was *al-Khandaq* and he was present at all following battles. He died in the year 36H.

Shaddād bin Aws: bin Thābit al-Anṣārī al-Khazrajī, Abū Ya'lā. He was famous for his knowledge and wisdom and died in the year 58H.

Ṭalḥah: bin 'Ubaydullāh bin 'Uthmān bin 'Amr al-Qurashī, Abū Muḥammad, one of the ten promised Paradise. He witnessed

Uḥud and the following battles. He died in the year 36H.

'Umar bin al-Khaṭṭāb: Abū Ḥafs 'Umar bin al-Khaṭṭāb bin Nufayl al-Qurashī al-'Adawī, the second Rightly Guided *Khalīfah* and one of the ten promised Paradise. He accepted Islām five years before the *Hijrah* and his acceptance was a great victory for the Muslims. He witnessed every battle that the Prophet (ﷺ) witnessed. He was martyred in the year 23H.

Umm Ayman: Barakah bint Tha'labah bin 'Amr. She married 'Ubaid bin al-Ḥārith and gave birth to Ayman. Then she was married to Zaid bin Ḥārithah and gave birth to 'Usāmah bin Zayd. She died in the year 11H.

Umm Sulaym: Her name is differed over, she was the daughter of Mil'ān al-Anṣārī. She was initially married to Mālik and when he died she married Abū Ṭalḥah. She used to accompany the Messenger (ﷺ) on his military expeditions. She died in the year 30H.

Usayd bin Huḍair: bin Sammāk bin 'Amr al-Qays al-Anṣārī al-Ashhalī, Abū Ya'yā, he witnessed the pledge of *Uqbah*, the battle of *Uḥud* and the following battles. He had a beautiful recitation and died in the year 20H.

'Uthmān bin 'Affān: *Dhu an-Nurayn* 'Uthmān bin 'Affān bin Abū al-'Ās bin Umayyah al-Qurashī al-Amawī, the third Rightly Guided *Khalīfah* and one of the ten promised Paradise. He was known for his generosity and freely giving in the Way of Allāh. He was married to two daughters of the Prophet (ﷺ), Ruqayyah and after her death, Umm Kulthūm. He was martyred in the year 35H.

Az-Zanīrah: ar-Rumī. She was one of those slaves who would be tortured by the polytheists, who Abū Bakr bought and freed.

Az-Zubair: bin al-Awām bin Khuwaylid bin Asad al-Qurashī al-Asadī, Abū 'Abdullāh. He migrated to Abysinnia on both the migrations there and accompanied the Messenger on all his military expeditions. He was one of the ten promised Paradise and died in the year 36H.

The Successors

'Āmir bin 'Abd Qais: 'Āmir bin 'Abdullāh al-Quḍayrī, famously know as 'Āmir bin 'Abd Qais al-Baṣrī. He was known for his knowledge and piety and died in the year 55H.

'Abd-al-Malik bin Marwān: bin al-Hakam, Abū al-Walīd, the Leader of the Believers. He was a Legal Jurist and possessed knowledge of the religion. He died in the year 86H.

Abū Muslim al-Khawlānī: 'Abdullāh bin Thawb, the Legal Jurist, worshipper and ascetic. He was trustworthy and precise. He accepted Islām before the death of the Prophet (ﷺ) but did not get to see him. He died in the year 62H.

Al-Ahnaf bin Qais: bin Mu'āwiyah at-Tamīmī as-Sa'dī. He lived during the time of the Prophet (ﷺ) but did not see him. He was known for his gentle, forbearing nature and was trustworthy and precise. He died in the year 67H.

'Amr bin 'Utbah bin Farqad: al-Qurashī, known for his worship and asceticism.

Awais al-Qarnī: bin 'Āmir, the famous ascetic. He lived during the time of the Prophet (ﷺ) but did not get to see him. He was trustworthy and precise and died in the year 37H.

Al-Awzā'ī: 'Abdur-Raḥmān bin 'Amr bin Muḥammad, Abū 'Amr, one of the great scholars of his time. He was well versed in ḥadīth, *fiqh* and the military expeditions undertaken by the Prophet (ﷺ). The Muslims have agreed as to his excellence and being an *Imām*. His *fiqh* dominated Spain for a time and he died in the year 158H.

Aḍ-Ḍaḥḥāk: bin Muzāhim al-Hilālī, Abū al-Qāsim al-Khurasānī, the *Imām* of *tafsīr*. He was trustworthy and precise and a student of Sa'īd bin Jubair. He died in the year 105H.

Fuḍayl bin 'Ayāḍ: bin Mas'ūd at-Tamīmī, Abū 'Alī, the *shaykh* of Mecca and one of the righteous worshippers. He was trustworthy and precise, noble, having *wara'* and narrated many *aḥādīth*. He died in the year 187H.

Al-Ḥajjāj bin Yusūf: bin Abū 'Aqīl bin Mas'ūd ath-Thaqafī, Abū Muḥammad, known for his spilling of innocent blood. He died in the year 95H.

Al-Ḥasan al-Baṣrī: Al-Ḥasan bin Abū al-Ḥasan al-Anṣārī. He was trustworthy and precise, noble and famous. He was a great scholar and narrated many *aḥādīth*. He died in the year 110H close to the age of ninety.

Ibn Abī Mulaykah: bin 'Abdullāh bin Jud'ān al-Madanī. He met thirty Companions and was trustworthy and precise, a Legal Jurist.

Ibrāhīm bin Adham: bin Manṣūr at-Tamīmī, the famous ascetic who was known for his precision in ḥadīth. He died in the year 161H.

Ibrāhīm at-Taimī: bin Yazīd bin Sharīk, Abū al-Aʿmash. He was known for his worship and asceticism. Aḥmad said that he was truthful (*ṣadūq*). He died in the year 92H.

Muṭarraf bin ʿAbdullāh bin ash-Shakhayyir: He was born during the time of the Prophet (ﷺ) and was known for his worship, asceticism and keen intellect. He was trustworthy and precise and died in the year 87H.

Saʿīd bin al-Musayyab: bin Ḥazn, Abū Muḥammad. He excelled in ḥadīth and *fiqh*, and was known for his worship and asceticism. He was one of the 'Seven Legal Jurists' of Madīnah and Imām Aḥmad regarded him to be the most virtuous of the Successors. He was trustworthy and precise and narrated many *aḥādīth*. He died in the year 94H.

Ash-Shaʿbī: ʿĀmir bin Sharāḥīl ash-Shaʿbī al-Ḥumayrī, Abu ʿAmr, the *Ḥāfiẓ*, Legal Jurist and poet. He died in the year 103H.

Silah bin Ashīm: al-ʿAdawī, the famous successor and some mentioned him amongst the Companions. He died in the year 35H.

Sufyān ath-Thawrī: bin Saʿīd bin Masrūq, Abū ʿAbdullāh ath-Thawrī, one of the great *Imāms* and worshippers of this nation. He was titled 'The Leader of Believers in Ḥadīth' and was well versed in *tafsīr*. He was the teacher of Abū Ḥanīfah and Mālik amongst others and died in the year 161H.

Urwah: bin az-Zubair bin al-ʿAwām al-Asadī, Abū ʿAbdullāh. He was trustworthy and precise, a Legal Jurist, a scholar, and he narrated many *aḥādīth*. He died in the year 94H.

ʿUtbah al-Ghulām: bin Abān, one of the ascetics of Baṣrah. He was martyred during the war against ar-Rum.

Az-Zuhrī: Muḥammad bin Muslim bin 'Ubaydullāh al-Qurasahī, Abū Bakr, one of the *Imāms* of this nation. He was one of the most knowledgeable people of his time of ḥadīth and the Qur'ān. He was trustworthy and precise and narrated many aḥādīth. He died in the year 124H.

Others

'Āmir bin at-Ṭufail: bin Mālik al-Āmirī. He died in the year 11H. as a disbeliever.

'Abdullāh bin Sayyād: His father was a Jew and it was thought by some that he was the *Dajjāl*. He was born during the time of the Prophet (ﷺ) and was one-eyed - later it was proven that he was not the *Dajjāl*. It is said that he accepted Islām after the death of the Messenger (ﷺ) and he died in the year 63H.

'Abdul-Wāḥid bin Zayd: The *shaykh* of the *Ṣūfīs* at his time, his supplications were answered. He is trustworthy and precise and died in the year 177H.

Abū al-'Abbās bin 'Aṭā': Aḥmad bin Muḥammad bin Sahl bin 'Aṭā' al-Admī, from the *shaykhs* of the *Ṣufis*. He died in the year 309H or 311H.

Abū 'Abdur-Raḥmān as-Sulamī: Muḥammad bin Mūsā Abū 'Abdur-Raḥmān as-Sulamī an-Naisābūrī. Author of a number of unique works on *Ṣūfism* and devoted to ḥadīth. Al-Ḥākim reported from him but he was regarded to be ḍa'īf in ḥadīth. He died in the year 412H.

Abū 'Amr bin Nujaid: Ismā'īl bin Nujaid bin Aḥmad as-Sulamī Abū 'Amr, from the *shaykhs* of the *Ṣūfīs* and he met al-Junaid. He was one of the greatest scholars of his time and died in the year 366H.

Abū Dāwūd: Sulaymān bin al-Ash'ath bin Isḥāq bin Bashīr, Abū Dāwūd as-Sijistānī, the *Imām*, *Ḥāfiẓ* and author of the famous *Sunan*. He died in the year 275H.

Abū Ḥāmid al-Ghazālī: Muḥammad bin Muḥammad al-Ghazālī at-Ṭūsī, Abū Ḥāmid, he excelled in many sciences and authored a number of works such as *Iḥyā Ulum ad-Dīn* and *Tahāfat al-Falāsifah*. He was known for his worship and asceticism and died in the year 505H.

Abū Ḥātim al-Bustī: see ibn Ḥibbān.

Abū Ḥanīfah: Nu'mān bin Thābit at-Tamīmī al-Kūfī, one of the great *Imāms* of this nation and the earliest of the Four *Imāms*. He commenced his studies in philosophy and scholastic theology, but later abandoned them to study *fiqh*. He died in the year 150H.

Abū Jahl: 'Amr bin Hāshim bin al-Mughīrah al-Makhzūmī al-Qurashī, one of the greatest enemies of the Prophet (ﷺ). He was killed at *Badr* in the year 2H.

Abū Nu'aym: The great *Ḥāfiẓ* and *Muḥaddith* of his age, Aḥmad bin 'Abdullāh bin Aḥmad bin Isḥāq bin Mūsā bin Mahrān al-Asbahānī *as-Ṣūfīs*. He died in the year 430H at the age of ninety-four.

Abū Sa'īd al-Kharrāz: Ahmad bin 'Īsā, one of the *Ṣūfīs Imāms*. He died in the year 286H.

Abū Sulaymān ad-Dārānī: 'Abdur-Raḥmān bin Aḥmad bin 'Aṭiyyah al-'Īsā ad-Dārānī, Abū Sulaymān, the famous ascetic. He died in the year 215H.

Abū 'Uthmān an-Naysābūrī: Sa'īd bin Ismā'īl bin Sa'īd al-Ḥayrī an-Naysābūrī, Abū 'Uthmān, the famous ascetic known for his excellent manners. It was through him that *Ṣūfism* spread in Naysābūr. He died in the year 298H.

Aḥmad: bin Muḥammad bin Ḥanbal bin Hilāl ash-Shaybānī, Abū 'Abdullāh, the *Imām* of the *Sunnah* and author of the famous *Musnad*. He was known for his knowledge of ḥadīth, *fiqh*, and his *taqwā* and asceticism. He died in the year 241H.

Alexander the Great: 356-323BC. A great military leader and king who thought himself to be a god. His empire spanned from Greece to India.

Aristotle: 384-322BC. Born in Greece and a student at Plato's Academy, and eventually taught there for some twenty years. He was the author of a philosophical and scientific system that moulded Western thought and influenced many Muslims.

Al-Aswad al-Ansī: Abhalah bin Ka'b bin Awf al-Ansī. He initially accepted Islām and then apostated during the lifetime of the Prophet (ﷺ) and claimed Prophethood for himself. His was the first apostasy that took place in Islām, and many of the people of his country, Yemen, then followed suit. When the Prophet (ﷺ) heard of this, he ordered the Muslims in Yemen to kill him. They finally killed him in the year 11H.

Bukhārī: Muḥammad bin Ismā'īl bin Ibrāhīm bin al-Mughīrah, Abū 'Abdullāh. He was born in the year 194H and became one of the *Imāms* of ḥadīth and was nicknamed 'The Leader of the Believers in Ḥadīth.' He died in the year 256H.

Dāwūd adh-Ẓāhirī: bin 'Alī bin Khalaf al-Aṣbahānī, Abū Sulaymān, the *Imām* of the *ẓāhirī* School of Thought and one of the *Mujtahids*. He died in the year 270H.

Ad-Durr al-Qunawī: Muḥammad bin Isḥāq bin Muḥammad al-Qunawī ar-Rumī, the *Ṣūfīs* and one of the greatest students of ibn Arabī. He was the teacher of at-Talmasānī and authored a number of works such as a commentary to *Sūrah al-Fātiḥah*. He died in the year 673H.

Al-Ḥallāj: Al-Husain bin Manṣūr, initially he was a devout worshipper but then he took to the extreme *Ṣufis* ways and left the religion, studying magic and showing people various miraculous feats. The scholars passed the verdict that his blood was lawful and so he was killed in the year 309H.

Ibn al-'Arabī: *Muḥiy ad-Dīn* Muḥammad bin 'Alī bin Muḥammad bin 'Arabī at-Ṭā'ī, Abū Bakr, the heretical *Ṣūfīs*. He authored a number of works containing explicit disbelief and many scholars actually called him a disbeliever. He died in the year 638H.

Ad-Dāruquṭnī: 'Alī bin 'Umar bin Ahmad, the *Imām* of his era in hadīth, knowledge of the defects of *aḥādīth* and author of the famous *Sunan*. He was well versed in the various recitations of the Qur'ān, *fiqh*, language and poetry. He died in the year 385H.

Al-Ḥārith ad-Dimashqī: bin Sa'īd. He was a worshipper who would articulate eloquent statements when praising Allāh, so Shayṭān came and misguided him into thinking that he was a Prophet. He used to go to the Mosque and show the people amazing things. His affair was conveyed to ʿAbdul-Malik who sought him out and finally killed him and crucified him in the year 69H.

Iblīs: see Shayṭān.

Ibn al-Fāriḍ: ʿUmar bin ʿAlī bin Murshid bin ʿAlī, Abū Ḥafs al-Ḥamawī, the poet who took to the ways of the extreme *Ṣūfis*. He has been severely criticised by more than one scholar. He died in the year 632H.

Ibn Ḥibbān: Abū Ḥātim Muḥammad ibn Ḥibbān al-Tamīmī al-Bustī, the *Ḥāfiẓ*, *Mujtahid* and author of the famous *Ṣaḥīḥ ibn Ḥibbān*. He died in the year 354H.

Ibn al-Jawzī: ʿAbdur-Raḥmān bin ʿAlī bin Muḥammad, Abū al-Faraj al-Qurashī at-Tamīmī, the *Ḥāfiẓ* and *Imām*. He was a prolific writer and authored around three hundred works. He died in the year 587H.

Ibn Sabʿīn: ʿAbdul-Ḥaqq bin Ibrāhīm bin Muḥammad ar-Raqwaṭī, the philosopher. He believed that Prophethood could be attained by anyone and would hence withdraw to cave *Hirā'* hoping to receive revelation just as it had come to the Prophet (ﷺ) before him. He died in the year 669H.

Ibn Sīnā: Abū ʿAlī al-Husain bin Sīnā, philosopher and a remarkable physician. He was severely criticised for a great deal of his beliefs due to his delving into philosophy. He died in the year 428H.

Isḥāq bin Rāhawayah: al-Ḥanẓalī at-Tamīmī al-Marwazī, Abū Yaʿqūb, the scholar of Khurasān of his time and one of the *Mujtahid Imāms*. He taught Aḥmad, Bukhārī, Muslim, at-Tirmidhī, an-Nasā'ī and others. He died in the year 238H.

Al-Junaid: bin Muḥammad az-Zujjāj, Abū al-Qāsim. He was a Legal Jurist who followed the school of Abū Thawr and was known for asceticism. He died in the year 297H.

Ka'b bin al-Ashraf: at-Ṭā'ī, a poet from the days of *Jāhiliyyah*. He incited many people against the Prophet (ﷺ) and the Muslims, and the Prophet (ﷺ) ordered him killed. Five of the *Anṣār* left to kill him and killed him in the year 3H.

Khiḍr: He is the companion of Moses, it is said that he was a Prophet or a righteous servant - however the majority are of the opinion that he was a Prophet. This is because the realities behind his actions can only be known through revelation and because a person does not learn or follow except one who is above him and it is not possible that a non-prophet be above a Prophet. His name and life are greatly differed over and this difference is detailed by ibn Kathīr. Refer to: *'Tafsīr al-Qurtubī'* [11/16] and *'al-Bidāyah wan Nihāyah'* [1/355].

Al-Layth bin Sa'd: bin 'Abdur-Raḥmān al-Fahmī, Abū al-Ḥārith, the *Imām* of Egypt in ḥadīth, *fiqh* and language. He was trustworthy and precise and narrated many *aḥādīth*. Ash-Shāfi'ī regarded him to be a better jurist than Mālik. He died in the year 175H.

Mālik bin Anas: ibn Mālik ibn Abū 'Amr al-Asbāhī. The *Imām* of Madīnah in his time, one of the great *Imāms* of Islām and author of the famous *Muwaṭṭa*. His virtues are many and the scholar's praise of him is abundant. He died in the year 179H.

Ma'rūf al-Karkhī: bin Fairoz, Abū Ma'fūẓ, one of the *shaykhs* famous for asceticism and one whose supplication would be answered. He died in the year 200H.

Muḥammad bin ʿAlī al-Ḥakīm at-Tirmidhī: From the great scholars of Khurasān who authored some famous works and was devoted to ḥadīth. He died in the year 320H.

Al-Mukhtār bin Abū Ubaid: bin Masʿūd ath-Thaqafī, Abū Isḥāq, who claimed Prophethood for himself. He was killed by Muṣʿab in the year 67H.

Musaylamah: bin Thumāmah bin Kabīr bin al-Ḥanafī al-Wāʾilī, Abū Thumāmah, the great liar. He initially accepted Islām, then apostated and claimed Prophethood for himself and gained a following. He was fought by the Muslims and was killed in the year 12H.

Muslim: bin al-Ḥajjāj bin Muslim al-Qushayrī, Abū al-Ḥusain an-Naisābūrī, the *Ḥāfiẓ* and one of the great *Imāms* of this nation. He is the author of the Ṣaḥīḥ which is the most authentic book of ḥadīth after Bukhārī. He died in the year 261H.

Najdah al-Ḥurūrī: bin ʿĀmir al-Ḥanafī. He was one of the *Khawārij* who was unique, even amongst them, because he thought that it was obligatory to kill anyone who held an opposing view to him. He was killed in the year 69H.

Philip the Macedonian: 383-336BC. A great warrior and brutal king who was responsible for turning the Macedonian army into the greatest fighting force of its time.

Plato: 427-347BC. He studied under Cratylus and was a close friend of Socrates. Later he studied mathematics under the students of Pythagoras and came to believe that mathematics was the highest possible expression of thought. At about 387BC he founded his Academy, which was a school devoted to philosophy and the physical sciences.

Pythagoras: 569-475BC. Born in Greece, he was a genius in mathematics and an astronomer. He founded a school called the Semicircle wherein political discussions were held, and he himself taught philosophy in a cave which he used as a base for his research into mathematics. He later moved to Italy and founded another school there devoted to philosophy.

Ṣafwa bin Murr bin Add bin Ṭābikha: He lived in the days of *Jāhiliyyah*.

Sahl bin 'Abdullāh: bin Yunūs Abū Muḥammad at-Tustorī, one of the *Ṣūfis* scholars. He died in the year 283H.

Ash-Shāfi'ī: Muḥammad bin Idrees bin al-'Abbās bin Shāfi'ī al-Hāshimī al-Qurashī, Abū 'Abdullāh, the *Mujaddid* of his era and one of the great *Imāms* of this nation. He died in the year 204H.

Shayṭān: Also called *Iblīs*. He is a Jinn and the enemy of mankind, devoted to leading them astray in any way that he can. The word Shayṭān is derived from the verb *shaṭana* which means to be distant, and indeed Shayṭān is distant from all good.

Ṭalḥa al-Asadī: bin Khuwaylid bin Nawfal. He initially accepted Islām at the hands of the Prophet (ﷺ) and then apostated, claiming Prophethood for himself. Many of the Arabs followed him and Abū Bakr sent Khālid bin Walīd to him who fought him. Ṭalḥa was defeated and fled to Syria where he eventually accepted Islām again. It is said that he was martyred at *Nahāwund* in the year 21H.

At-Talmasānī: Sulaymān bin 'Alī bin 'Abdullāh bin 'Alī, the *Ṣūfis* poet who authored various works on language, manners and *Usūl*.

He was a follower of the way of ibn ʿArabī and was accused of grievous beliefs some of which were pure disbelief. He died in the year 690H.

At-Tirmidhī: Muḥammad bin ʿĪsā bin Sawrah bin Mūsā bin ad-Ḍaḥḥāk as-Sulamī at-Tirmidhī, the *Imām*, *Ḥāfiẓ* and the author of the famous *Sunan*. He was trustworthy and precise and one of the students of Bukhārī. He died in the year 279H.

INDEX OF PLACE NAMES

ʿArafah: a plain 12 miles south-west of Mecca, a little beyond Muzdalifa. It is one of the culminating stations of Ḥajj.

Ardabīl: A city in north-west Iran.

Al-Ahwāẓ: A city situated on the outskirts of Iran.

Badr: Situated 90 miles south of Madīnah.

Baghdād: Capital of Iraq, situated on the river Tigris.

Baṭn Nakhla: A place falling between Mecca and Ṭāʿif.

Dome of the Rock: shrine in Jerusalem. The dome stands over the rock on the temple Mount. The rock is 18 metres by 14 metres.

Harrān: An old city within the Arabian Peninsula between Syria and Iraq.

Hijāẓ: the area from the Red Sea coast of Arabia, from south of Mecca, north beyond Yenbo and inland as far as Madīnah.

Hirā': cave at the summit of mount Hirā', a few miles from Mecca.

Al-Hurra: A place just outside Madīnah.

Hudaybiyyah: on the road from Jeddah to Mecca, just a few miles outside the *Ḥaram*.

Jimār: Name of monuments, representing Shayṭān, that are stoned during the *Ḥajj*. They are situated in Mina, a valley near Mecca.

Madīnah: Situated in western Saudi Arabia, 330km north of Mecca.

Al-Marwa: Hill in Mecca, near the Kaʿbah and included in one of the rites of *ʿUmrah* and *Ḥajj*.

Mecca: Situated in Saudi Arabia, 80km from the Red Sea coast and founded upon the well of *Zamzam*.

Mount al-Fatḥ: A mountain in Egypt.

Mount Lebanon: This is a range of mountains stretching from Hijāz to Syria. The part in Palestine is called Mount *al-Haml*, the part in Jordan is called Mount *al-Khalīl*, the part in Damascus is called Mount *Sinīr* and the part in Aleppo and Homs is called Mount Lebanon. This range also crosses Antakya (southern Turkey) where it is called Mount *Lukām*.

Mount al-Lukām: see under Mount Lebanon.

Mount Nahāwund: Nahāwund is a great city in Iran that was conquered by the Muslim in 20H.

Mount Qāsiyūn: Situated in east Damascus.

Mount Sabalān: Situated in north-west Iran, near to Ardabīl.

Mount Sahl: Famous mountain in Syria.

Muzdalifah: Situated between Mina and Arafah.

Naṣībayn: A city falling between Damascus and Mosul, northern Iraq. It was conquered by the Muslims in the 18H.

Ṣafā: Hill in Mecca, near the Ka'bah and included in one of the rites of *'Umrah* and *Ḥajj*. It is 394 metres from al-Marwā.

Ṣuffah: An area in the northern part of the Prophet's Mosque, in which the poor or homeless Muslims resided.

Ṭā'if: City in eastern Saudi Arabia situated on a plateau and slightly east of Mecca, famous for its grapes.

Tabrīz: Situated in North-West Iran at about 1400 meters above sea-level.

Tigris: River of Turkey, Syria and Iraq. It is 1850 km long and has two principle sources, Lake Hazer and Lake Van, both in Turkey.

Uḥud: a volcanic hill on the western outskirts of Madīnah.

'Ukāẓ: site in Hijāz in the region of Tā'if, south-east of Mecca. Before Islām, once a year, a fair would be held there in the beginning Dhūl Qa'dah where poetry would be read.

INDEX OF QUR'ĀNIC VERSES

INDEX OF ḤADĪTH

INDEX OF SECTS

AHLU'L-KALĀM: Adherents to speculative theology, people seeking to explain the articles and premises of belief and to give evidences for them based on philosophy and logic.

BĀṬINIYYAH: A sect of the Shī'a, the followers of Ismā'īl ibn Ja'far. They were of the belief that the legal texts were merely superficial expressions carrying inner meanings that oppose what is outwardly understood of them, examples lie with their explanations of Paradise, Hell and the Last Day.

ḤASHWIYYAH: A term frequently used by the innovators to refer to Ahlu'l-Sunnah, the Ahl'l-Ḥadith, those who affirmed the Attributes of Allāh. The first to use this term was 'Amr ibn 'Ubaid al-Mu'tazilī who said that 'Abdullāh ibn 'Umar ibn al-Khaṭṭāb was a Ḥashwī.

JABARIYYAH: Followers of the school of Jahm ibn Ṣafwān in his belief that all actions are decreed by Allāh and man has no control over them at all, instead he is forced to do what he does.

JAHMIYYAH: Followers of Jahm ibn Ṣafwān in his denial of the Names and Attributes of Allāh.

KARRĀMIYYAH: Followers of Muḥammad ibn Karrām (d. 255H), they divided into many sub-sects and were famous for their likening of Allāh to His creation (*tashbīh*).

MUTAKALLIMŪN: Speculative Theologians, adherents to *kalām*.

MU'TAZILA: Followers of Wāṣil ibn 'Aṭā' al-Ghazzāl who abandoned the circles of Ḥasan al-Baṣrī. They negated the Attributes of Allāh for fear of likening Him to His creation, yet affirmed His Names. From amongst their beliefs was that a person who committed a major sin was neither a believer nor a disbeliever, rather of a station between the two stations, but he would be consigned to Hellfire forever. They were from the rank and file of the Mutakallimūn and gave precedence to their intellects over the divine texts.

QADARIYYAH: Those who held the belief that man has complete free will in all that he does and that Allāh has no control over him.

QARĀMIṬA: A sect holding the same belief as the Bāṭiniyyah and followers of Maymūn ibn Daysān.

FALĀSIFA: Those philosophers who promoted the 'wisdom' of the Greeks, the Greek philosophers who did not believe in the Resurrection as it is mentioned in the Book and Sunnah, nor did they affirm the Names and Attributes of Allāh. From amongst their leaders was Aristotle, the student of Plato and from amongst their latter proponents was al-Fārābī and ibn Sīnā.

GLOSSARY OF ARABIC TERMS

Āla: apparatus.

'Ārif: The one possessing knowledge. *Ṣūfī*: the one who knows Allāh and the true realities.

'Ashūrā': 10th Muḥarram, the 1st month of the Islāmic calender.

Āyah: pl. *āyāt*. Sign, miracle, example, lesson, verse.

'Abd: pl. *'ebād*. slave, servant, worshipper.

Al-Abdāl: sing: badal. *Ṣūfī*: the Substitutes.

Abrār: righteous.

Adhān: *fiqh*: the call to prayer.

Aflāq: *phil*: celestial spheres.

Ahl al-Ma'rifah wal-Ithbāt: *Ṣūfī*: The people of knowledge and substantiation. Those endowed with the higher knowledge and verification amongst the *Ṣūfis*.

Anfāl: spoils of war. The property appropriated from the polytheists while at war with them.

'Araḍ: purpose, *phil*: accidental property.

'Aṭā: bestowal of provision/sustenance.

'Awn: assistant, aid.

Al-Awtād: *Ṣūfī*: the Poles, a category of the *Awliyā'*.

Barzakh: barrier, obstruction, an isthmus. *fiqh*: a barrier placed between a person who has deceased and this worldly life.

Bay'atul Riḍwān: The Pledge of Allegiance with which Allāh was well Pleased. A reference to the pledge given under the tree after *Ḥudaybiyyah*.

Bid'ah: innovation, *fiqh*: that which is newly introduced into the religion of Allāh.

Ḍaʿīf: weak. A ḥadīth that has failed to meet the criteria of authenticity.
Dīn: religion, way of life.
Adh-Dharāʾiʿ: *fiqh*: means.
Dhawq: taste, *Ṣūfīs*: direct experience of the truth.
Dhikr: remembrance, *fiqh*: making mention of Allāh.
Dhimmi: protected person, *fiqh*: a non-Muslim living under the protection of the Islāmic state. He must pay *jizya*.
Duʿā: supplication, invocation.
Faiʾ: Property legally appropriated by the Muslims by way of land tax and *jizya*.
Fatḥ adh-Dharāʾiʿ: *fiqh*: Facilitating the Means.
Fanāʾ: oblivion, absorption, extinction. *Ṣūfī*: to die before dying, annihilation in Allāh, death of the ego, to die in this world and subsist (*baqāʾ*) in Allāh.
Faqīh: pl. *fuqahāʾ*. *fiqh*: an expert in Islāmic law, a Legal Jurist.
Faqīr: poor, needy person. *Ṣūfīs*: initiate in a *Ṣūfī* order, the graduate from such an order is called a *Ṣūfī*.
Faqr: poverty, need.
Farḍ: see *wājib*.
Fasād: corruption, decay, and invalidity.
Fatwā: *fiqh*: legal ruling.
Fiqh: understanding and comprehension. *fiqh*: of the rulings and legislation of Islām.
Fisq: pl. *fusūq*. Immorality, transgression, wickedness.
Fitnah: pl. *fitan*. Trial, tribulation, civil strife.
Fiṭrah: primordial nature, the harmony between man, creation and Creator.
Ghanīmah: pl. *ghanāʾim*. See *Anfāl*.
Gharāmah: infatuation.
Ghayb: the Unseen, those matters beyond our senses.
Ghubṭa: envy, referring to the permissible form of envy where the envier wishes to have the same blessings as the envied but without desiring to see them removed from the envied. This is opposed to *ḥasad*, the blameworthy form of envy where the envier wishes to see the blessings removed from the envied.
Ḥāfiẓ: pl. *ḥuffāẓ*. Ḥadīth Master, commonly referred to one who has memorised at least 100 000 *aḥādīth*.

Ḥāl: pl. *aḥwāl*, state or condition. *Ṣūfī*: spiritual state, a spiritual realisation that is fleeting or temporary.

Ḥāll: *phil*: subsistent.

Ḥadīth: pl. *aḥādīth*, speech, report, account. *fiqh*: a narration describing the sayings, actions, character, physical description and tacit approval of the Prophet (ﷺ).

Ḥajj: *fiqh*: pilgrimage, one of the pillars of Islām.

Ḥalāl: released. *fiqh*: permissible.

Ḥanīf: pl. *Ḥunafā'*. Upright and Devout. One who leaves the false religions and beliefs for the truth and does not swerve from it. His outward rectitude reflects what is inside him.

Ḥaqīqah: truth, reality, state of things as they are. sufee: a route to Allāh, for his elite that is beyond the *Sharī'ah*.

Ḥarām: forbidden, sacred, restricted. *fiqh*: unlawful, that which the legally responsible person is rewarded for leaving and sinful for doing.

Ḥasad: see *Ghubṭa*.

Ḥasan: good. *fiqh*: a ḥadīth that has met the criteria of authenticity to a sufficient level as would allow it to be used as legal proof.

Hawā': base desires.

Ḥawḍ: the Fount.

Hayūlā: *phil*: primal matter, *materia prima*.

Hudūd: limits, boundaries. *fiqh*: limits ordained by Allāh, prescribed punishments.

Ḥulūl: settling, descent. *phil*: settling of a superior faculty upon a support, incarnation.

Idtibā': placing the middle of the upper garment under the right arm and the ends of it over the left shoulder during *tawāf*.

Iḥrām: the ceremonial state of making Ḥajj or the Ḥajj garments themselves.

Ijtihād: striving and exerting. *fiqh*: striving to attain the Islāmic ruling on an issue, after certain preconditions have been met by the person.

Ilḥād: deviation, atheism.

Imām: model, exemplar. *fiqh*: religious leader, one who leads the congregational prayer or leads a community.

Īmān: faith that also comprises a meaning of submission. Its place is the heart, the tongue and the limbs and it increases with obedience and decreases with disobedience.

'Irfān: *Ṣūfī*: esoteric knowledge.
'Ishk: passionate love.
Isnād: chain of narration.
Ittiḥād: *phil*: unification.
Izār: lower cloth of *Iḥrām*.
Jāhiliyyah: Pre-Islāmic Ignorance. Technically this refers to the condition of a people before the guidance of Allāh reaches them, or the state of a people that prevents them from accepting the guidance of Allāh.
Janābah: *fiqh*: state of major impurity.
Janāzah: *fiqh*: funeral prayer, funeral procession.
Jawhar: pl. *jawāhir*. material substance, essence.
Jihād: striving in the Way of Allāh to make His Word supreme.
Jinn: another creation besides mankind who are invisible to us. They are also subject to the laws of Islām and will be judged in the Hereafter according to how they lived in this life.
Jism: physical body.
Junub: *fiqh*: one who is in a state of major impurity.
Juz'iyyāt: *phil*: details, particulars.
Kāfir: a rejecter of faith, disbeliever.
Kalām: speech, discourse. *phil*: dialectics, scholastic theology.
Karāmah: pl. *karāmāt*. Miracles performed by those not Prophets.
Khāriqul 'Ādah: miraculous feats, supernatural occurrences.
Khalwah: *ṣūfī*: solitary retreat.
Khalīfah: pl. *khulafā'*. Successor, representative. *fiqh*: of the Prophet (ﷺ), head of the Islāmic state. Also called *Amīr al-Mu'minīn* or Leader of the Believers.
Khawf: fear.
Khuṭbah: sermon, lecture. *fiqh*: Friday sermon.
Kulliyyāt: *phil*: generalities, universals.
Lisān al-Ḥāl: *ṣūfī*: tongue of the spiritual state.
Makrūh: *fiqh*: disliked, reprehensible, that which the legally responsible person is rewarded for leaving but not punished for doing.
Maqāmāt: sing: *maqām*, station. *ṣūfī*: spiritual stations, a permanent spiritual realisation.
Maqdūr: foreordained.
Maṣāliḥ al-Mursalah: *fiqh*: Public Interest.
Matrūk: abandoned. This refers to a narrator of a ḥadīth who is aban-

doned due to being accused of lying.

Mawḍu': fabricated ḥadīth. That ḥadīth which is a lie against the Prophet (ﷺ).

Mu'jizah: pl. *mu'jizāt*. Miracles performed by Prophets.

Mufassir: pl. *mufassirūn*. Exegete, commentator. *fiqh*: one who explains the Qur'ān.

Muhājir: pl. *Muhājirūn*. One who perform *hijrah*. *fiqh*: the Companions who migrated from Mecca to Madīnah.

Muḥaddith: pl. *muḥaddithūn*. Scholar of Ḥadīth.

Mujtahid: one who performs *ijtihād*. *fiqh*: that level of scholar who can deduce independent verdicts directly from the primary Islāmic sources.

Mukhāṭabah: *ṣūfī*: disclosure of hidden realities - the *ṣūfī* hearing things via extraordinary means.

Mukāshafah: *ṣūfī*: unveiling of hidden realities - the *ṣūfī* attaining knowledge through extraordinary means.

Mushāhadah: *ṣūfī*: vision of hidden realities - the *ṣūfī* seeing things via extraordinary means.

Mukallaf: morally responsible person.

Mulḥid: heretic.

Munāfiq: hypocrite. *fiqh*: one who outwardly displays Islām but inwardly conceals disbelief. This is the worst type of hypocrisy and its possessor is the worst type of disbeliever, there are other lesser types.

Munqaṭi': a ḥadīth whose *isnād* is not connected, meaning that has a narrator missing. This is a sub-category of the *ḍa'īf* ḥadīth.

Murābaḥah: *fiqh*: resale with specification of gain.

Murīd: one who wants, desires, aims for something. *ṣūfī*: a devotee to a *ṣūfī shaykh*.

Mursal: a ḥadīth whose *isnād* has the name of the Companion missing, i.e. a Successor reports directly from the Prophet (ﷺ). In the eyes of the majority of scholars such a ḥadīth is a sub-category of the *ḍa'īf* ḥadīth.

Mutashābih: unclear and ambiguous. *fiqh*: an *āyah* of the Qur'ān that is not clear and conclusive in meaning from the wording of the text itself.

Naṣīḥah: Sincere/Faithful advice.

Nidd: peer.

An-Nujabā': *ṣūfī*: the Nobles, a category of the *Awliyā'*.

An-Nuqabā': *ṣūfī*: the Leaders, a category of the *Awliyā'*.

Qaḍā: see *qadar*.

Qadar: Allāh's decree of all matters in accordance with His prior knowledge and as dictated by His wisdom.

Qiblah: *fiqh*: direction to which the Muslims pray, towards the *ka*ʿ*bah*.

Qiyās: *fiqh*: Analogy.

Al-Quṭb: *ṣūfī*: the Axis, the greatest of the *Awliyā*ʾ.

Raghabah: fervent desire.

Rahbah: dread.

*Rajā*ʾ: reverential hope.

Ramaḍān: ninth month of the Islāmic calendar.

Riḍā: contentment and pleasure.

*Riyā*ʾ: an act of worship undertaken by someone to be seen and praised by others and not purely for Allāh.

Ruqyā: recitation used to cure an illness or disease. It can only be done in the Arabic tongue, in words whose meaning is understood, using verses of the Qurʾān or supplications of the Prophet combined with the belief that it is only Allāh who in reality gives the cure.

Sabābah: fervent longing.

Ṣabr: patience, steadfastness.

Sadd adh-Dharāʾi: *fiqh*: Blocking the Means.

Ṣaḥīḥ: healthy, sound, authentic, correct. A ḥadīth that has met the criteria of authenticity and can be used as a legal proof.

Ṣalāh: *fiqh*: the second pillar of Islām, the prayer.

Salaf: predecessors, commonly employed to refer to the first three generations of Muslims.

Ṣawm: *fiqh*: fasting, one of the pillars of Islām.

Shaghafah: crazed passion.

Shahādah: testification, witness. The declaration that none has the right to be worshipped save Allāh and that Muḥammad (ﷺ) is the Messenger of Allāh.

Shahwā: carnal lusts.

Sharīʿah: divine Islāmic law as ordained by Allāh.

Sharīk: partner, associate.

Shaykh: old man. *fiqh*: learned person, scholar. *ṣūfī*: a guide along the spiritual path.

Shayṭān: Satan, Iblīs, a devil.

Shirk: polytheism, associating partners with Allāh in matters that are exclusive to Allāh.

Sunan: a compilation of *aḥādīth*.

Sunnah: habit, customary practice, norm and usage as sanctioned by tradition. *fiqh*: the sayings, commands, prohibitions, actions, and tacit approvals of the Prophet (ﷺ).

Sūrah: chapter of the Qur'ān.

Ṣūrah: image, form, face.

Ṭāghūt: all that is falsely worshipped besides Allāh.

Tafsīr: elucidation, clarification, explanation. *fiqh*: of the Qur'ān.

Takalluf: affectation, going beyond bounds.

Taklīf: liability, obligation.

Taqdīr: fore-ordainment.

Taqwā: fearful awareness of Allāh, pious dedication, being careful not to transgress the bounds set by Allāh.

Ṭarīqah: path, *ṣūfī*: spiritual path.

Tatayyuma: worshipful love.

Ṭawāf: circumambulation of the Ka'bah

Ṭawāf Al-Ifāda: *ṭawāf* for Ḥajj.

Ṭawāf Al-Widā: farewell *ṭawāf*.

Tawakkul: trust and absolute reliance.

Tawḥīd: the foundation stone of Islām, the absolute belief in the Oneness of Allāh - His being the sole Creator and Sustainer, His being the only One deserving worship and His being unique with respect to His Names and Attributes.

Ummah: nation, the Muslim nation.

'Urf: *fiqh*: Customary Usage.

Wājib: *fiqh*: obligatory, that which a legally responsible person is rewarded for doing and sinful for leaving. In the eyes of the majority *wājib* has the same meaning as *farḍ*.

Wajd: *ṣūfī*: spiritual ecstasy.

Waliy: pl. *Awliyā'*. Friends, Allies, Saints - those who have faith and *taqwā*.

Wuḍu': *fiqh*: ritual ablution.

Zakāh: *fiqh*: one of the pillars of Islām, an obligatory tax levied on a Muslim wealth subject to certain criteria.

Zindīq: heretic, *fiqh*: Ḥanafī - one who does not adhere to a religion; Others ñ one who is a disbeliever pretending to be a Muslim.

Zuhd: asceticism.